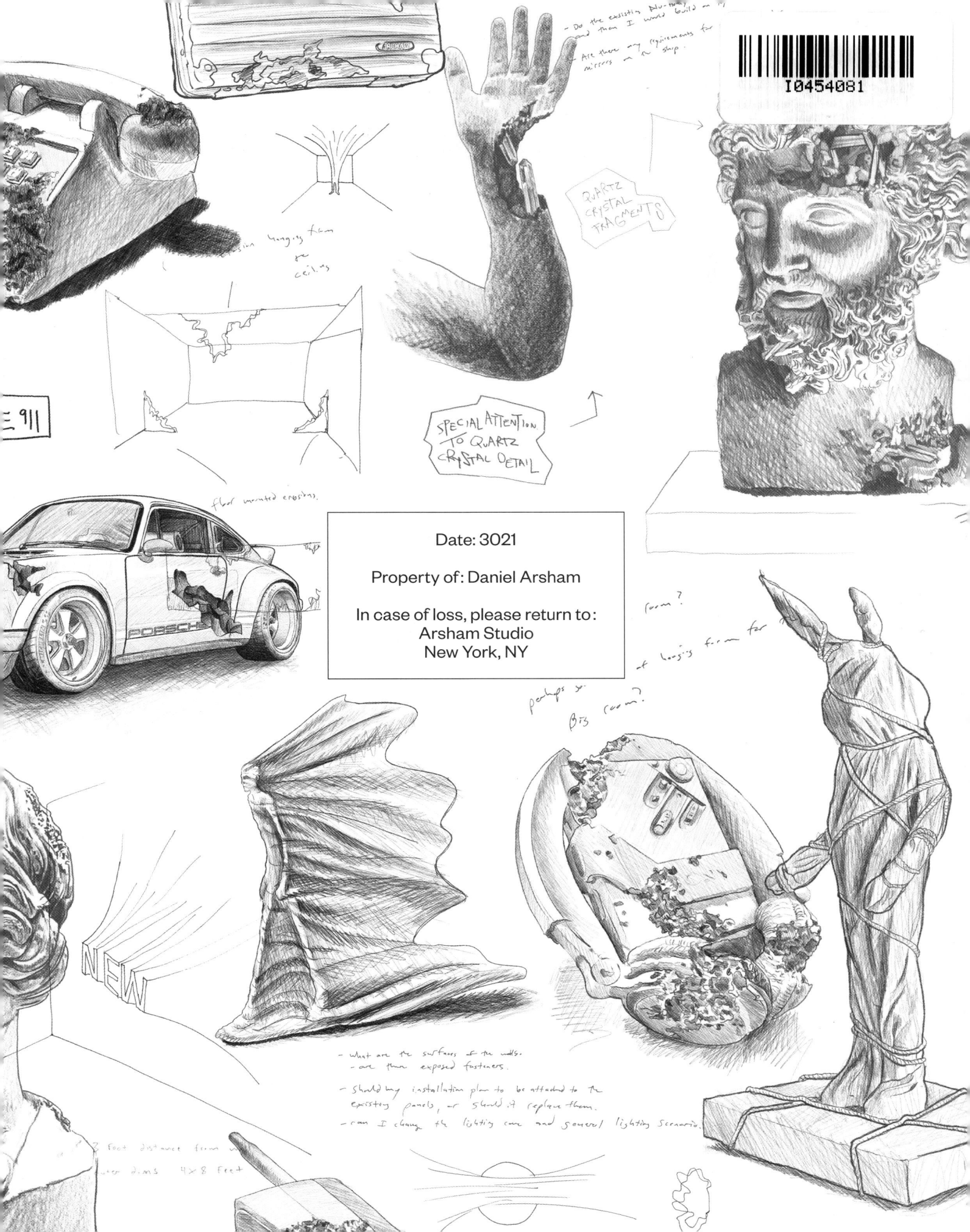

Date: 3021

Property of: Daniel Arsham

In case of loss, please return to:
Arsham Studio
New York, NY

Daniel Arsham
Sketchbook

Daniel Arsham
Sketchbook

Edited by
Larry Warsh

Published by
Princeton University Press

in association with
No More Rulers

Requests for permission to reproduce material from this work should
be sent to permissions@press.princeton.edu

Published by Princeton University Press
41 William Street, Princeton, New Jersey, 08540
6 Oxford Street, Woodstock, Oxfordshire , OX20 1TR

press.princeton.edu

In association with No More Rulers
nomorerulers.com
@nomorerulers

NO MORE RULERS

ISBN: 978-0-691-23426-7

Library of Congress Control Number: 2021944722

British Library Cataloging-in-Publication Data is available

Photographic Credits
Guillaume Ziccarelli
Nanzuka Gallery
Perrotin Gallery
Tanguy Beurdeley

Design
Arsham Studio

Cover
Drawings by Daniel Arsham

This book has been composed in Founders Grotesk

Printed on acid-free paper.

Printed in China

10 9 8 7 6 5 4 3 2 1

# Introduction

Creativity may come in many forms, but as the following pages illustrate, drawing and sketching are two modes essential to Daniel Arsham's creative process and artistic practice. Although Arsham is well-known for his sculptural work with molds, his artistic origins are actually in painting and drawing—both of which he has returned to in recent years. An expert draftsman, Arsham exhibits a keen attention to detail in every aspect of his work, including the many drawings never intended to be seen outside the studio. Collected here for the first time, these sketches demonstrate the artist's technical skill and thought process, and flesh out his imaginary world.

Many of the sketches in this volume are more than just preparatory works, though, of course, they are that too—evidenced by the annotations he often includes on the page. Large-scale sculptures and architectural interventions require extensive planning and forethought. And for Arsham, both the early stages of a design and the deeper, more thorough planning processes take place on paper. Such can be seen in the drawings of architectural structures gone all loose and drippy; the unexpected ripple of a wall's surface, which is bunched up like a bedsheet, and partially enveloping a clock; cartoonishly oversized stairs; viscous goop dripping from an HVAC vent; and a standing figure, who has pressed through an elastic-looking white ceiling, and wears the architectural element like some comical ghost in reverse drapery: curiosities and wonders all, developed *first* on paper.

More than his paintings and sculptures, Arsham's sketches inspire me to think in terms of lists and categories; I can't help myself. As I leaf through them, I automatically think: cars (BMW, DeLorean, Mercedes, Porsche, Ferrari, Volkswagen); hats; cassette tapes; phones; Bugs Bunny and Mickey; Greek statues; keyboards; furniture; Pokémon; crystals; brands, brands, and more brands; cameras; and cartoons. The ideas seem individuated, less a cohesive whole than the rooms full of the three-dimensional works. It's so much easier to drill down on imagery in the sketches than it is in the bigger, more elaborate sculptural works. The ideas are plainer, more transparent.

While Arsham's sketches are vehicles and plans for his paintings and sculptures, they are also artworks in their own right. They manage to coexist as preparatory, formal, and artistic works. This counterintuitive coexistence is a through line and permeates much of Arsham's work and practice—for instance, in the ways he confounds by collapsing the space and time in between disparate points in history (a speculative, future history, even). There is a leveling of sorts that happens in the work, not unlike roaming an encyclopedic museum, and experiencing the incongruity of passing from one period room to the next.

There is often something inchoate about a sketch (even a framed one) that typically isn't present in a sculpture or a painting. (Examples from both categories tend to appear as fully formed, completed works. The sculpture sits on its plinth, waiting to be seen. The painting hangs on the wall and does the same.) In Arsham's case, however, sculpture is pulled back into a relationship with perceived time, with incompleteness, and becoming. And this is due to the simultaneous nature by which they seem to erode and decay, while also exhibiting crystalline growth. Their status is indeterminate, their objecthood laden with an unknown, fictional past (or future? or future past?).

Arsham's collapsing of time disrupts the generally agreed-upon time system, and thus the synchronicity that we often take for granted. It is exactly Arsham's *de*synchronicity that trips us up and forces us to question what we are seeing. At the same time, their very objecthood is held in a state of suspended disbelief: they are objects of fantasy, and yet we all know very well that they're works of contemporary art.

Arsham pulls the past into the present while passing the contemporary through a process of ruination, which gives it the appearance of an artifact. And though the objects appropriate the visual language of artifacts, they are in fact the opposite: the artworks are artifices, not artifacts. (They are *imaged* artifacts. This is, after all, "fictional archeology.")

So many ruins. So much detritus and ruination. And yet, all within settings decidedly nothing like the so-called trash heap of history. In one of Arsham's sketches, he has imagined a fragmented, standing figure with one arm pointed toward the sky. The figure's body has noticeably missing sections (part of a leg, parts of the arms), which are replaced by thin, solid lines, implying repairs. In his annotation on the page, we read, "Like a marble figure from antiquity that has stainless pipe completing the missing sections." While not a perfect analogy, this is reminiscent of Alfonso Cuarón's rendering of Michelangelo's *David* in his 2006 film *Children of Men*: there, housed in the Ark of the Arts, *David* stands upon an unceremoniously repaired leg, the missing marble between left ankle and knee replaced by a metal rod. For Cuarón's imaginary version of *David*, the figure has suffered damage and undergone repair, though not exactly restoration. Rather than a return to an idealized past (as implied in the act of restoration), the blunt nature of the repair forces us to grapple with the existence of objects in space across time. And this too is present in the sketches, this act of dragging material culture to and fro in a fantastical time span, and then examining the results. Ultimately, Arsham's world is uchronic and disturbs the mutually exclusive categories of reality and fiction. It's dynamic and ambiguous. Its metaphysics is speculative. In the sketches, we see these ideas in process, on the page.

Larry Warsh

# Bibliography

Arsham, Daniel. Daniel Arsham. https://www.danielarsham.
    com/collection/connectingtime.
Bojilova, Elvira. "The 'Value of Drawing' and the 'Method of Vision':
    How Formalism and Connoisseurship Shaped the Aesthetic of the
    Sketch." *Journal of Art Historiography*, no. 24 (June 2021).
Carstocea, George. "Uchronias, Alternate Histories, and Counterfactuals,"
    in *The Routledge Companion to Imaginary Worlds*, edited
    by Mark J. P. Wolf. New York: Routledge, 2017.
Galerie Perrotin. "Daniel Arsham *Paris, 3020* At Perrotin Paris." YouTube video, 7:51.
Posted March 12, 2020. https://youtu.be/OI_Estszew0.
_____. "Daniel Arsham *Time Dilation* at Perrotin New York." YouTube video,
    7:05. Posted January 27, 2021. https://youtu.be/L5PB5EGe9no.
_____. "Daniel Arsham Walkthrough of *Time Dilation* at Perrotin New York." YouTube
video, 25:23. Posted February 11, 2021. https://youtu.be/q4UFhrSo-6E.
Hypebeast. "Daniel Arsham on the Ideation and Creation of 'Fictional Archeology.'"
YouTube video, 3:25. Posted on September 25, 2015. https://youtu.be/oOMJbg-e-jQ.
Lloyd, Joe. "Daniel Arsham: *Paris, 3020*." *Studio International*, October, 2, 2020.
Morrissey, Siobhan. "Artist Daniel Arsham Does 'Archaeological Dig'
    at Locust Projects." *Miami Herald*, November 11, 2014.
Rodgers, David. "Capriccio," in *The Oxford Companion to Western Art*, edited
    by Hugh Brigstocke. New York: Oxford University Press, 2003.
Schmid, Helga. *Uchronia: Designing Time*. Basel: Birkhäuser,
    2020. doi.org/10.1515/9783035618112.

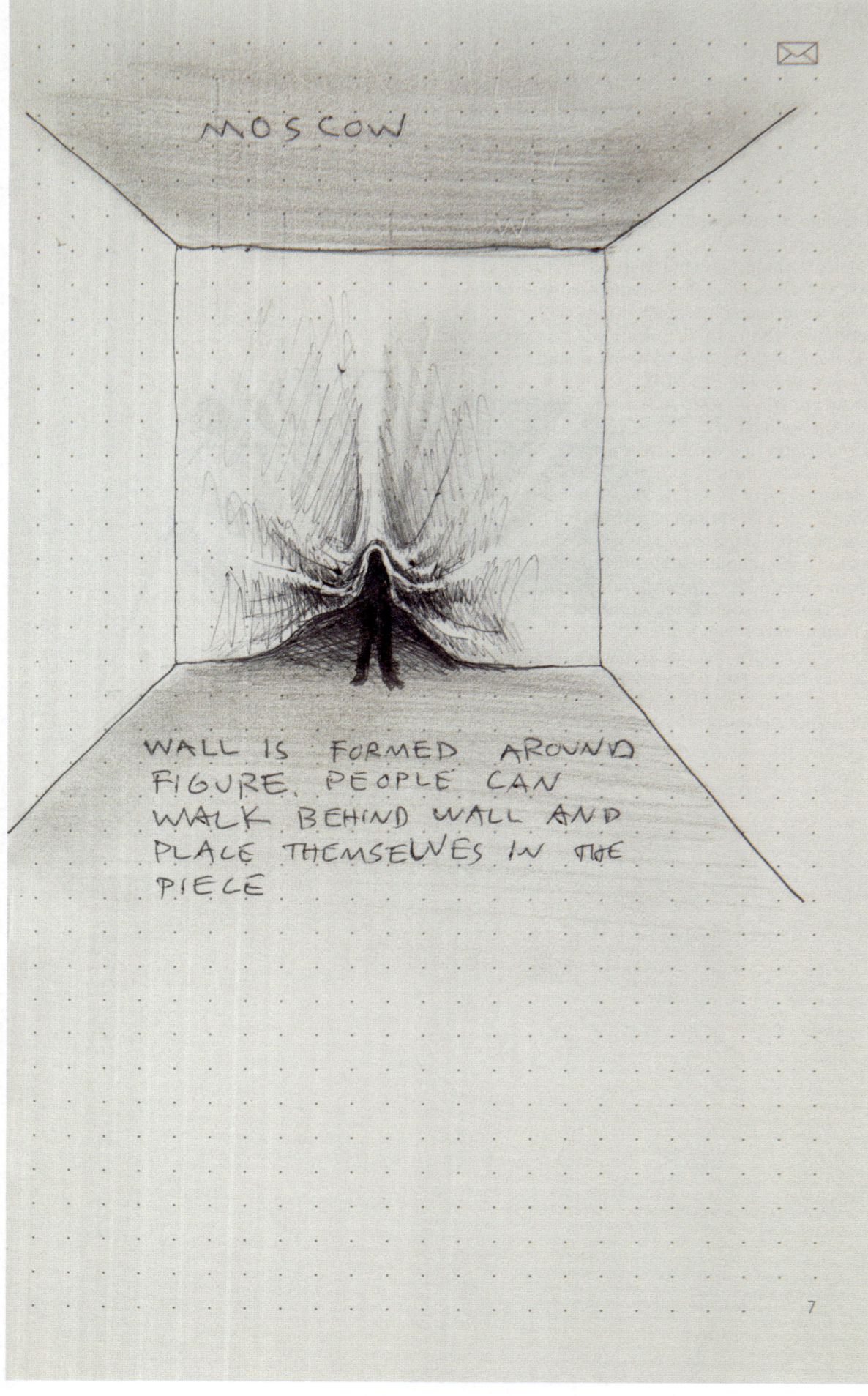

MOSCOW

WALL IS FORMED AROUND
FIGURE. PEOPLE CAN
WALK BEHIND WALL AND
PLACE THEMSELVES IN THE
PIECE

7

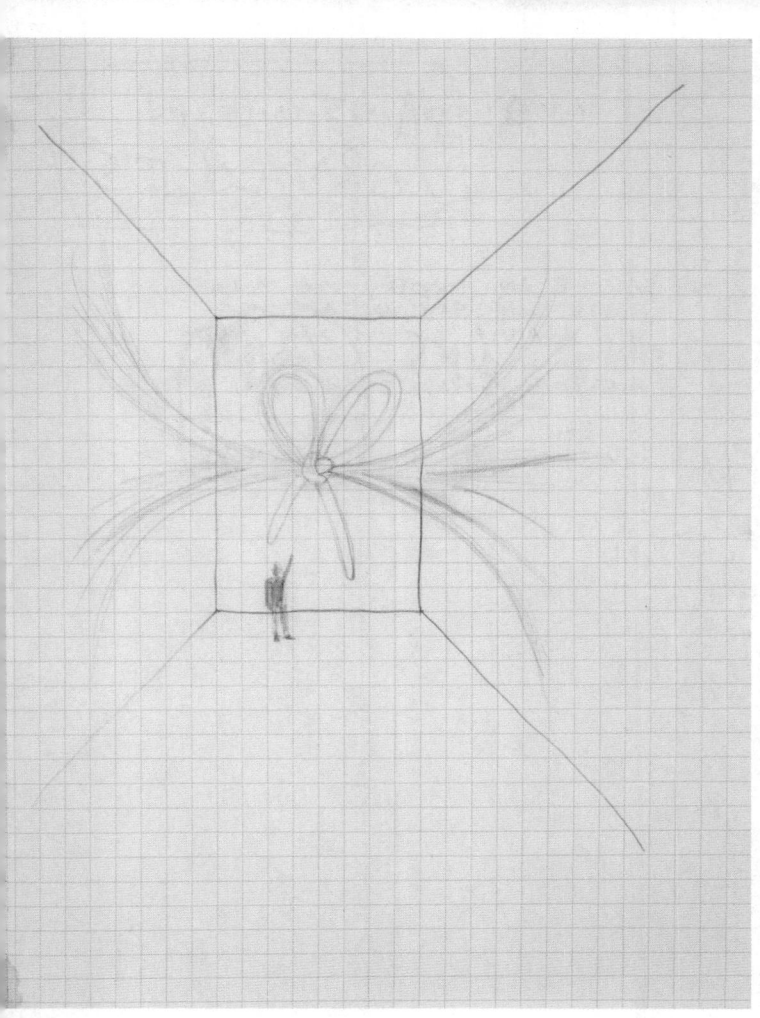 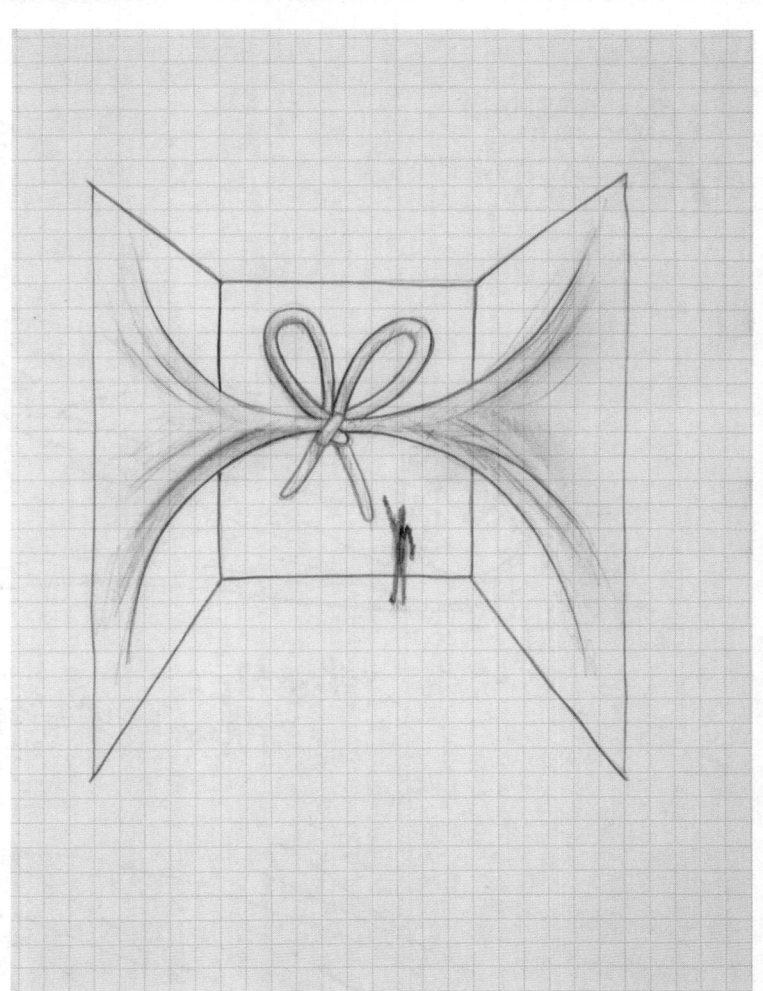

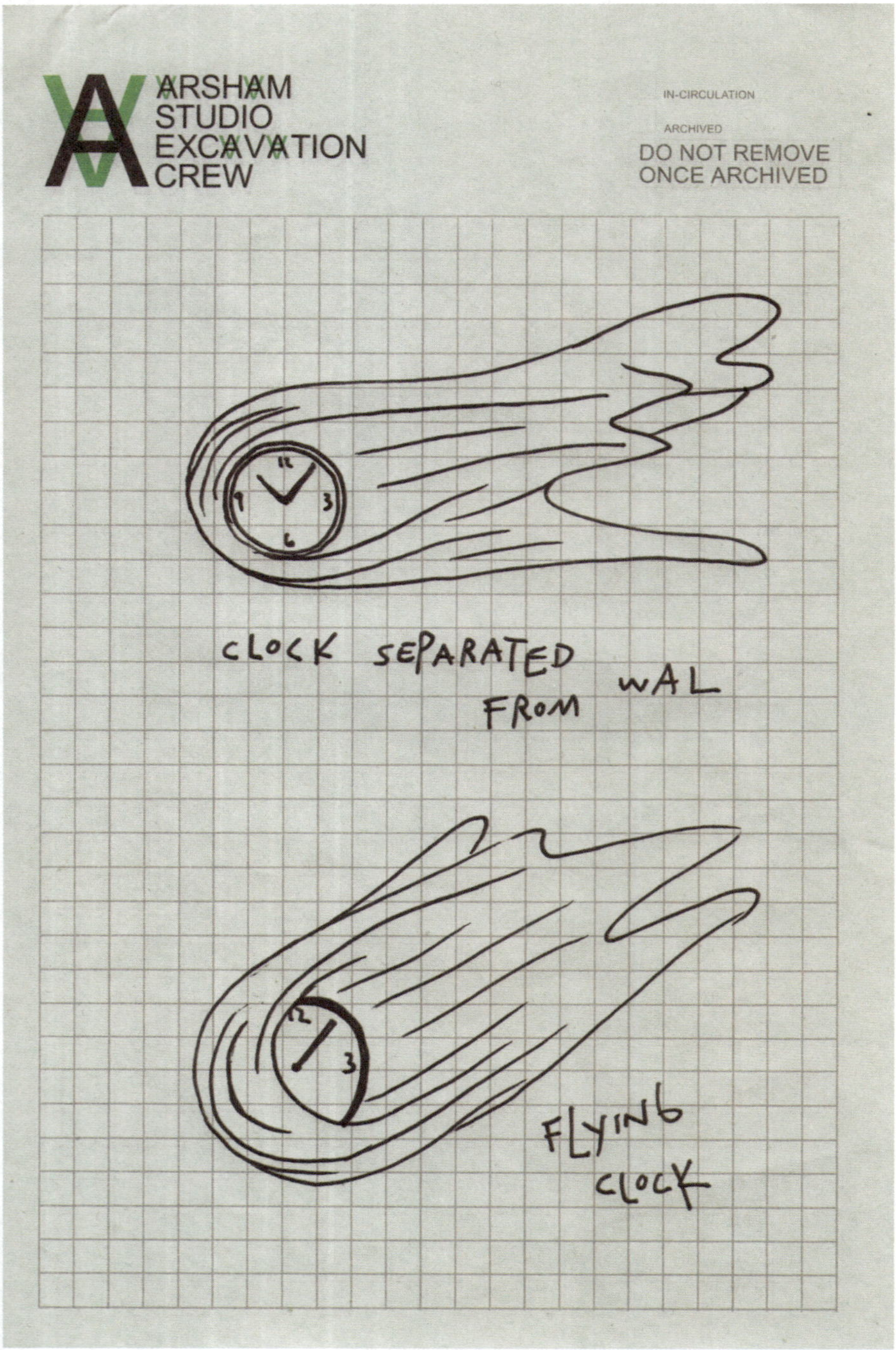

## ARSHAM
## STUDIO
## EXCAVATION
## CREW

IN-CIRCULATION

ARCHIVED

**DO NOT REMOVE
ONCE ARCHIVED**

CLOCK SEPARATED
FROM WAL

FLYING
CLOCK

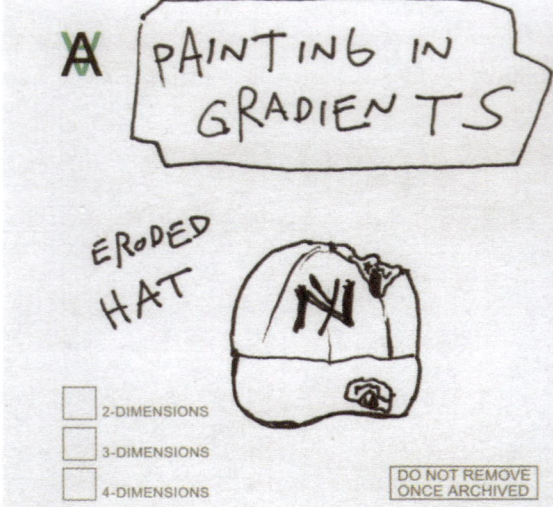

PAINTING IN
GRADIENTS

ERODED
HAT

☐ 2-DIMENSIONS

☐ 3-DIMENSIONS

☐ 4-DIMENSIONS

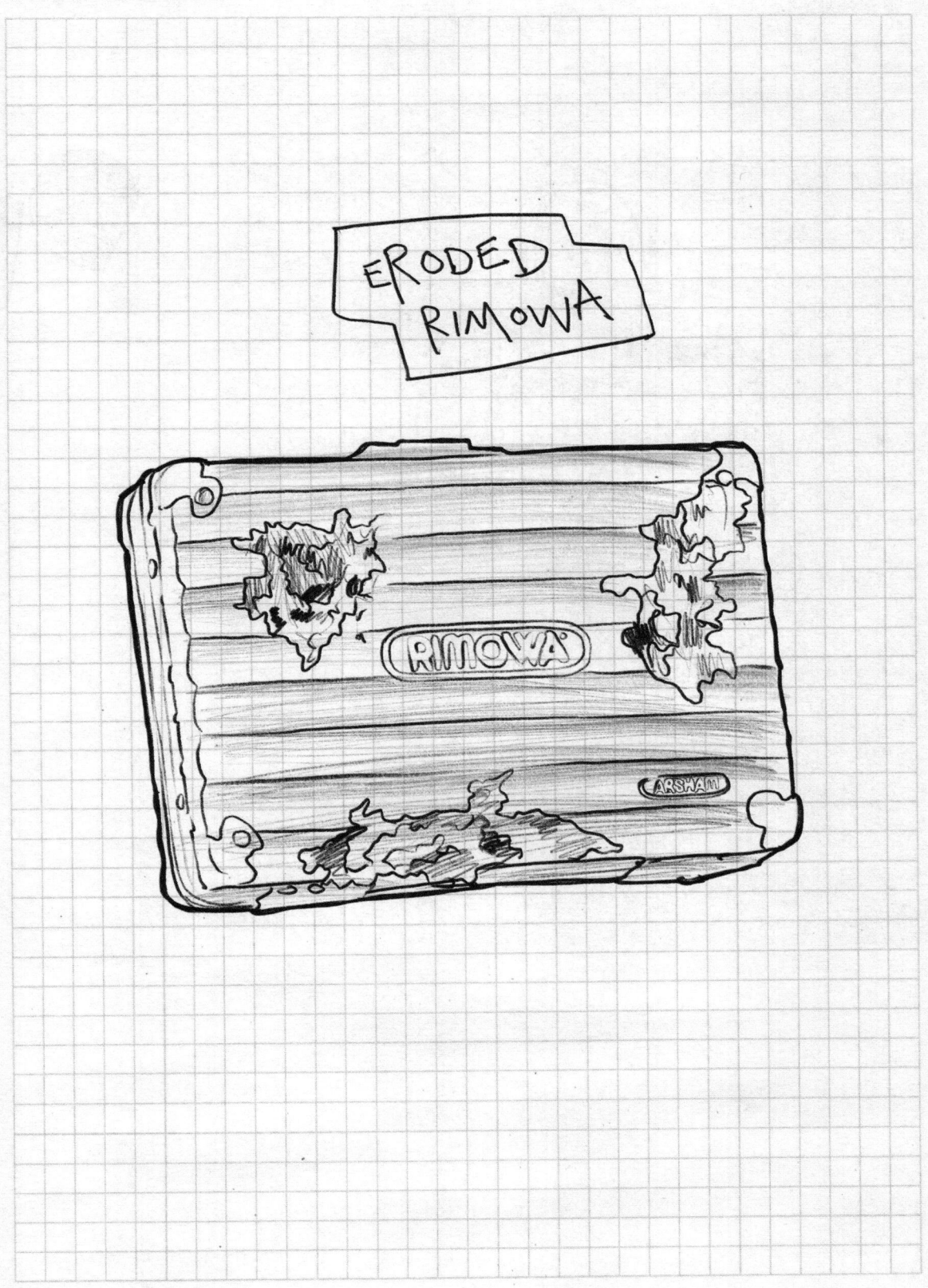

179 MOTT STREET, NEW YORK, NY

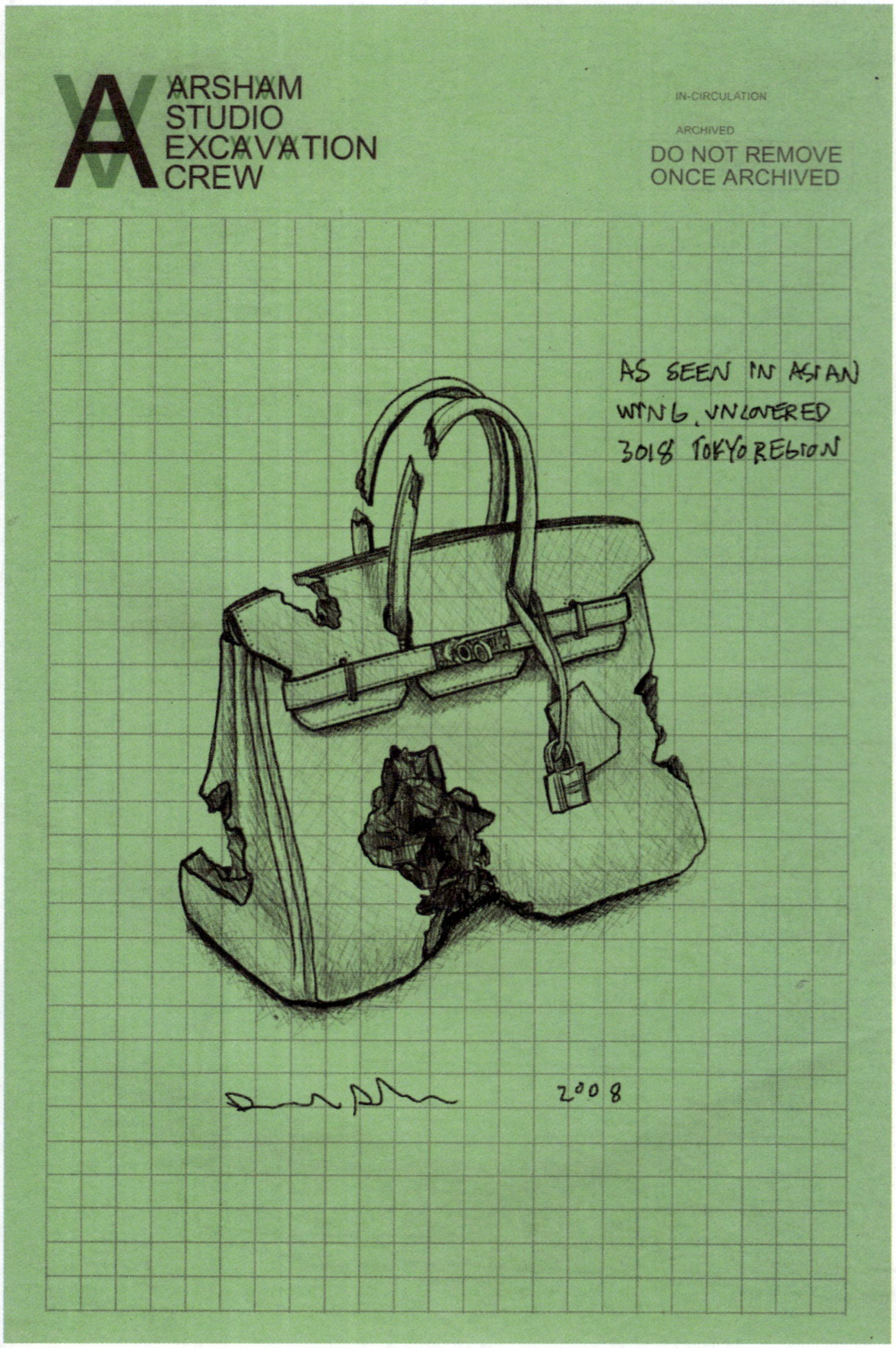

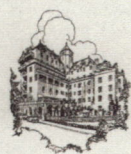

ARSHAM
STUDIO
EXCAVATION
CREW

AS SEEN IN ASIAN
WING. UNCOVERED
3018 TOKYO REGION

2008

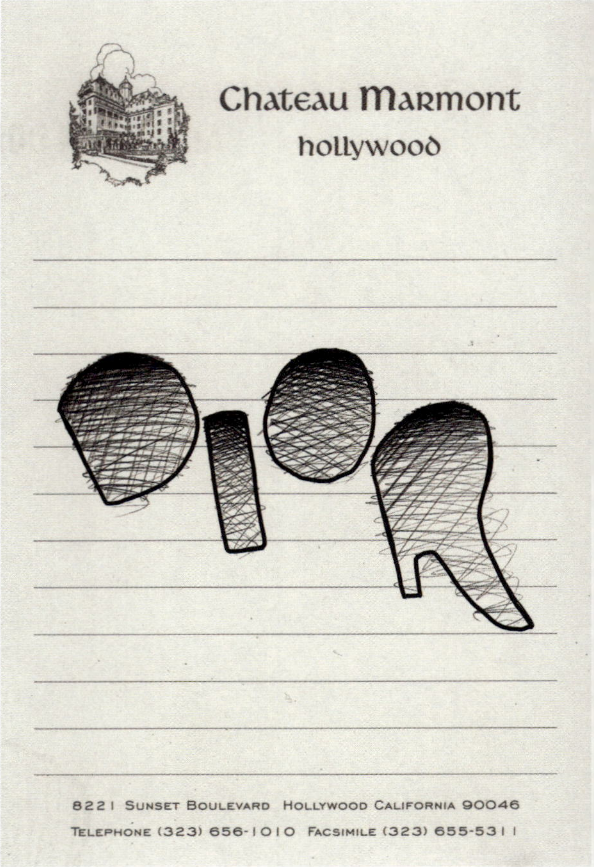

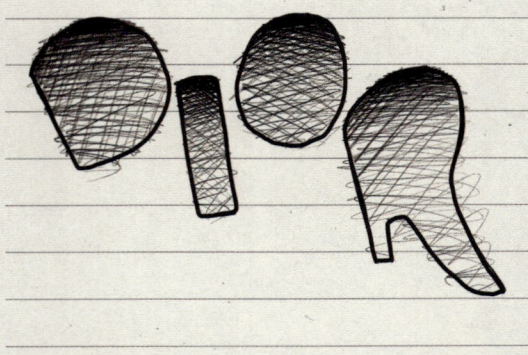

## Chateau Marmont
### hollywood

8221 Sunset Boulevard  Hollywood California 90046
Telephone (323) 656-1010  Facsimile (323) 655-5311

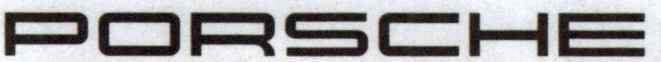

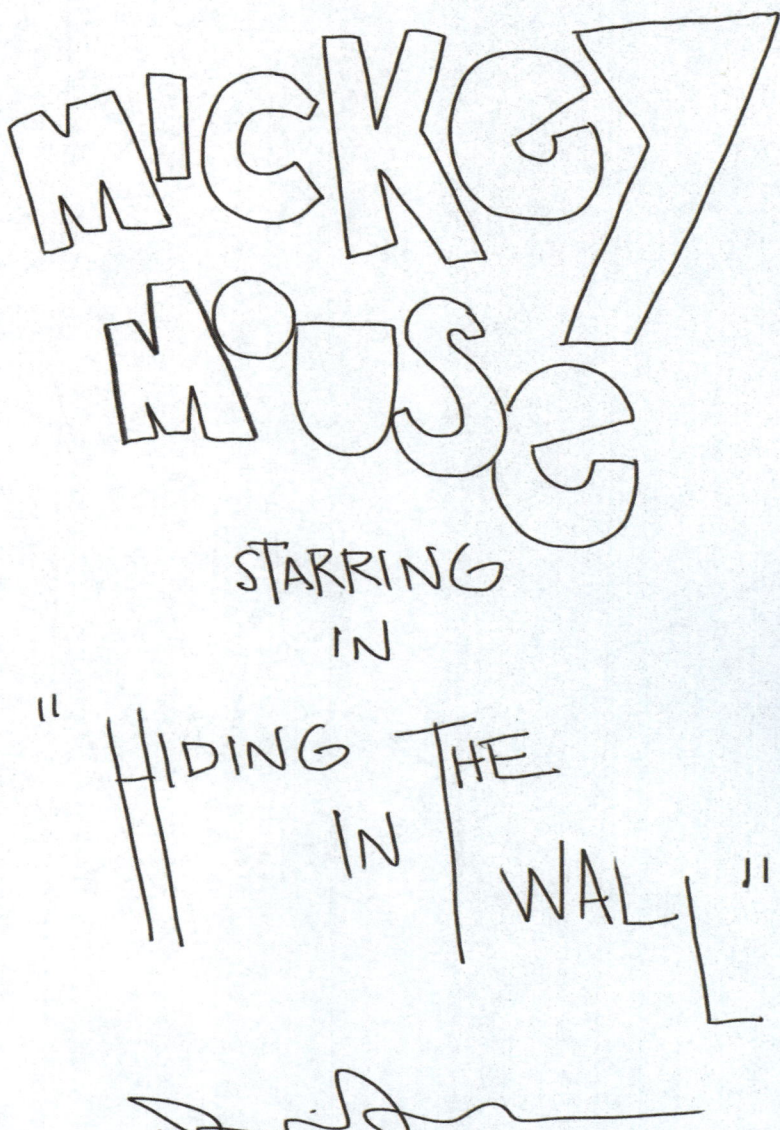

MICKEY MOUSE

STARRING IN

"HIDING THE IN WALL"

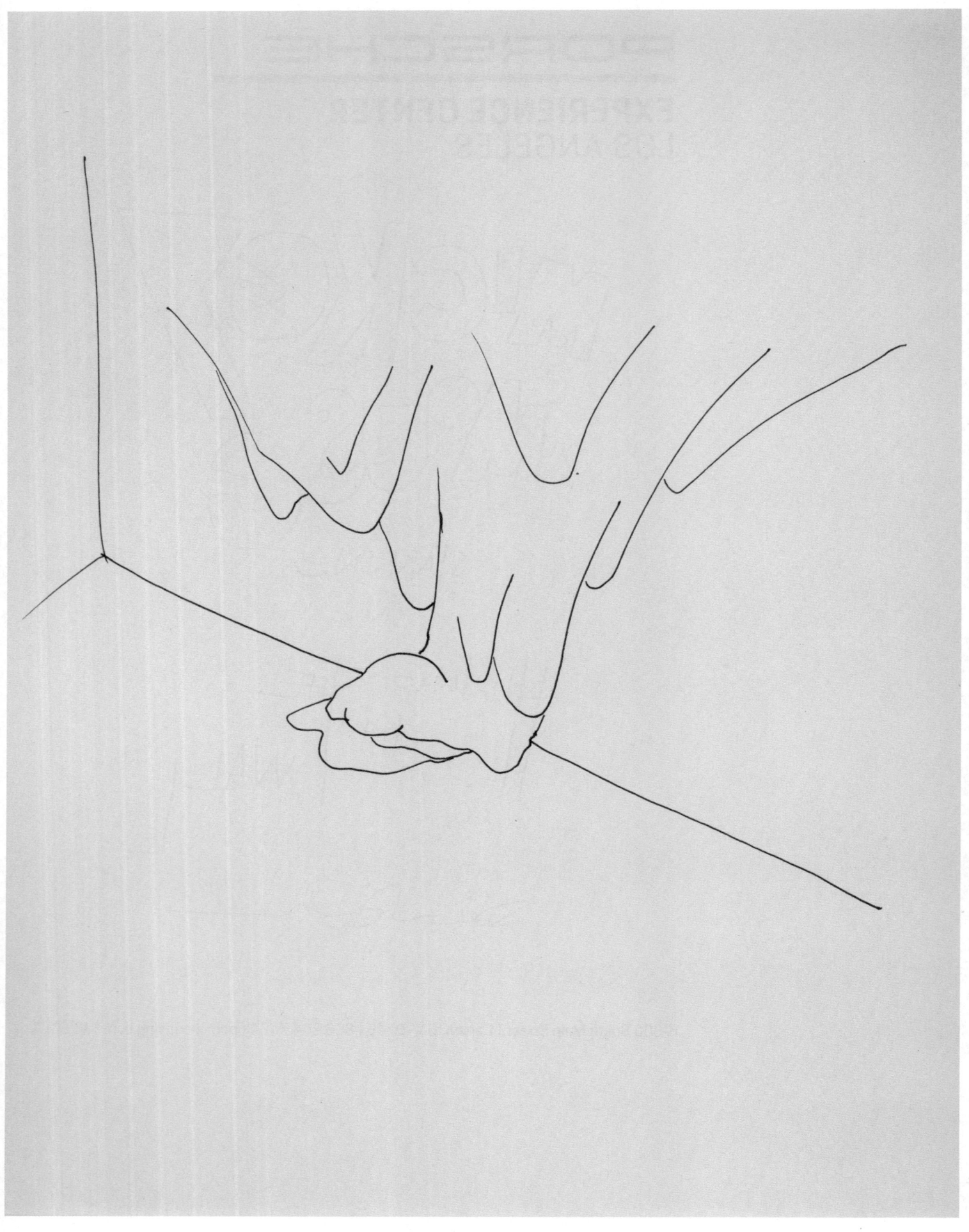

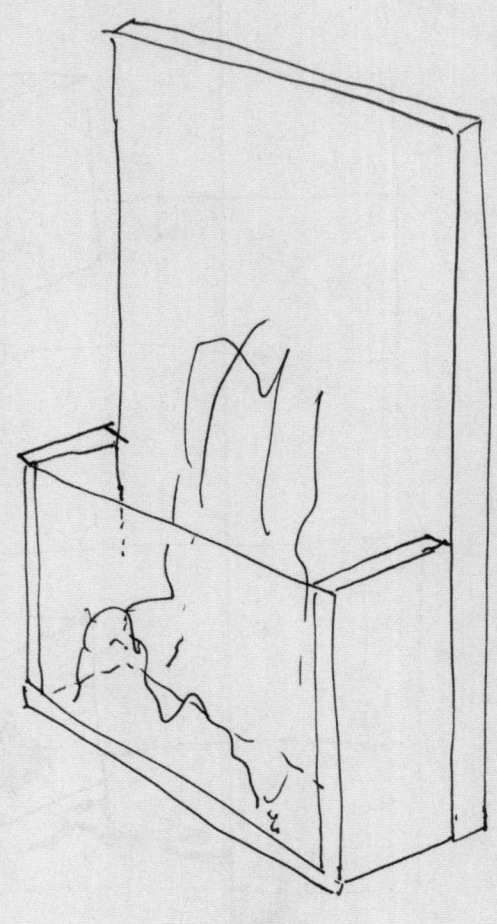

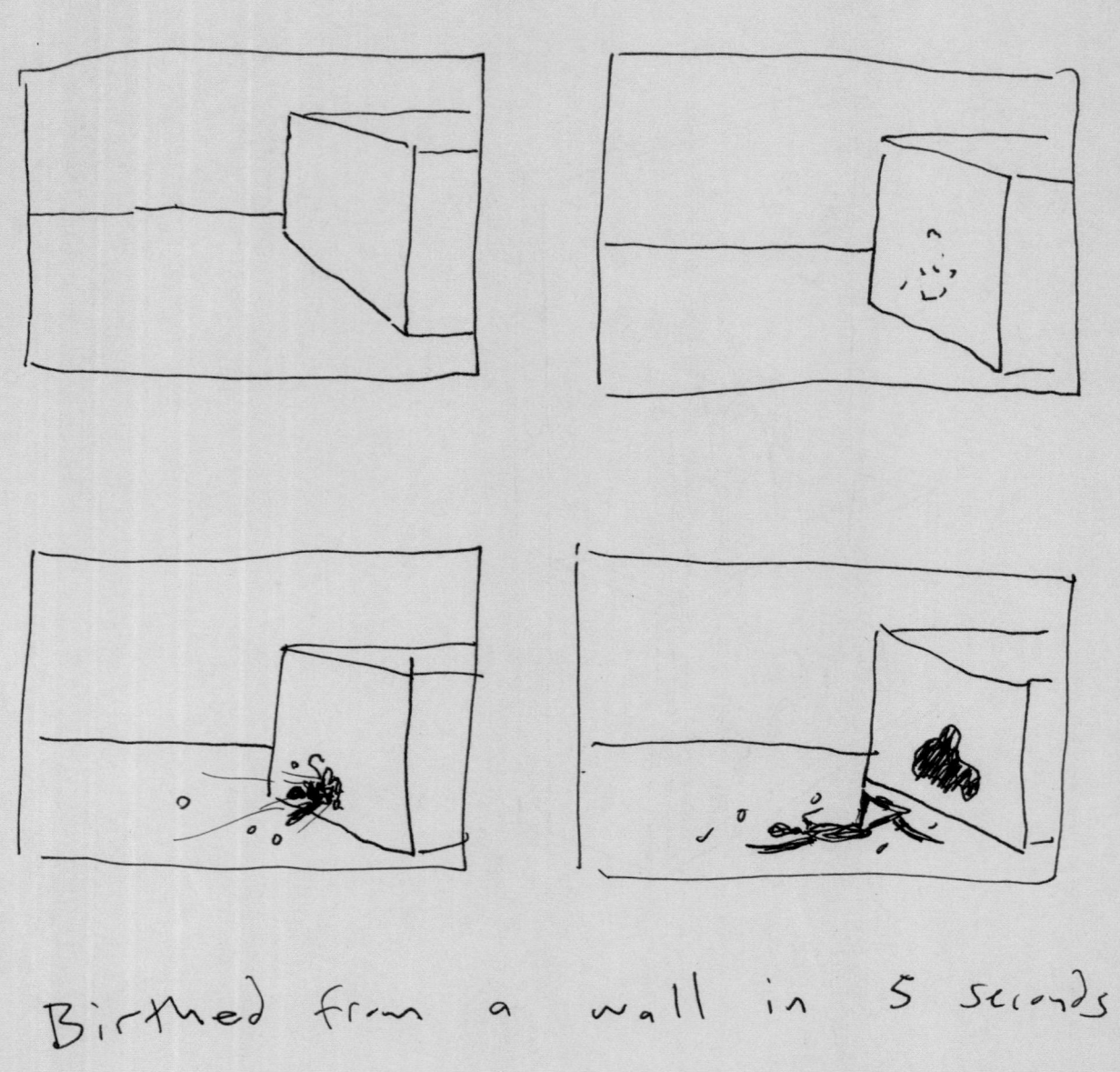

Birthed from a wall in 5 seconds.
ALL white. powder. different
size white cubes come out with
the explosion.

Duet with AN earth mover

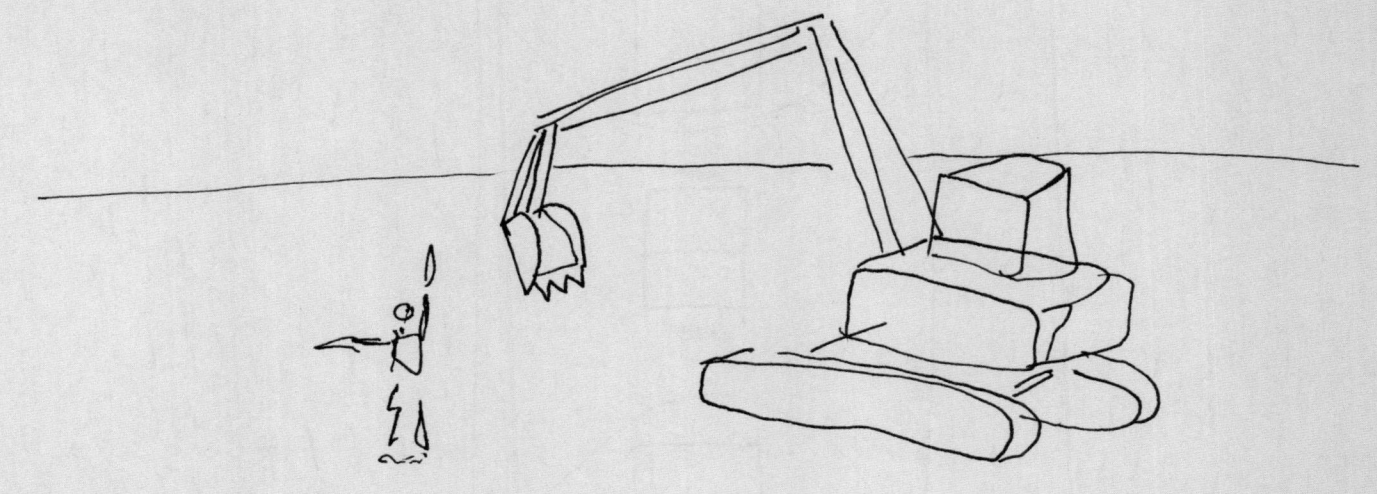

11-7-09

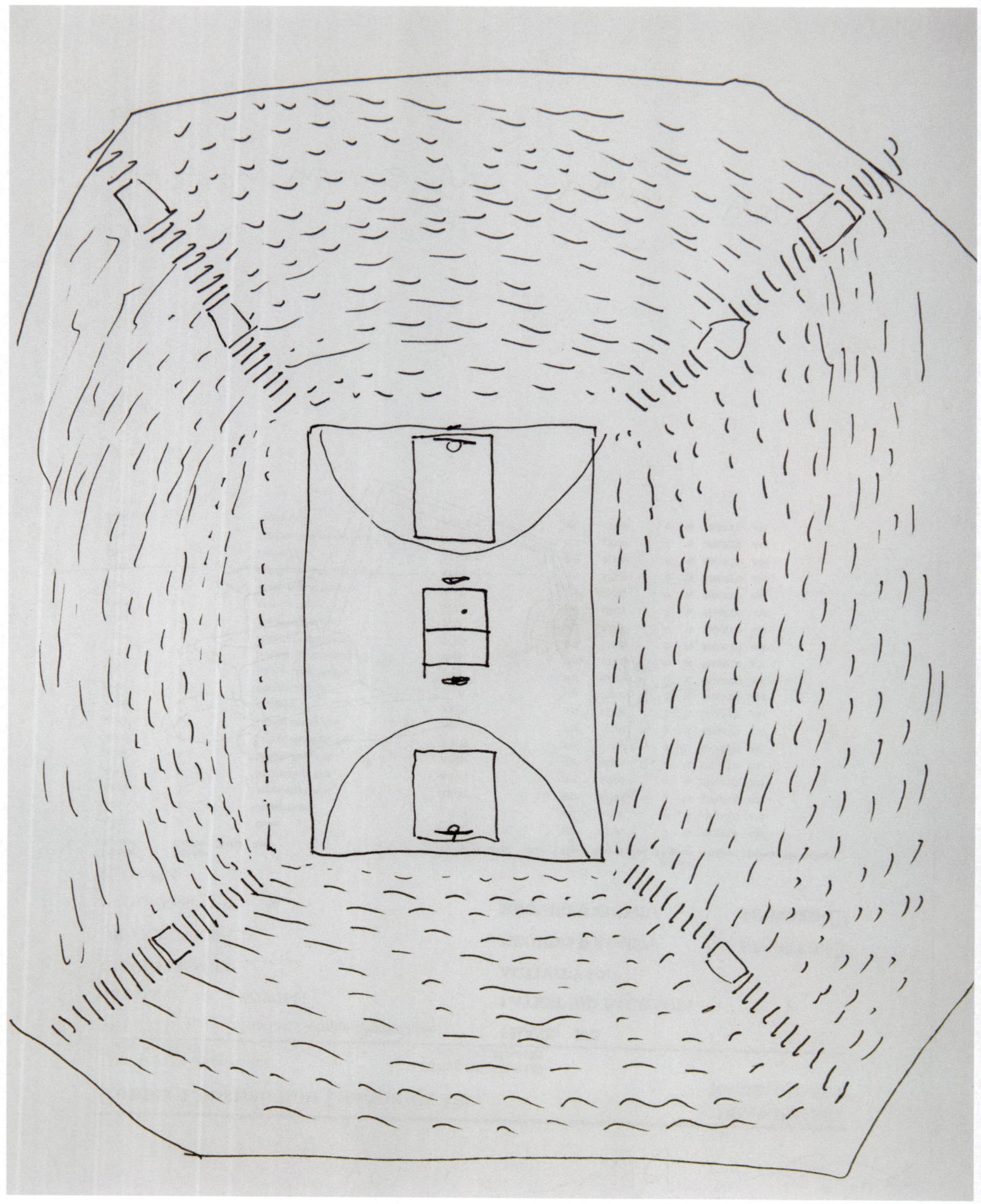

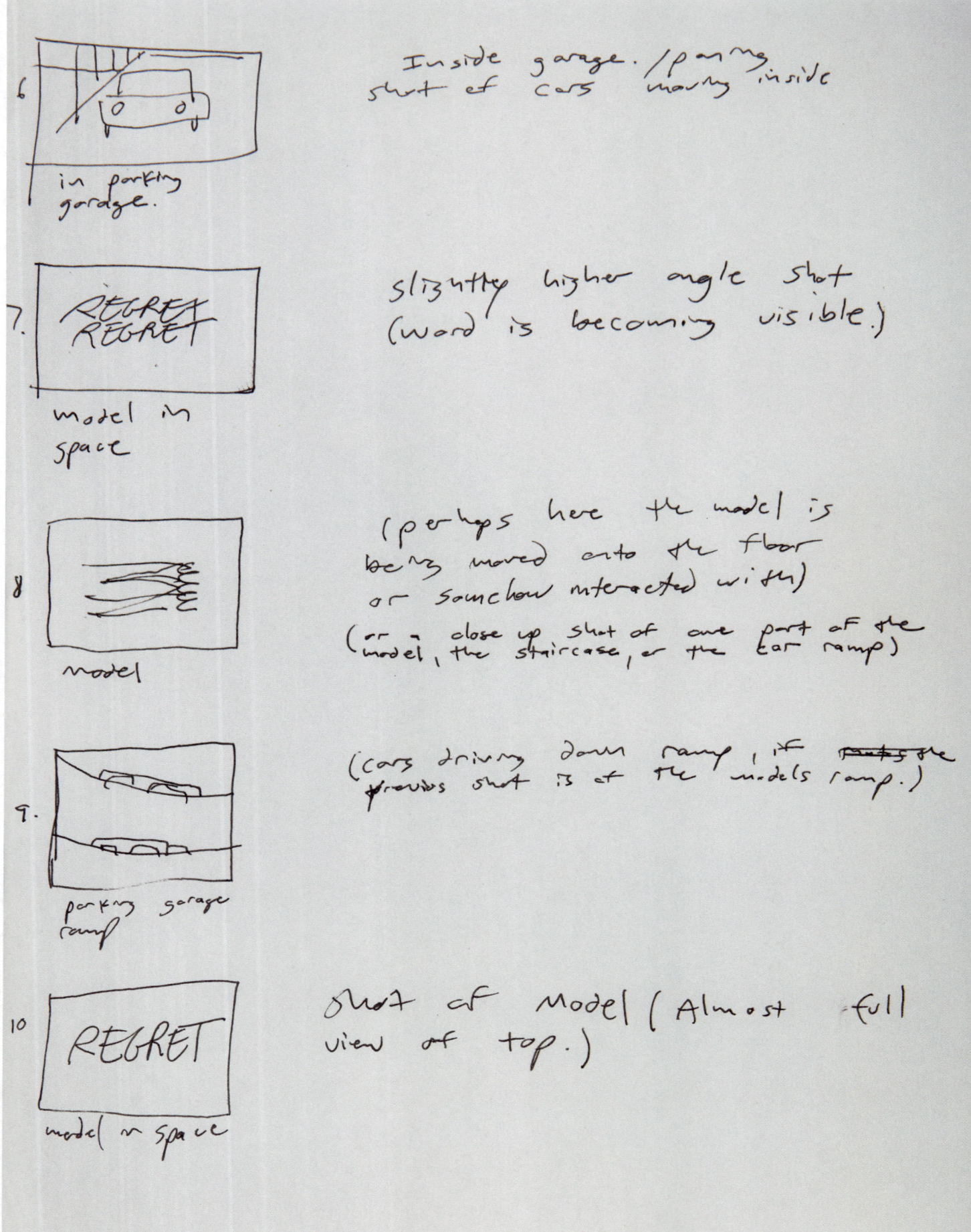

6  *in parking garage.*

Inside garage. / panning shot of cars moving inside

7.  *model in space*

slightly higher angle shot (word is becoming visible.)

8  *model*

(perhaps here the model is being moved onto the floor or somehow interacted with)

(or a close up shot of one part of the model, the staircase, or the car ramp)

9.  *parking garage ramp*

(cars driving down ramp, if possible previous shot is of the models ramp.)

10  *model in space*

shot of model (Almost full view of top.)

# SCENARIO 2

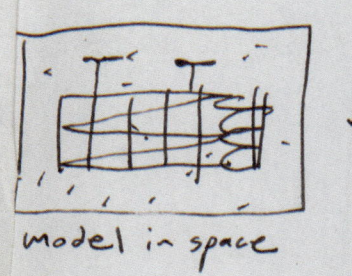

model in space

side view of model in space. (very little of top shows) Hard lighting

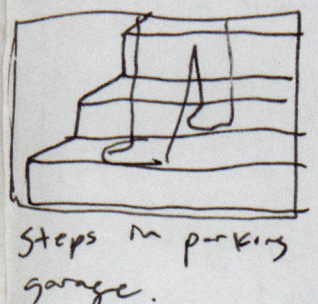

Steps in parking garage.

person walks down the steps in the parking garage. (color coded lighting if possible) pink and blue. pink here
(just a hint of the person on the stairs.) either just coming into frame, or moving out of frame.

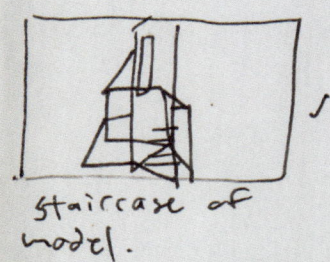

Staircase of model.

pan shot of staircase in the model. from bottom to top same color coding as previous shot.

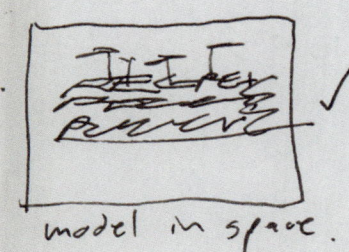

model in space.

Shot of model. slightly more exposed top. dramatic lighting remains constant. pink on the staircase.

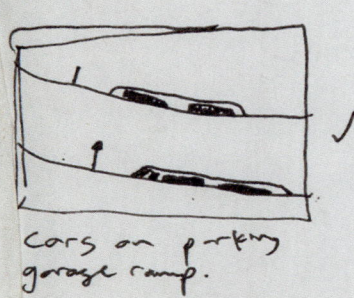

cars on parking garage ramp.

(going down in circles, ~~that with~~ close enough only to show the garage. No other buildings)

(Blue lighting)

note. this shot might need to be inside the building. Driving down the ramp for instance.

1998-849

23

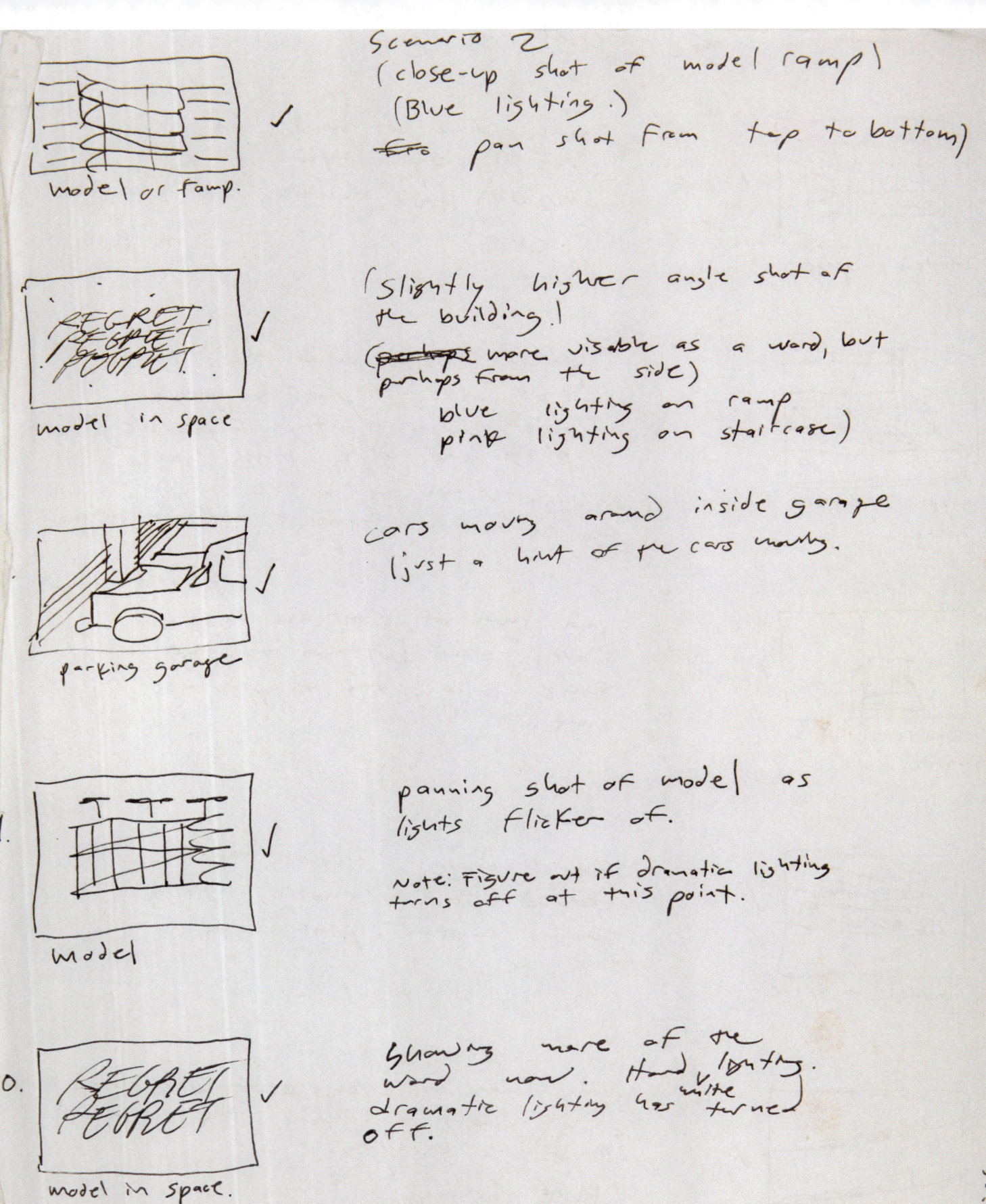

Scenario 2
(close-up shot of model ramp)
(Blue lighting.)
~~to~~ pan shot from top to bottom)

✓ model or ramp.

(slightly higher angle shot of
the building.)
(~~perhaps~~ more visable as a word, but
perhaps from the side)
blue lighting on ramp
pink lighting on staircase)

✓ model in space

cars moving around inside garage
(just a hint of the cars moving.

✓ parking garage

panning shot of model as
lights flicker of.

Note: Figure out if dramatic lighting
turns off at this point.

✓ model

Showing more of the
word now. Hand lighting.
dramatic lighting has white turned
off.

✓ model in space.

Note: The staircase is for people to move up and down. The ramp is for cars.
The staircase is the only part of the building that has a physical connection

bodies.

11.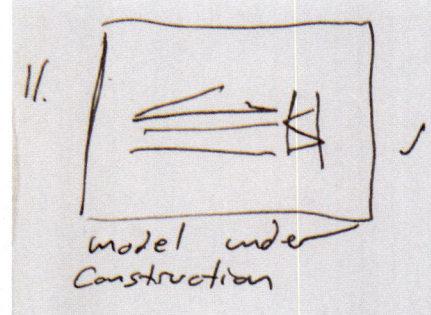

model under
construction

Scenario 2
with all the materials
and tools present
(without dramatic lighting)
(possibly some one working on it)

12.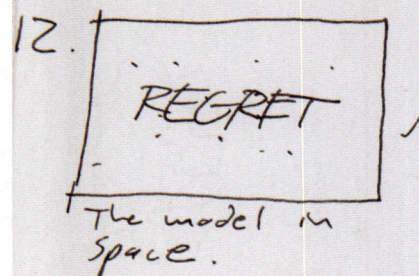

The model in
Space.

Hard lighting.

3.

The plans.

REGRET visible.
the t-square should move down
multiple times crossing over
the entire image.

Film strip.

Need to shoot moving down the staircase. and
the shops of the plans.

- what are the surfaces of the walls.
- are there exposed fasteners.

- should my installation plan to be attached to the existing panels, or should it replace them.
- can I change the lighting core and several lighting scenario.

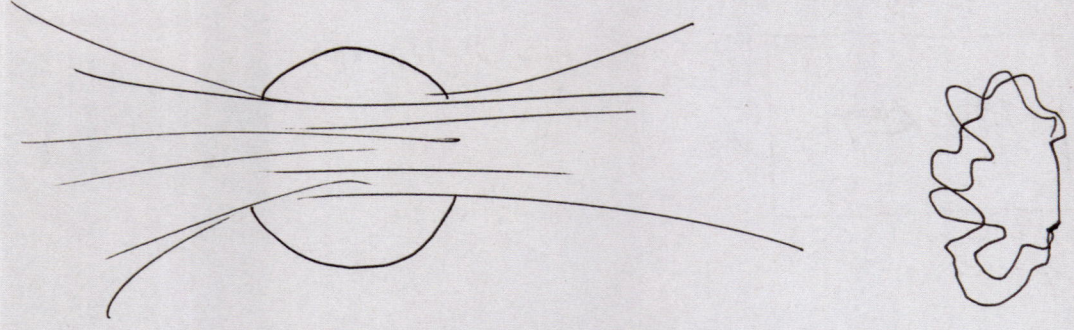

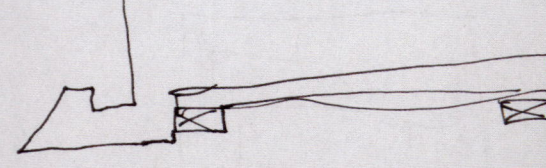

- Do the existing Alu-Honeycomb panels need to stay and then I would build on top of that?

- Are there any requirements for the use of glass mirrors on the ship.

_____Studio_____

- vent for heater?                          gravity boots?

- sink plumbing

- more boxes down

.                                            <u>Ross</u>
                                             discussion w/ Alex re.

<u>John</u>                    <u>Yadin</u>                    Yadin, John, Tim
3D ~~forms~~ cubes            - discuss the future            _____
mock-up donkey.               - review list.                  clean shop bring forms
                              - Eclipse recap                 down, dust, photograph etc.
                              - confer w/ oliver
                                about materials.
<u>Tim -</u>
- clean heater
- make air filter...
- move water to shop
- smoke detector.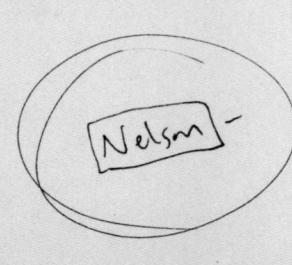

- Ana, prepare email description for Avalanche.
- poster for show...
- ~~prepare email for chong.~~
-email Mario -develop ideas for 1111
- ~~email Todd~~
- ~~Shira - Roanne.~~                    - email steven Matijcio
= Prepare images and Release for Annual Avalanche
- ~~email Jenany whiteside Scott Egg~~
- ~~email Jacob terms for fleess~~
- ~~email Ron.~~

- Avalanche /my piece./

- Ross does Renderings of cloud in Herzog.
- Air filter for studio

# Scenario 1

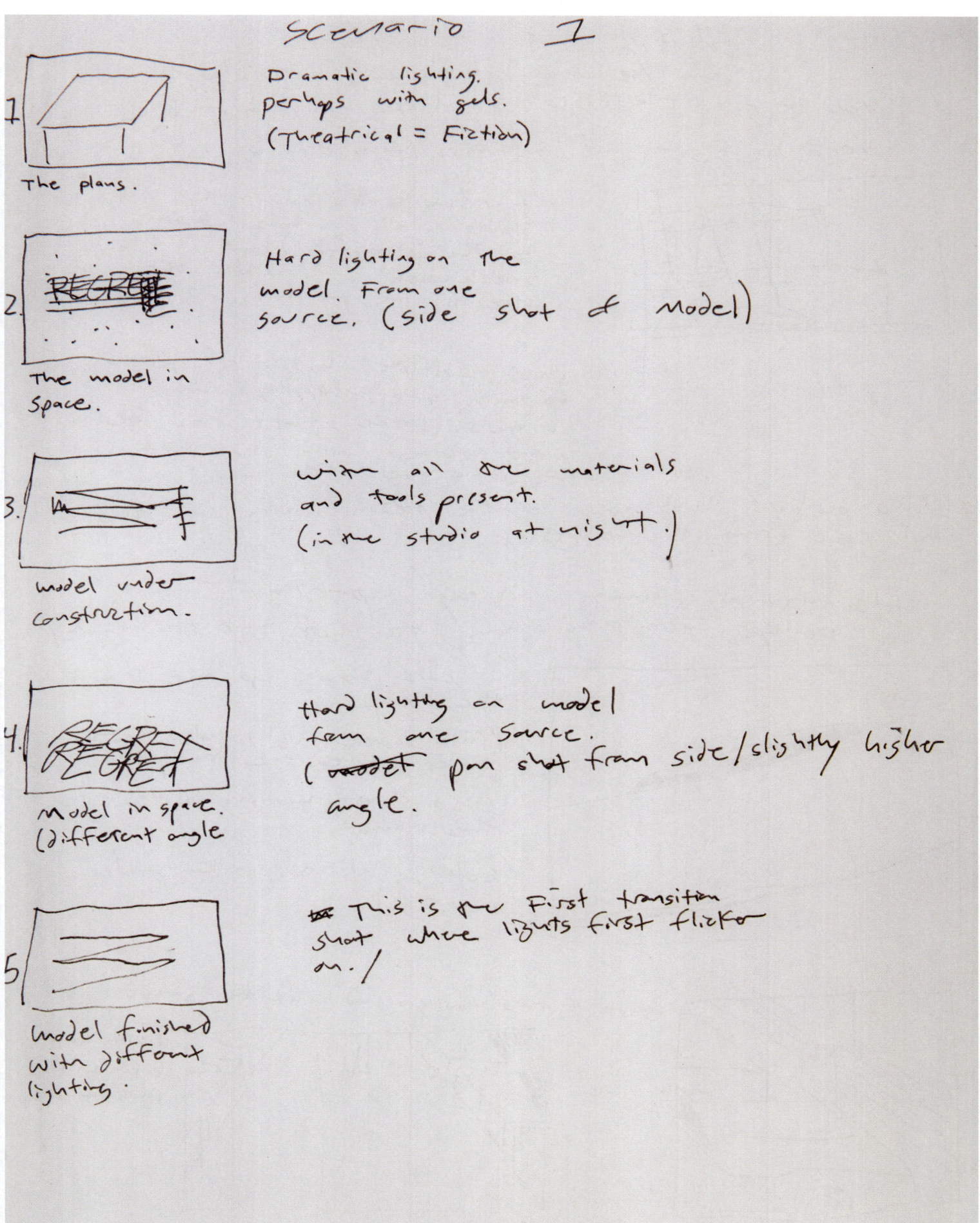

1. **The plans.**

   Dramatic lighting. perhaps with gels. (Theatrical = Fiction)

2. **The model in Space.**

   Hard lighting on the model. From one source. (side shot of model)

3. **model under construction.**

   with all the materials and tools present. (in the studio at night.)

4. **Model in space. (different angle**

   Hard lighting on model from one source. ( ~~model~~ pan shot from side/slightly higher angle.

5. **model finished with diffent lighting.**

   This is the First transition shot, where lights first flicker on. /

# Shots in Garage.

(can be done before model is finished)

Need to get TRIPOD. Perhaps bring bike

Need to figure out costumes if necessary.

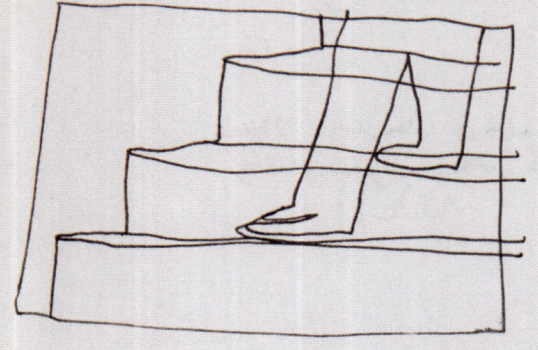

A person walks down the stairs in the garage. (Similar to the staircase descent in beetlegeuse). If possible use blue lighting on this.

shoot multiple shots of pans ~~up~~ down, and wrapping around corners. (these shots can be interspersed with shots of the staircase in the model.

(Also perhaps shoot some of the person moving down the stair case from the outside.

Height of camera : Very important perhaps everything from the height of the model

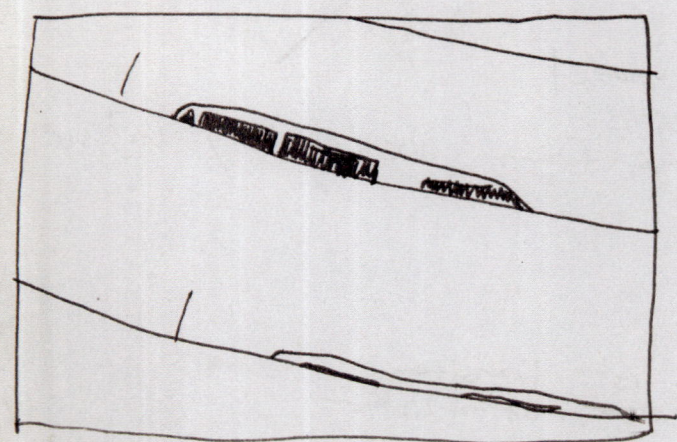

cars moving up and down the ramp.

(This scene might also take place inside the ramp)

Also shoot moving inside the ramp

(color with pink gel lights.)

shots of cars moving around inside the garage.

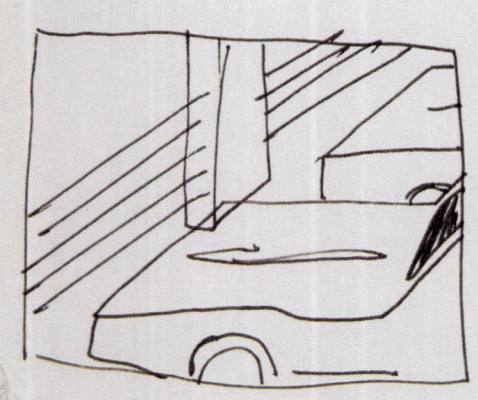

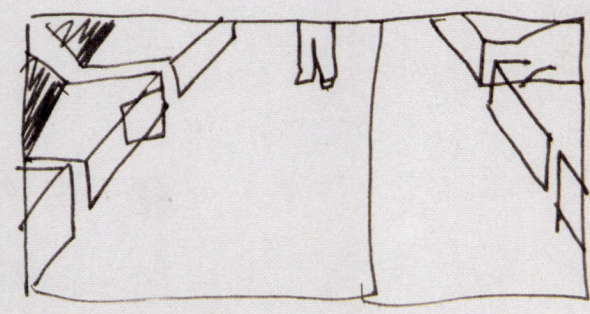

person walking between the rows of cars.

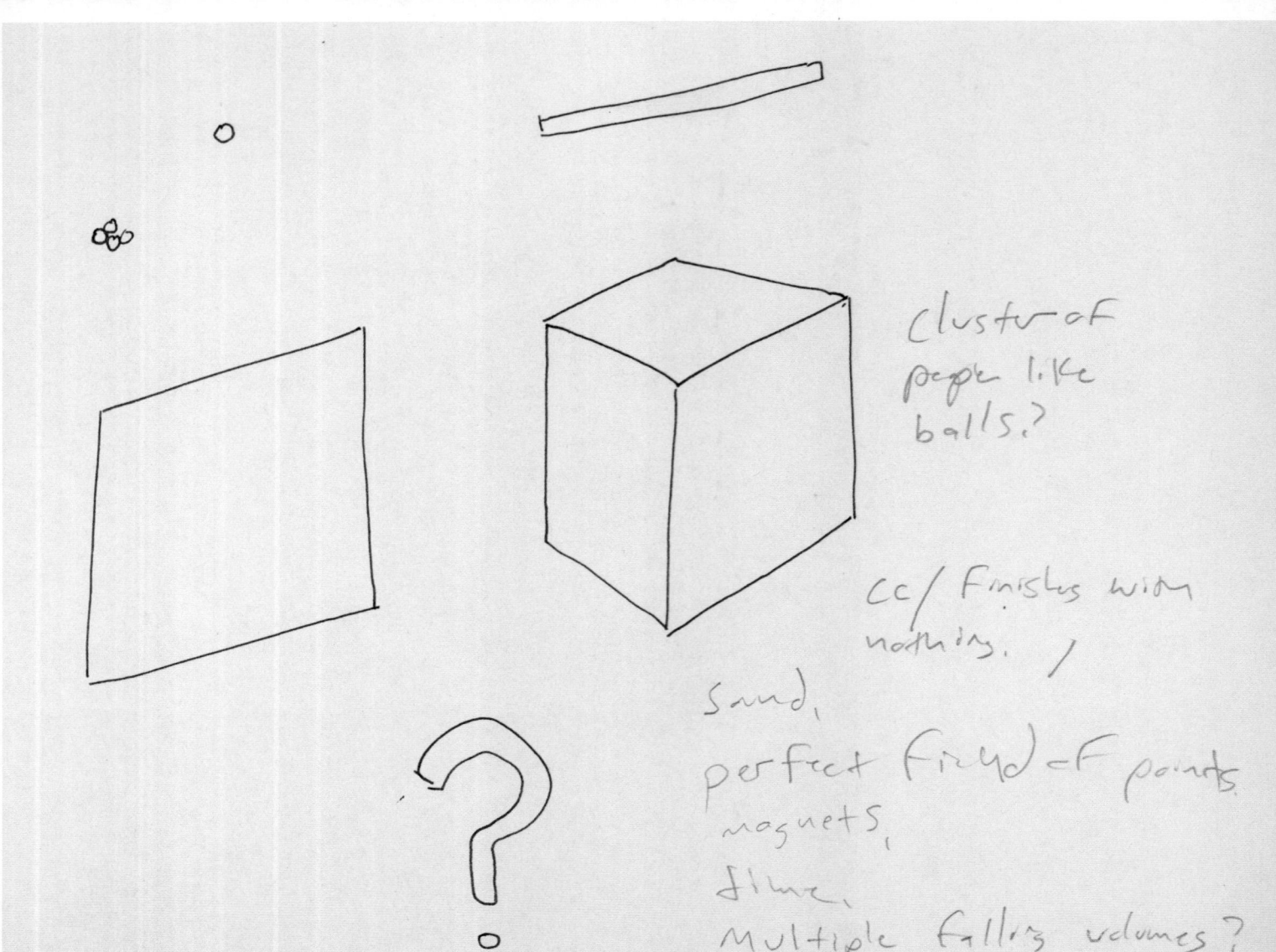

cluster of
paper like
balls?

cc/ finishes with
nothing. /

Sand,
perfect fire/ d-f points.
magnets,
time,
Multiple falling volumes?

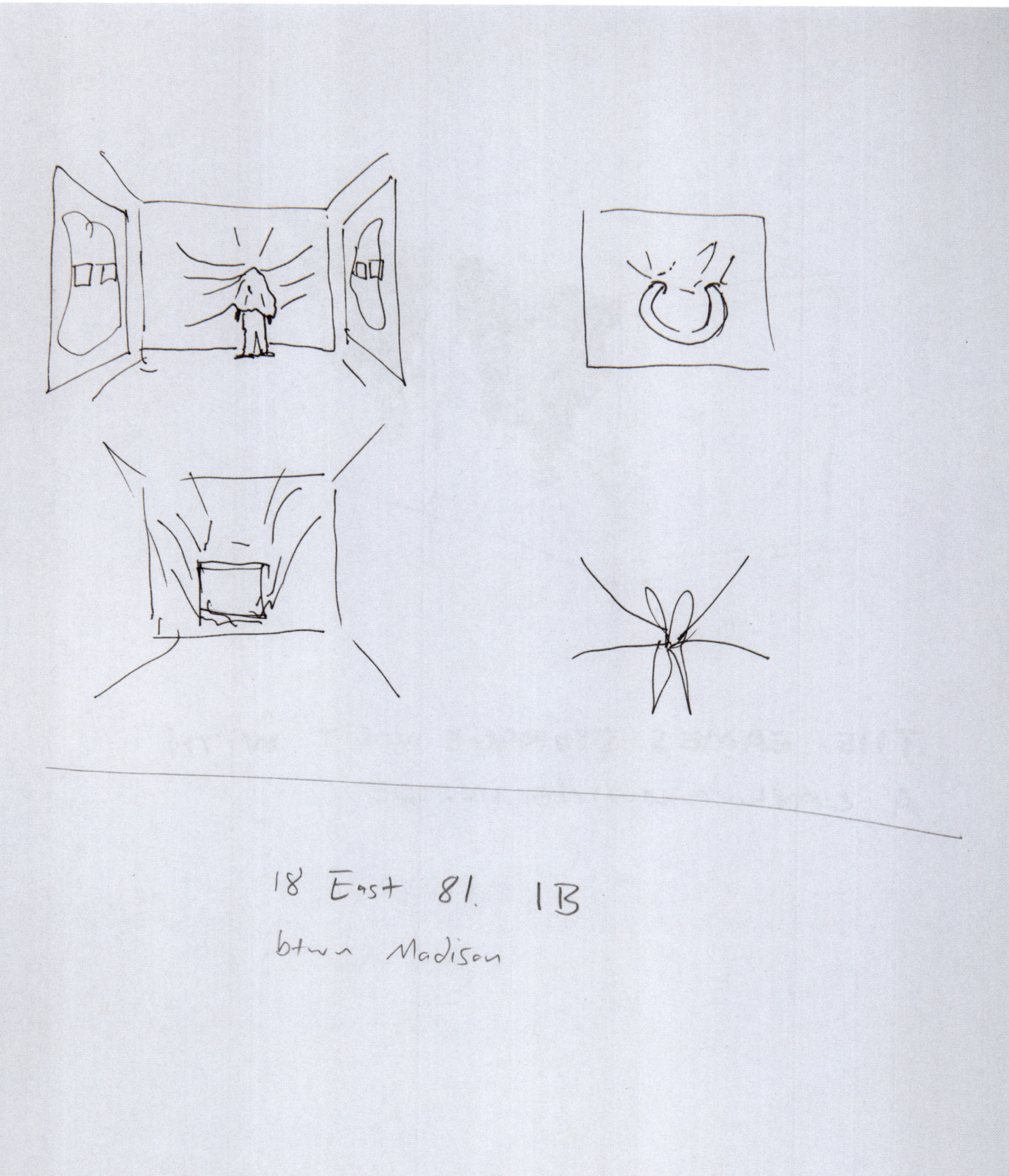

18 East 81. 1B
btwn Madison

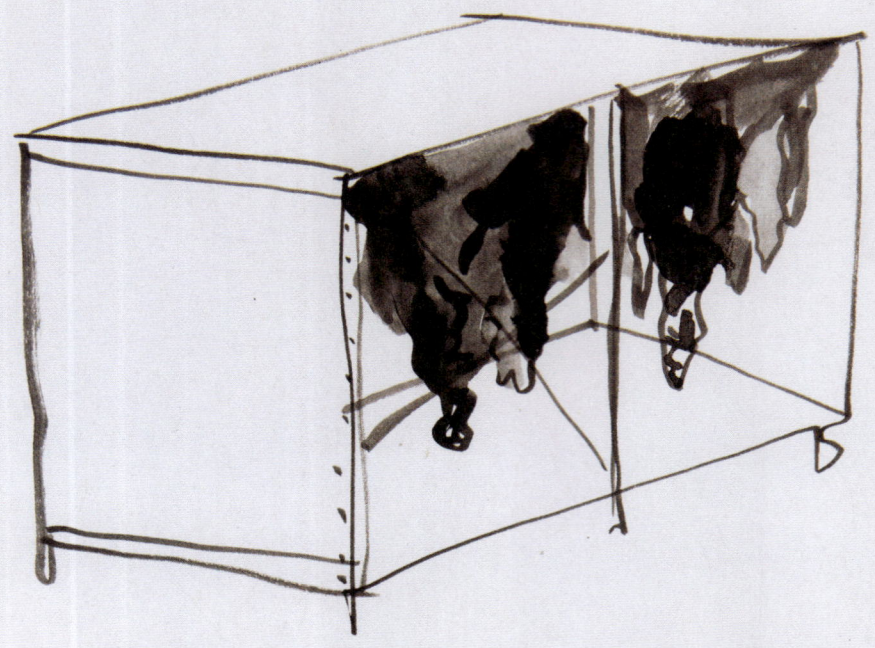

THE EAMES STORAGE UNIT WITH
A CAVE GROWING INSIDE

1-26-11

melting Eames chair with
white form filling in to make
chair functional again.

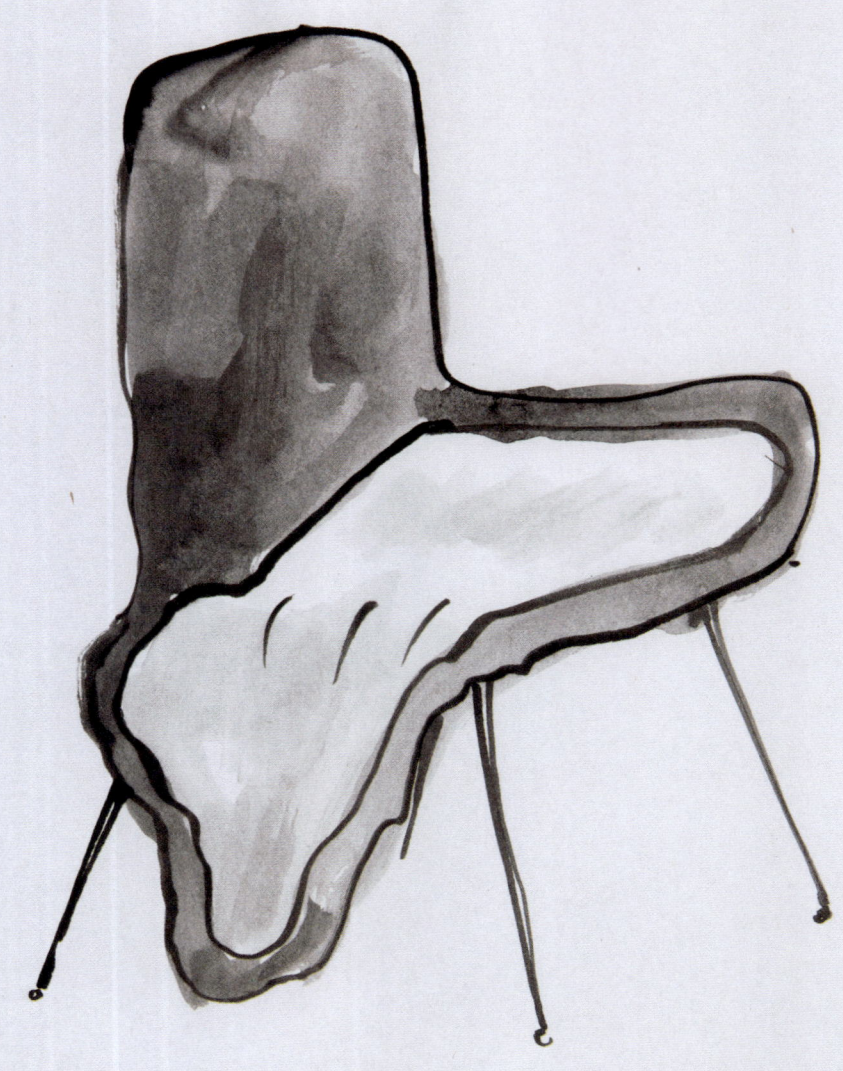

1-26-11

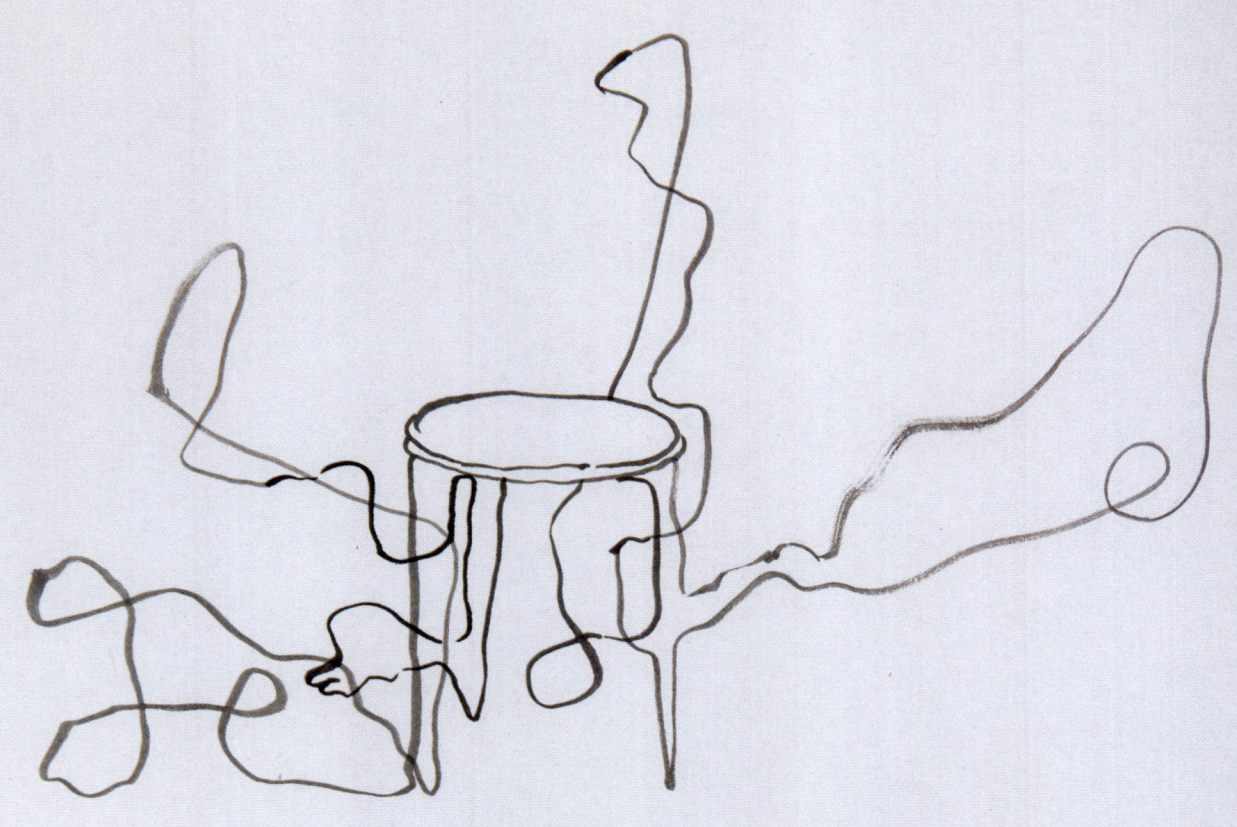

Florence Knoll Stool with Deviant legs

1.26.11

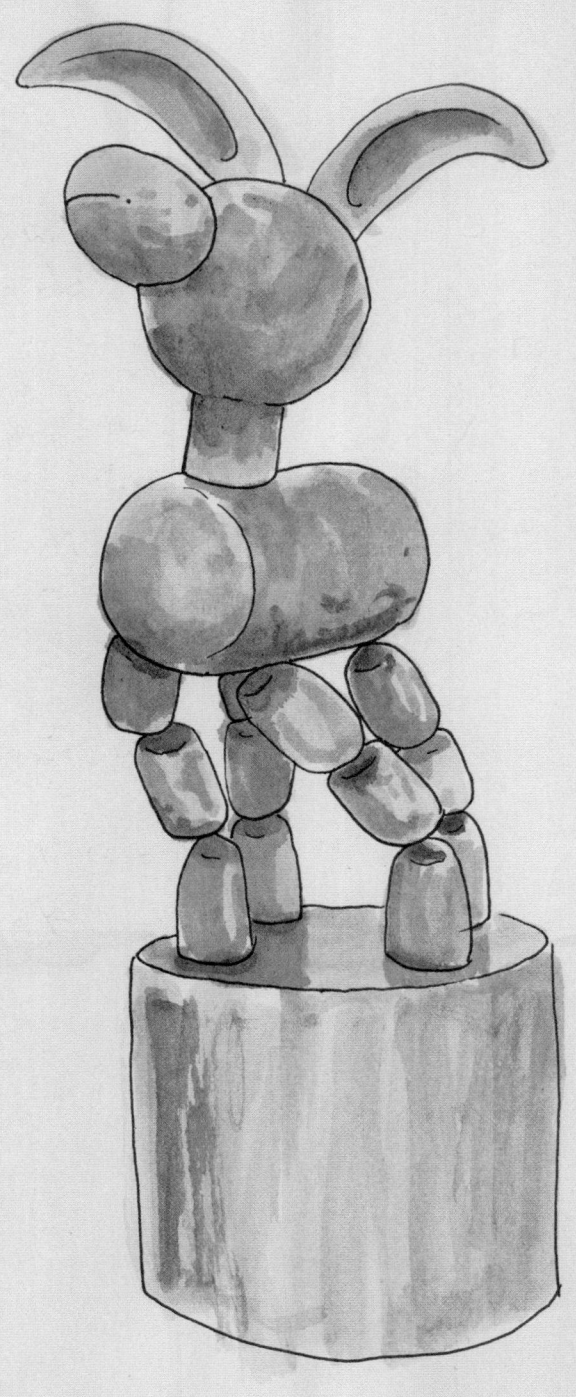

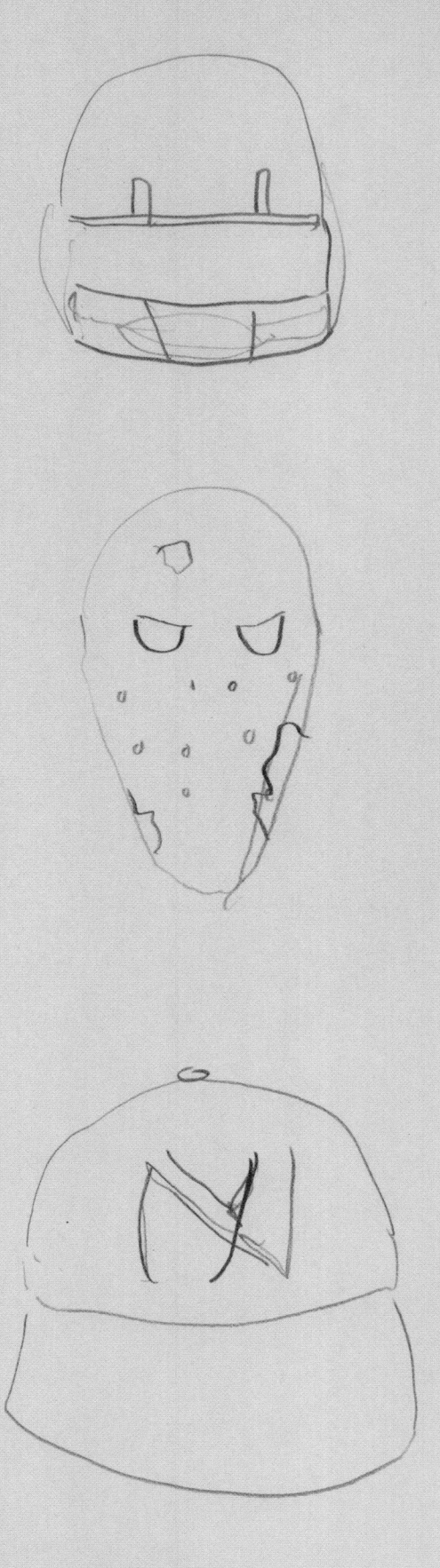

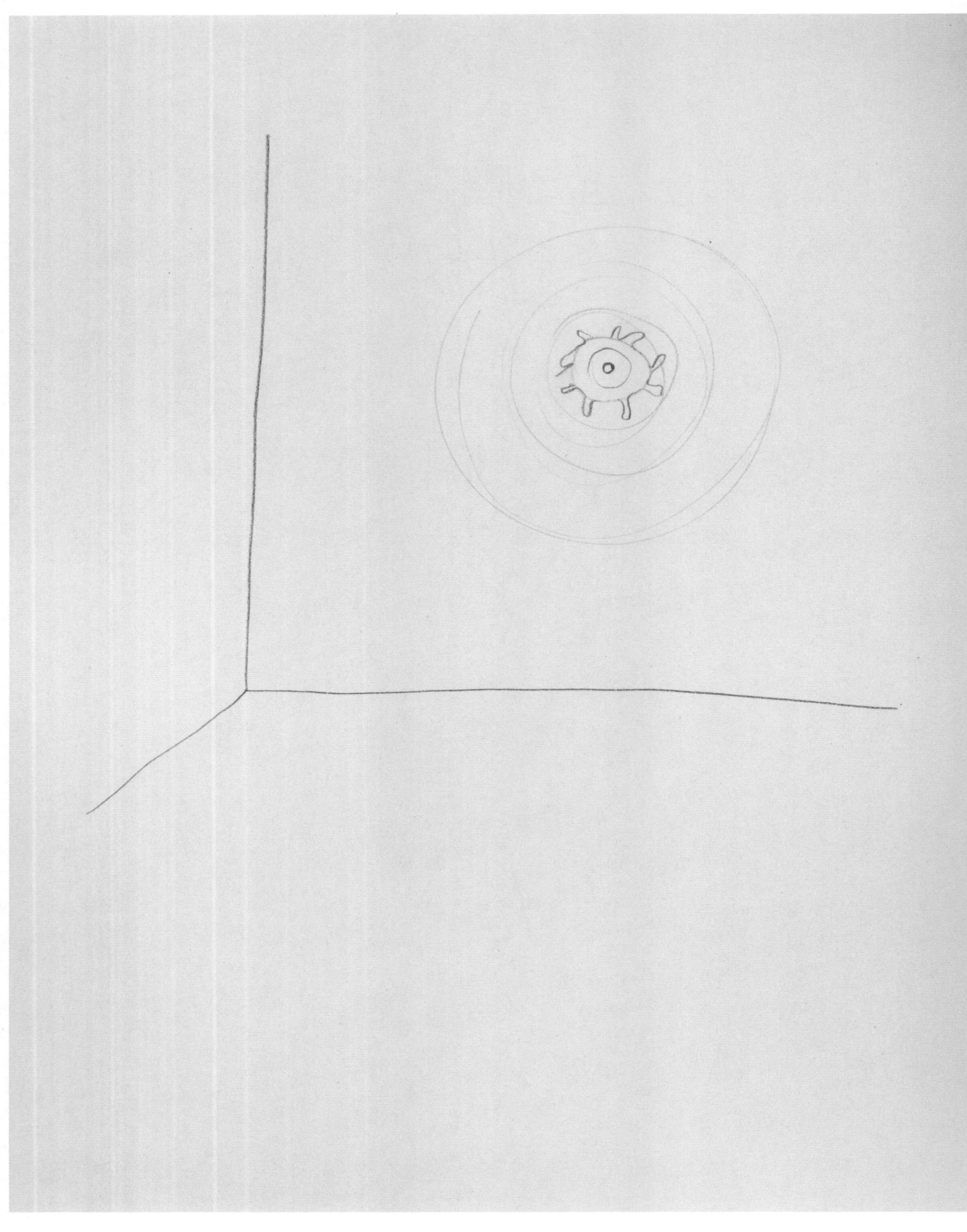

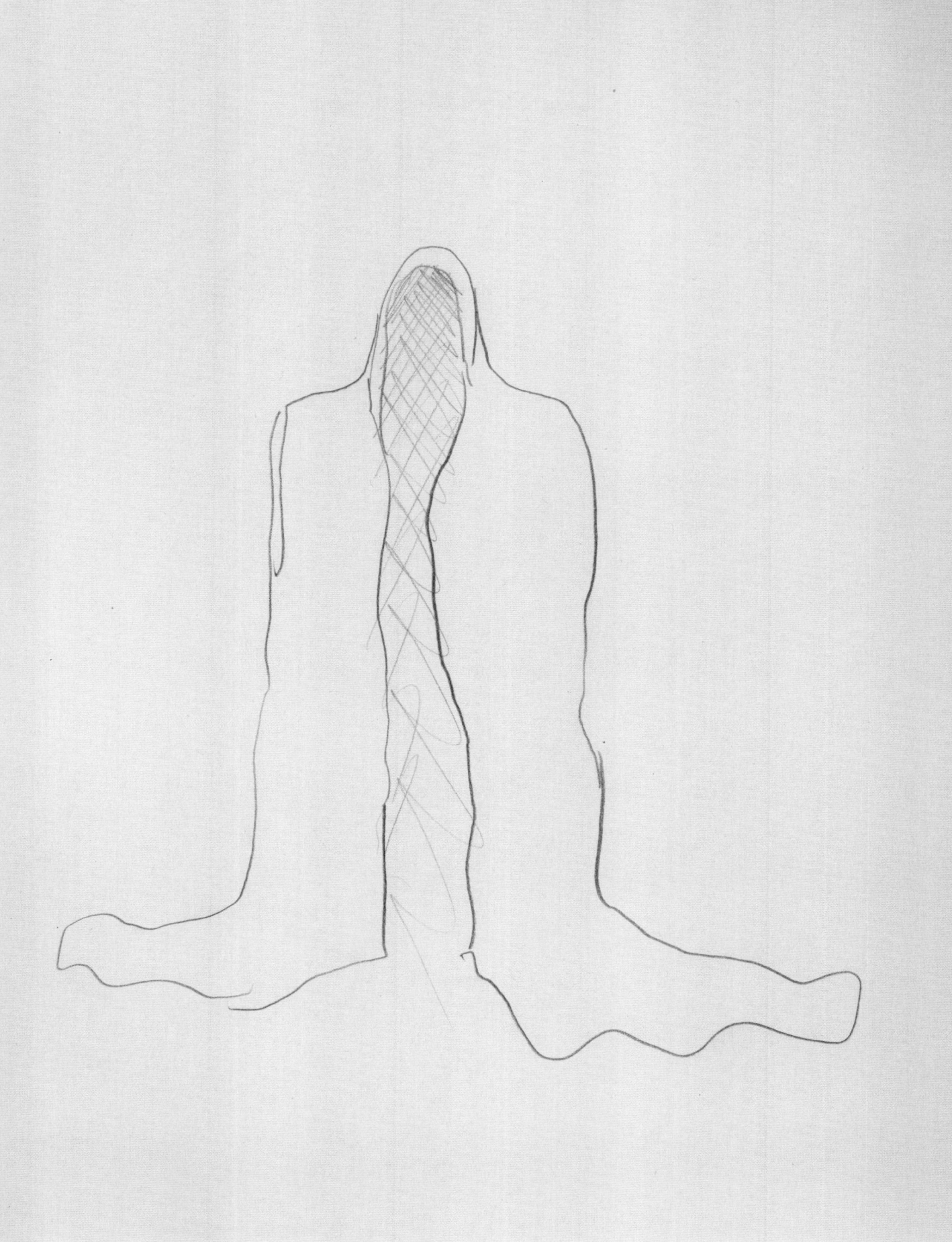

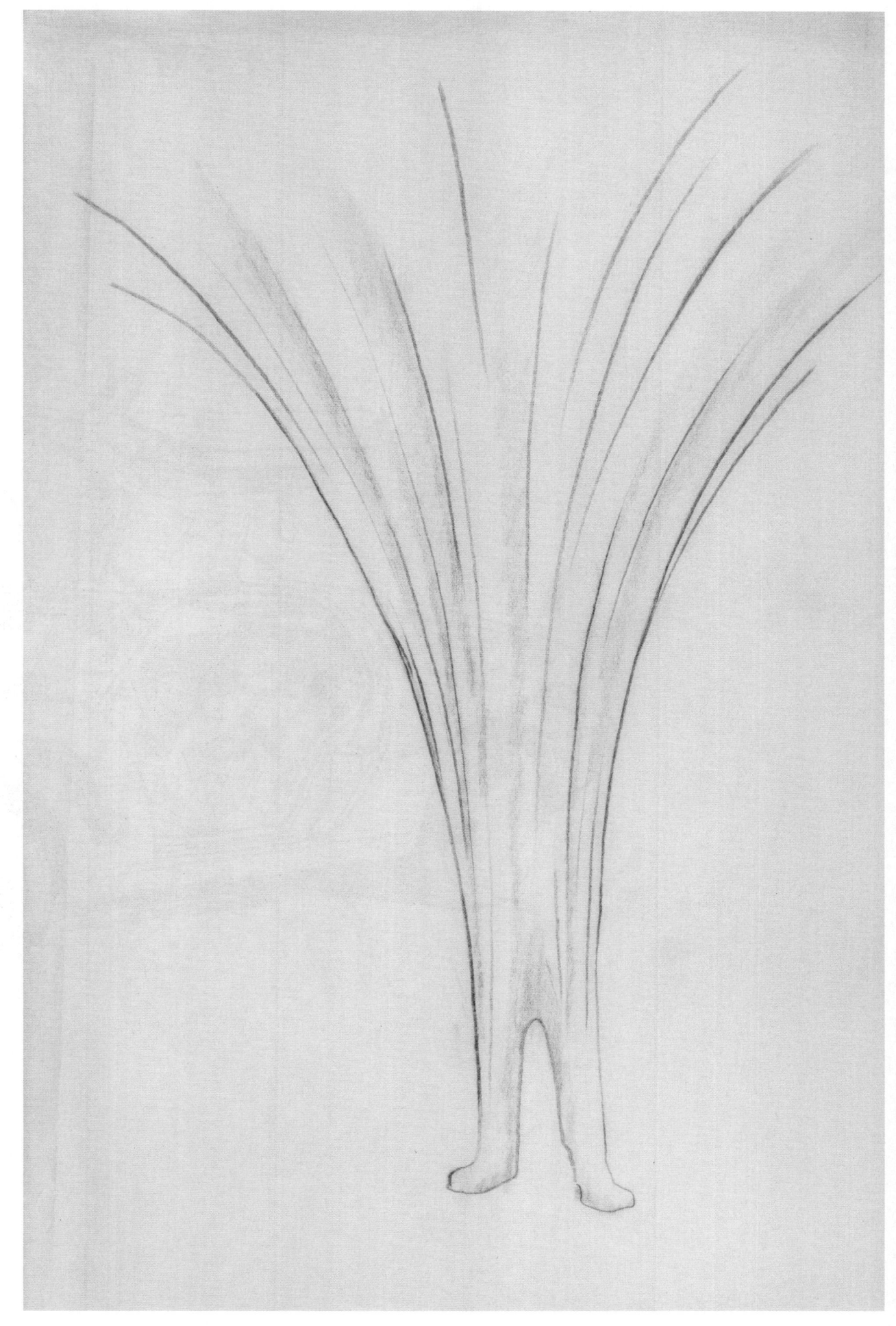

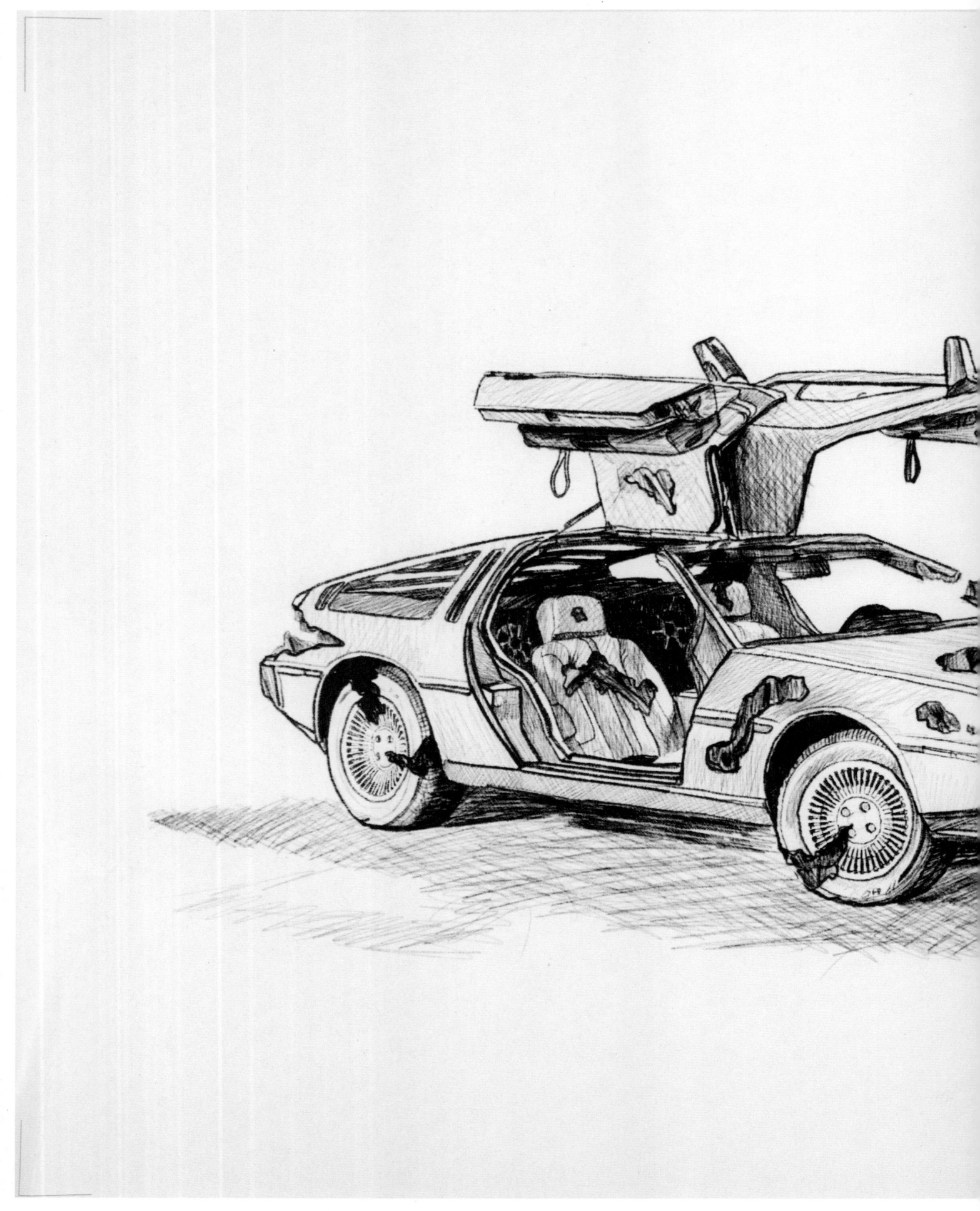

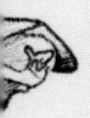

MAKE THIS IN
CRYSTAL + VOLCANIC
ASH.

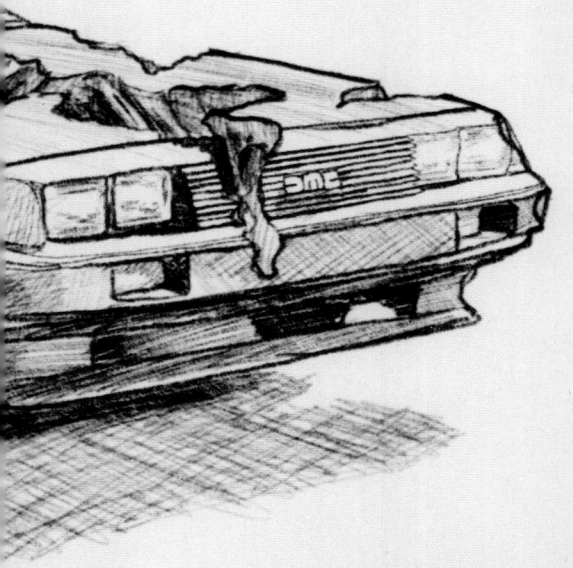

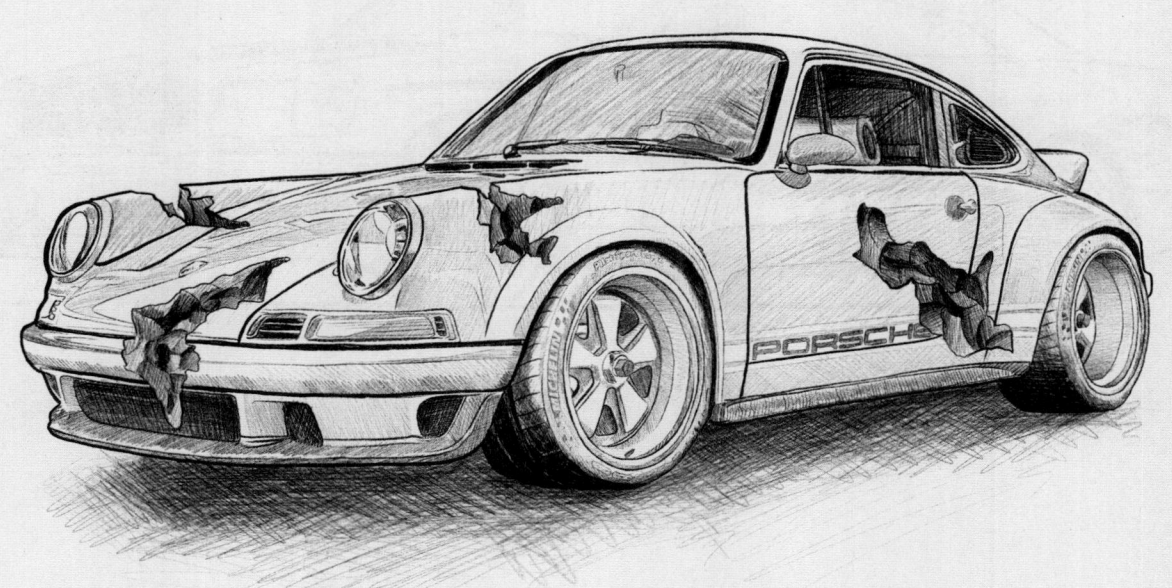

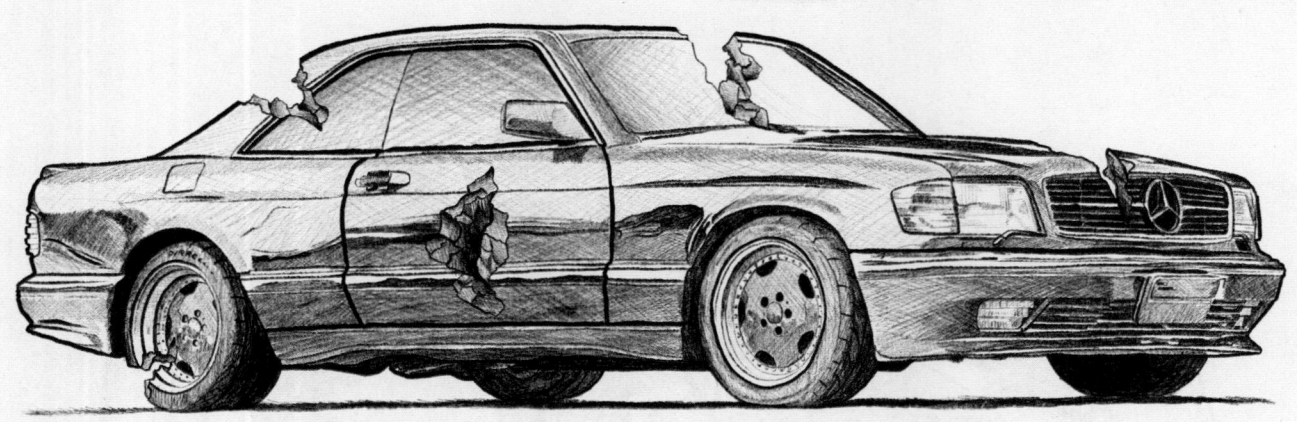

3019

CRYSTAL
ERODED
BMW E30

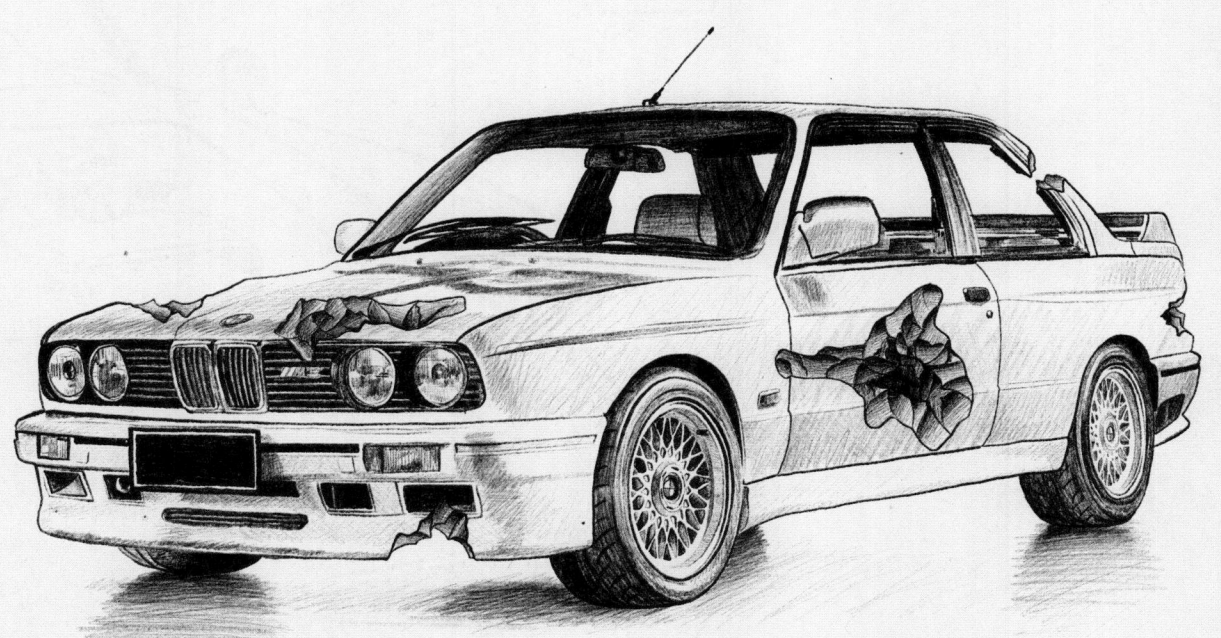

3019

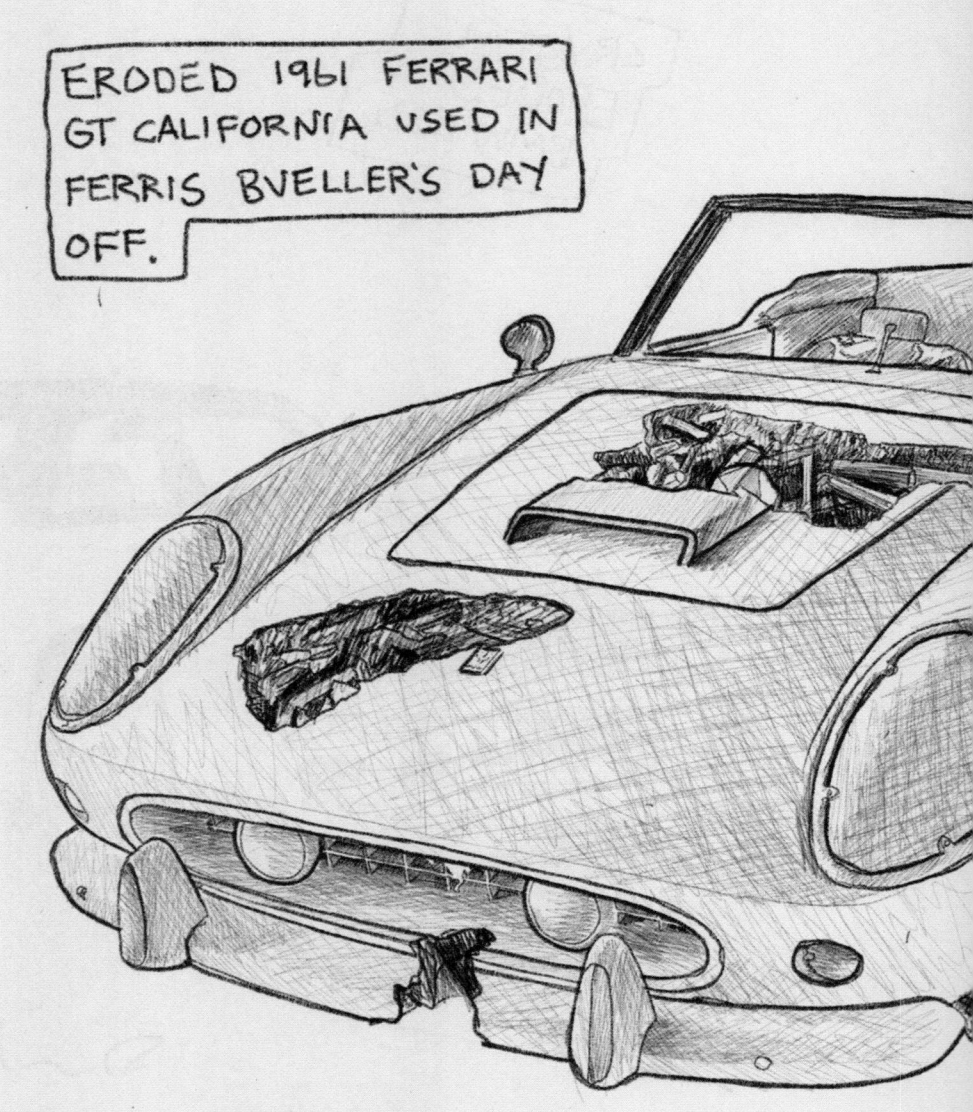

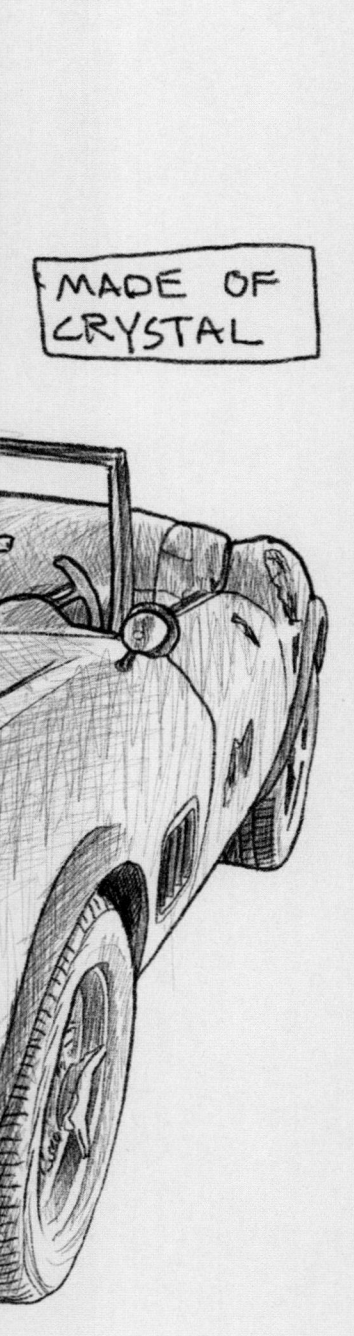

MADE OF
CRYSTAL

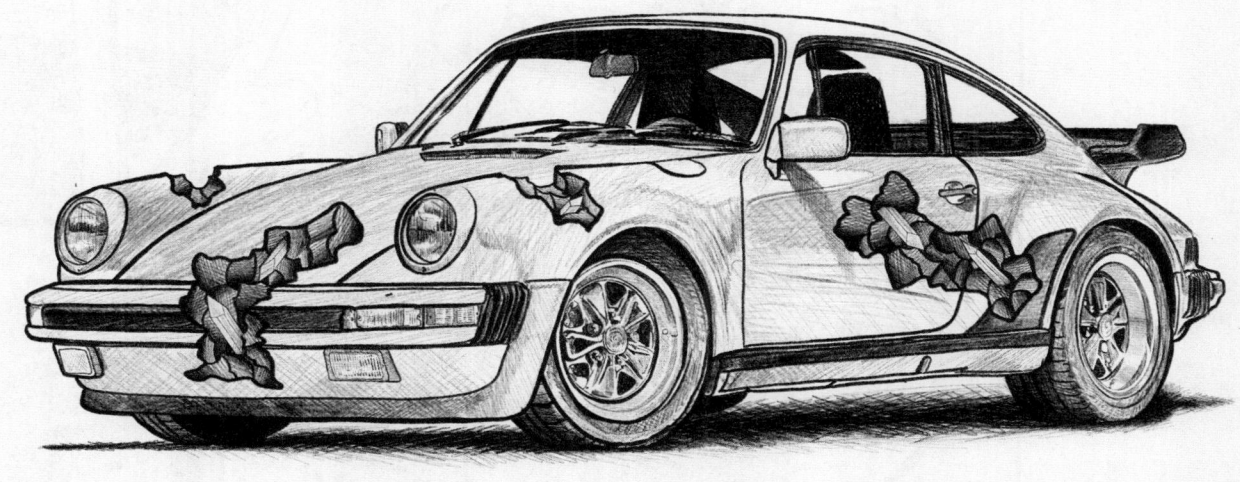

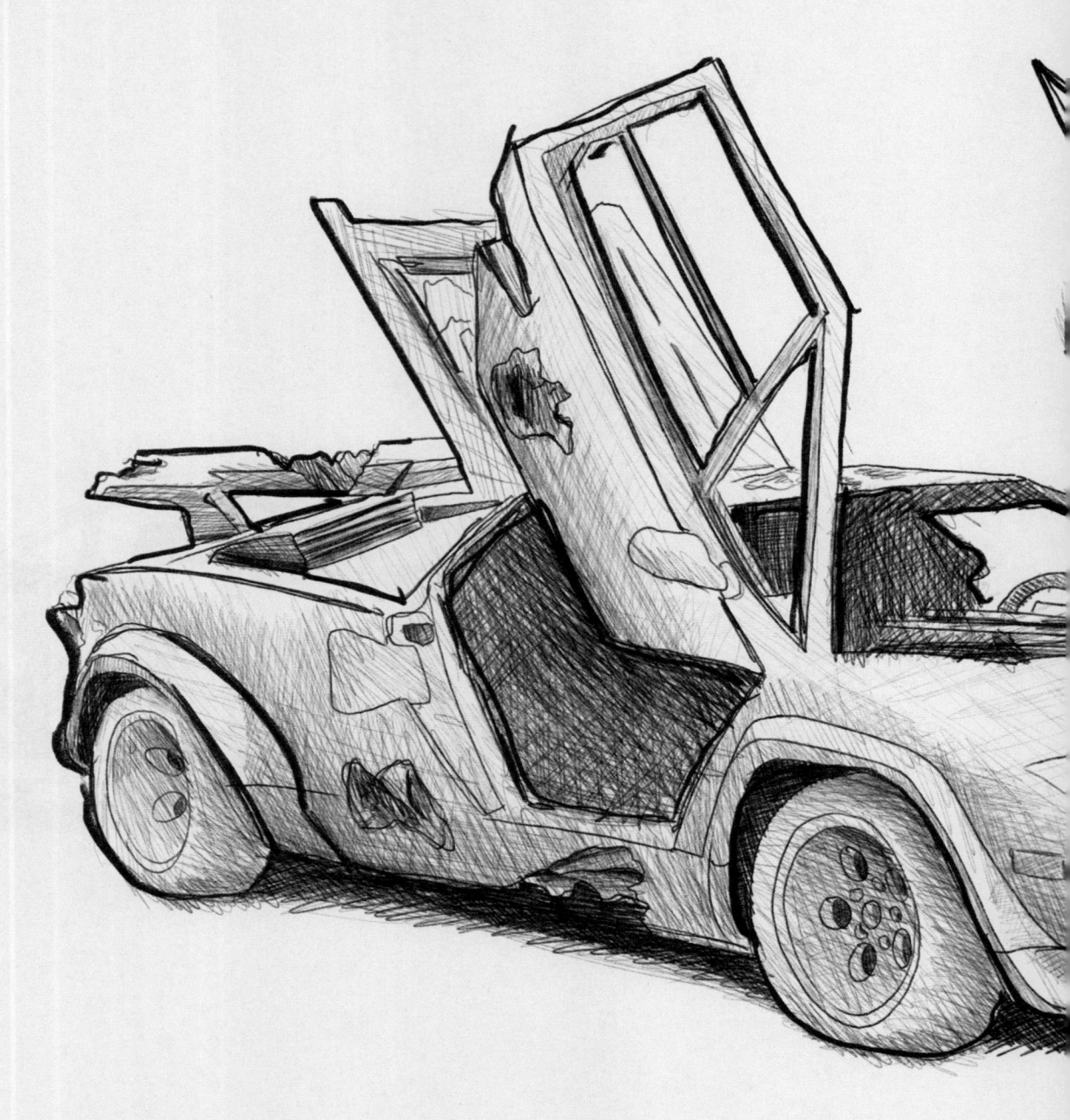

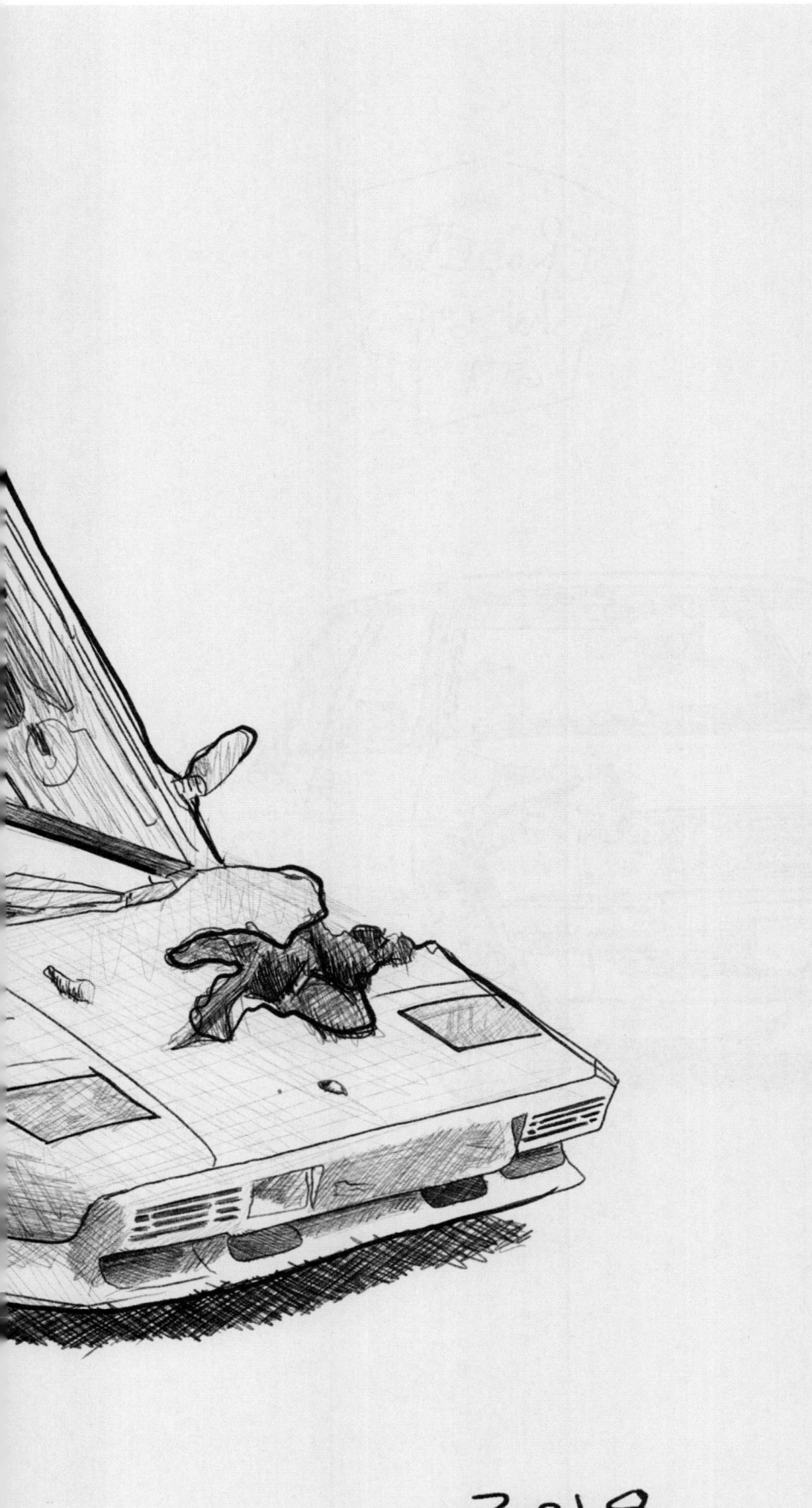

3018

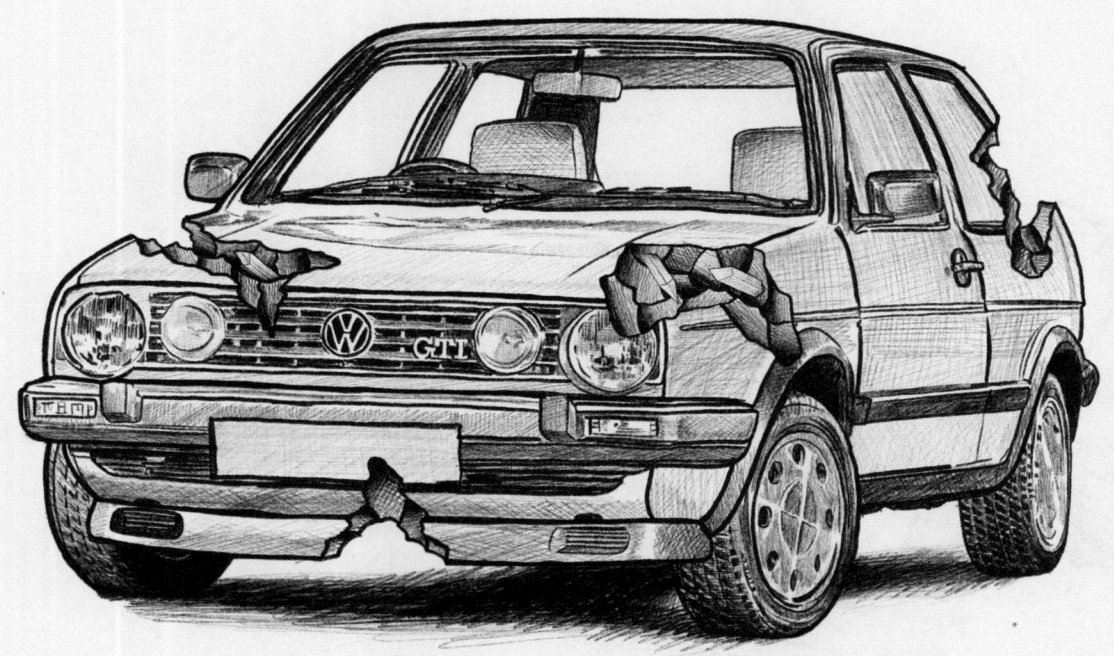

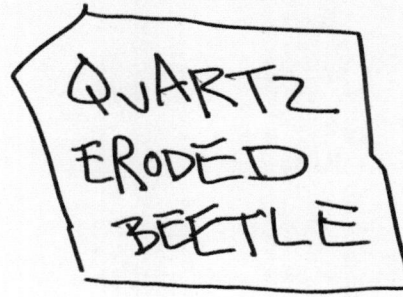

QUARTZ ERODED BEETLE

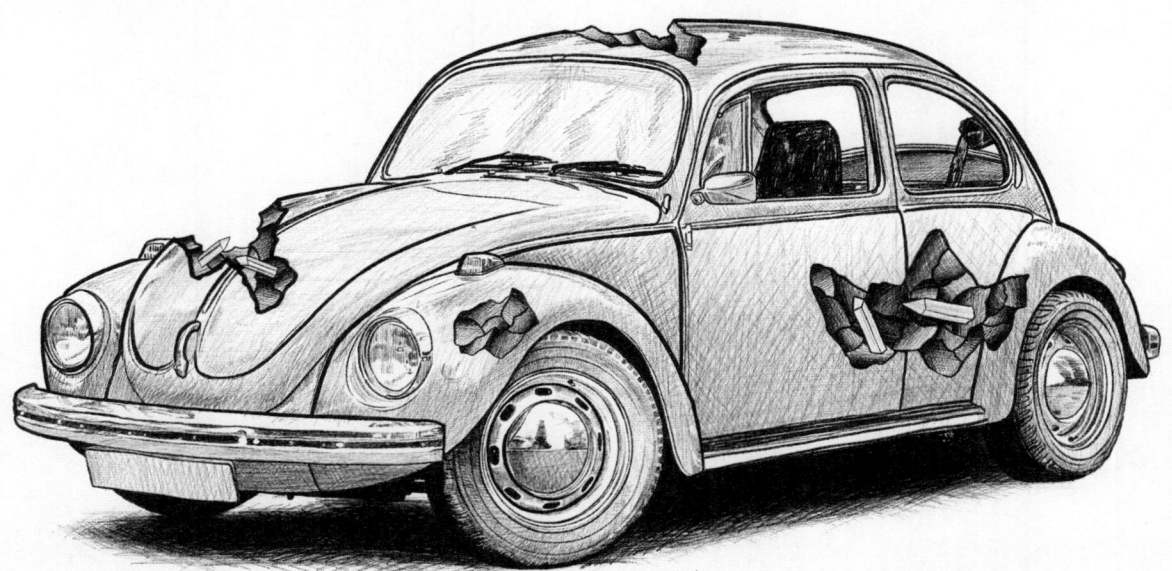

30|9

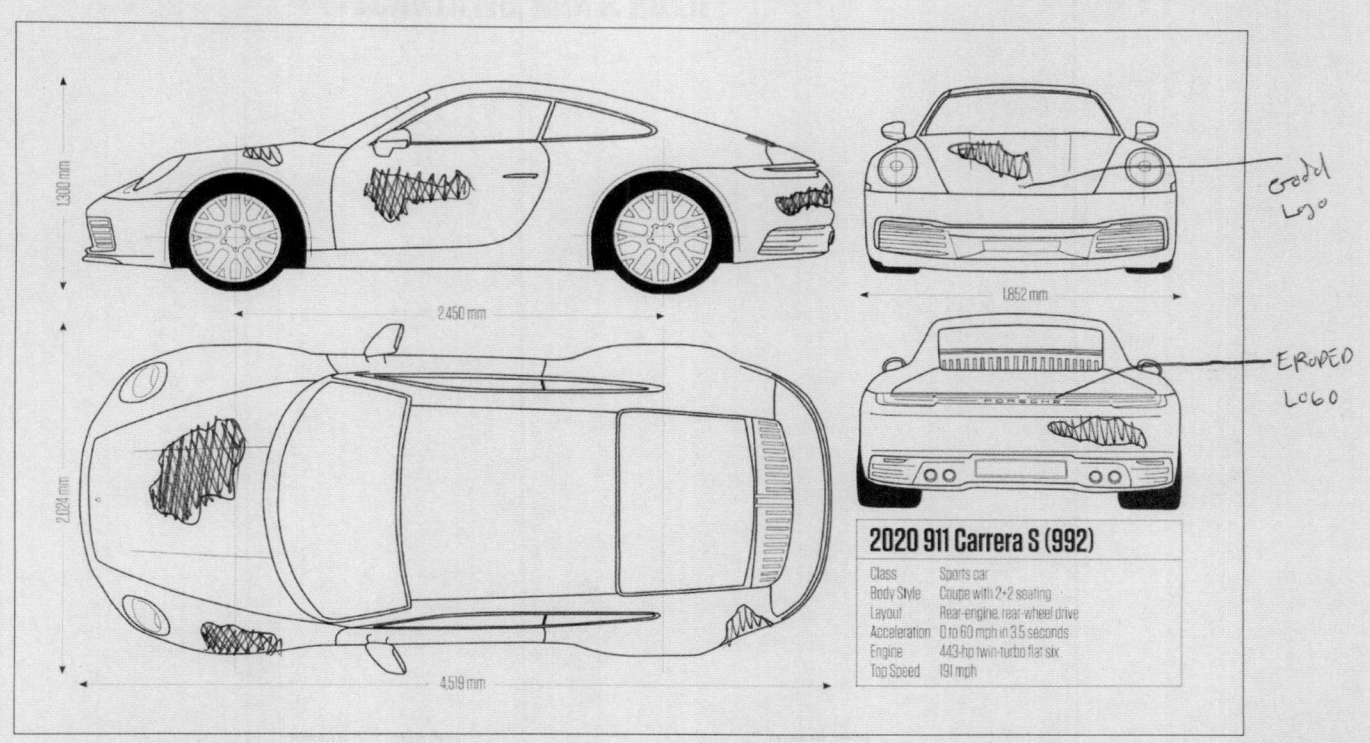

1,300 mm

2,450 mm

2,024 mm

4,519 mm

1,852 mm

### 2020 911 Carrera S (992)

| | |
|---|---|
| Class | Sports car |
| Body Style | Coupe with 2+2 seating |
| Layout | Rear-engine, rear-wheel drive |
| Acceleration | 0 to 60 mph in 3.5 seconds |
| Engine | 443-hp twin-turbo flat six |
| Top Speed | 191 mph |

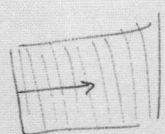

preparation for a 53-mile ride in the
California Sierra foothills, a 72-mile ride
around Lake Tahoe and the grand finale ride
of 100 miles at the Sacramento Century.

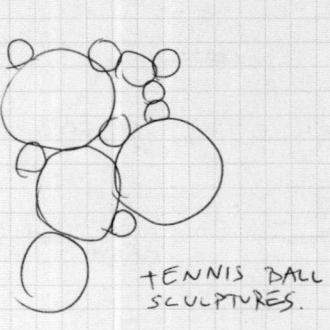

TENNIS BALL
SCULPTURES.

— THERE IS AN ARCHEOLOGICAL SITE
THAT IS CONTINUOUSLY EXCAVATED
AND COVERED IN SMALL PEBBLES
IT WOULD CREATE A SCENARIO
WITH HOLES IN THE FLOOR ON
THE 2ND FLOOR. AS THE MATERIAL
IS CLONED IT IS BROUGHT
UPSTAIRS. IT ALSO FUNCTIONS
LIKE A CLOCK.

JAPAN SHOW.

— VERY LARGE WHITE PLUSH TOYS

— OVERSIZE EMBROIDERED WHITE
HATS WITH PATCHES

— GIANT PATCHES EMBROIDERED
(MAYBE THESE SHOULD BE SCULPTED
IN CLAY? YOU COULD MAKE
INDIVIDUAL STRANDS AND IT WOULD
LOOK LIKE EMBROIDERY.

— VERY LARGE CAST WHITE TOYS

— AN ENTIRE SPACE WHERE THE
WALLS ARE COVERED IN A
GRADIENT OF ACTUAL PLUSH
TOYS.

— THE BIGGEST BEAR SHOULD
BE 10 FEET TALL

— A SERIES OF CAST BACKPACKS

— THIS SHOW COULD ALSO
PLAY WITH THE GRADIENT
FADE WITH THE AIRBRUSH.

— I WOULD LIKE TO WORK WITH
LOONY TUNES CHARACTERS.

# 3019 EXHIBITIONS + PROJETS

| | | |
|---|---|---|
| AMSTERDAM | - | JANUARY |
| TAIPEI | - | JANUARY |
| DETROIT | - | MARCH |
| HONG KONG | - | MARCH |
| AMSTERDAM | - | MAY |
| BASEL | - | JUNE |
| PARIS | - | JUNE |
| SHANGHAI | - | JUNE |
| ISTANBUL | - | SEPTEMBER |
| PARIS | - | OCTOBER |
| ST. BARTHS | - | DECEMBER |

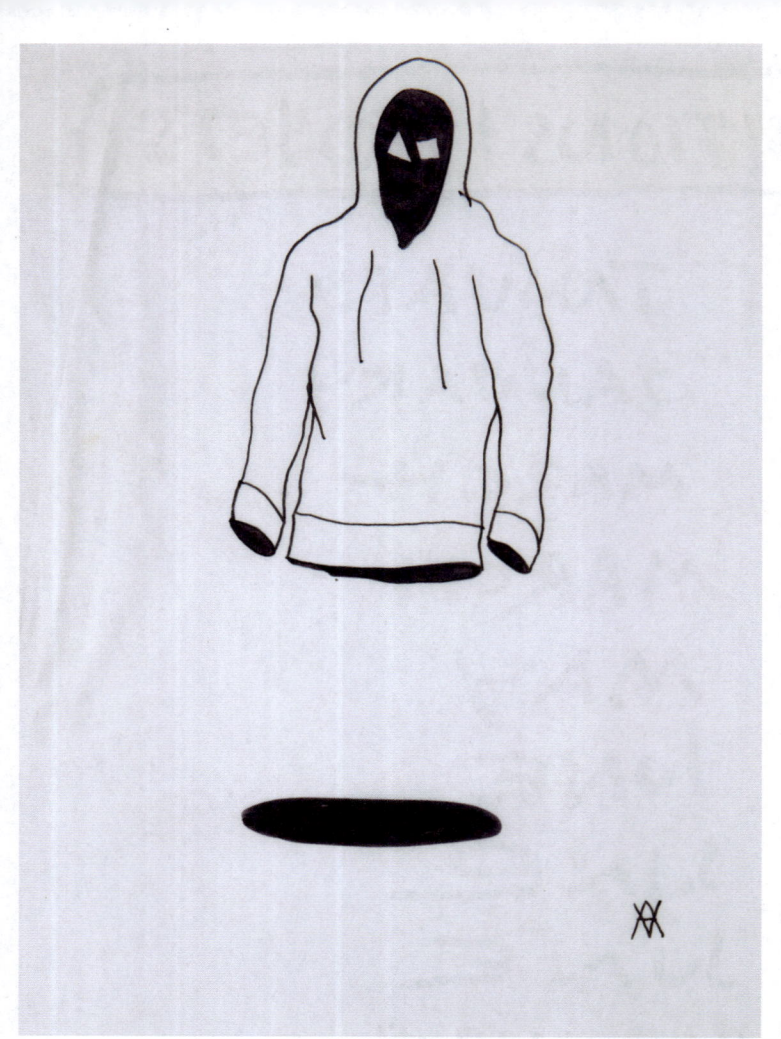 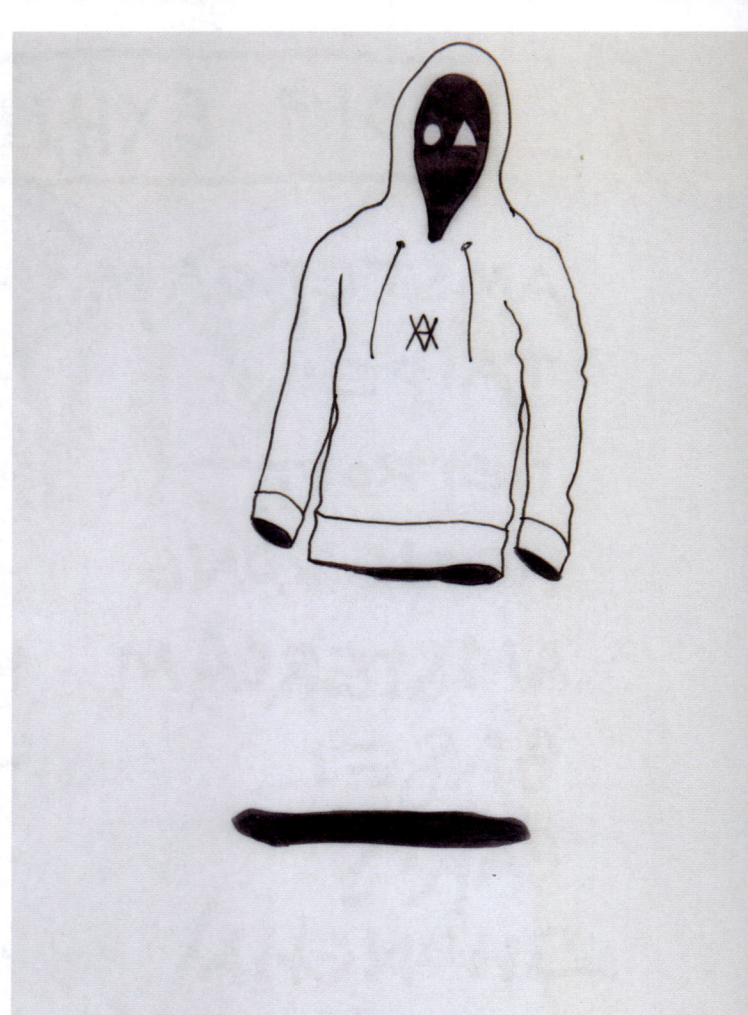

# QUARANTINE
# DAILY SCHEDULE
## (WEEKDAYS)

7:00 - WAKE UP

7:15-8:00 - BREAKFAST

8:00-8:30 ————————→ DISHES + CLEAN UP

8:30-9:30 - TRAINING

9:30-10:00 - SHOWER + NEWS

10:00-10:30 ——→ FACETIME CONNECT WITH TEAM

10:30-12:00 ·········→ WORK ON GRAPHITE DRAWINGS

12:00-12:45 ——————[FAMILY LUNCH]————————

12:45-1:00 ·········— MEDITATION·········

1:00-2:00 - WORK ON BOOK

2:00-4:00 ——→ HOMESCHOOLING BOYS

4:00-4:30 ——— RECESSES

4:30-5:00 - HOUSE CHORES, TOYS CLEAN UP ——→ BOYS SHOWER

5:00-6:00 - PREPARE DINNER

## 6:00 [OPEN A FUCKING BOTTLE OF SOMETHING]

6:00-7:00 — DINNER

7:00-7:30 MOVIE NIGHT WITH BOYS

7:30 - BOYS BEDTIME ☺

7:30-8:00 - DISHES + CLEAN UP

8:00-9:30 - (ATTEMPT TO CONVINCE STEPH TO WATCH A STARWARS MOVIE)

8:00-9:30 ——→ WATCH A MOVIE (NOT STARWARS)

9:30-10:00 — READ (CURRENTLY JOSEPH CAMPBELL THE POWER OF MYTH)

10:00 → GO TO SLEEP AND DREAM OF PORSCHES ··· CURRENTLY DREAMING OF THE 1972 911RS CARRERA 3.0 SAFARI

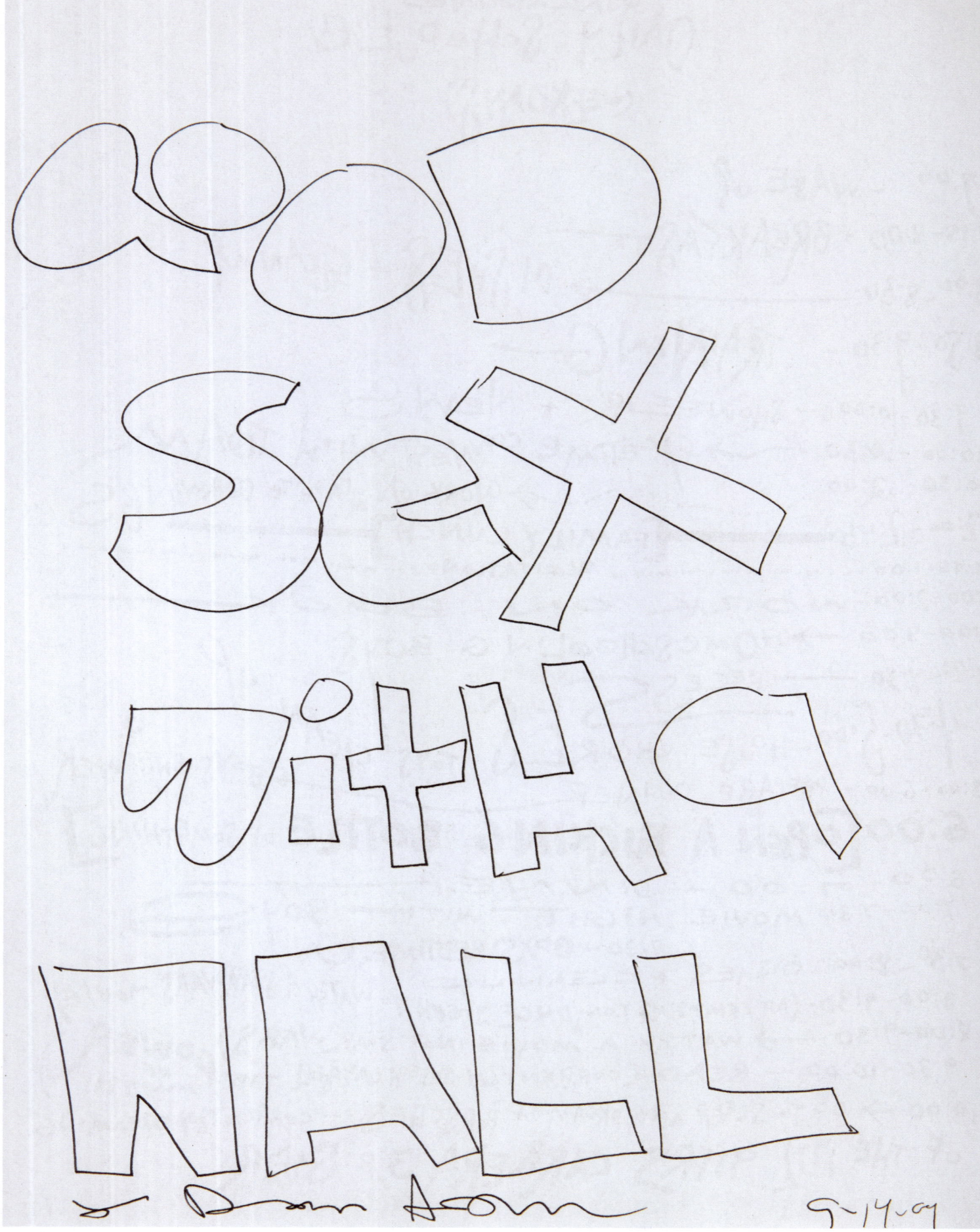

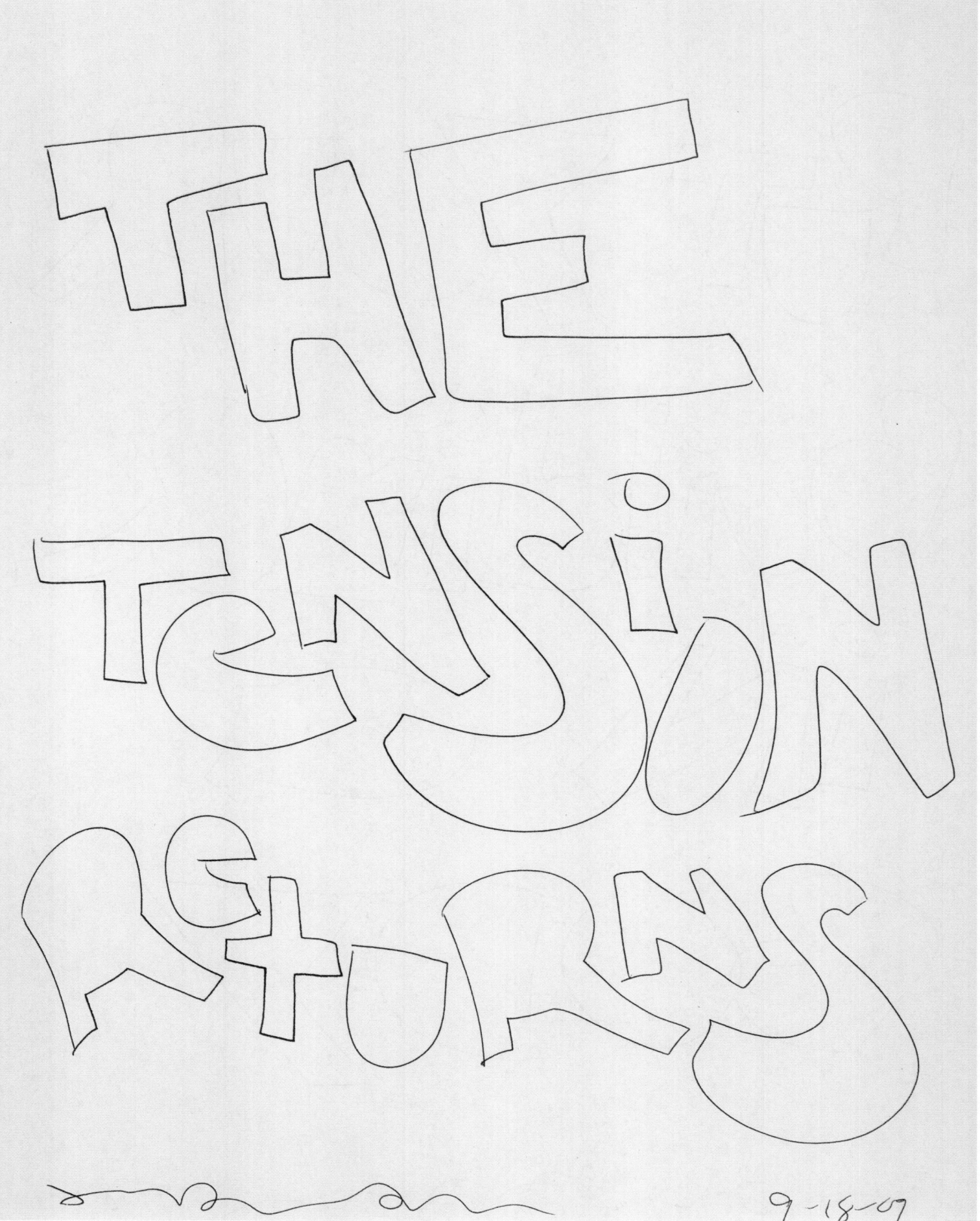

THE TENSION RETURNS

9-18-09

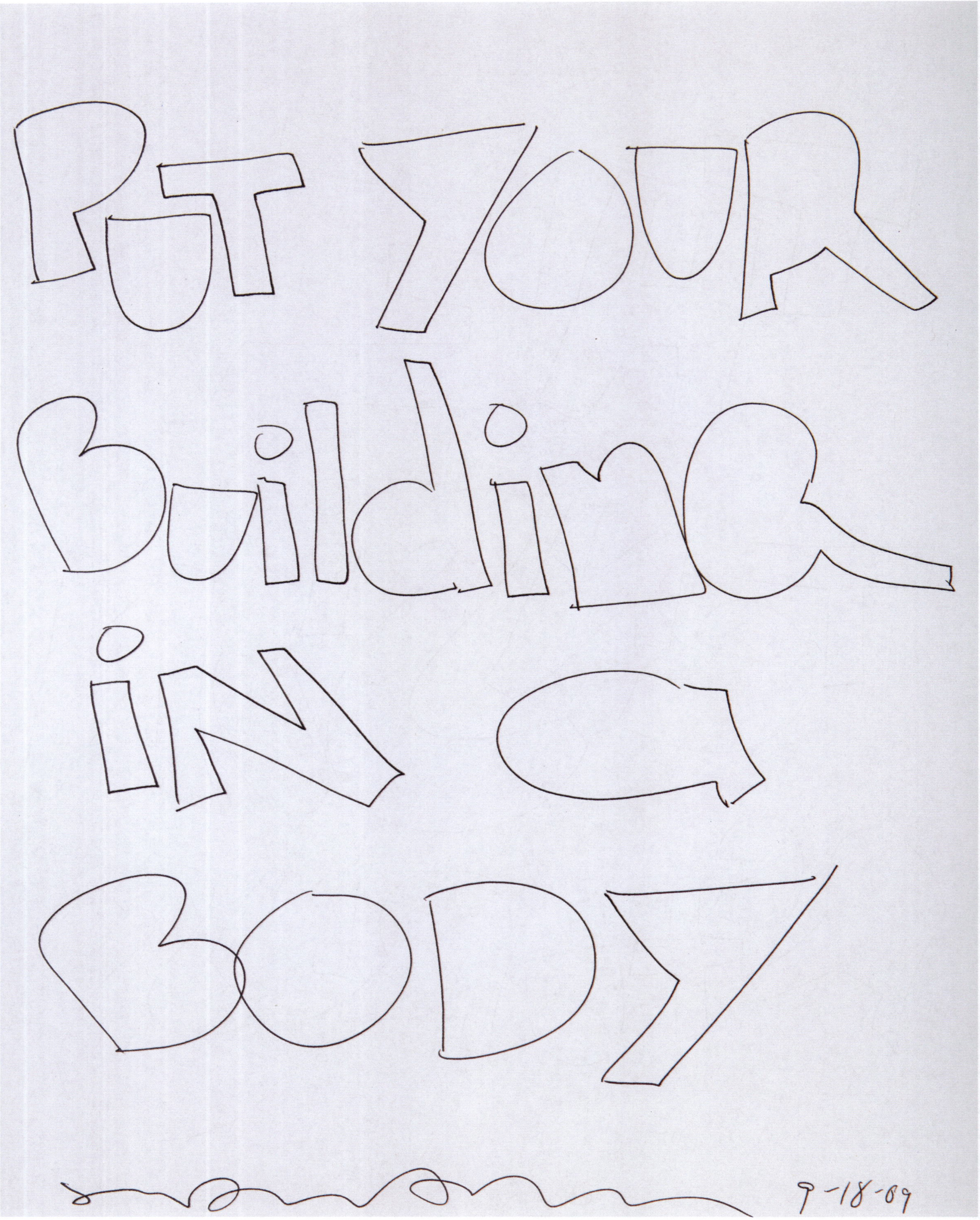

PUT YOUR
Building
iN a
BODY

9-18-09

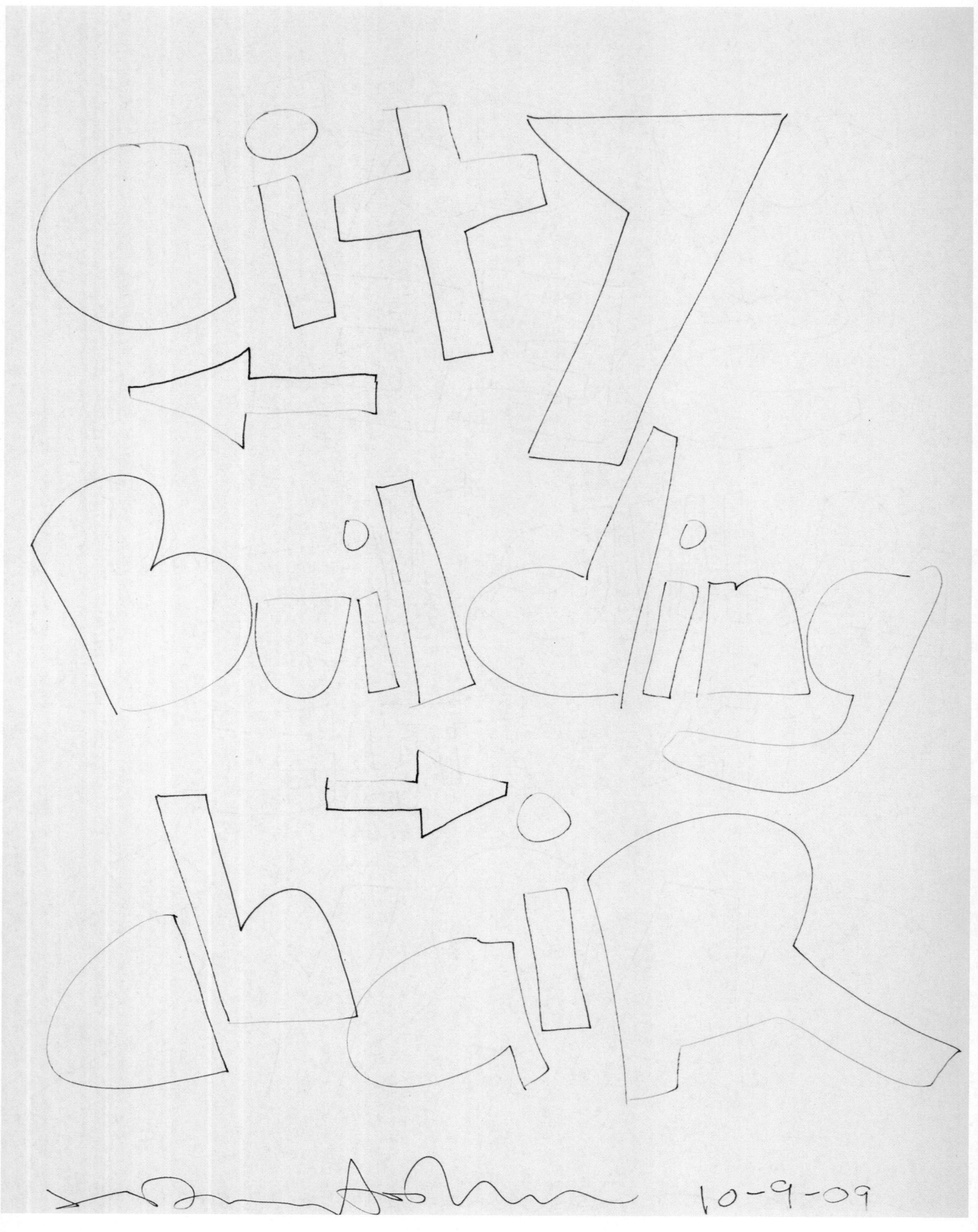

10-9-09

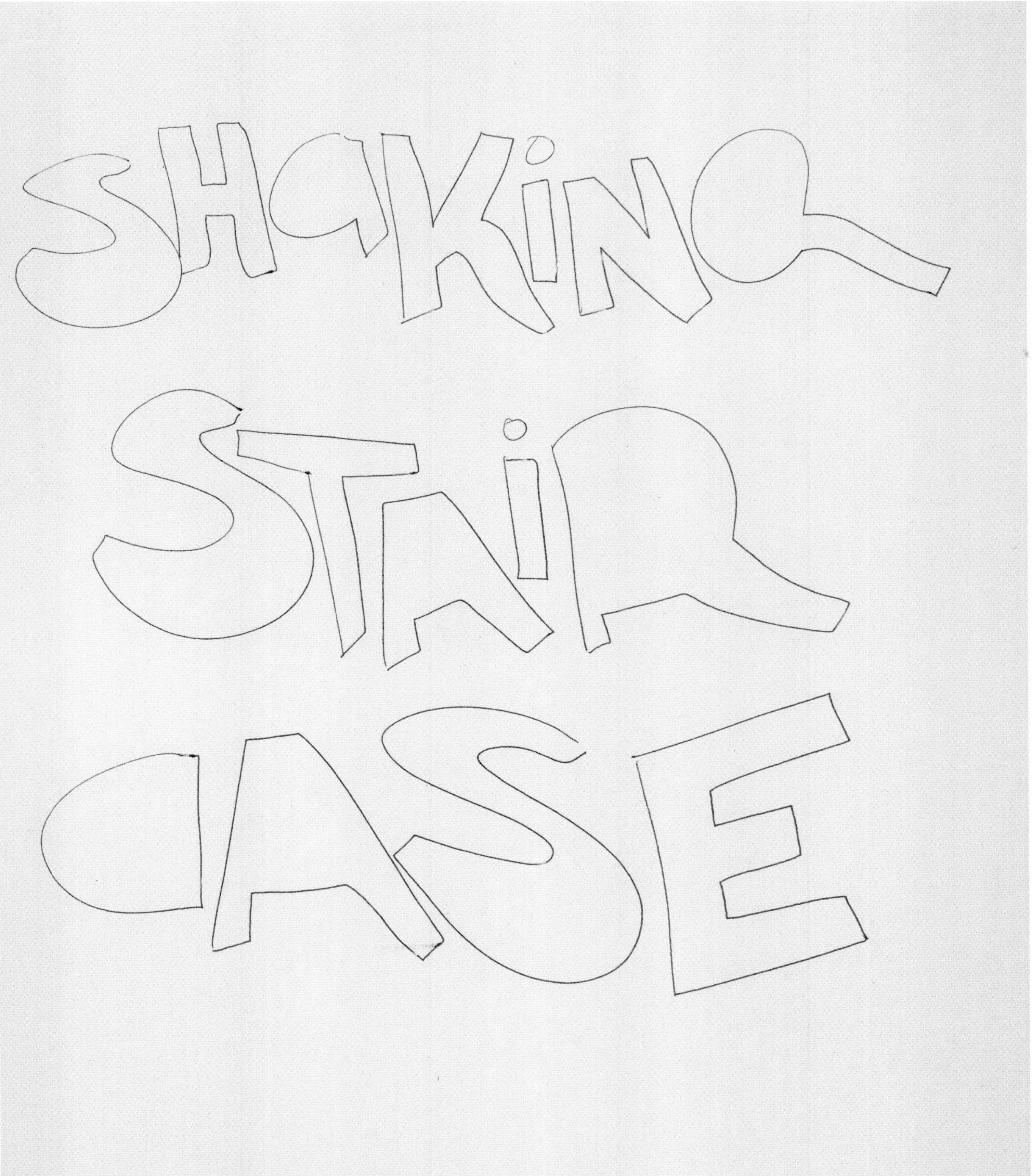

SHAKING
STAIR
CASE

10-11-09

ARCHITECTURE

IS

IMPORTANT

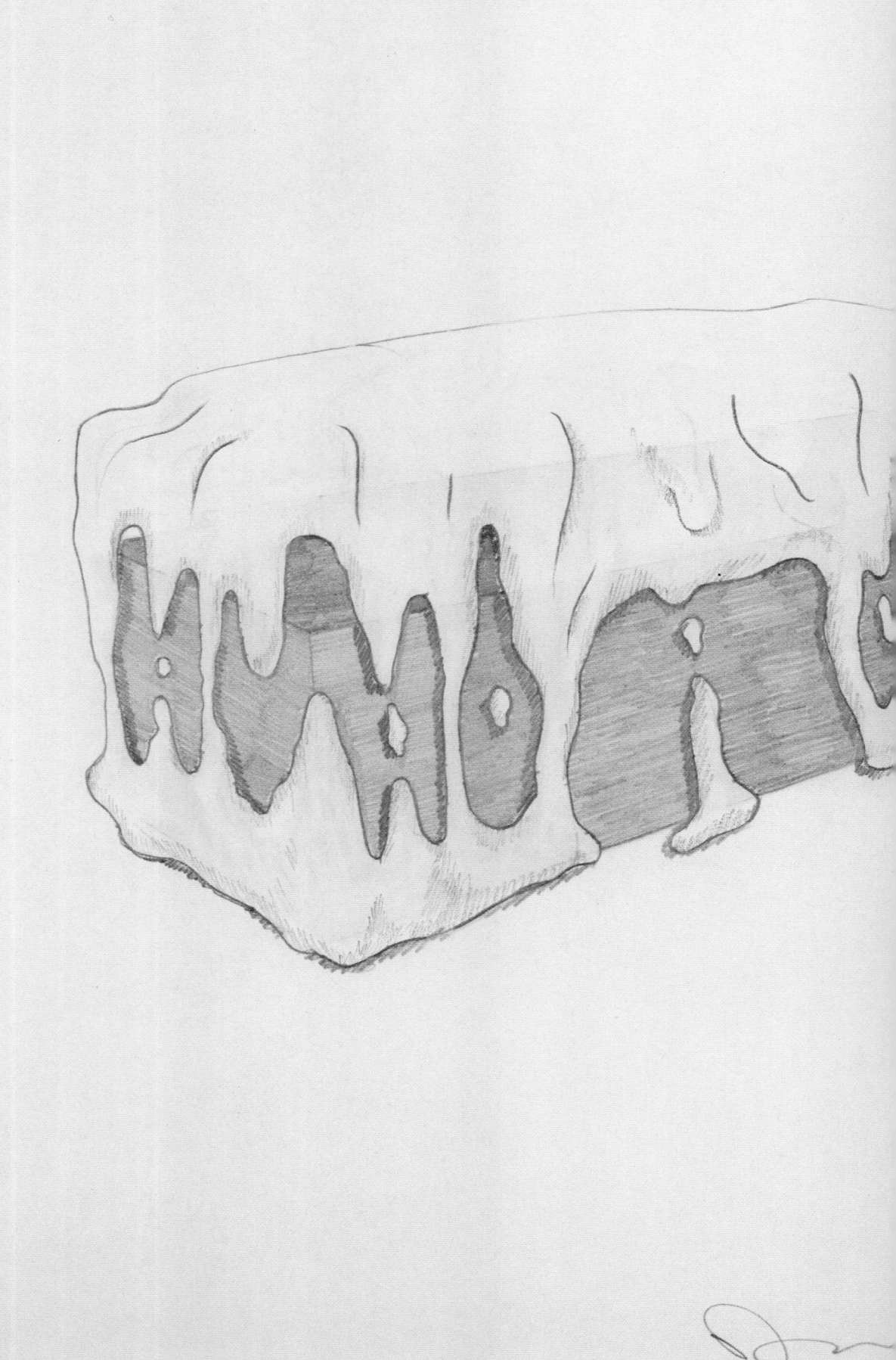

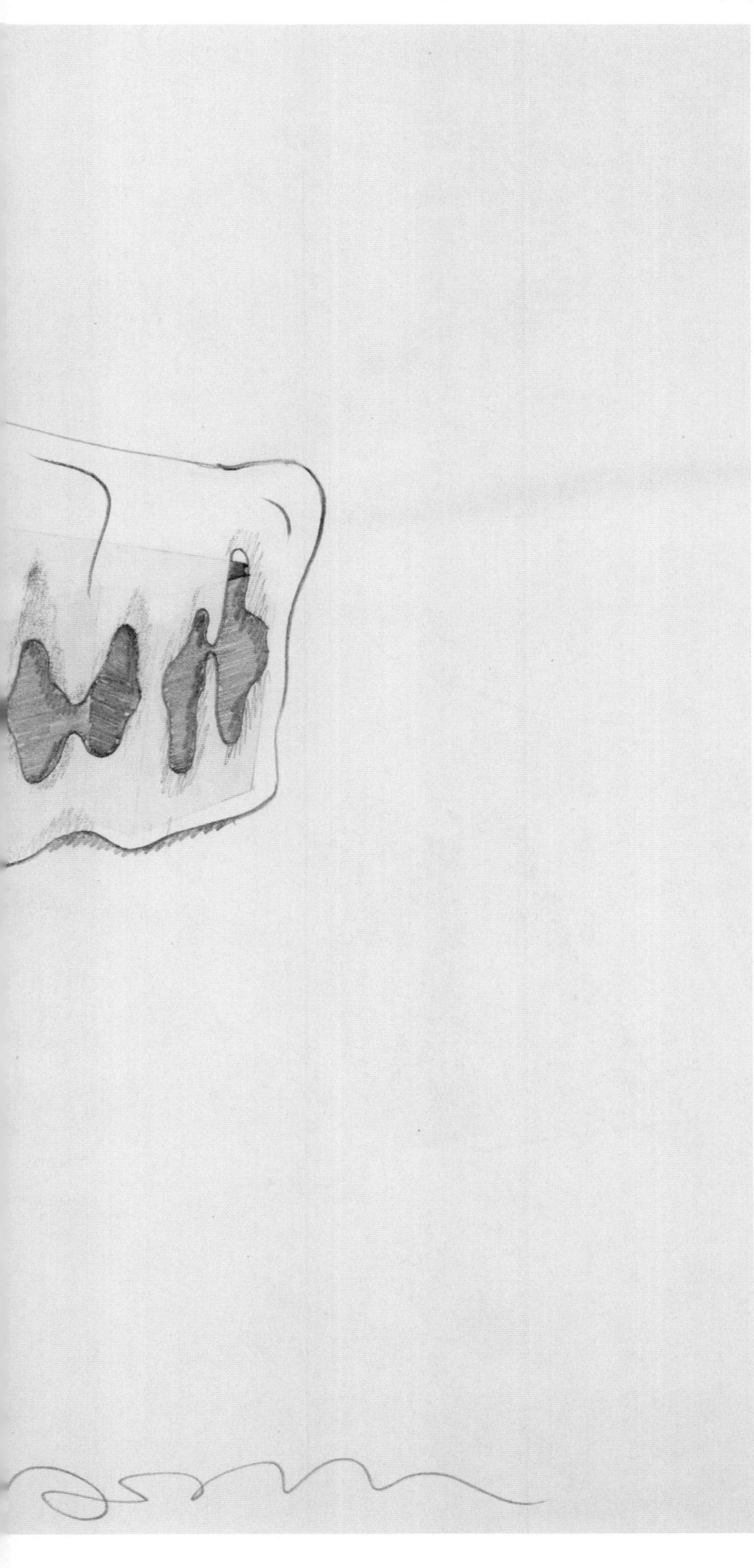

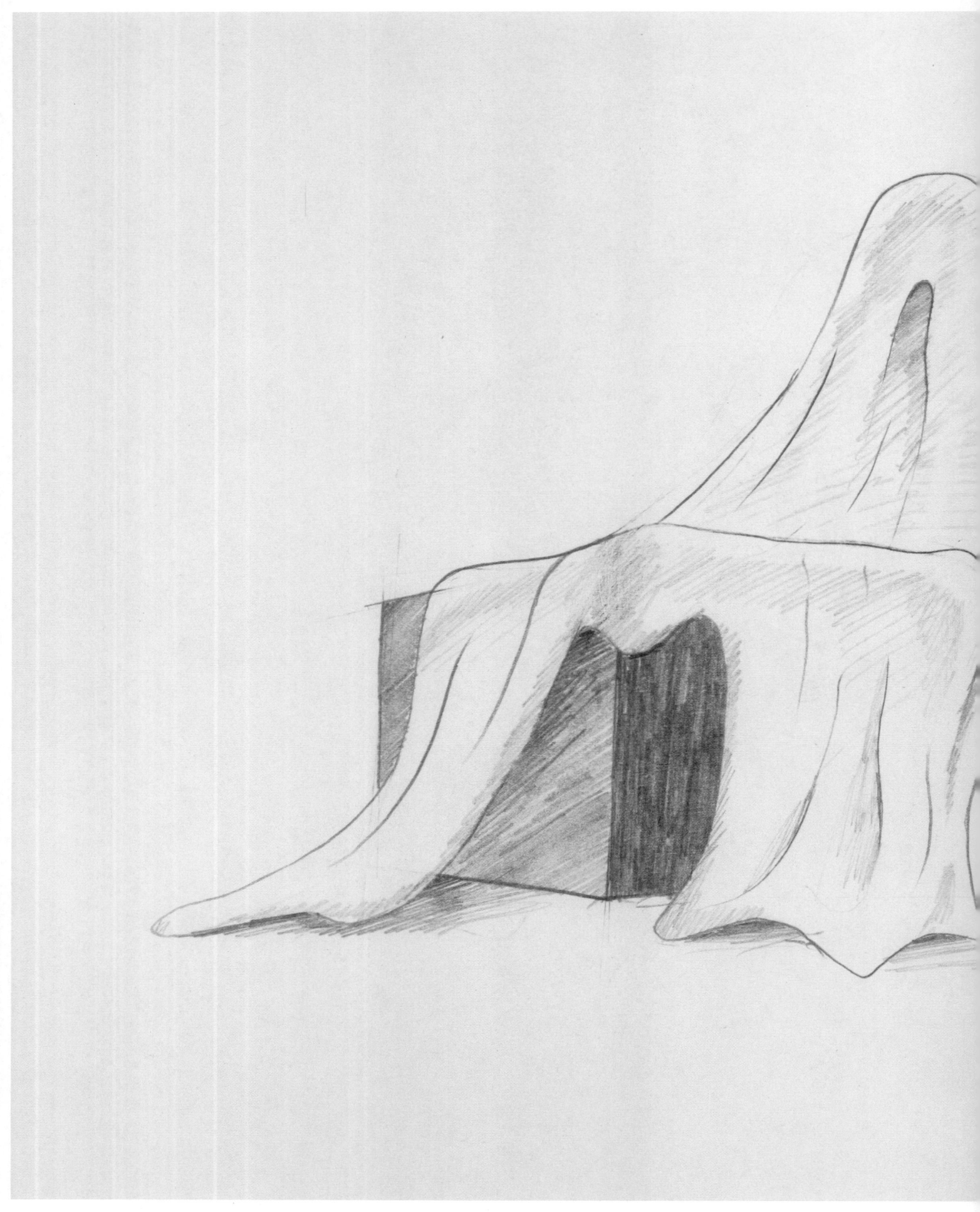

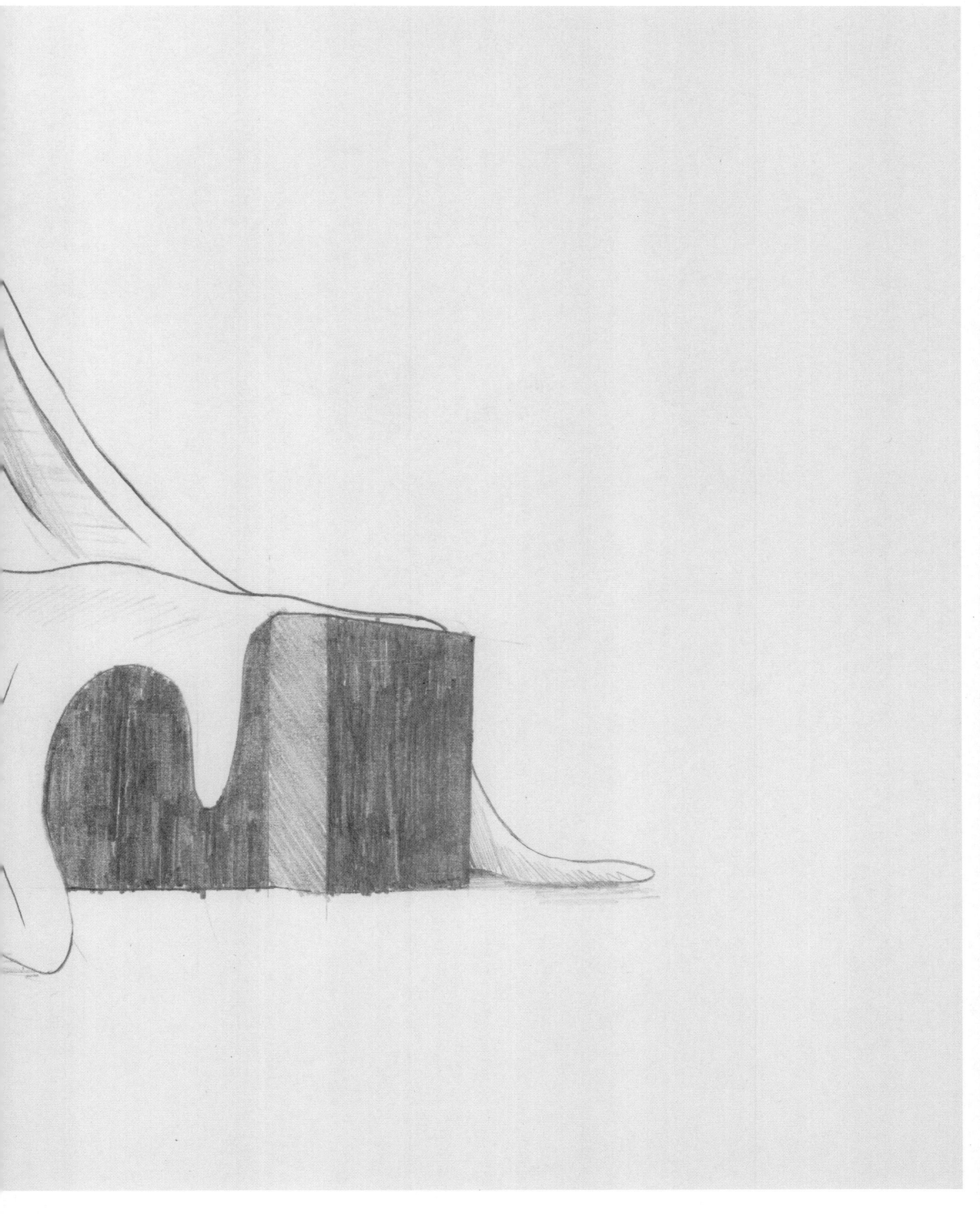

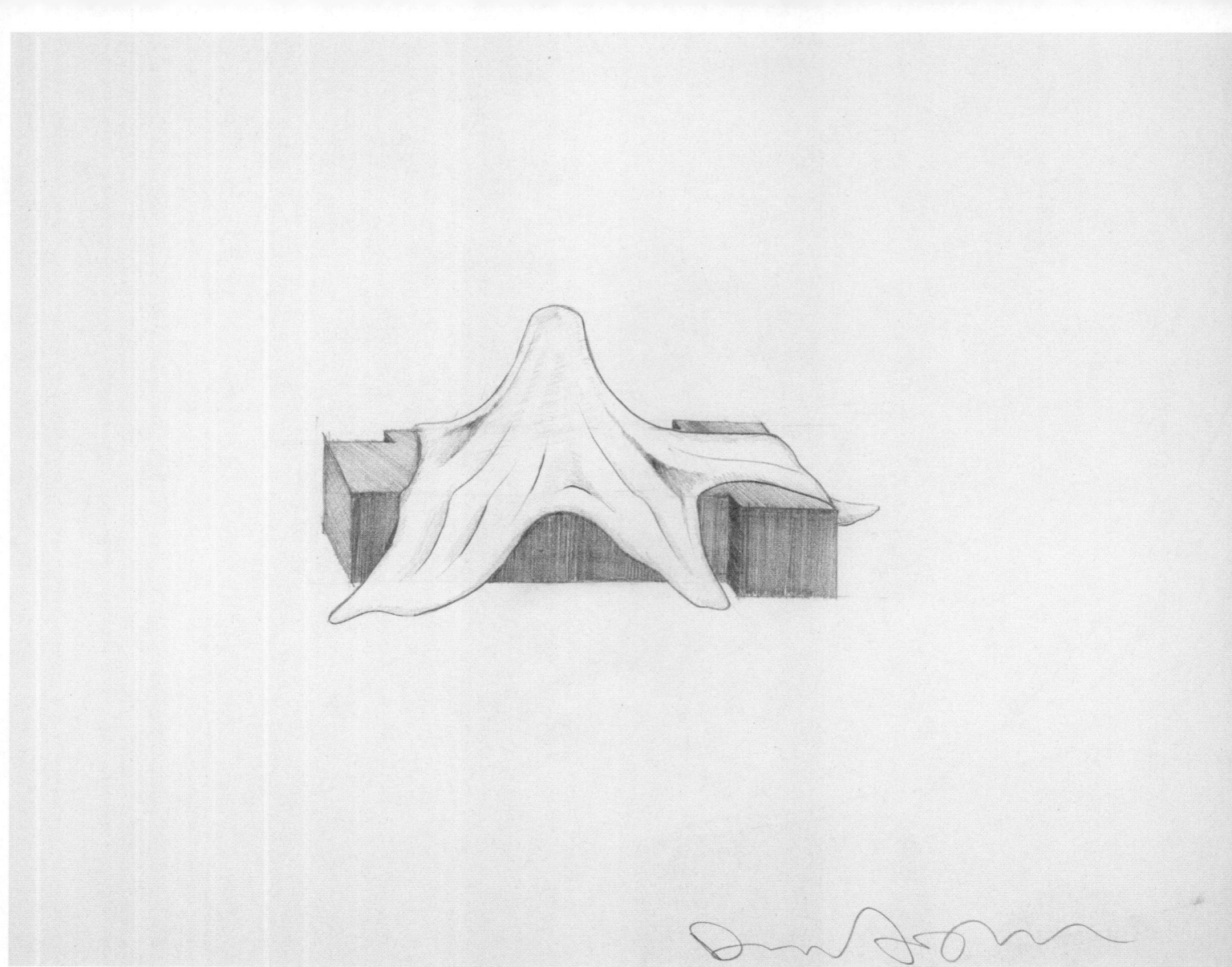

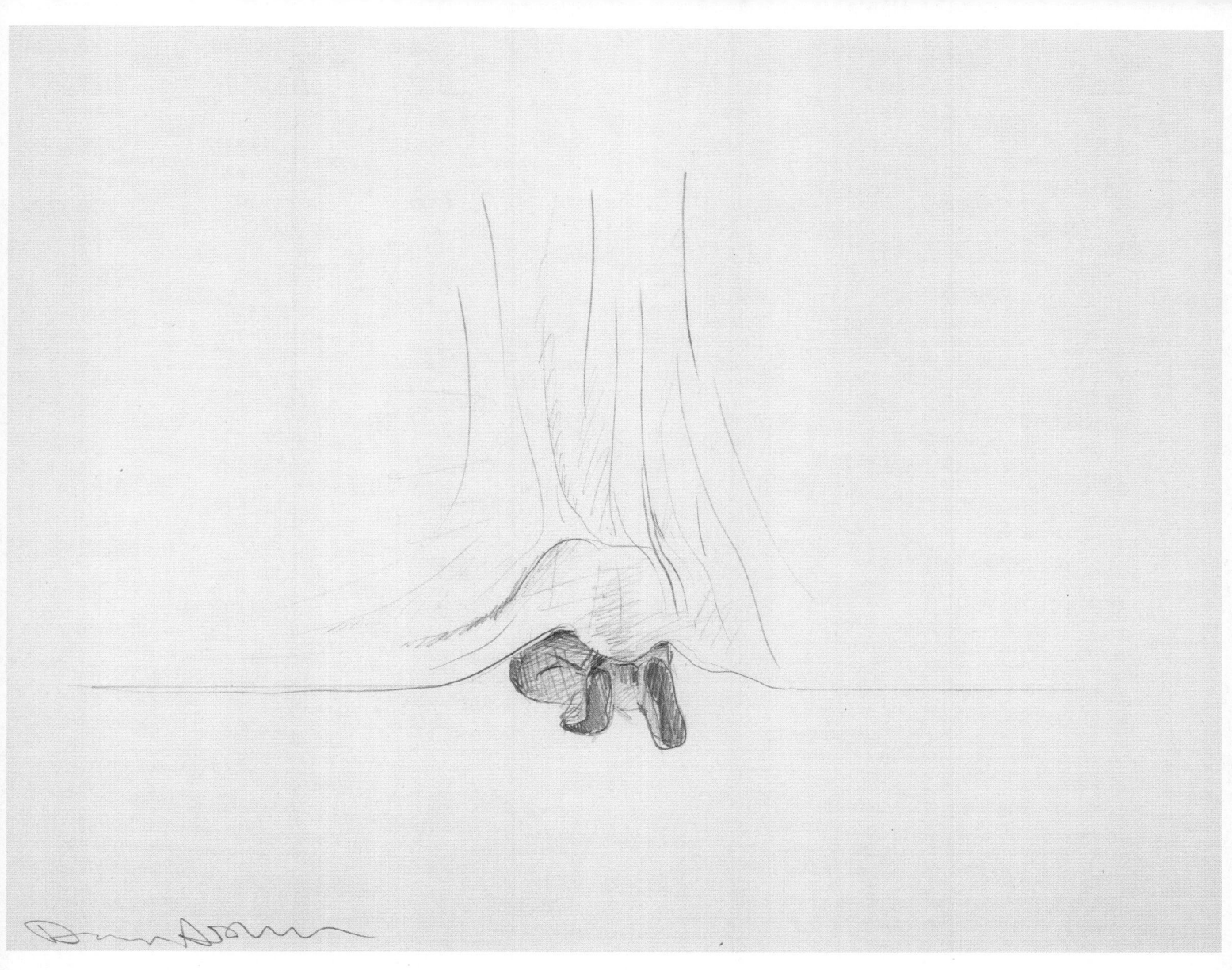

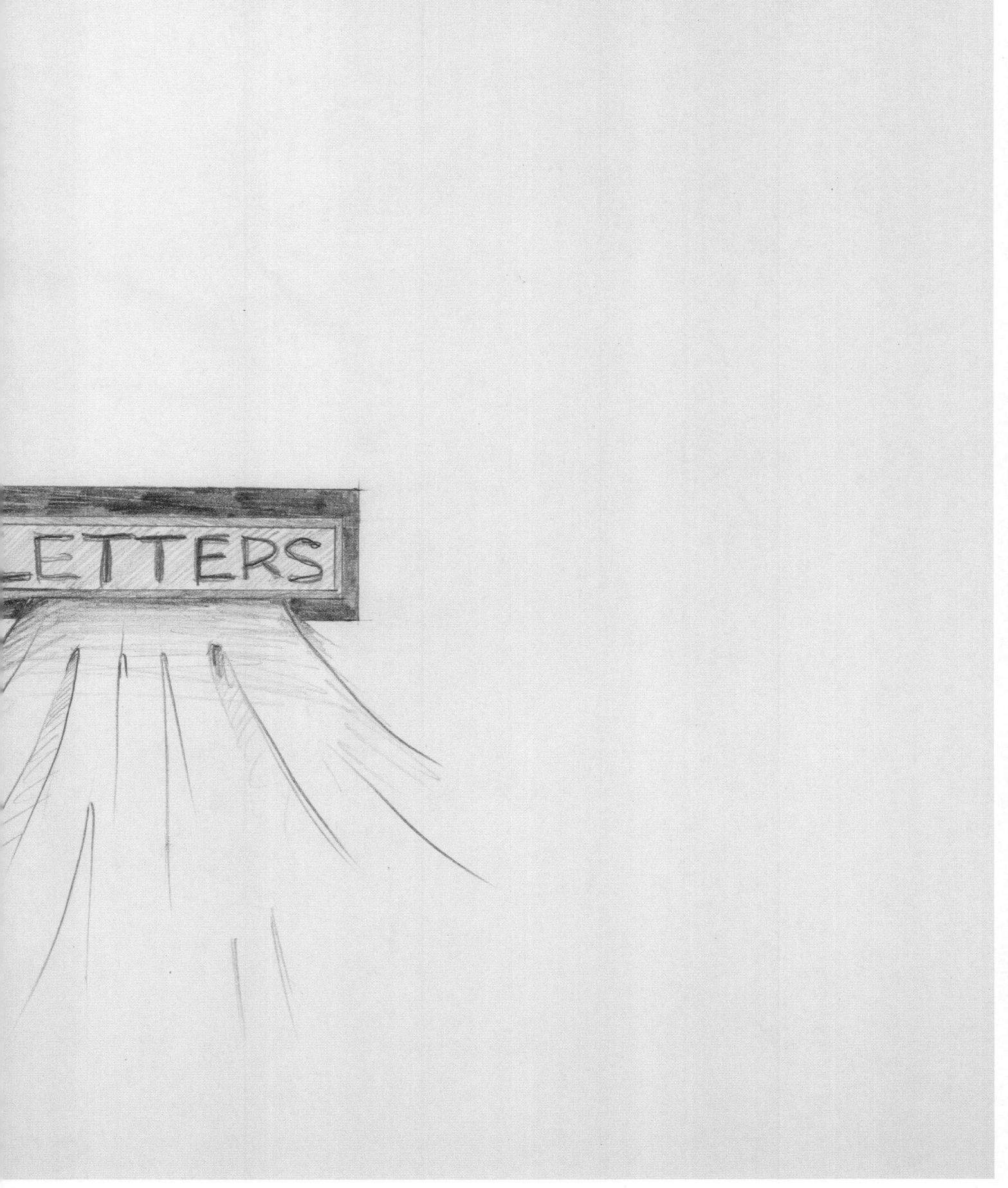

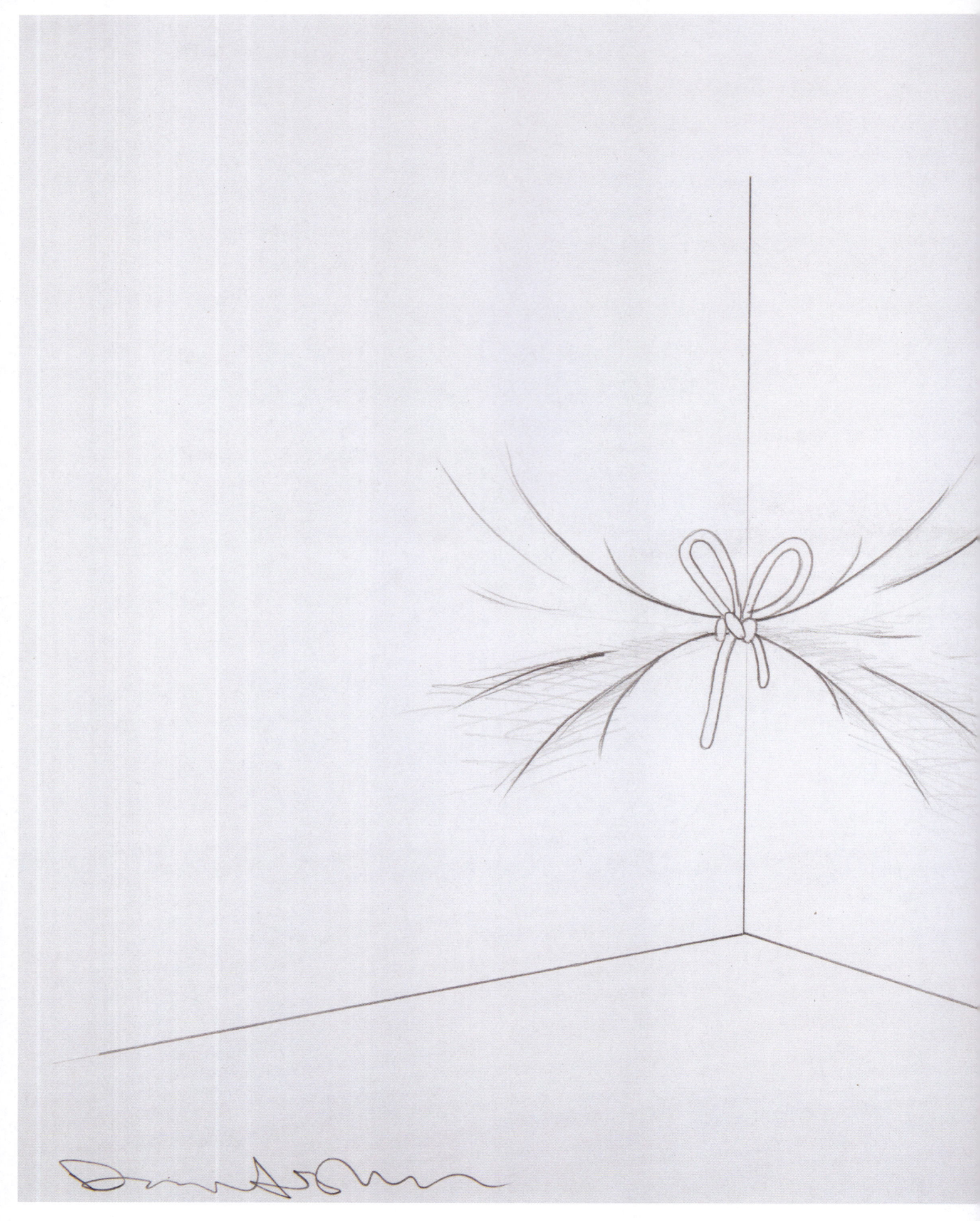

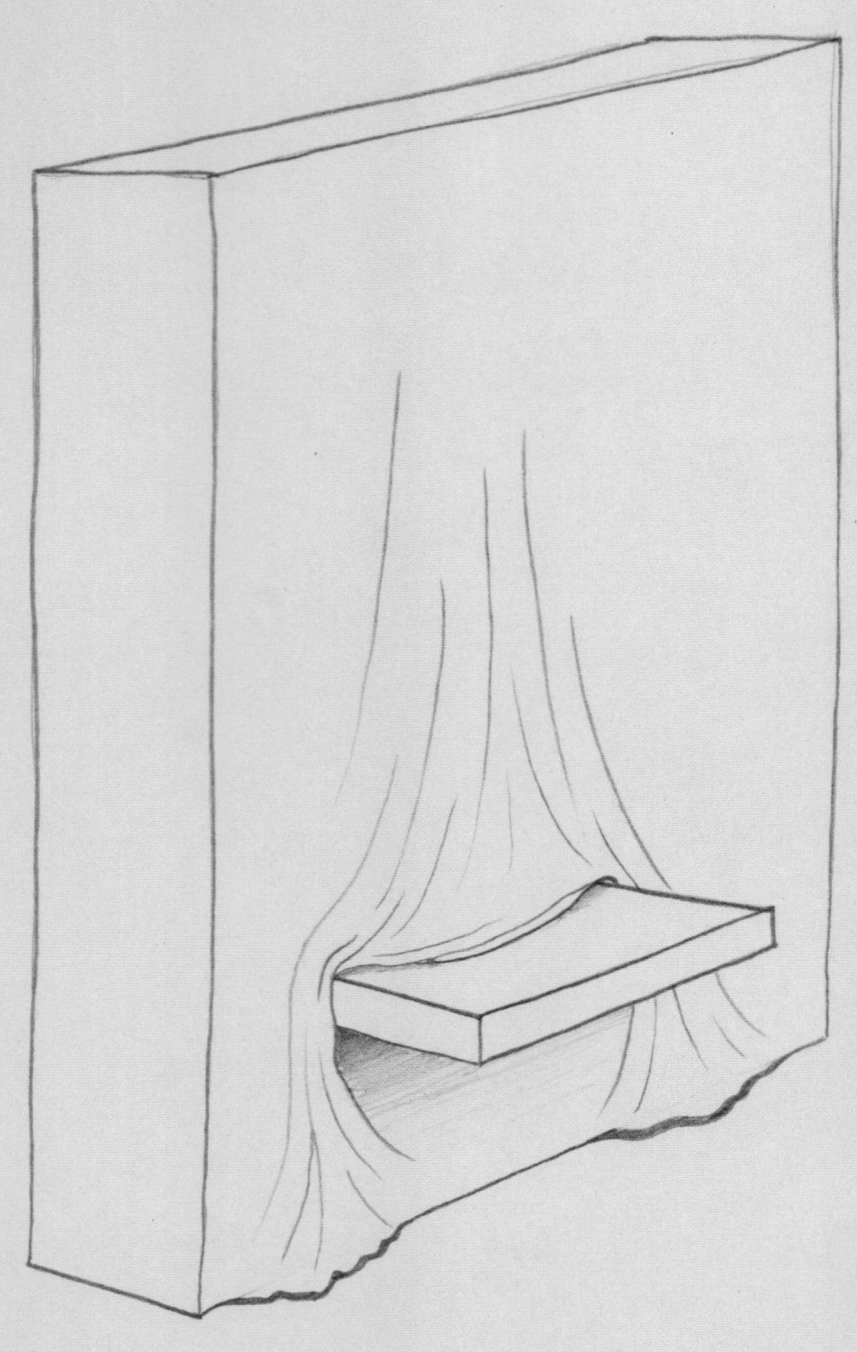

Sculpt // Bench wall curta

2009

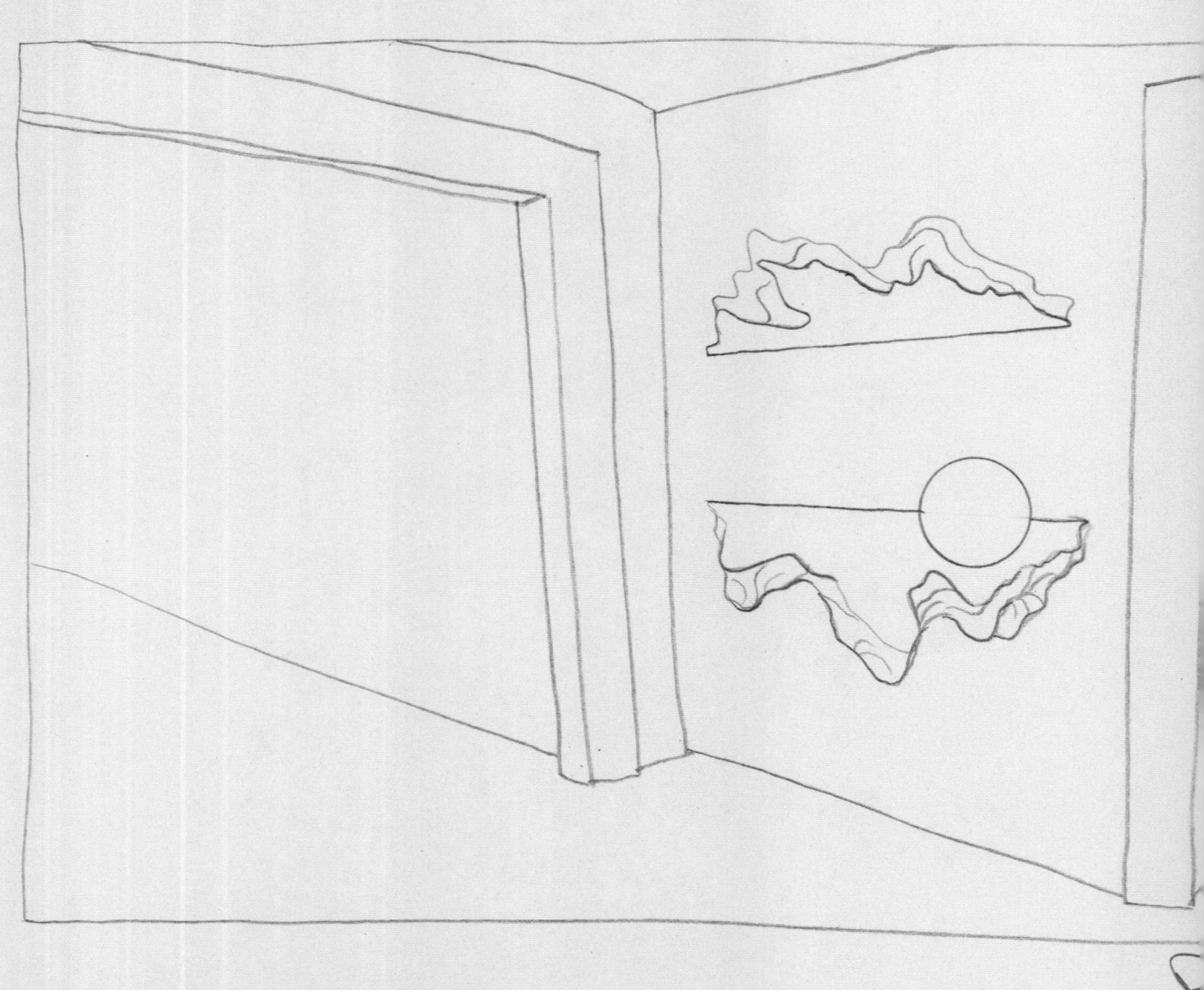

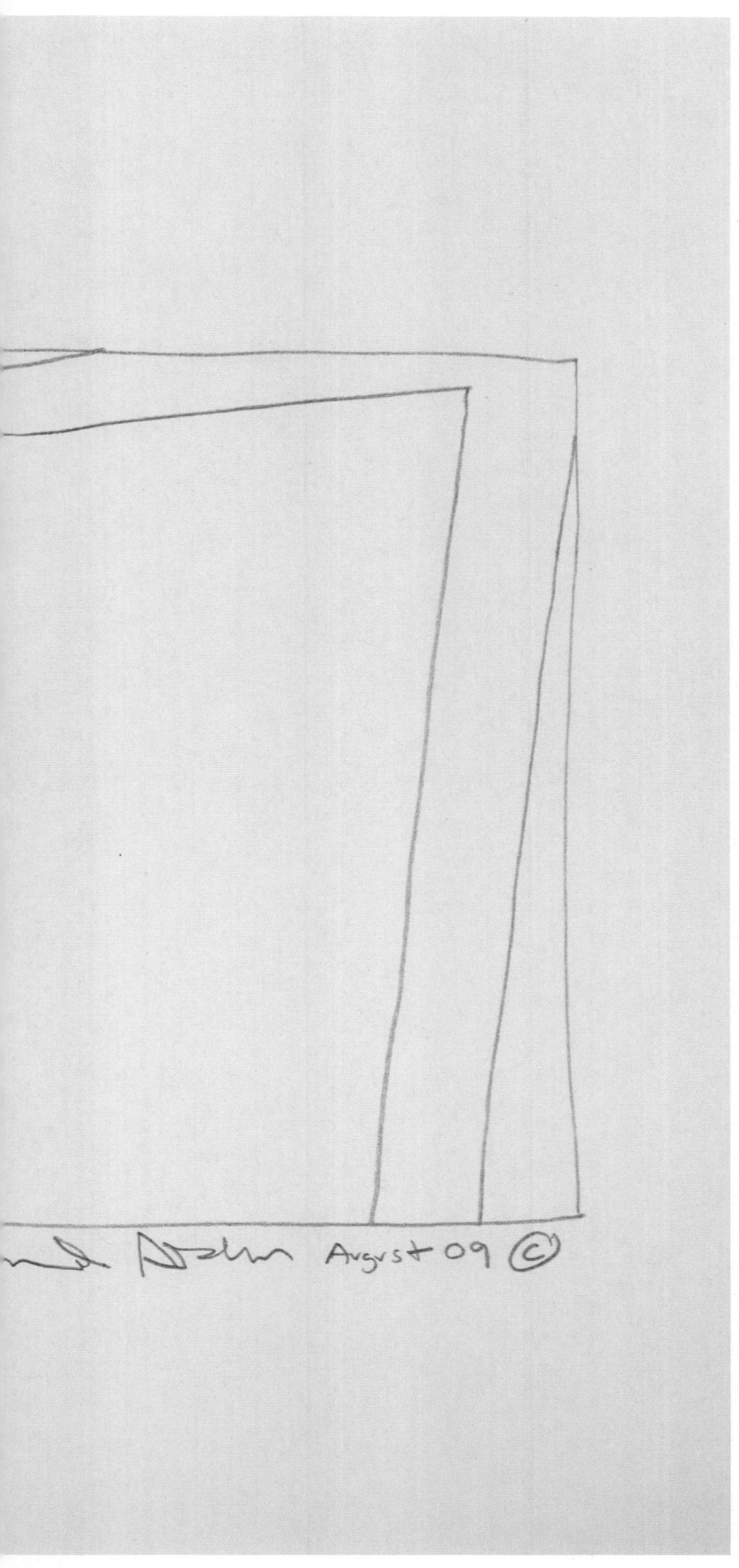

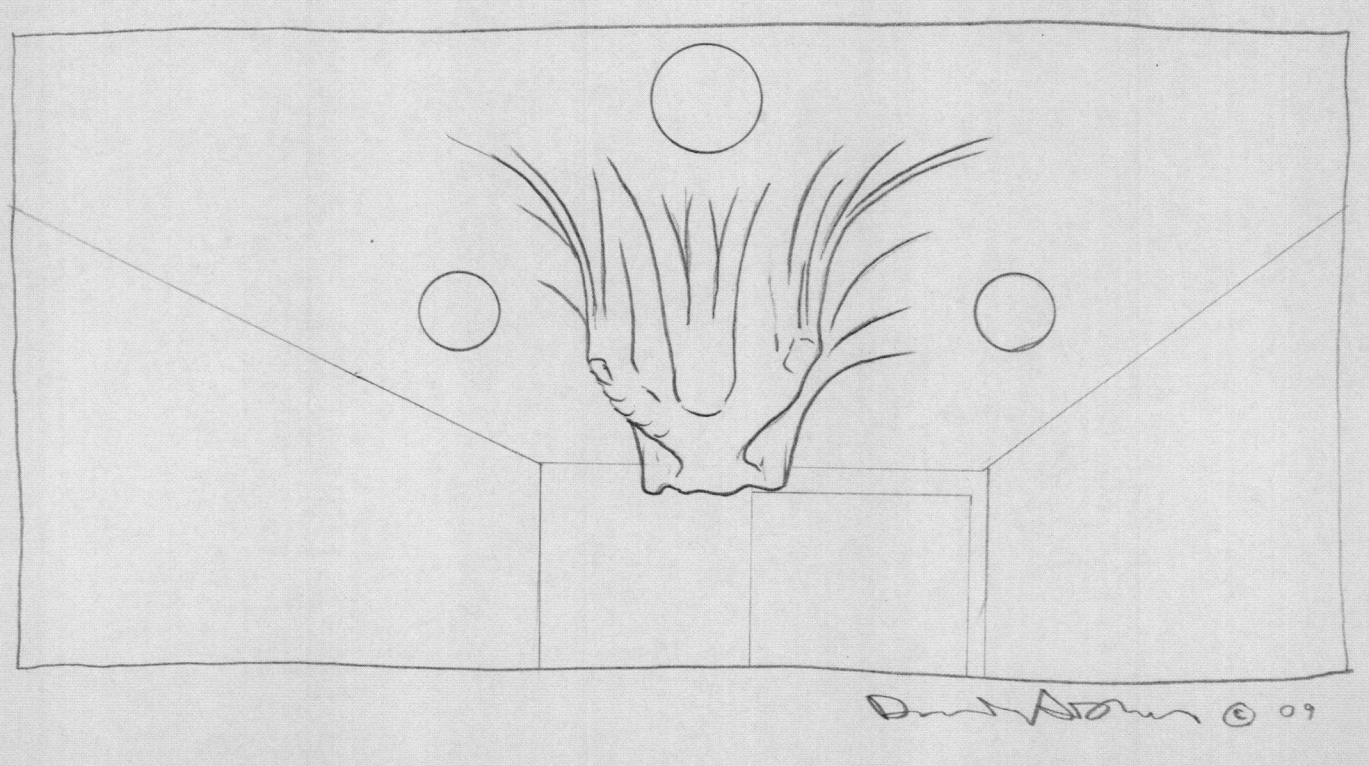

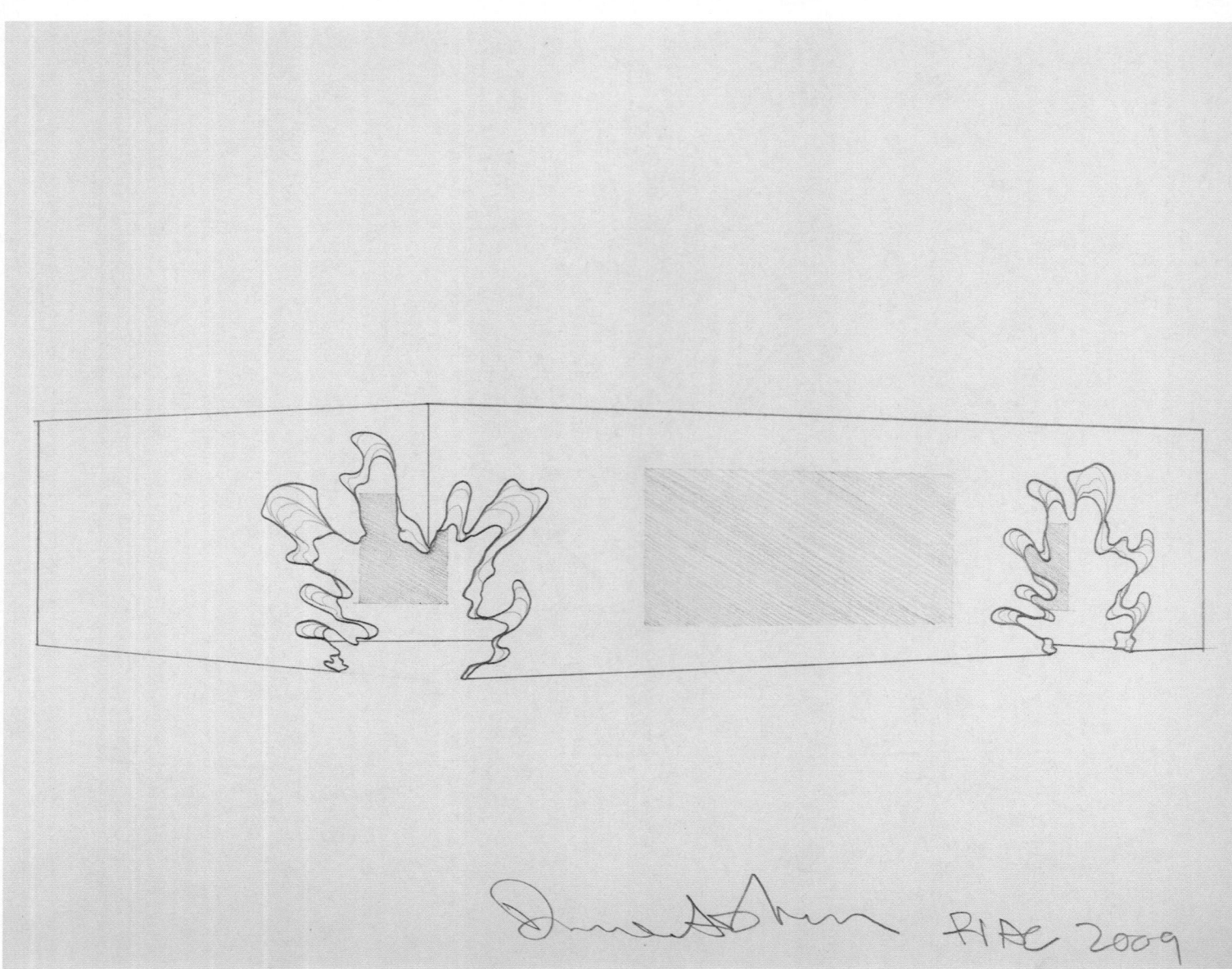

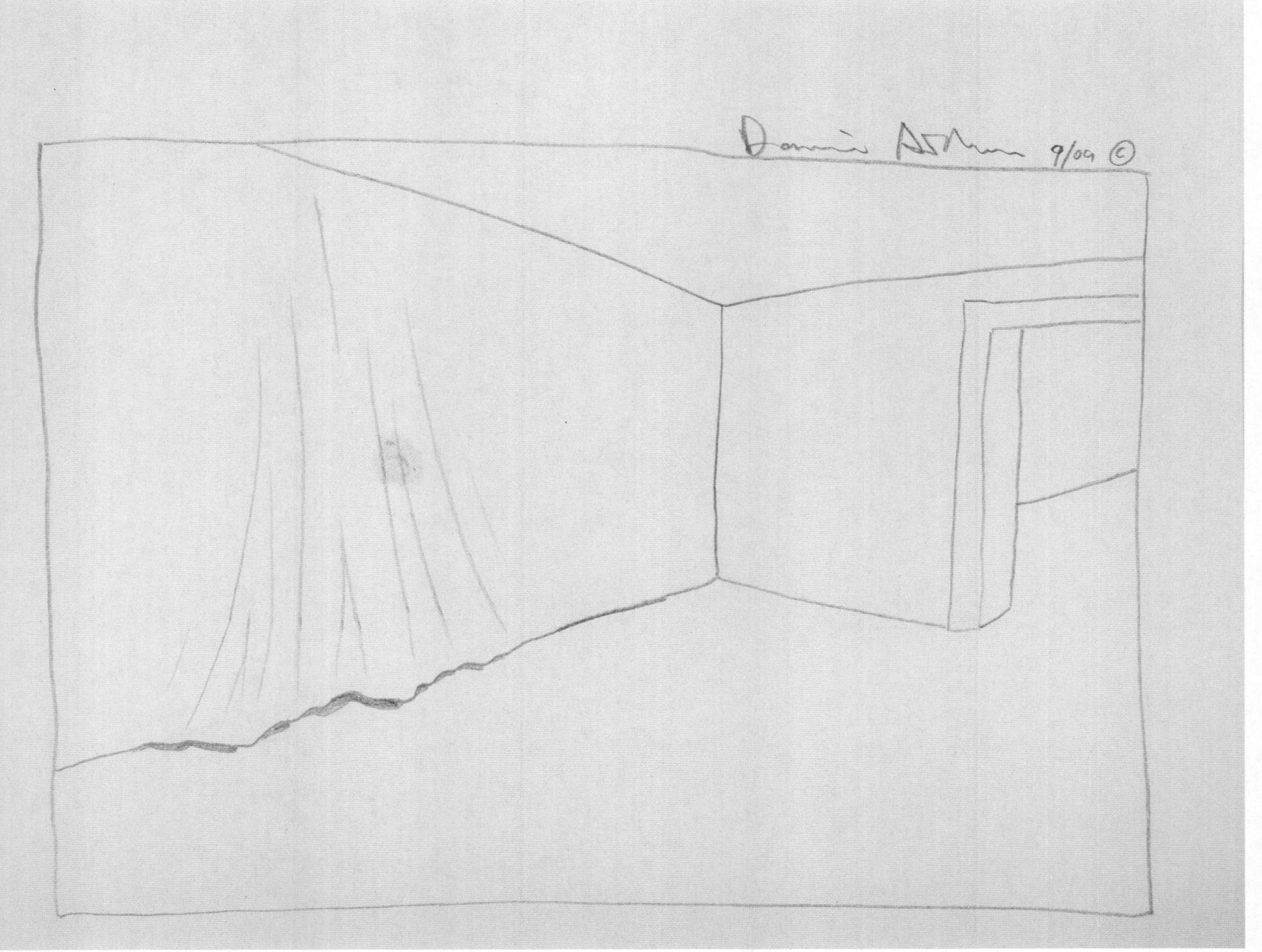

# Rocking Chair Design.

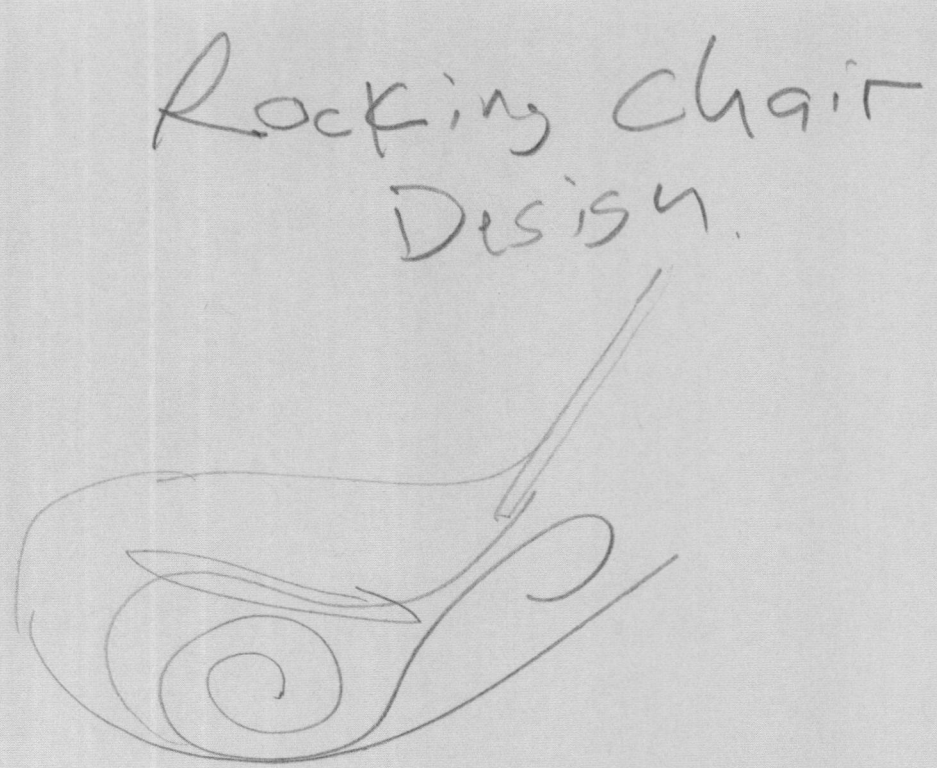

take the original profile of this chair
and extrude it laterally in foam, adjustments
will need to be made to account for back thickness.

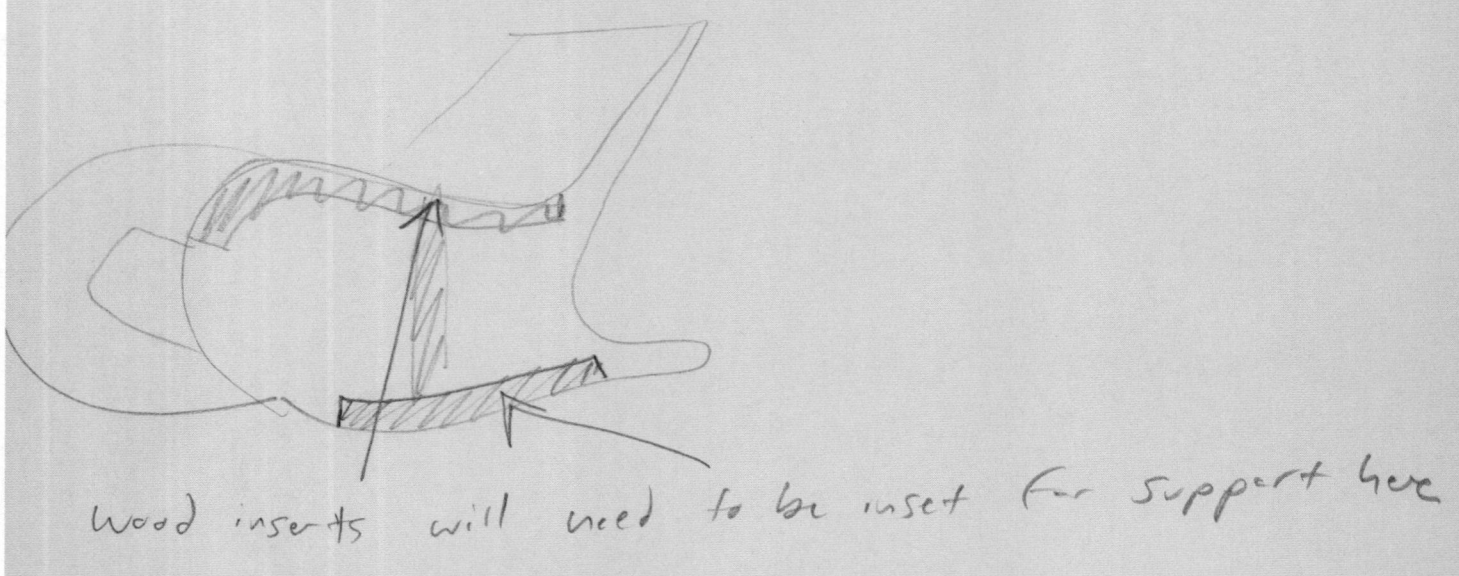

Wood inserts will need to be inset for support here

Once the general form has been constructed.
I will come back into the form and create
erosions into them

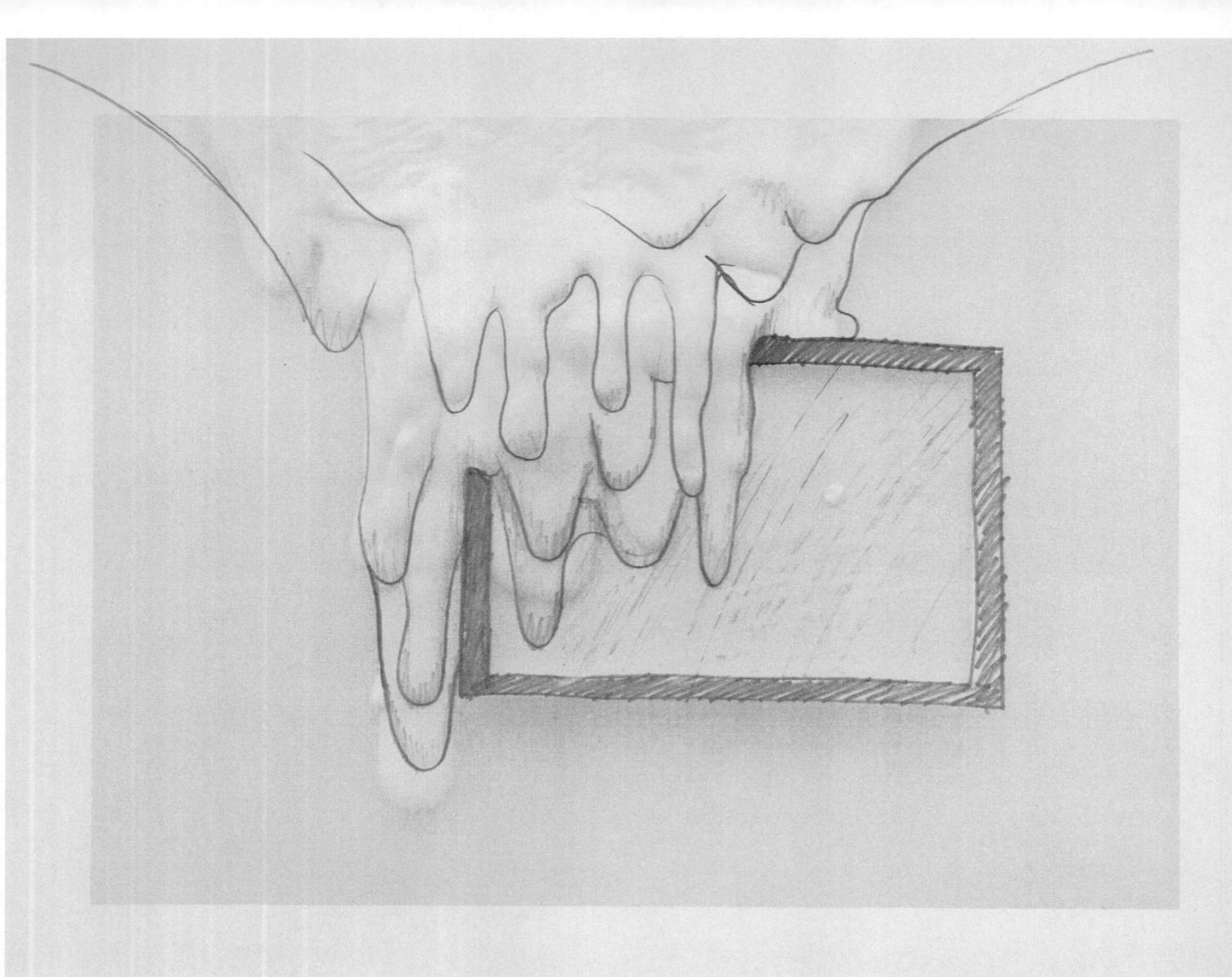

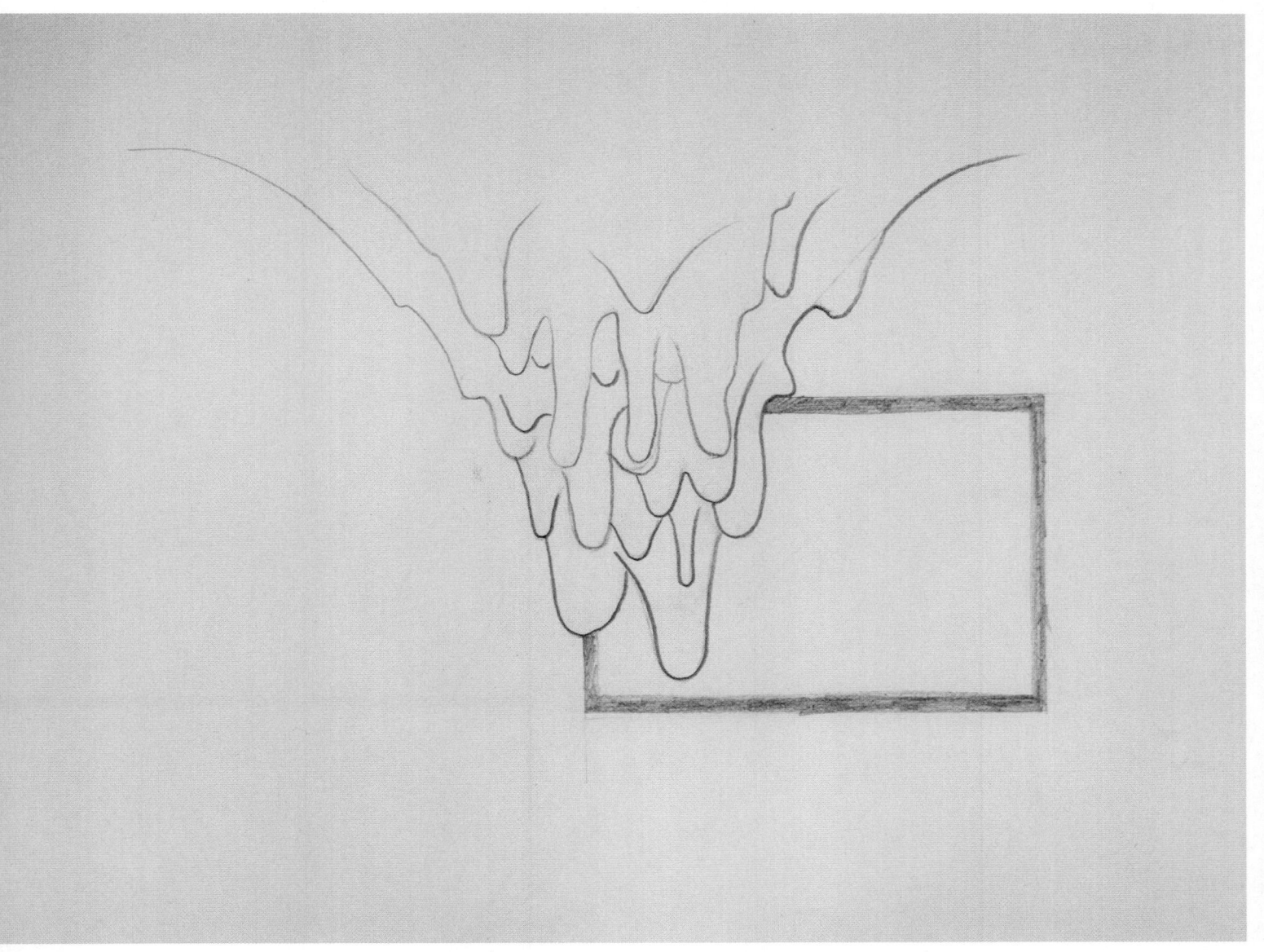

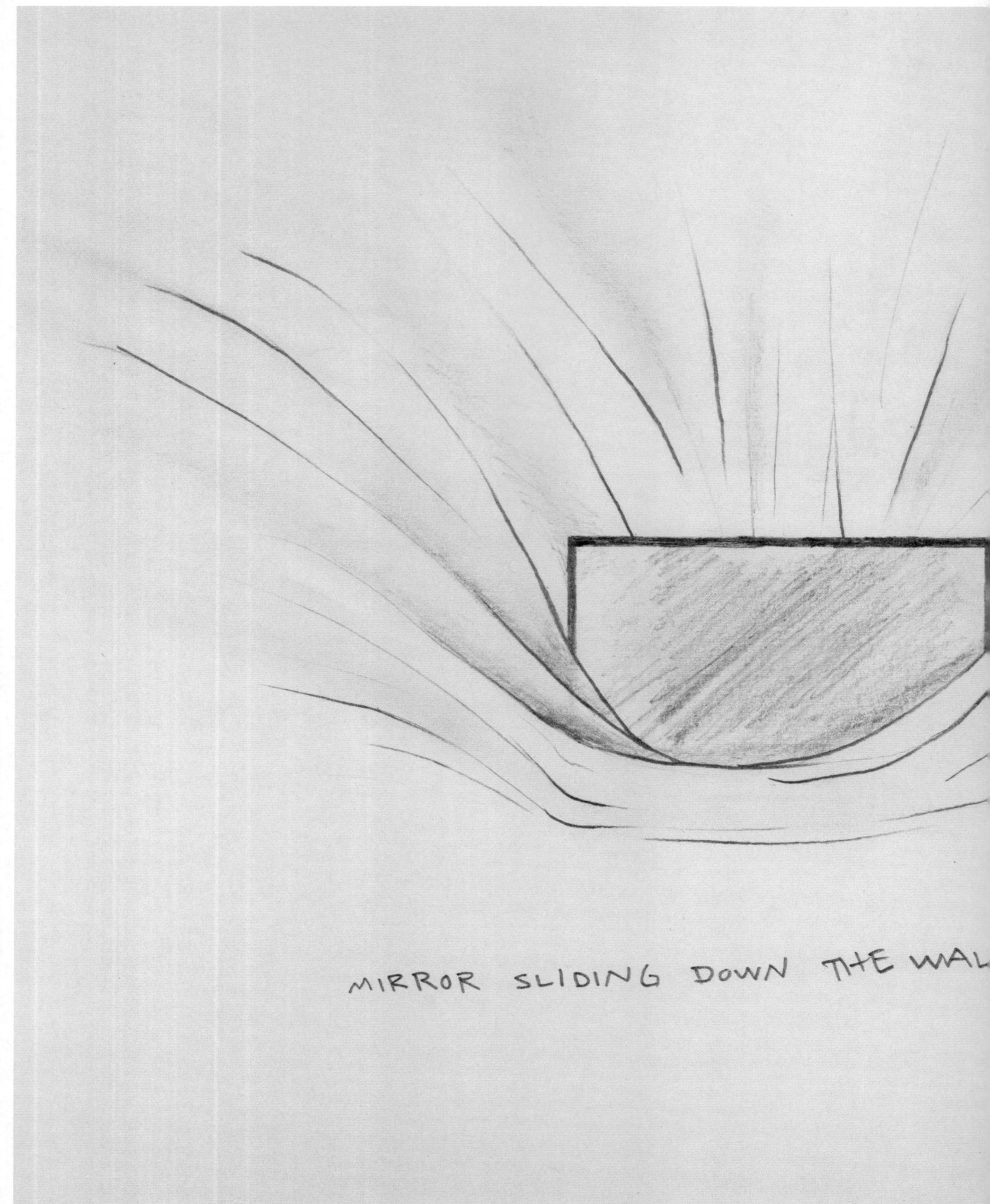

MIRROR SLIDING DOWN THE WALL

FOR JACK

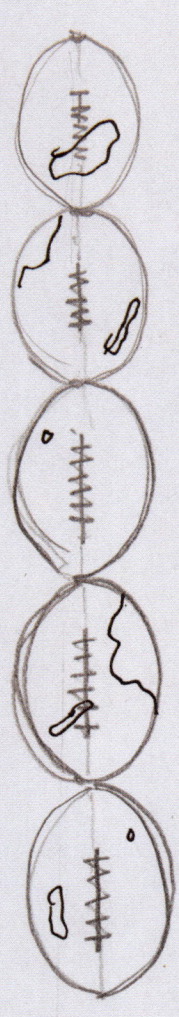

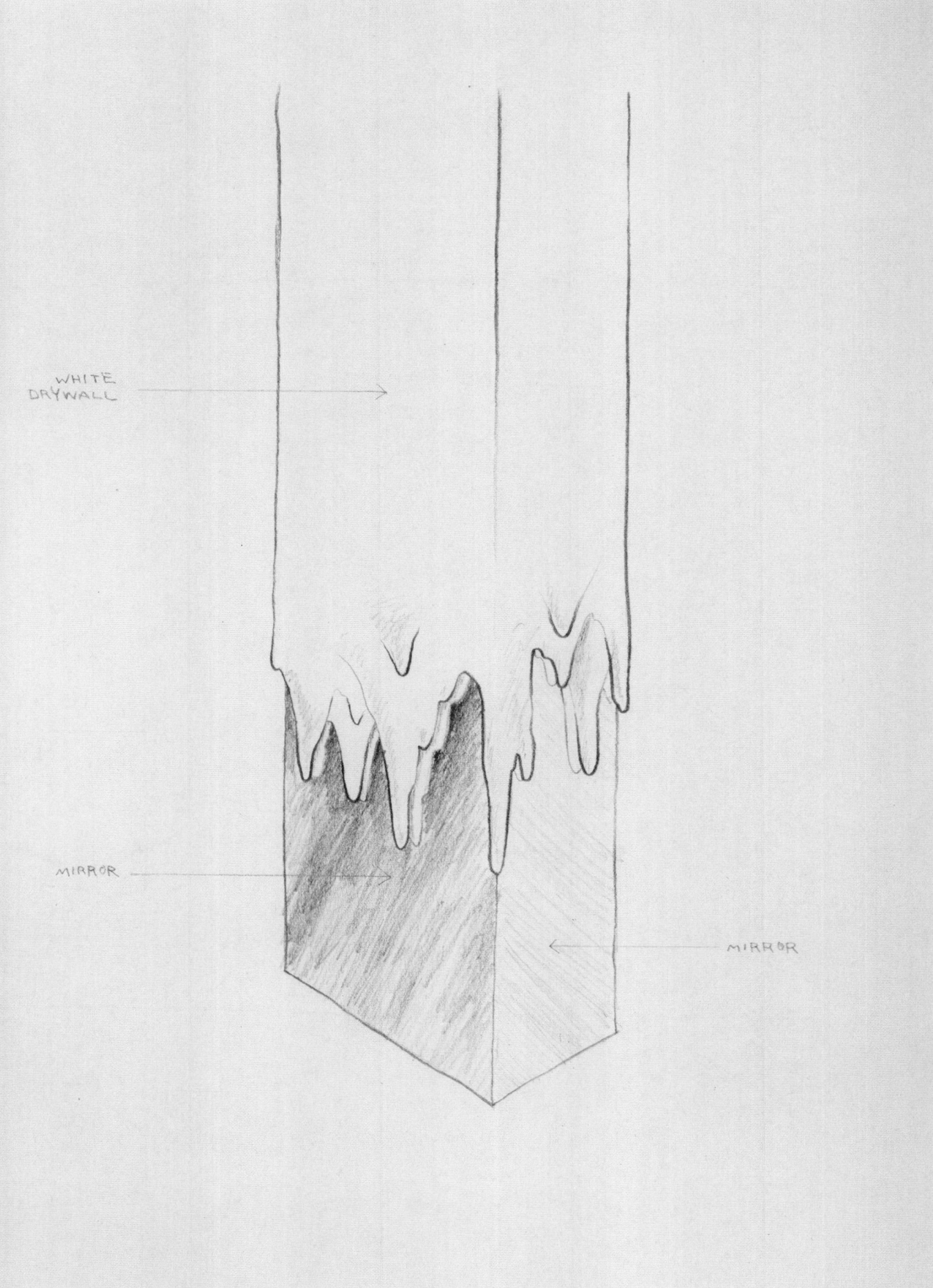

WHITE
DRYWALL

MIRROR

MIRROR

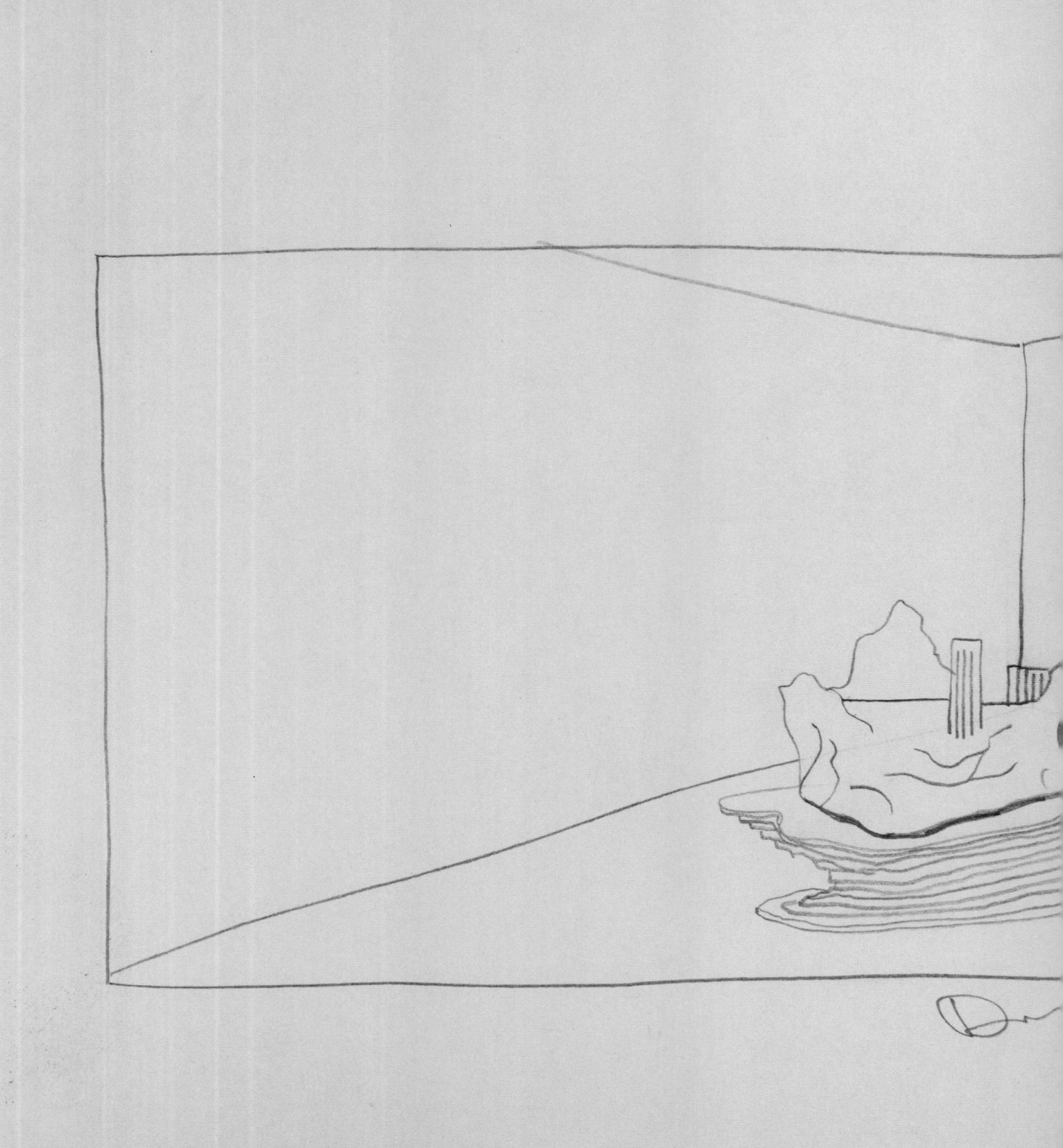

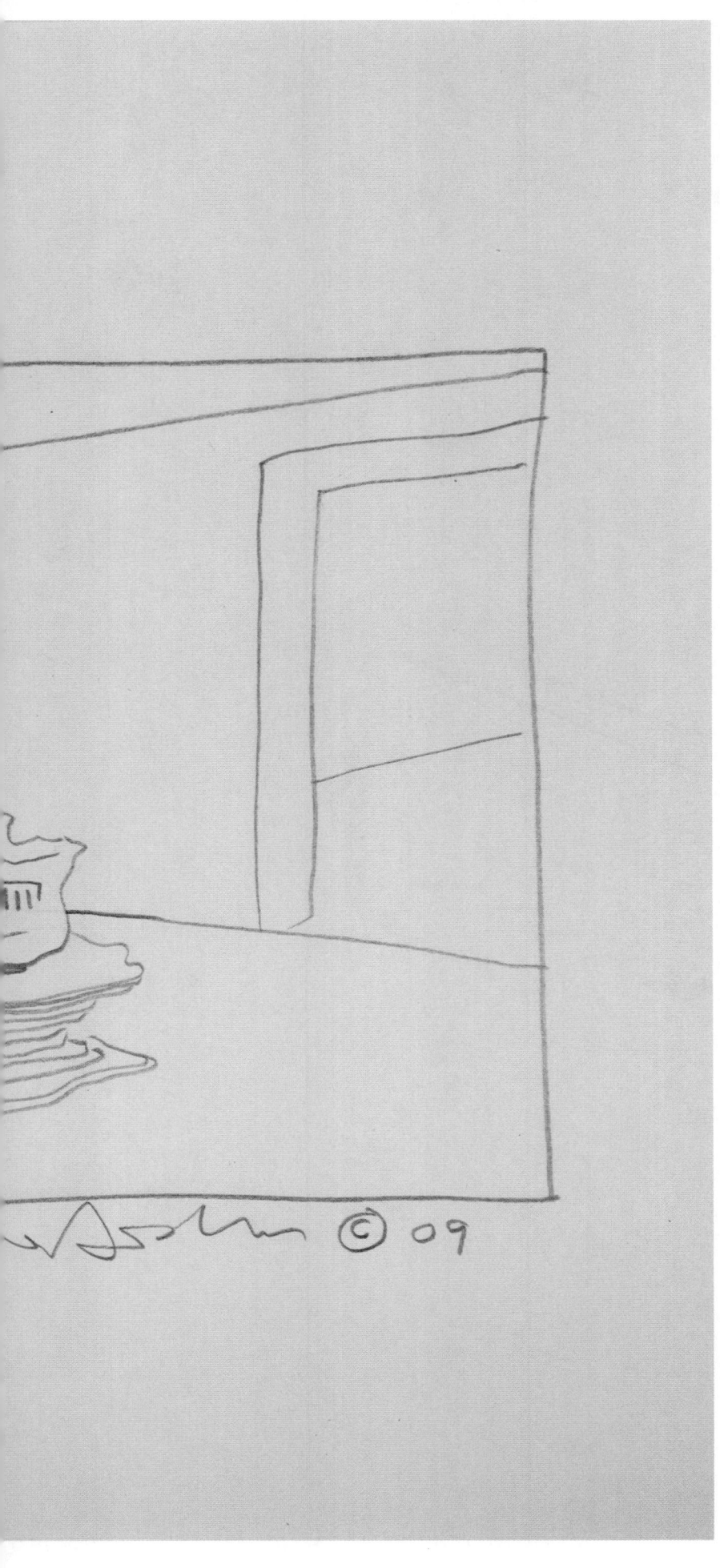

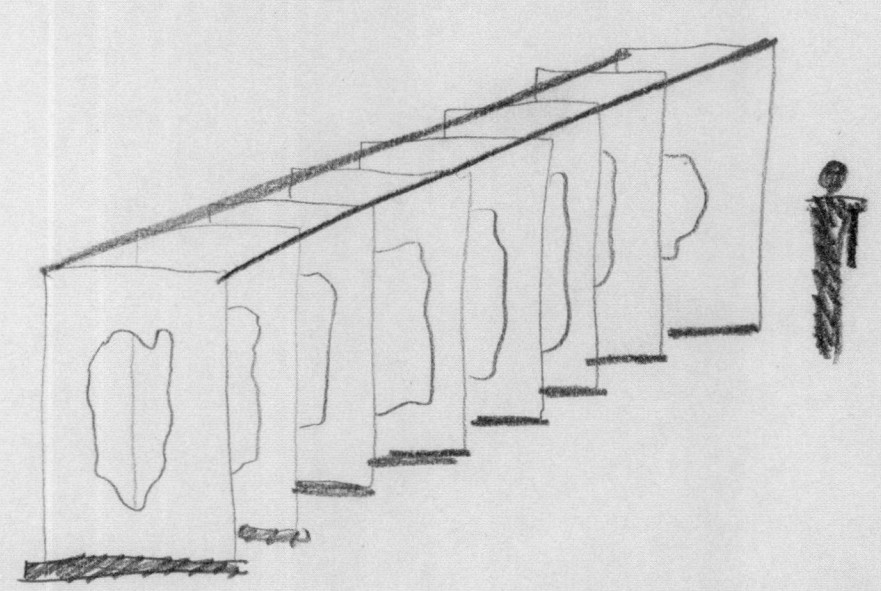

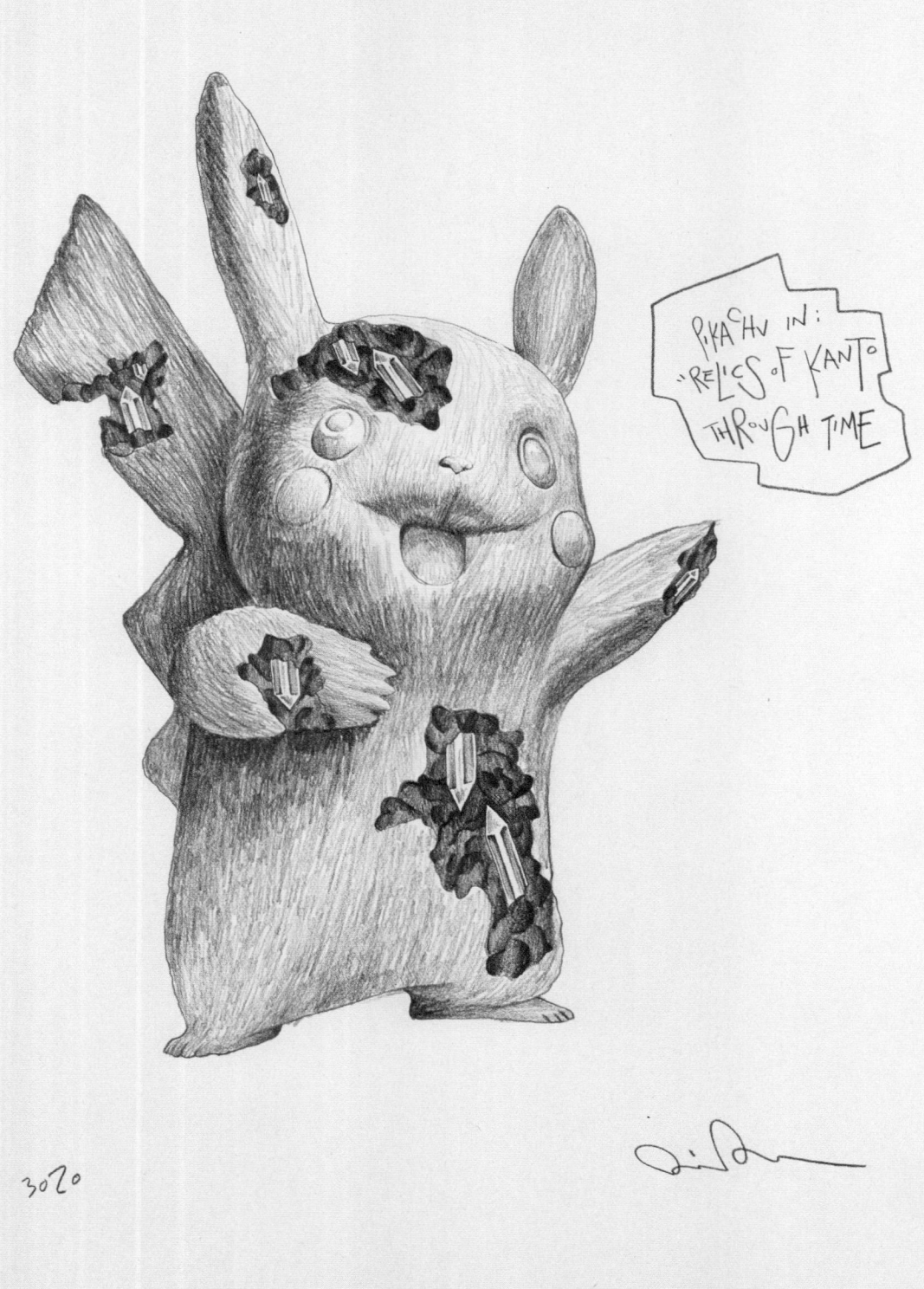

3020

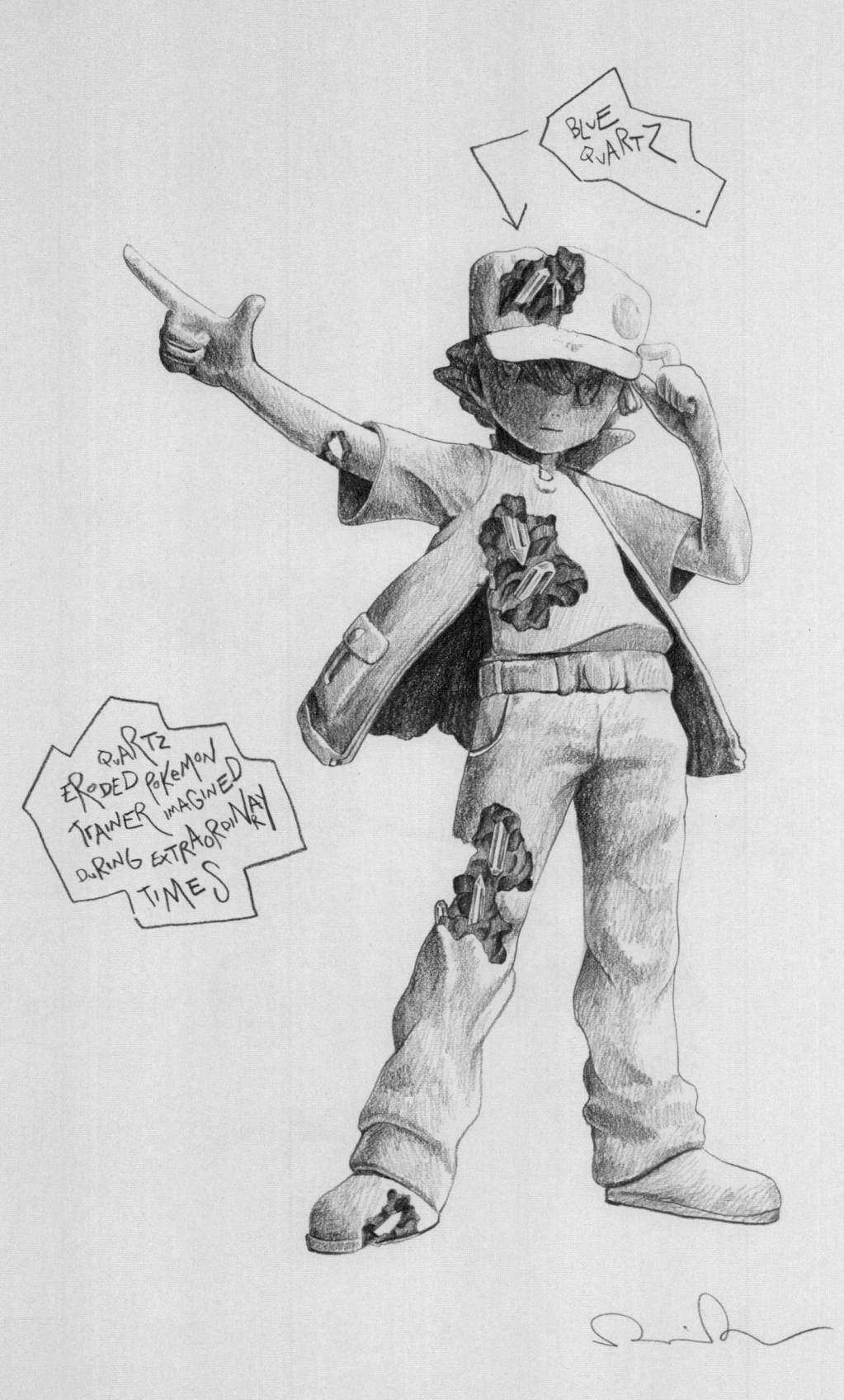

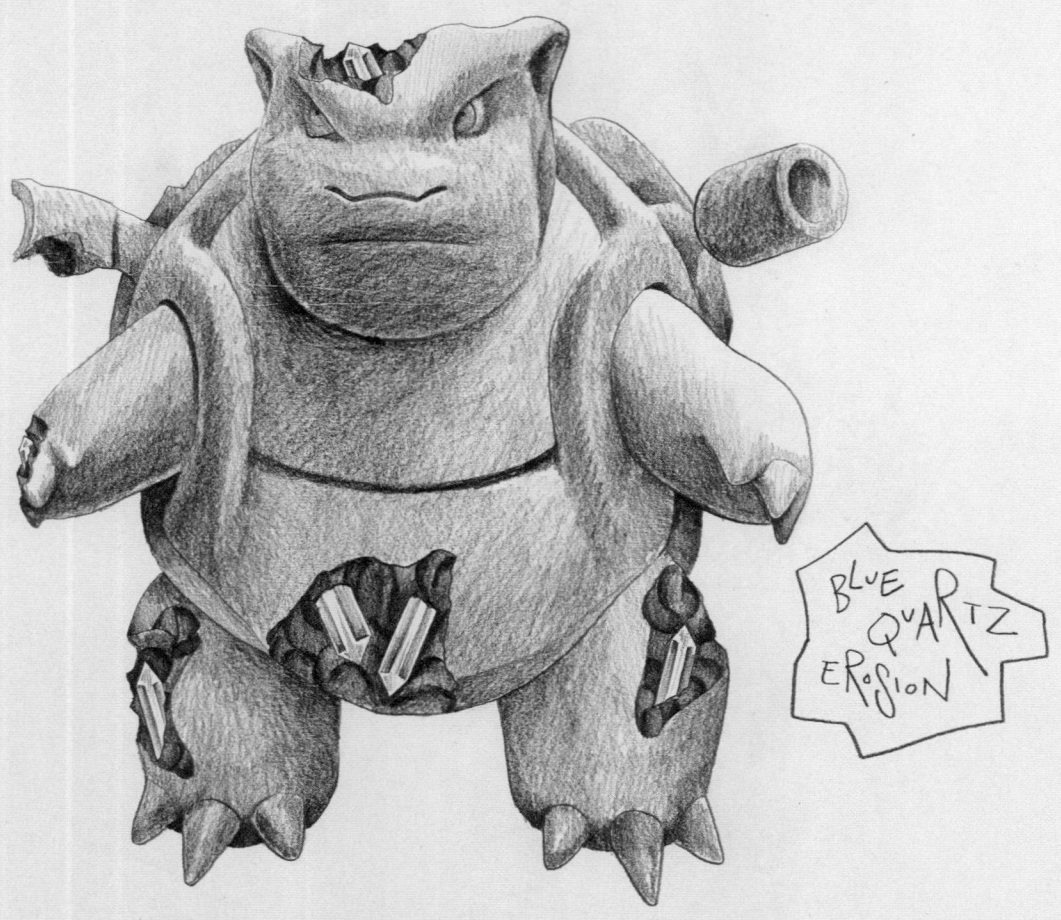

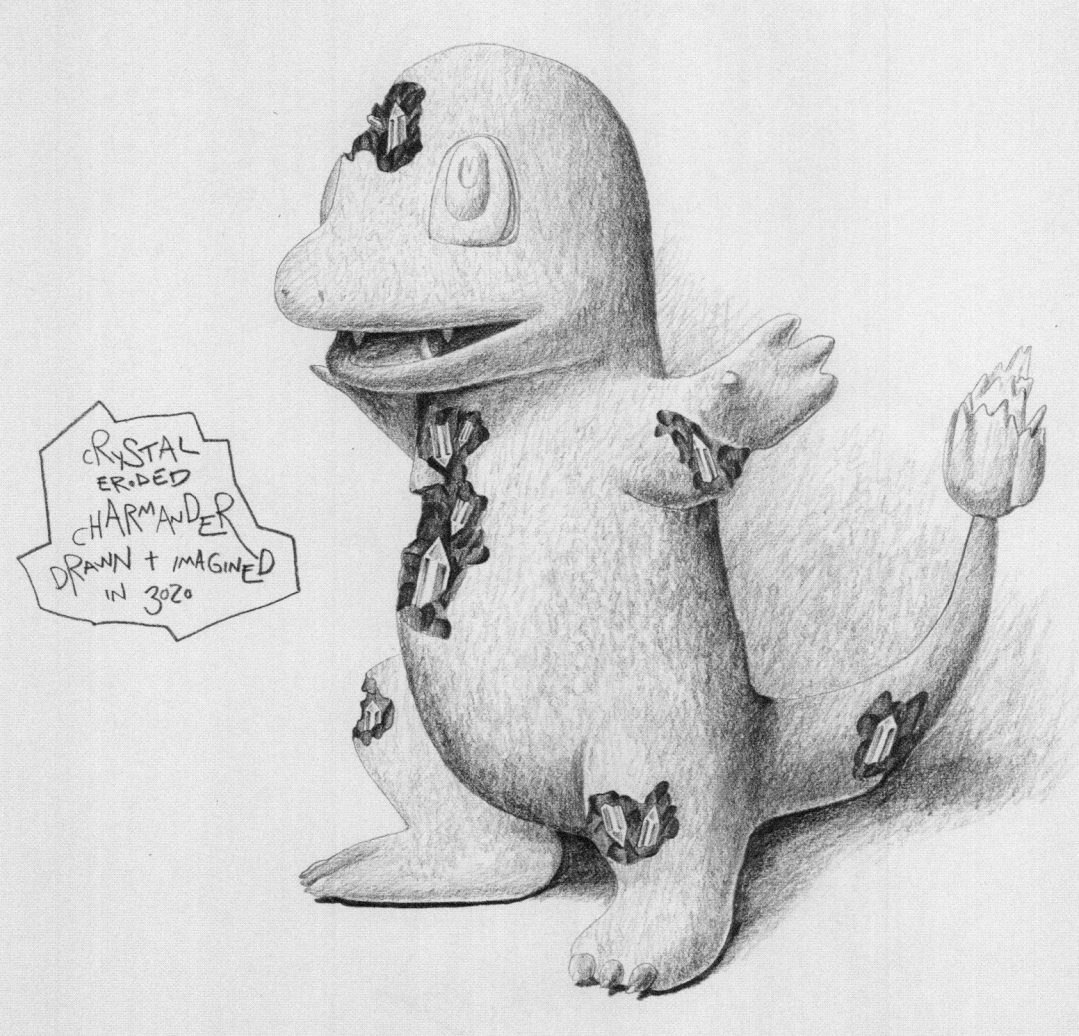

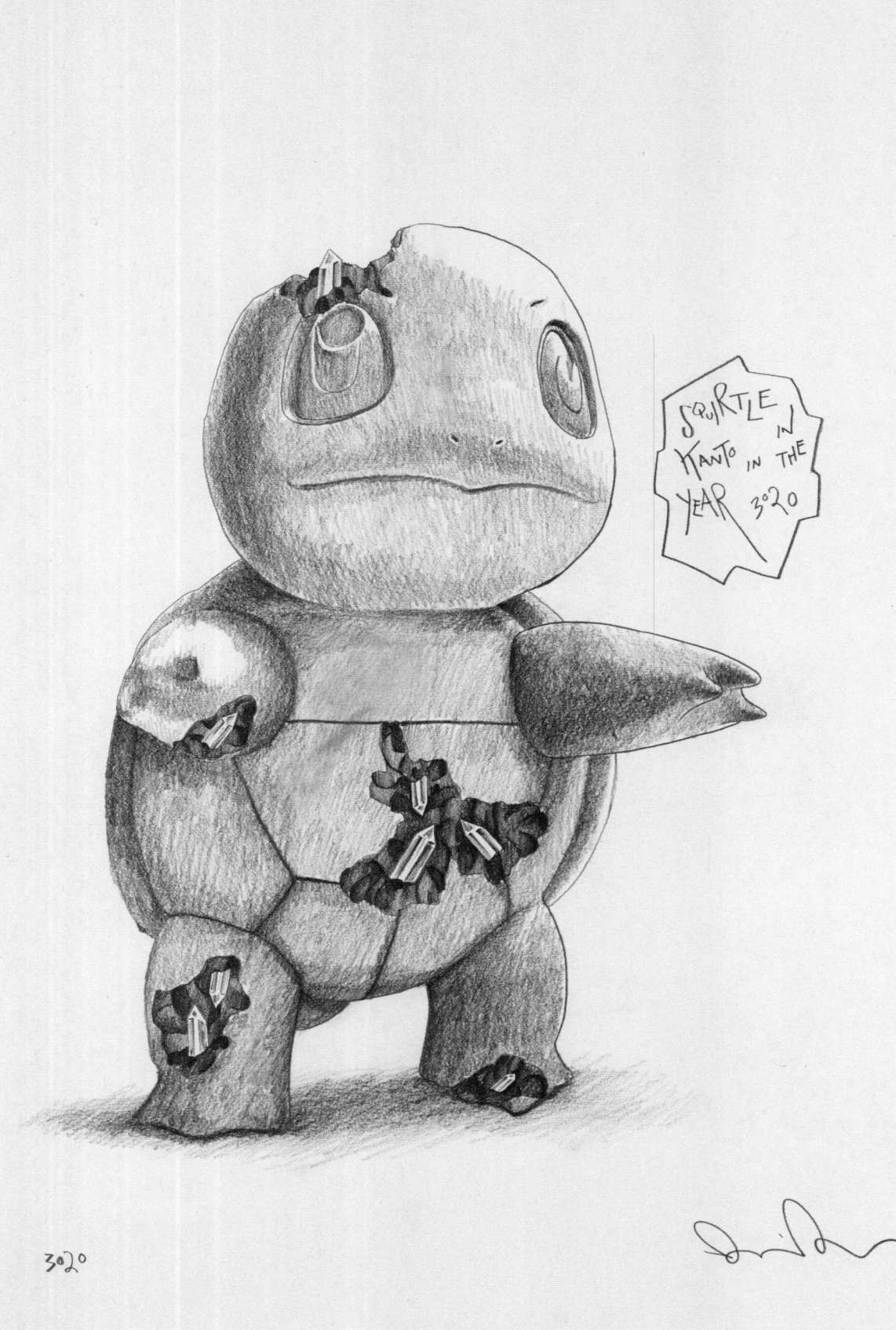

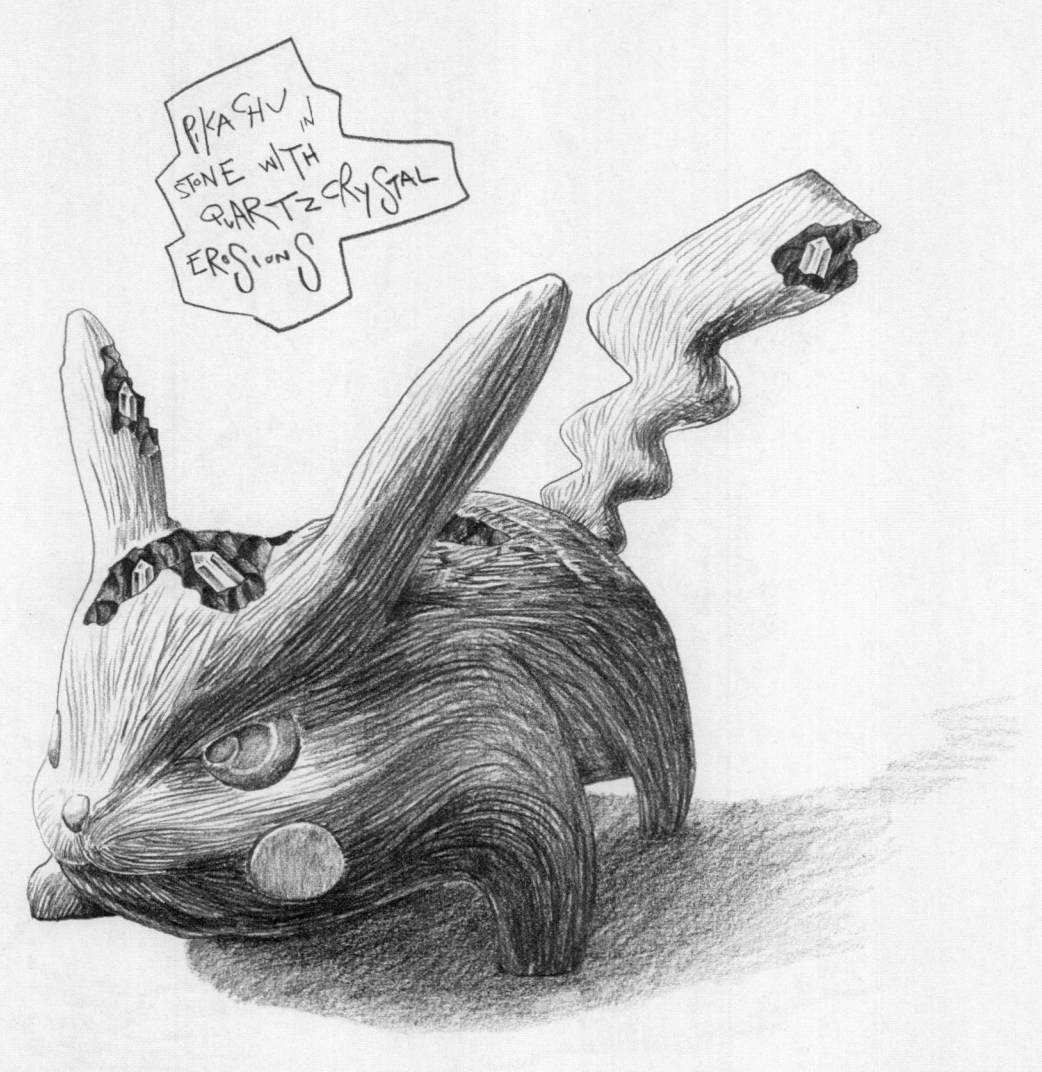

3020

113

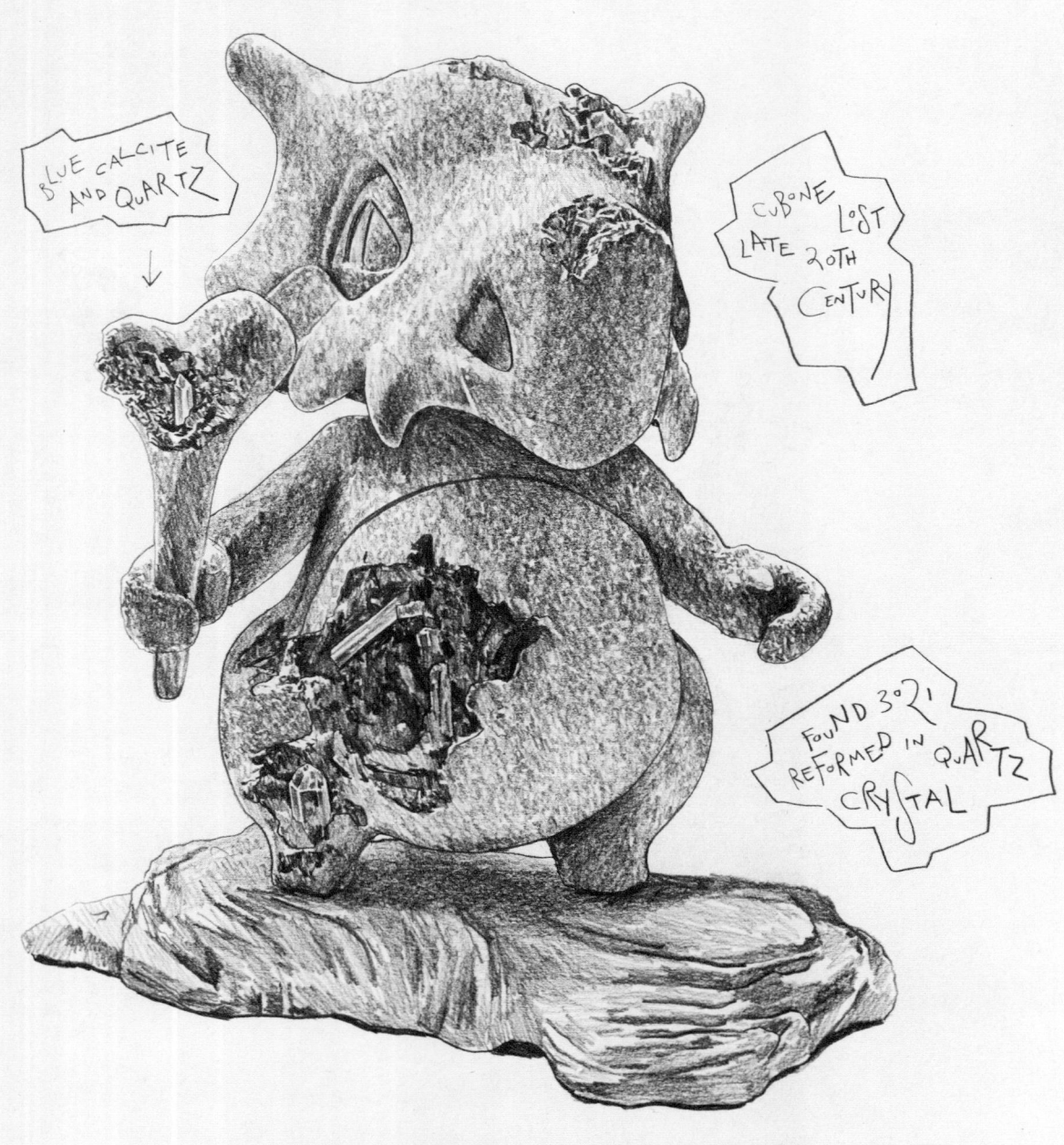

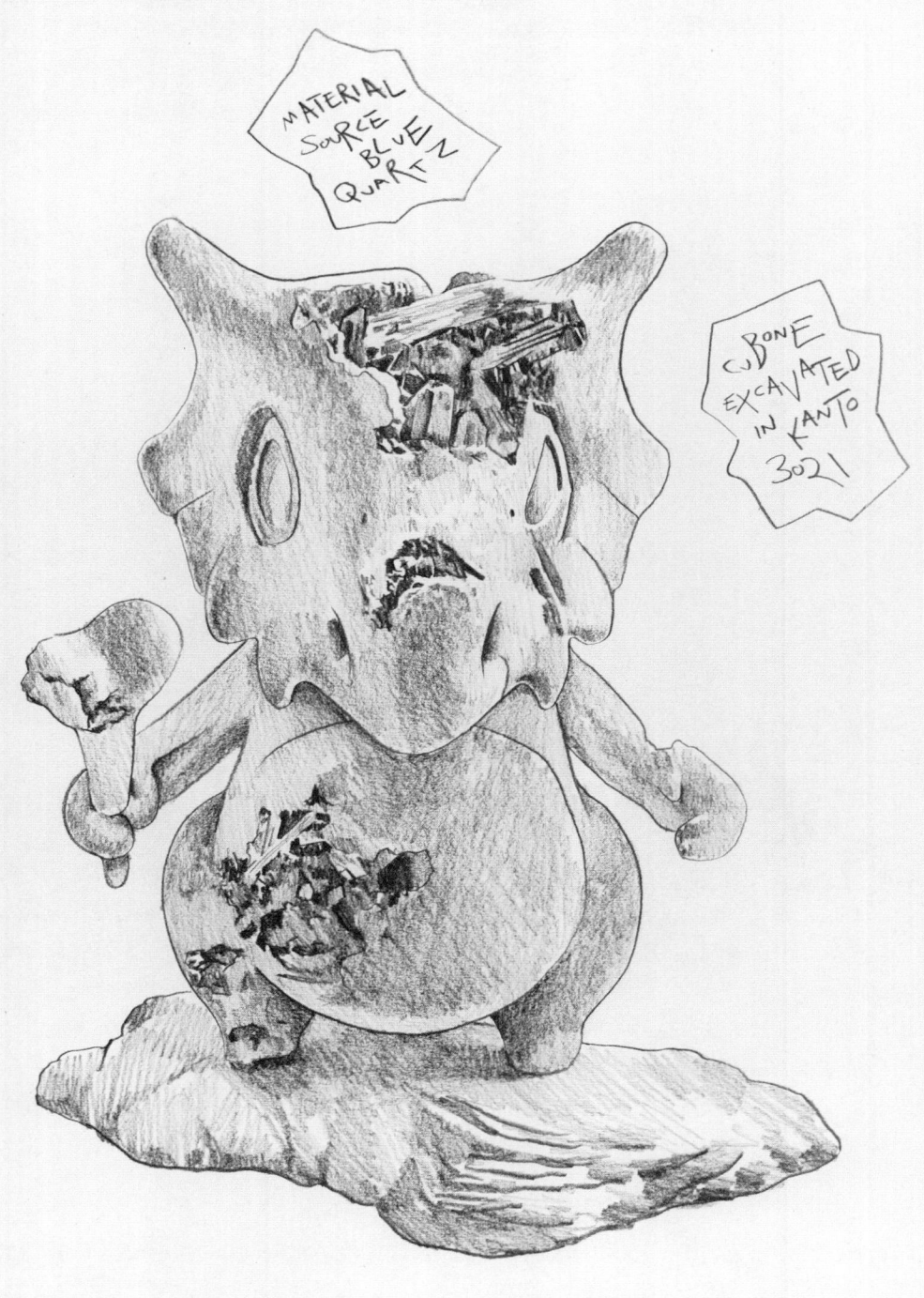

ERODED
LOGO

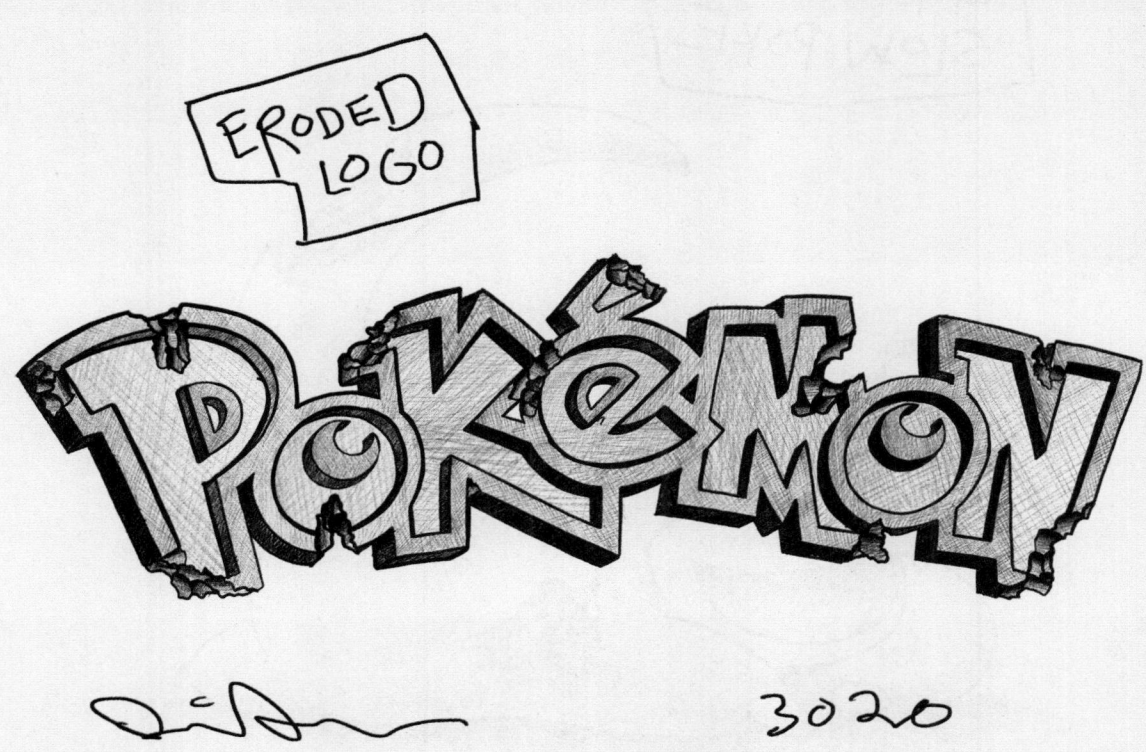

3020

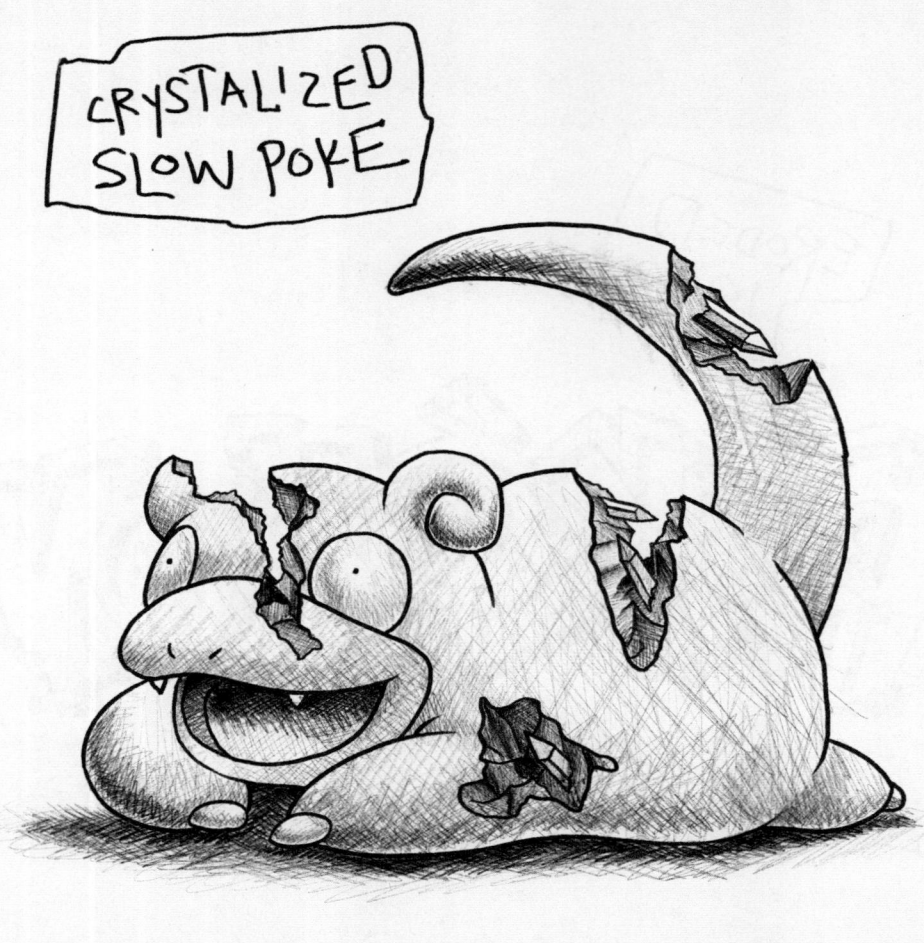

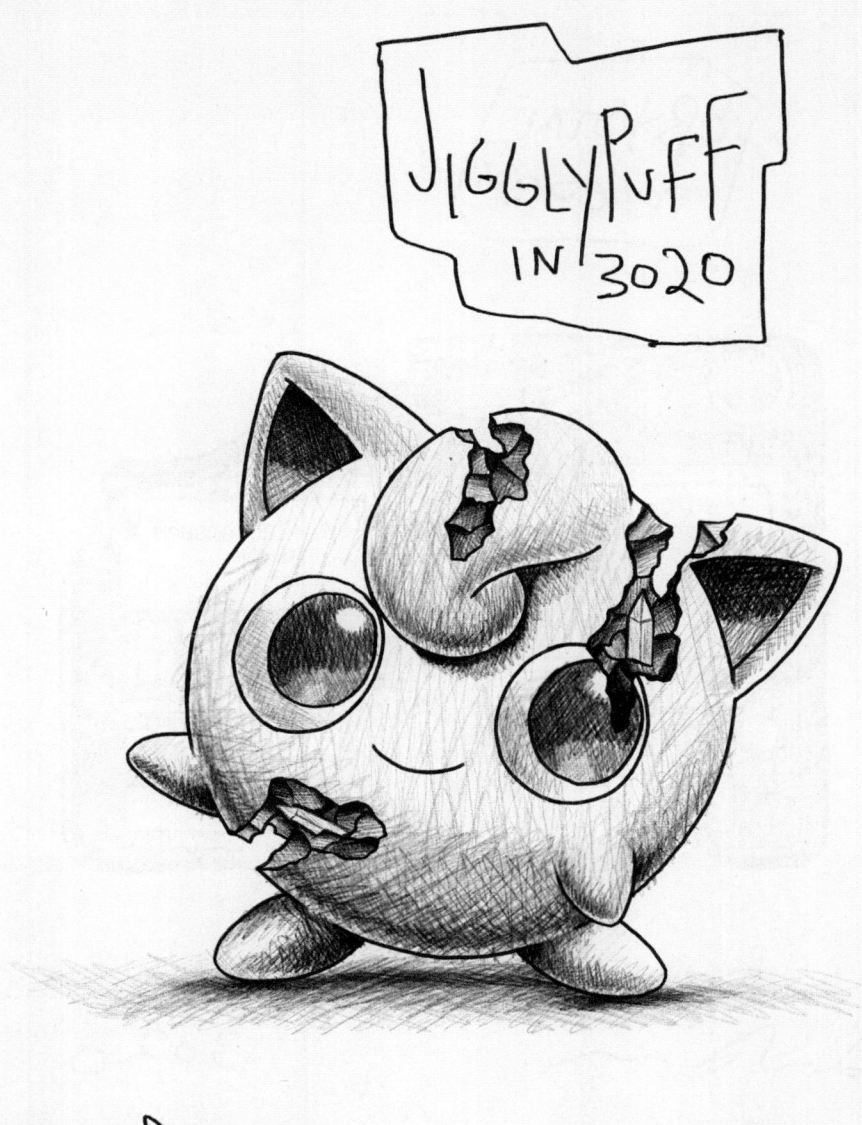

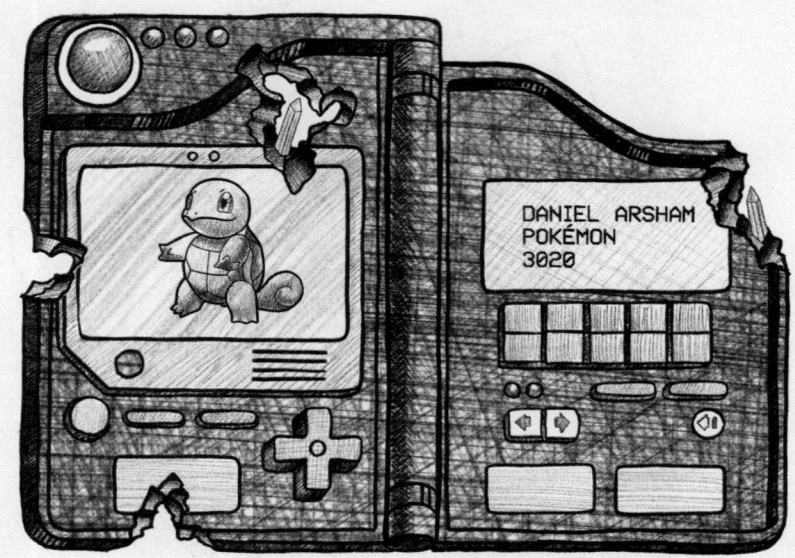

CRYSTAL POKEDEX

DANIEL ARSHAM
POKÉMON
3020

3020

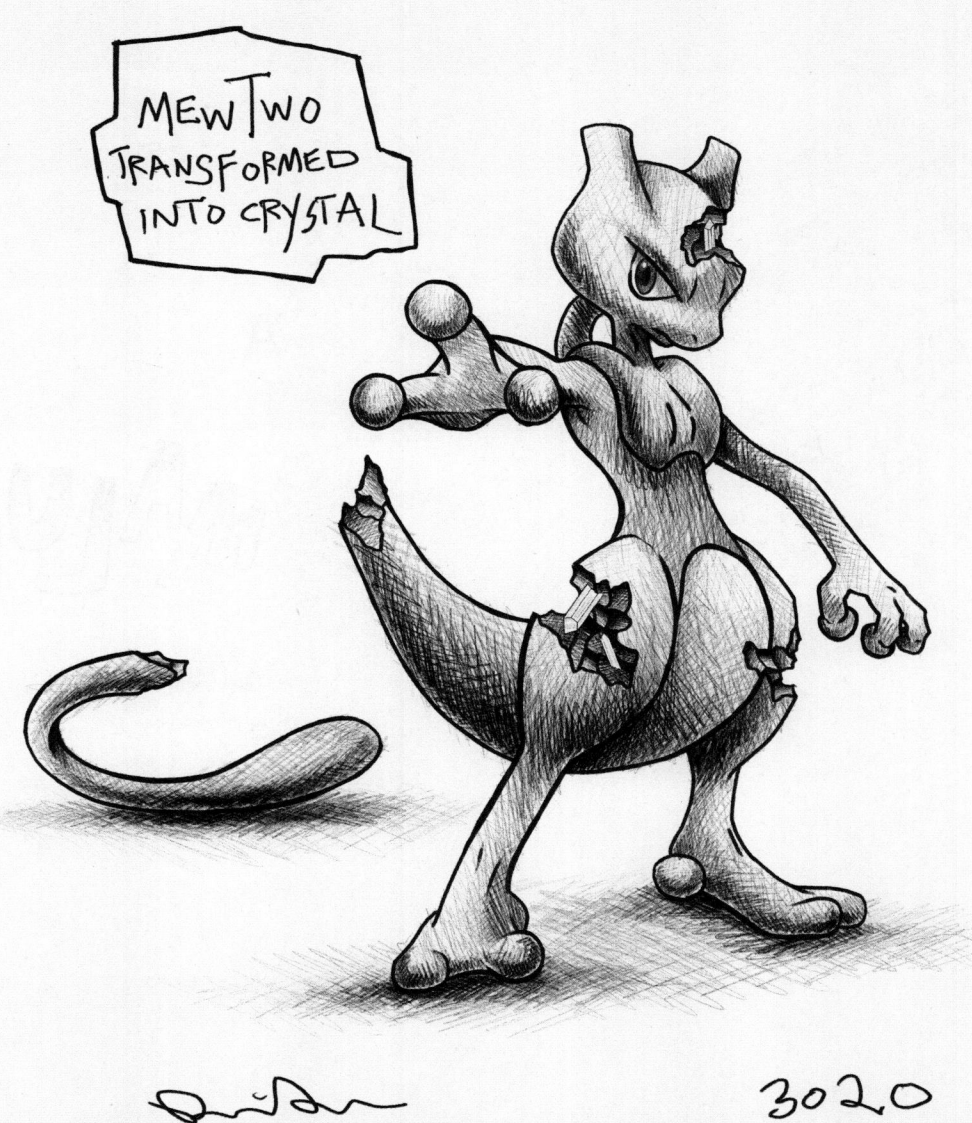

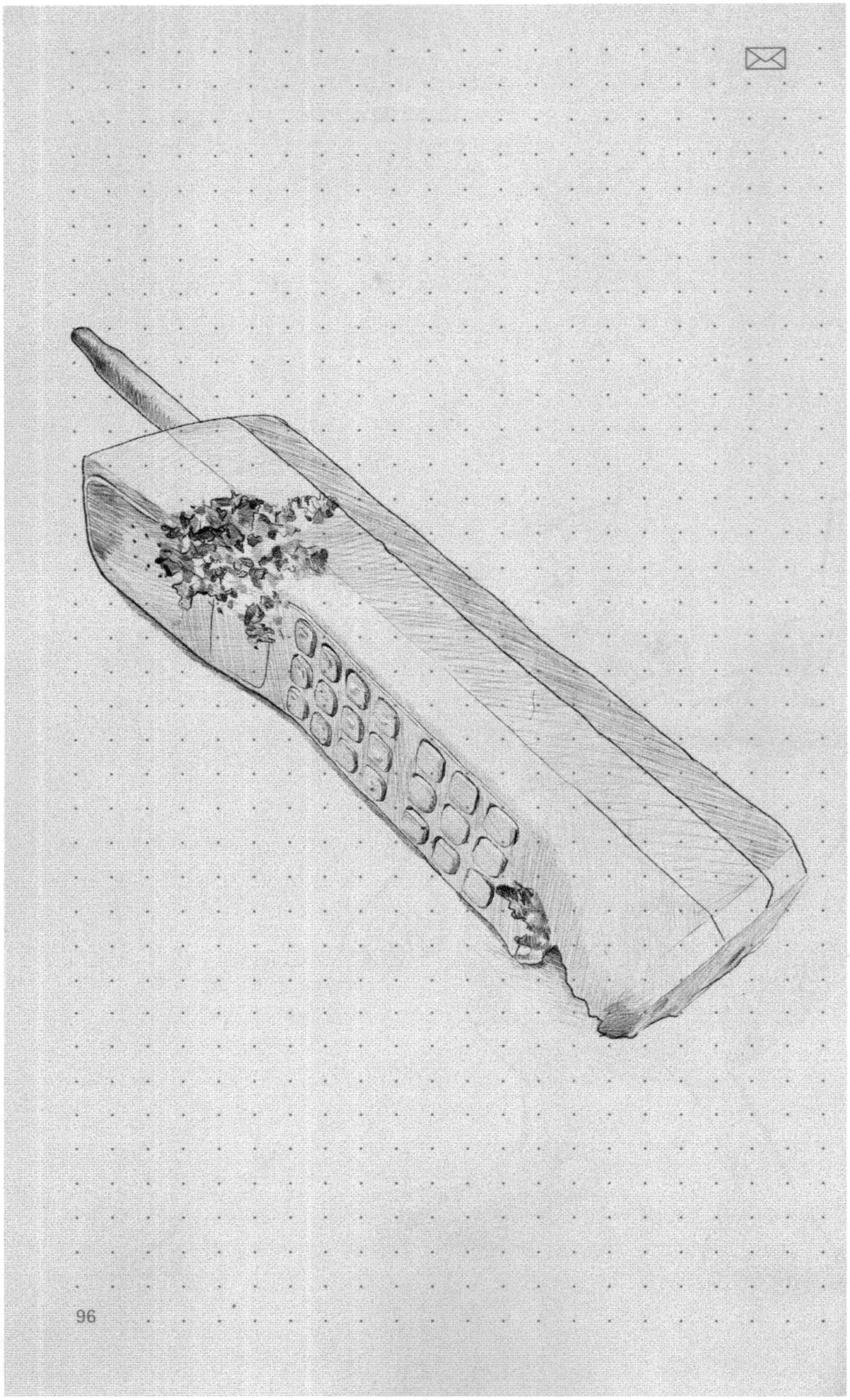

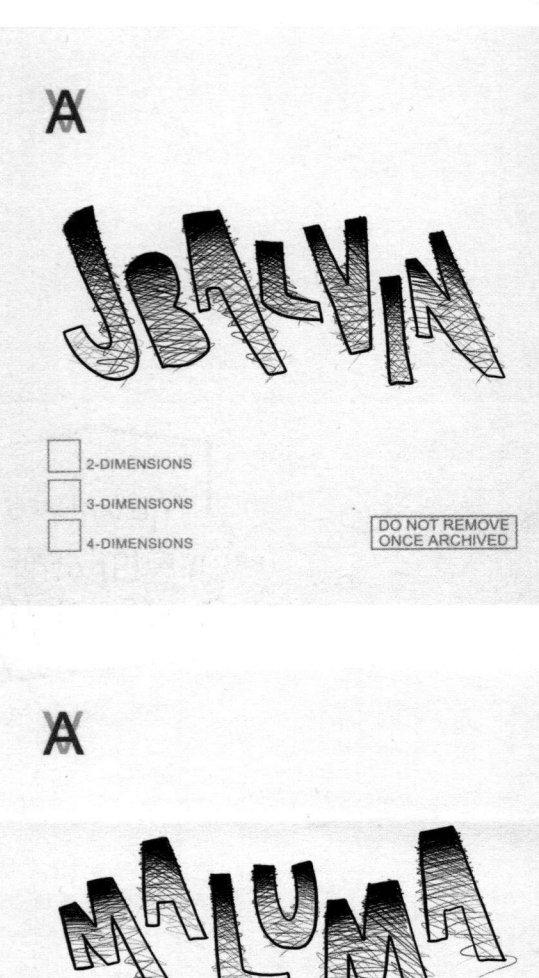

96

A

JBALVIN

☐ 2-DIMENSIONS
☐ 3-DIMENSIONS
☐ 4-DIMENSIONS

DO NOT REMOVE
ONCE ARCHIVED

A

MALUMA

☐ 2-DIMENSIONS
☐ 3-DIMENSIONS
☐ 4-DIMENSIONS

DO NOT REMOVE
ONCE ARCHIVED

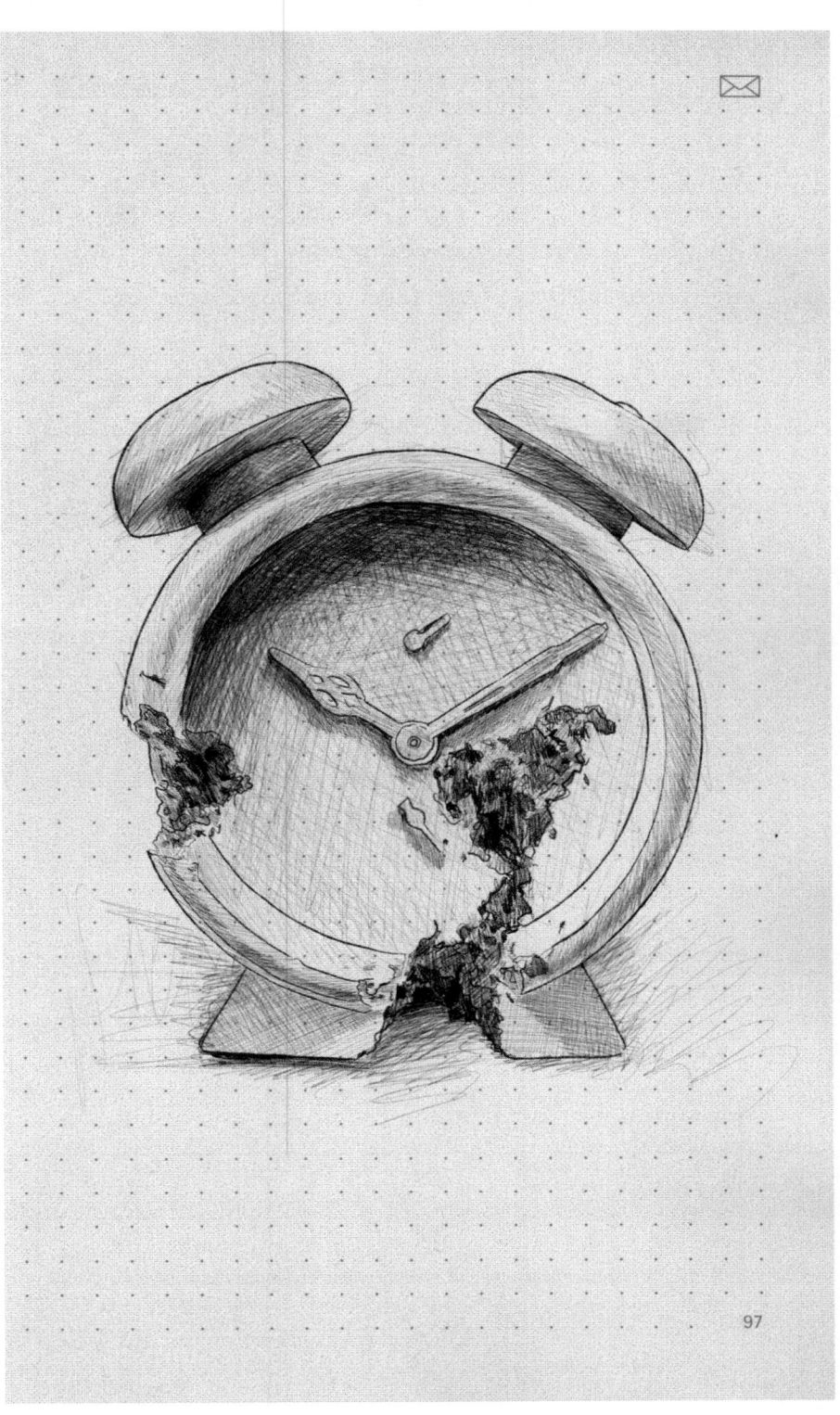

97

123

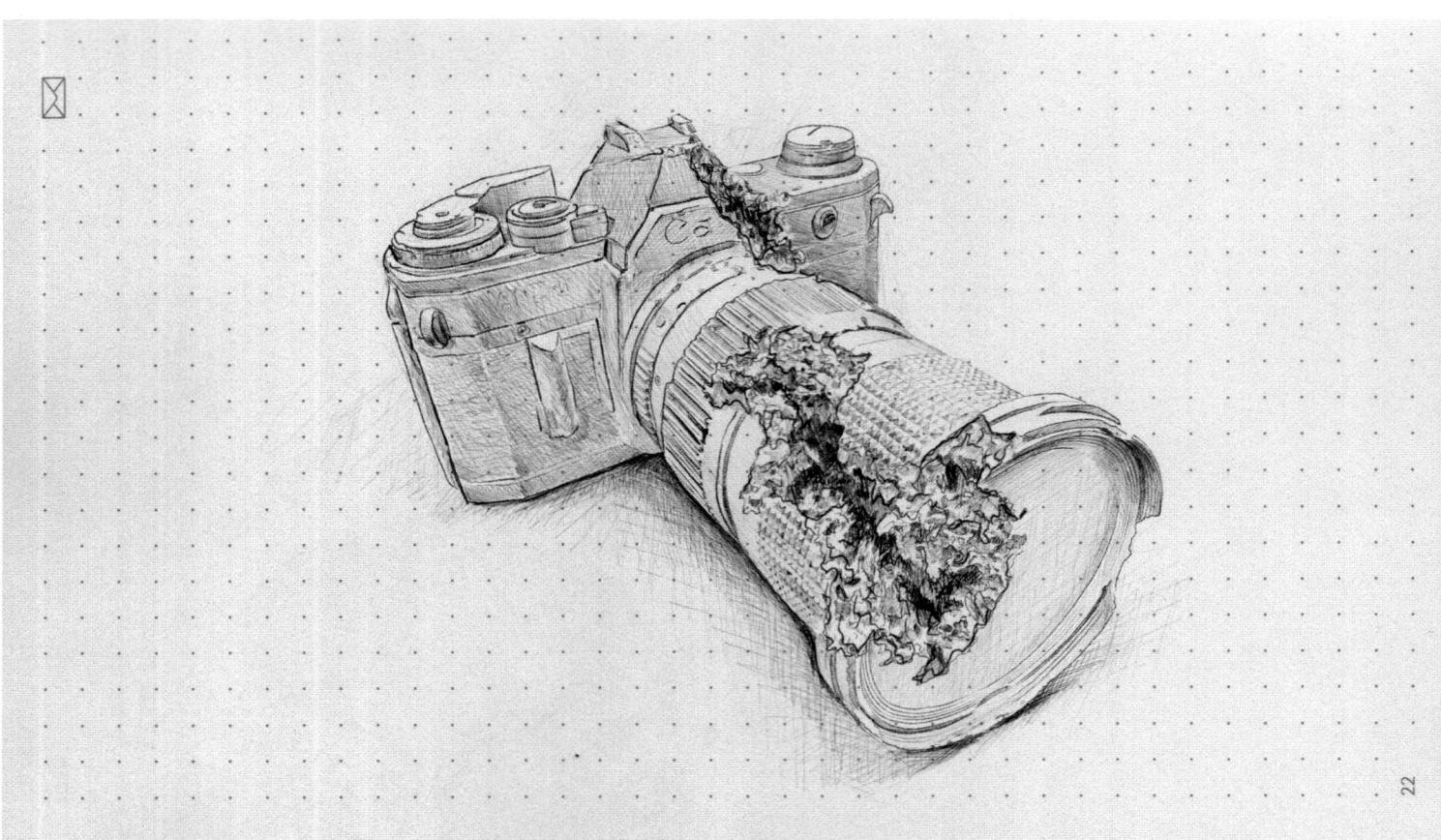

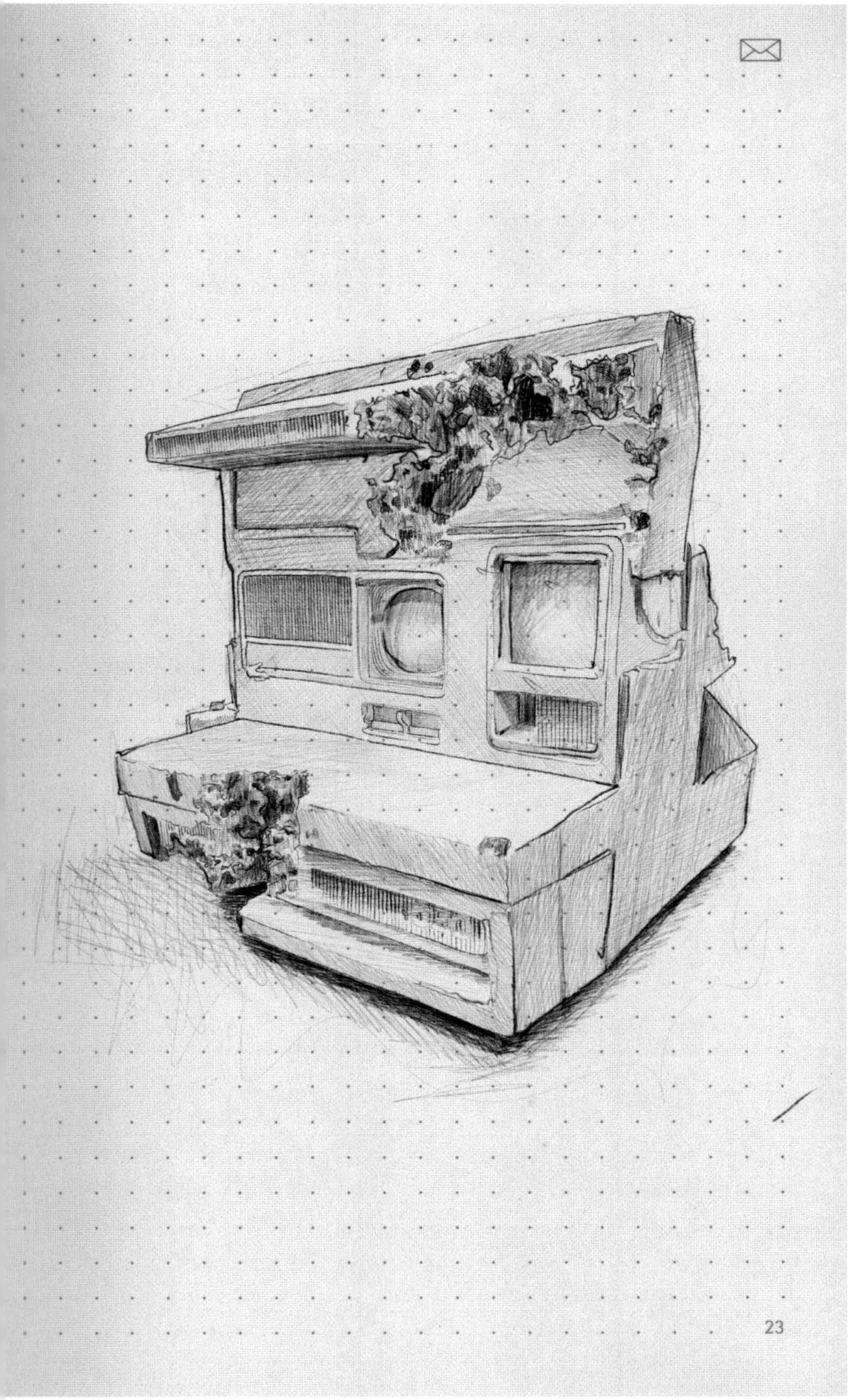

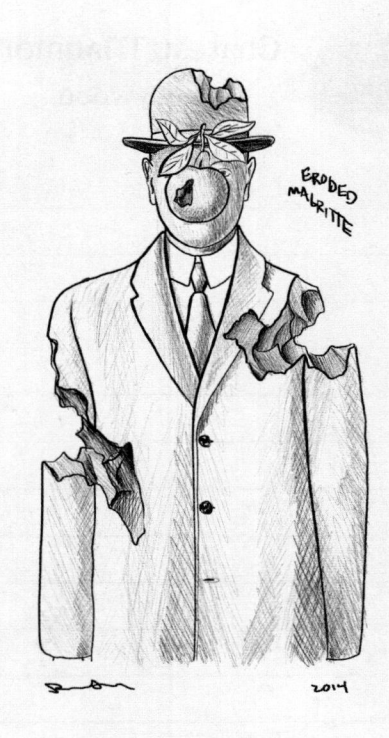

ERODED
MAGRITTE

2014

23

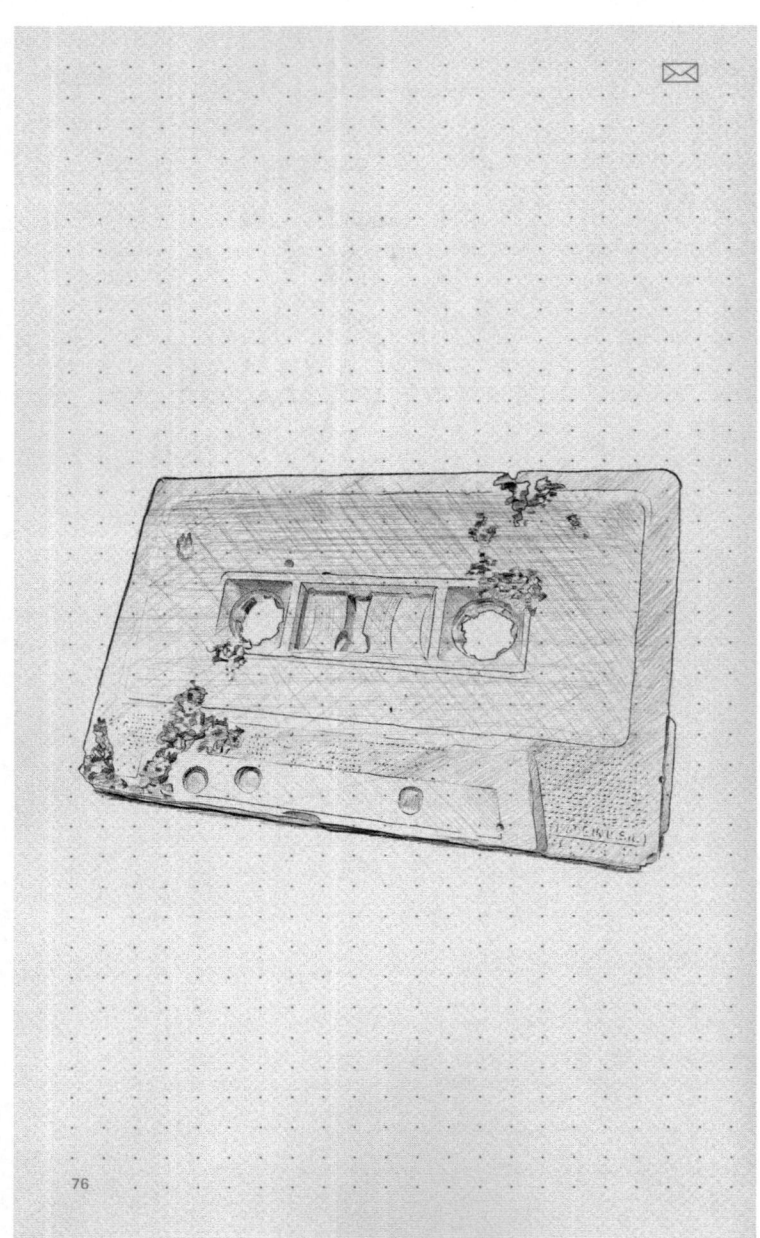

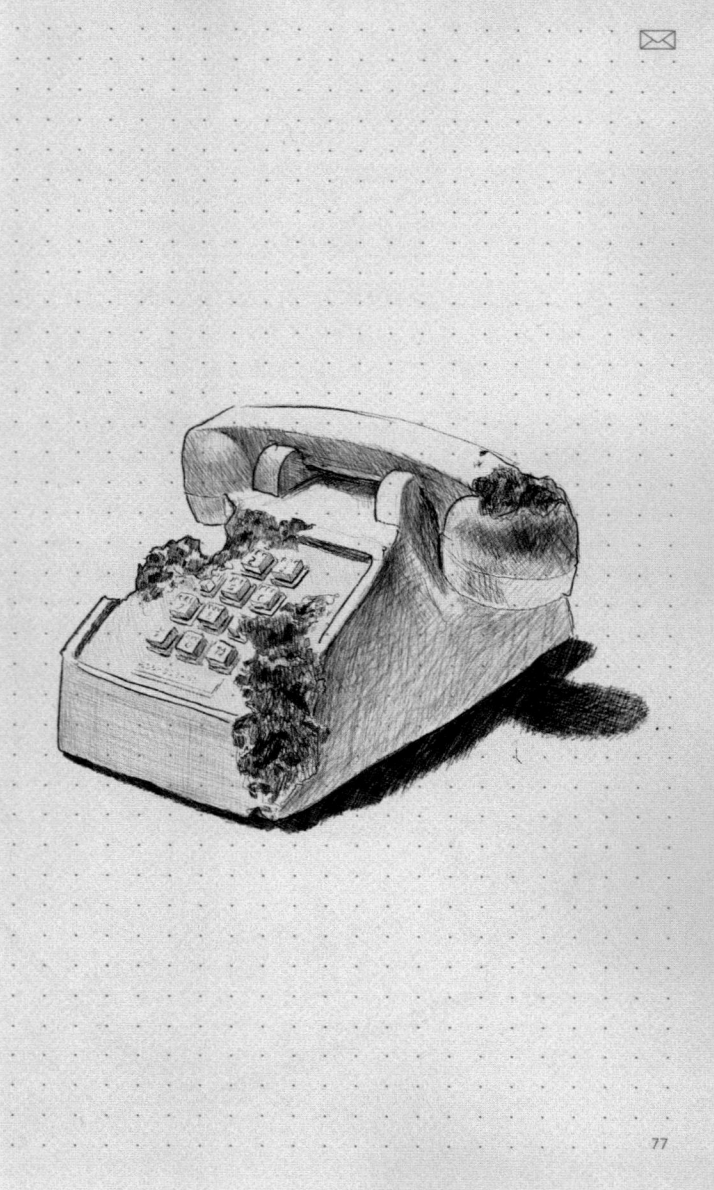

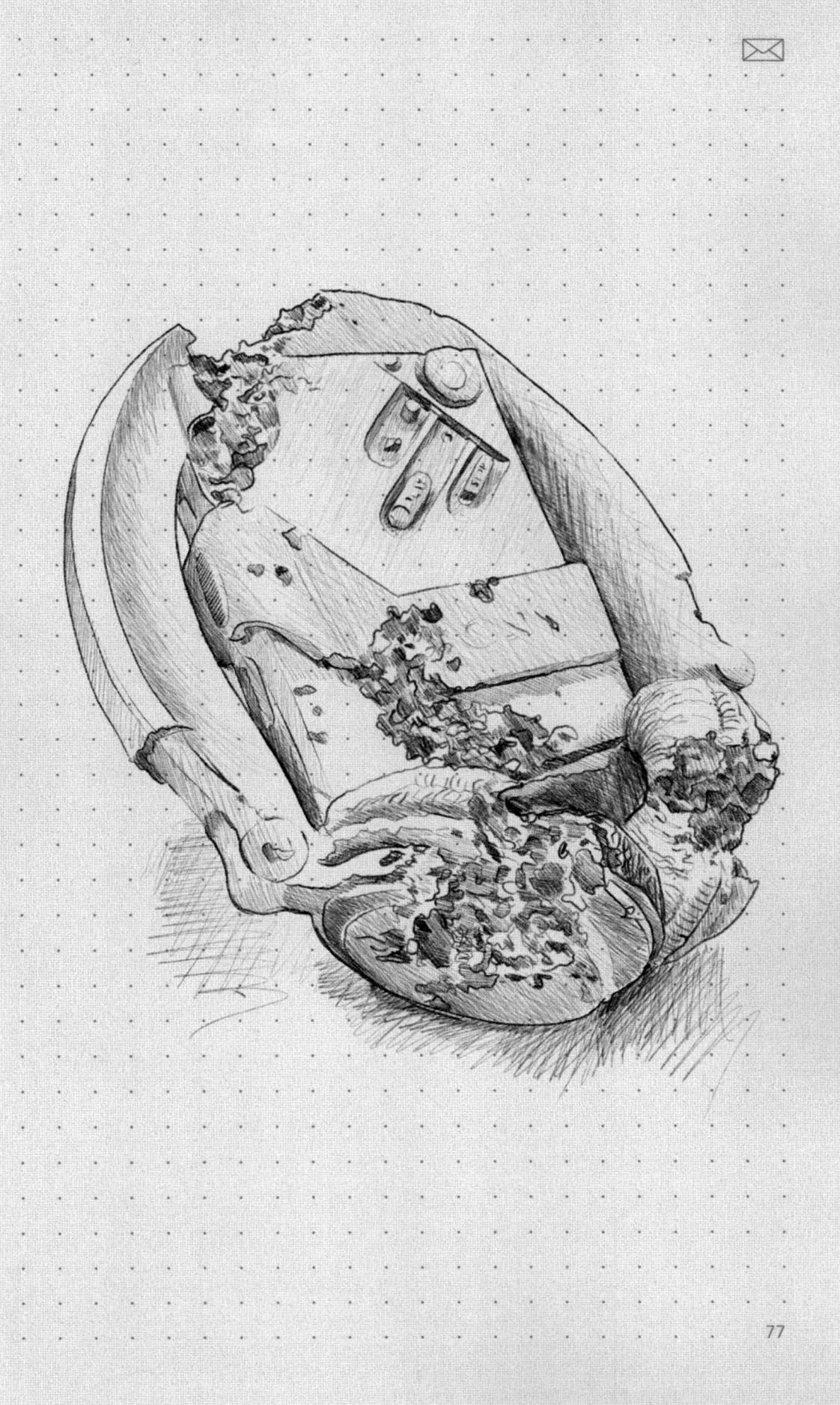

77

127

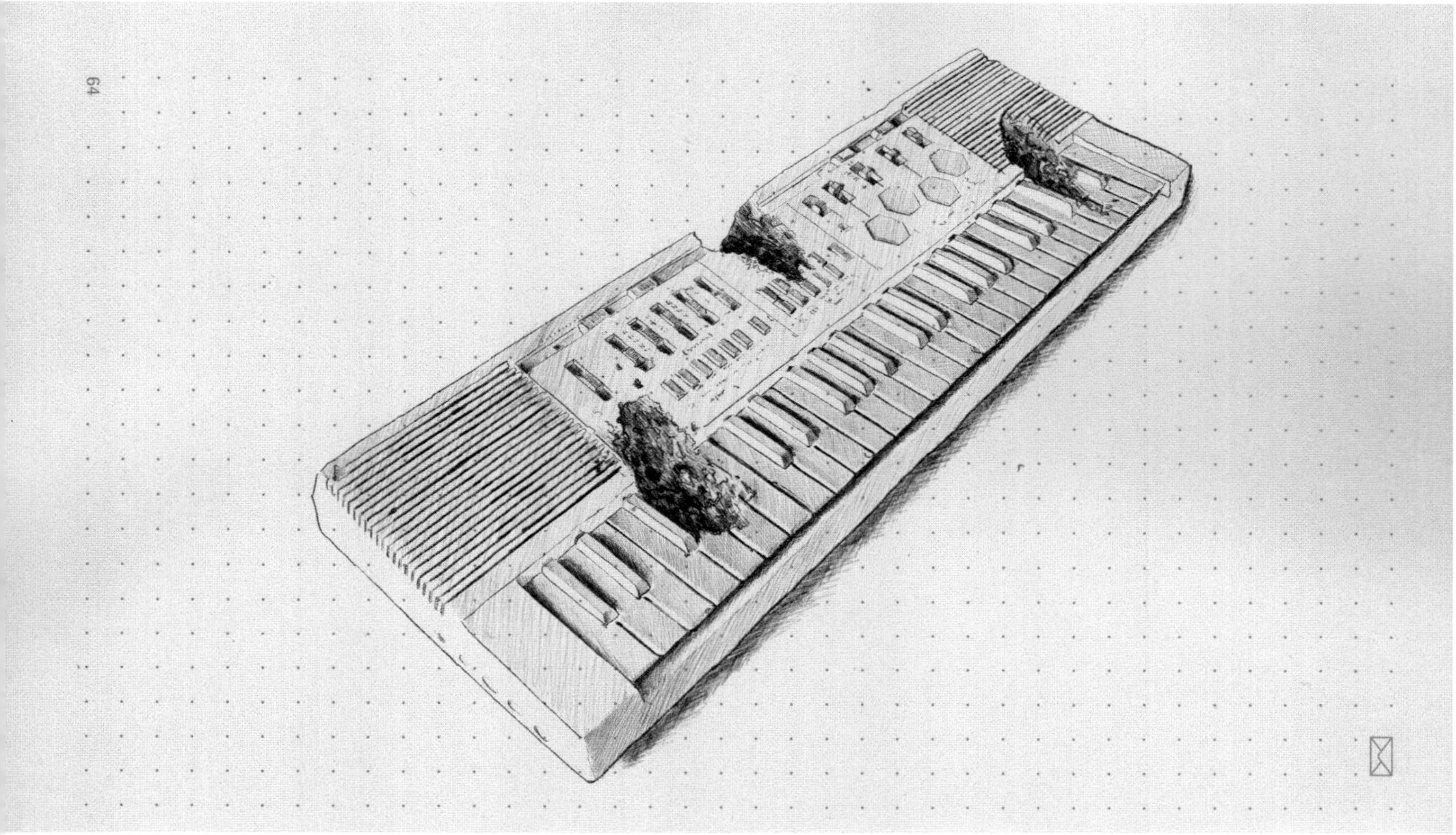
64

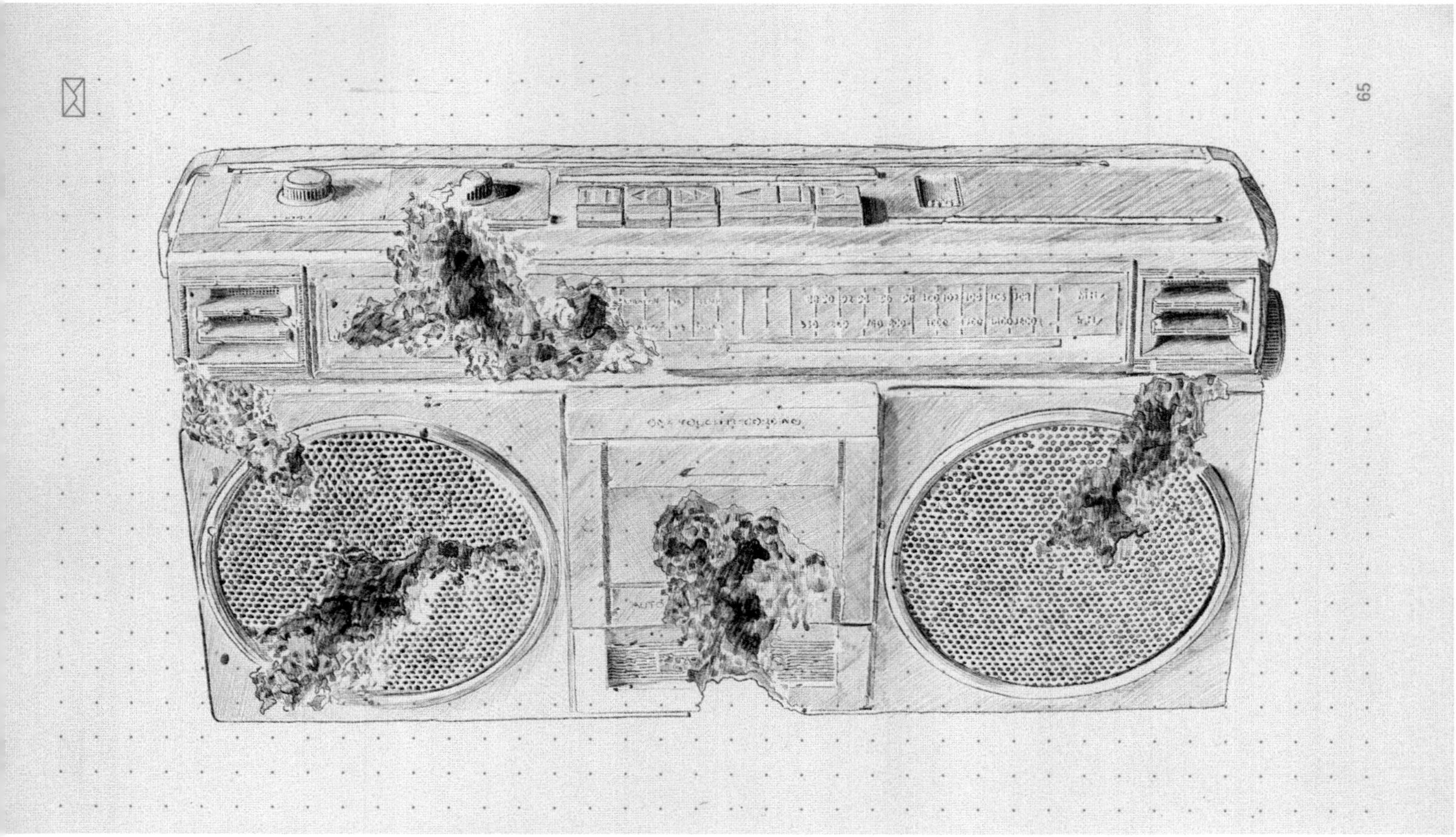
65

# COLOR BLIND PAINT INGS

4·21·11

1. MASSIVE DRIP
2. SAGGING MIRROR
3. PINK INSULATION PIECES
4. SINGING HOLE IN WALL
5. Electrical outlet extrusion
6. Singing elevator buttons
7. Deep hole elevator Buttons
8. Identical piles of Trash
9. Column splashes on chair
10. Directional Sign
11. Keyhole with singing light.
12. BURNED PORTRAITS
13. MOUSE HOLE
14. PEELING PAINT PORTRAIT

15. CLOCK MOVING THE WALL

16. FRAME IN CORNER

17. ANIMAL PUZZLES

18. Hurricane Andrew Sculpted in Pink Fiberglass insulation

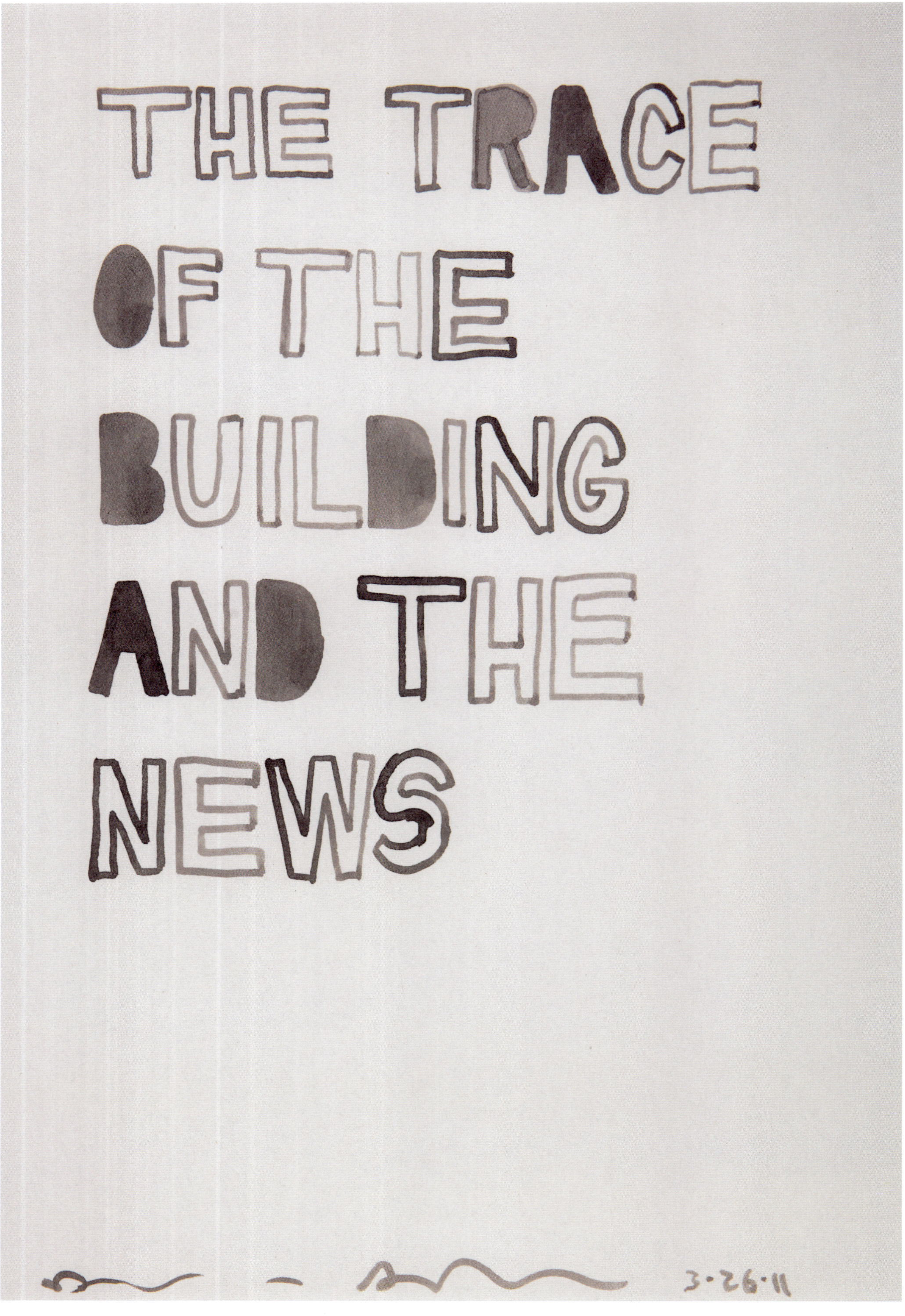

THE TRACE
OF THE
BUILDING
AND THE
NEWS

3·26·11

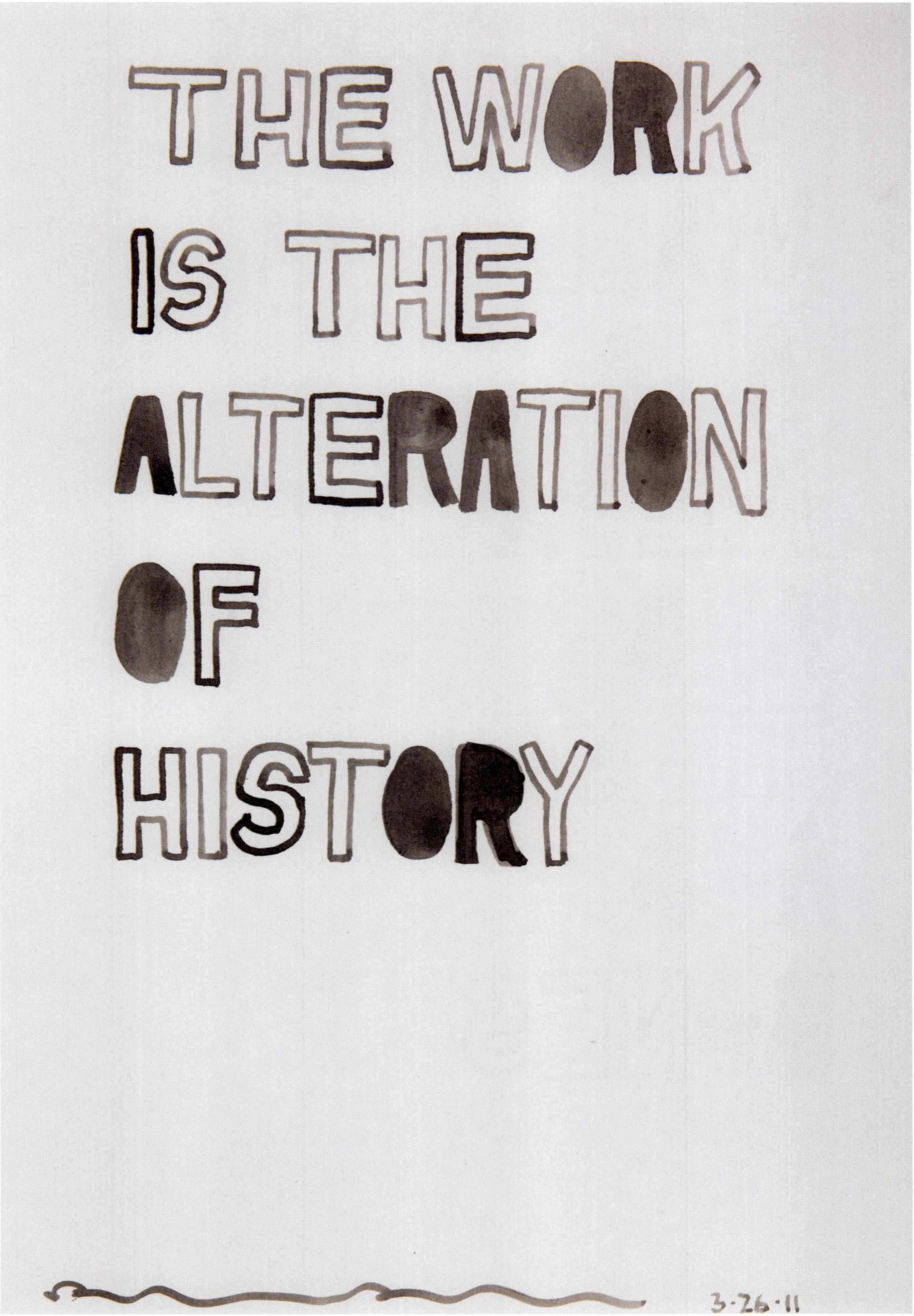

THE WORK
IS THE
ALTERATION
OF
HISTORY

3-26-11

# THROUGH WALLS AND METAL AND TEETH AND BONES

3·26·11

A PURPLE CAR IS PARTIALLY SUBMERGED IN MUD

3·27·11

STAR
ARCHITECT
DIVIDES

CALIFORNIA
CITY

4.1.11

# ECCENTRICITY GIVES WAY TO

# UNIFORMITY

3·27·11

IT GOES
TO          WHITE

THEN

I.

DISAPPEAR

4·18·11

143

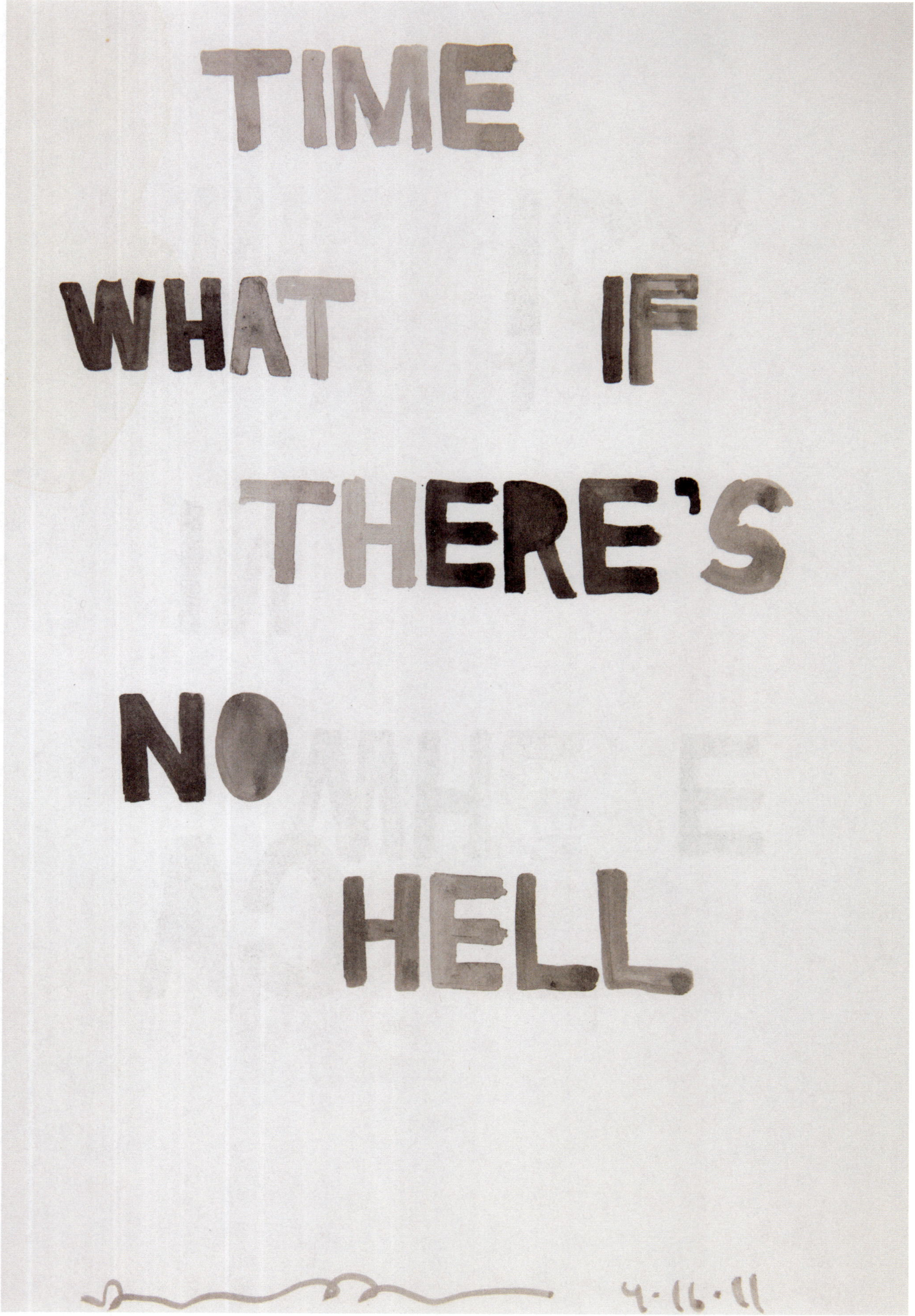

TIME

WHAT          IF

THERE'S

NO

HELL

4-16-11

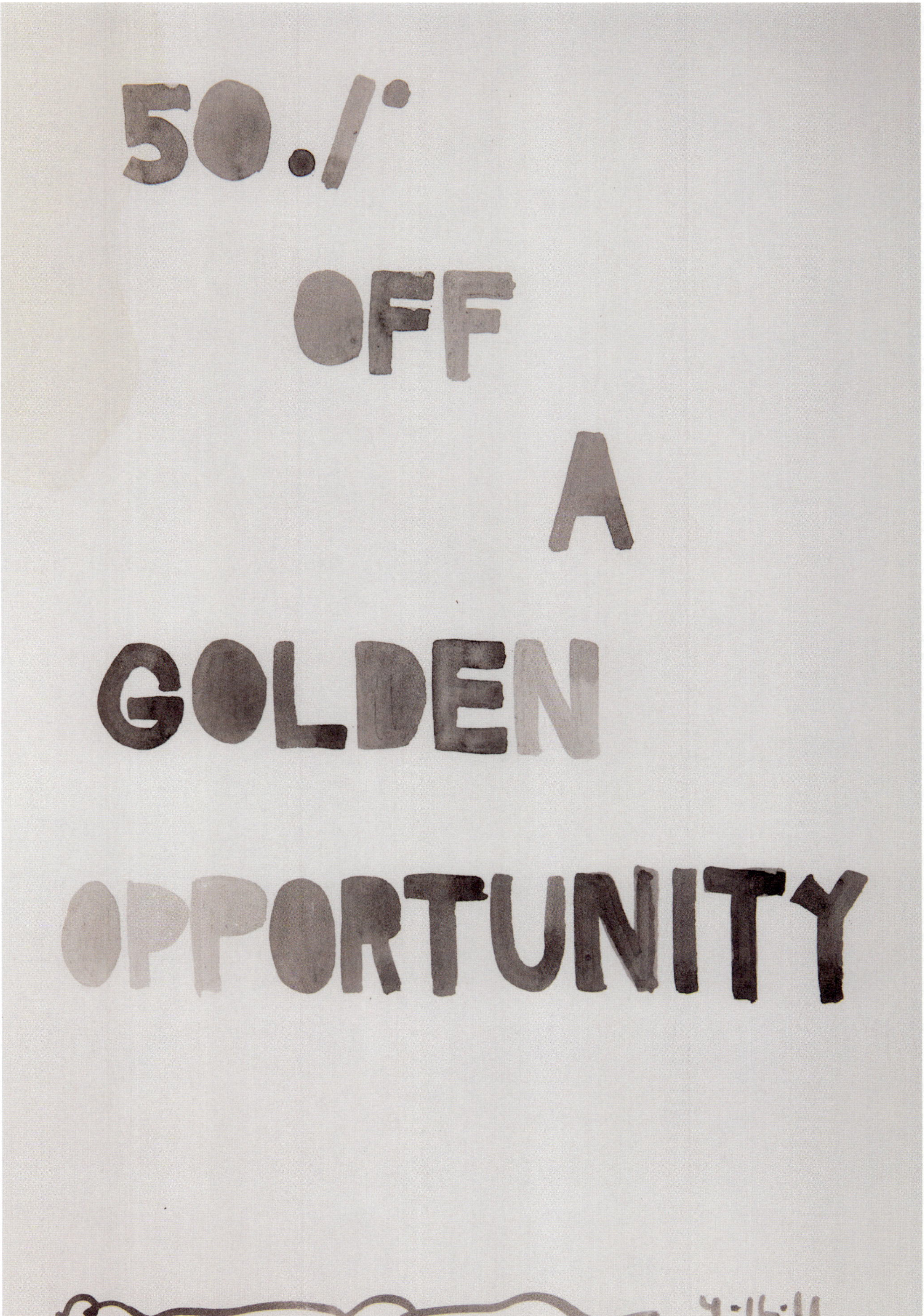

50.⁄°
OFF
A
GOLDEN
OPPORTUNITY

4-16-11

# RETHINKING THE PLAY GROUND

4-16-11

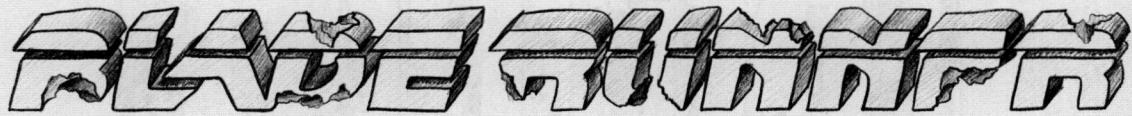

3018

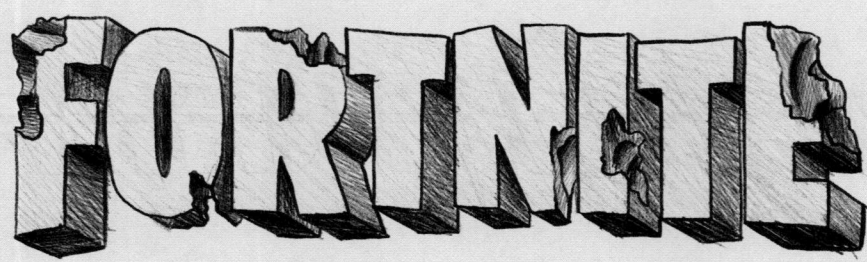

3018

# GoodFellas

3018

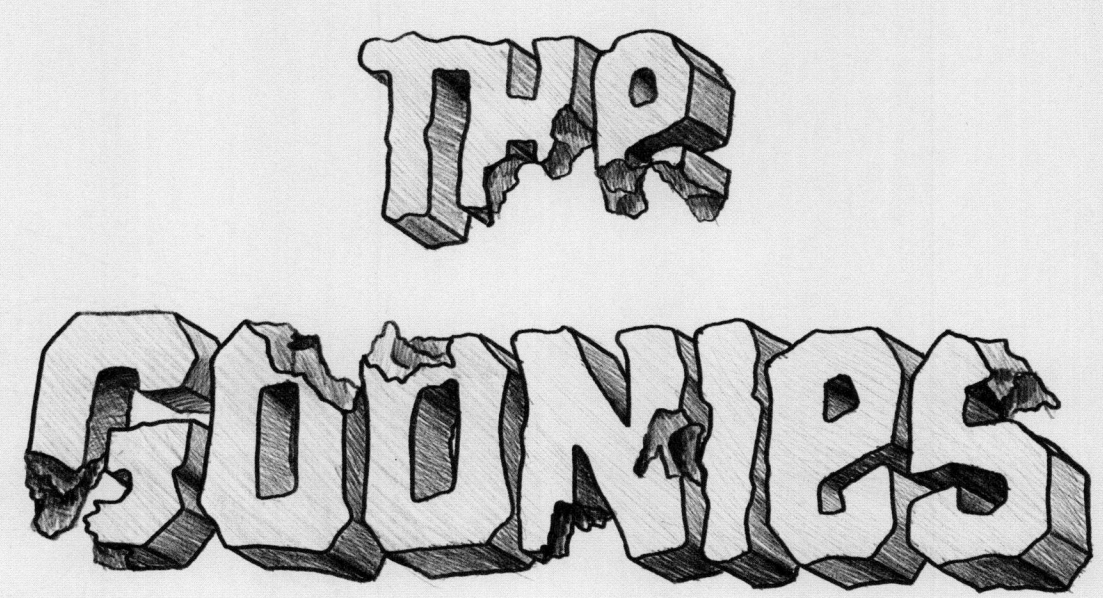

3018

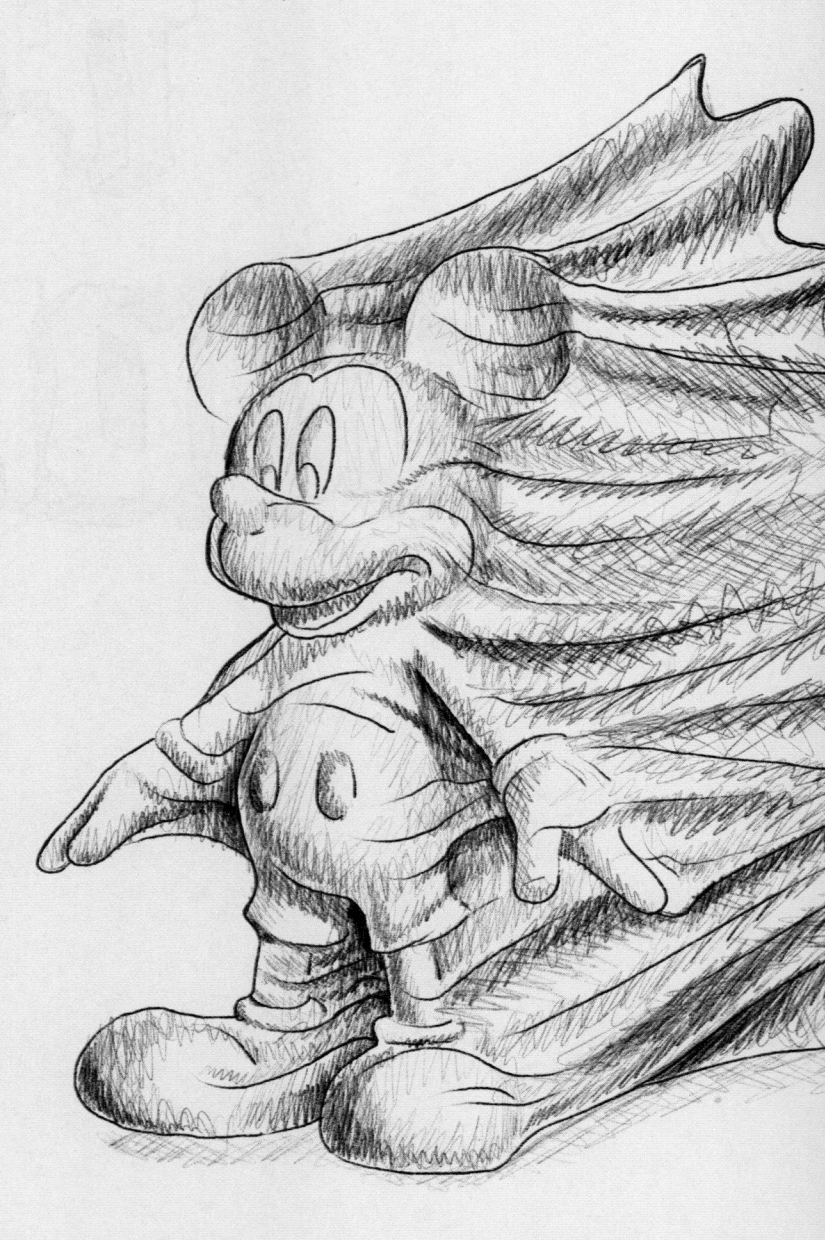

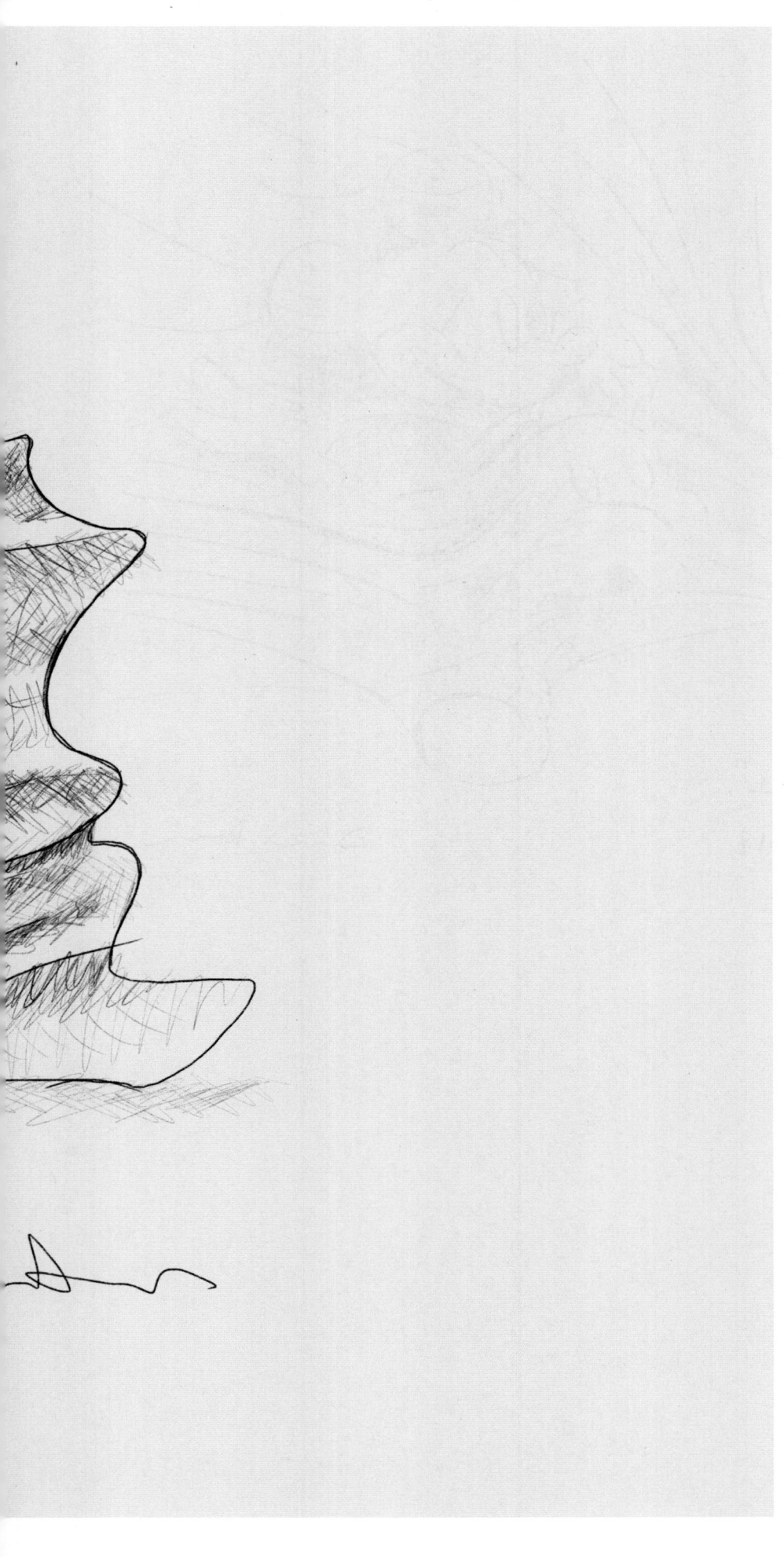

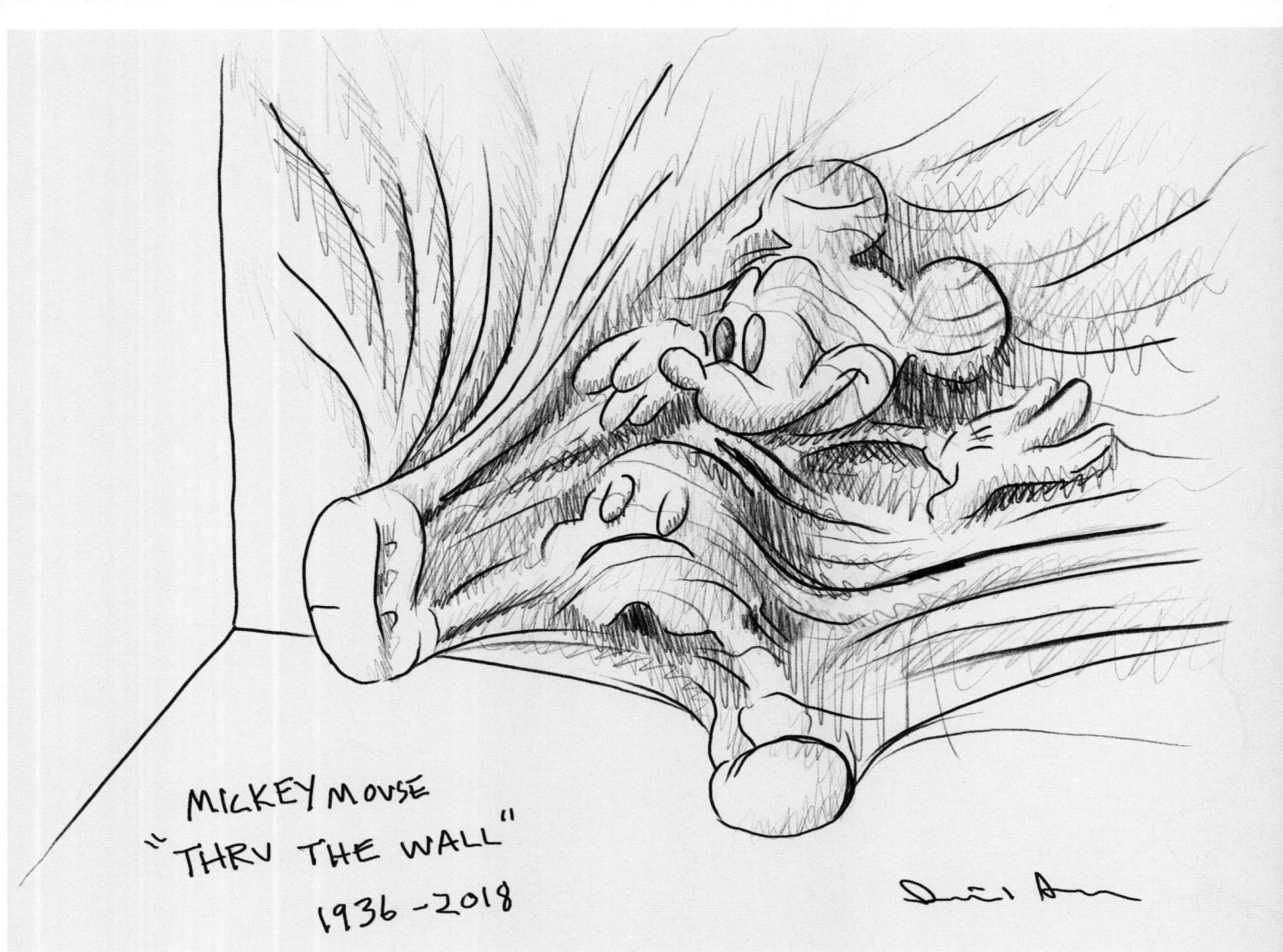

MICKEY MOUSE
"THRU THE WALL"
1936 - 2018

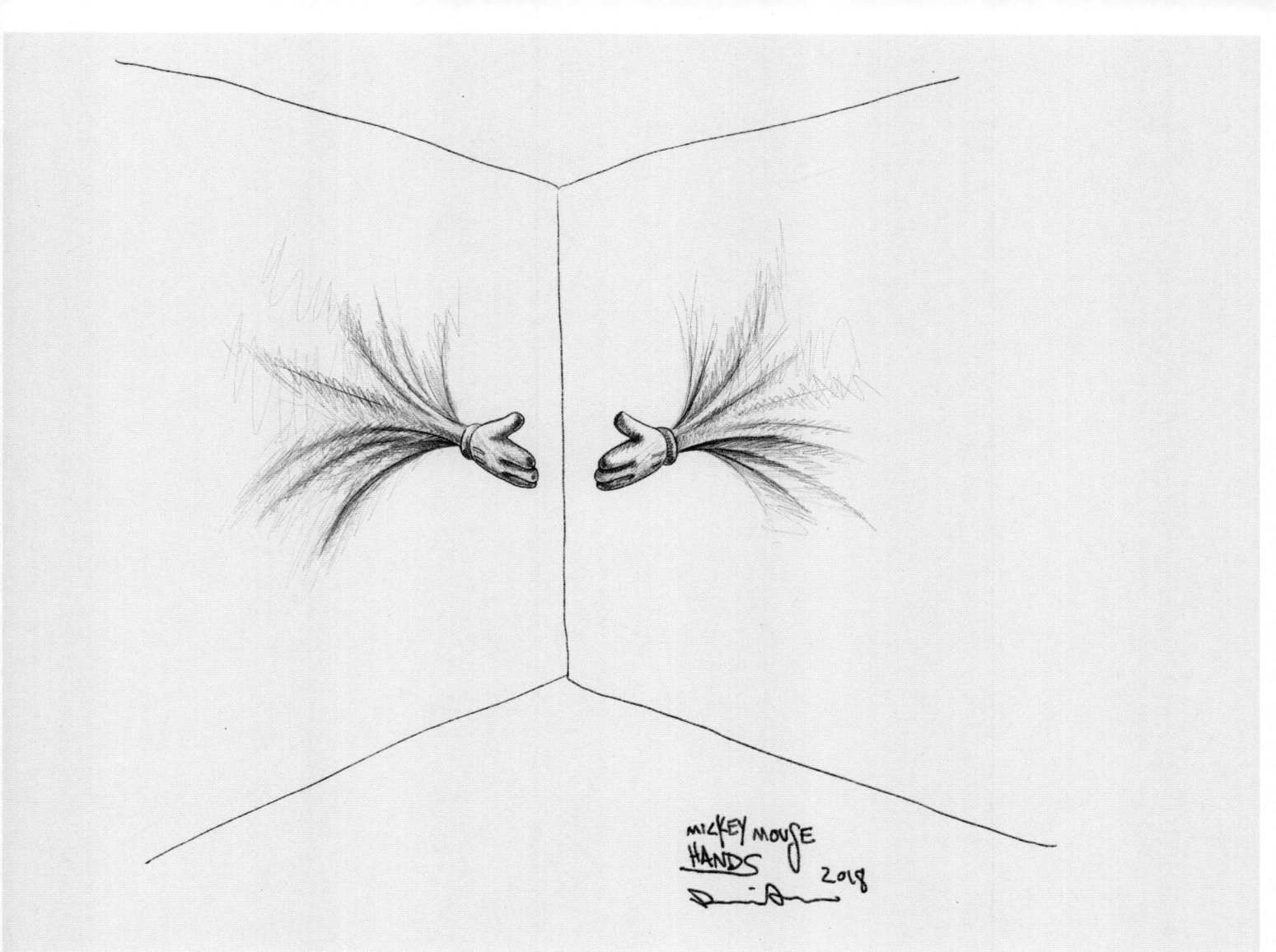

MICKEY MOUSE
HANDS    2018

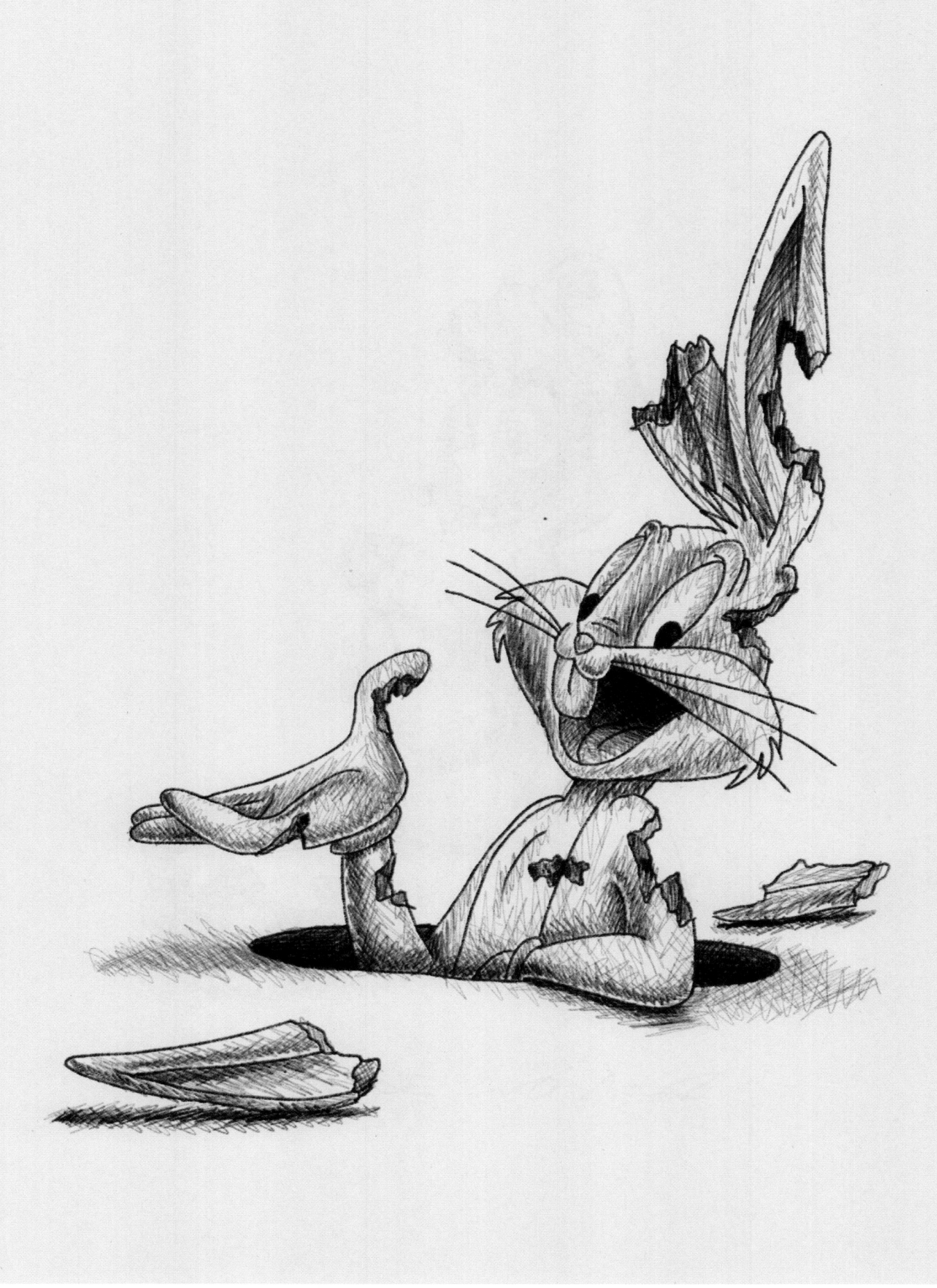

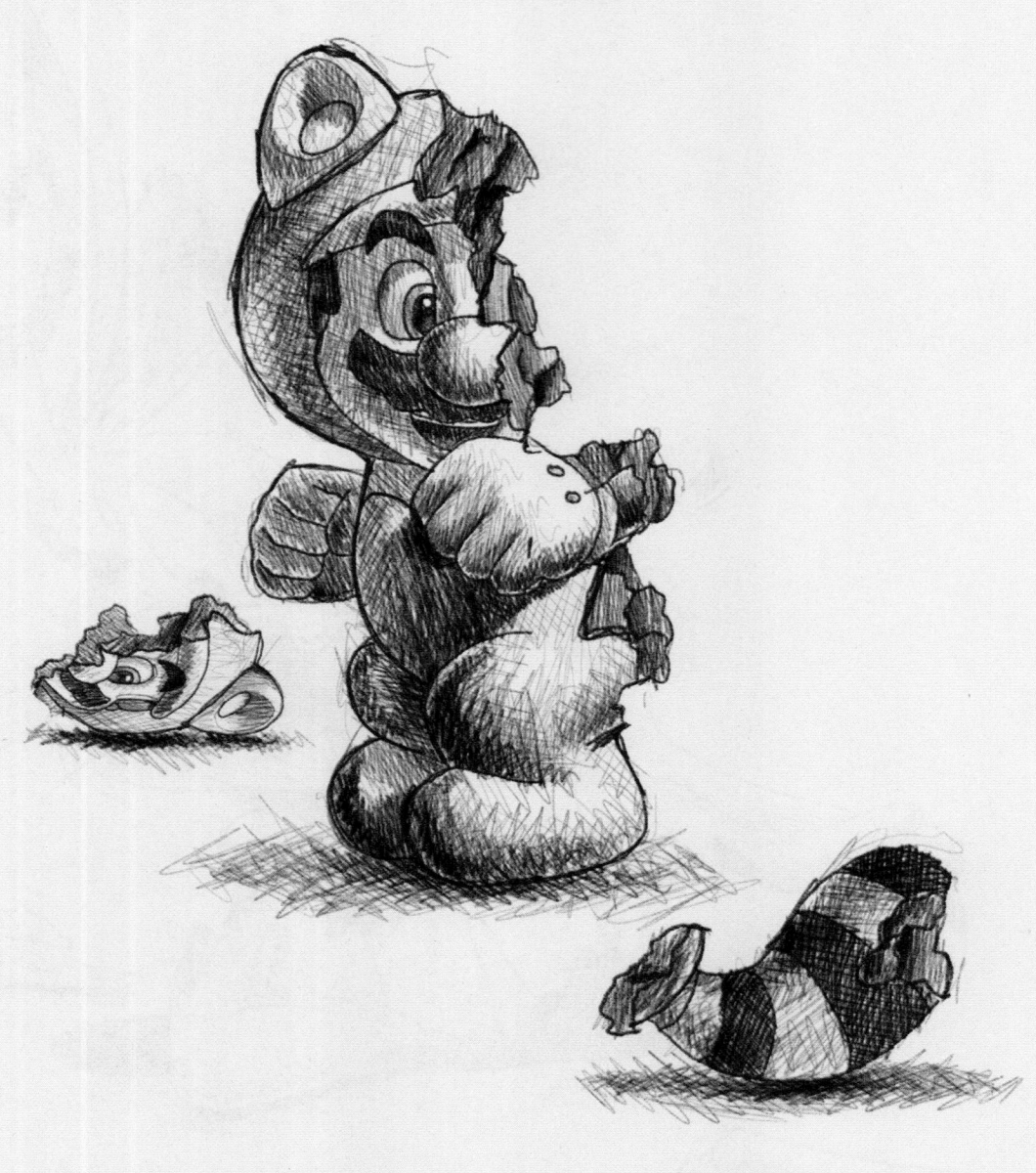

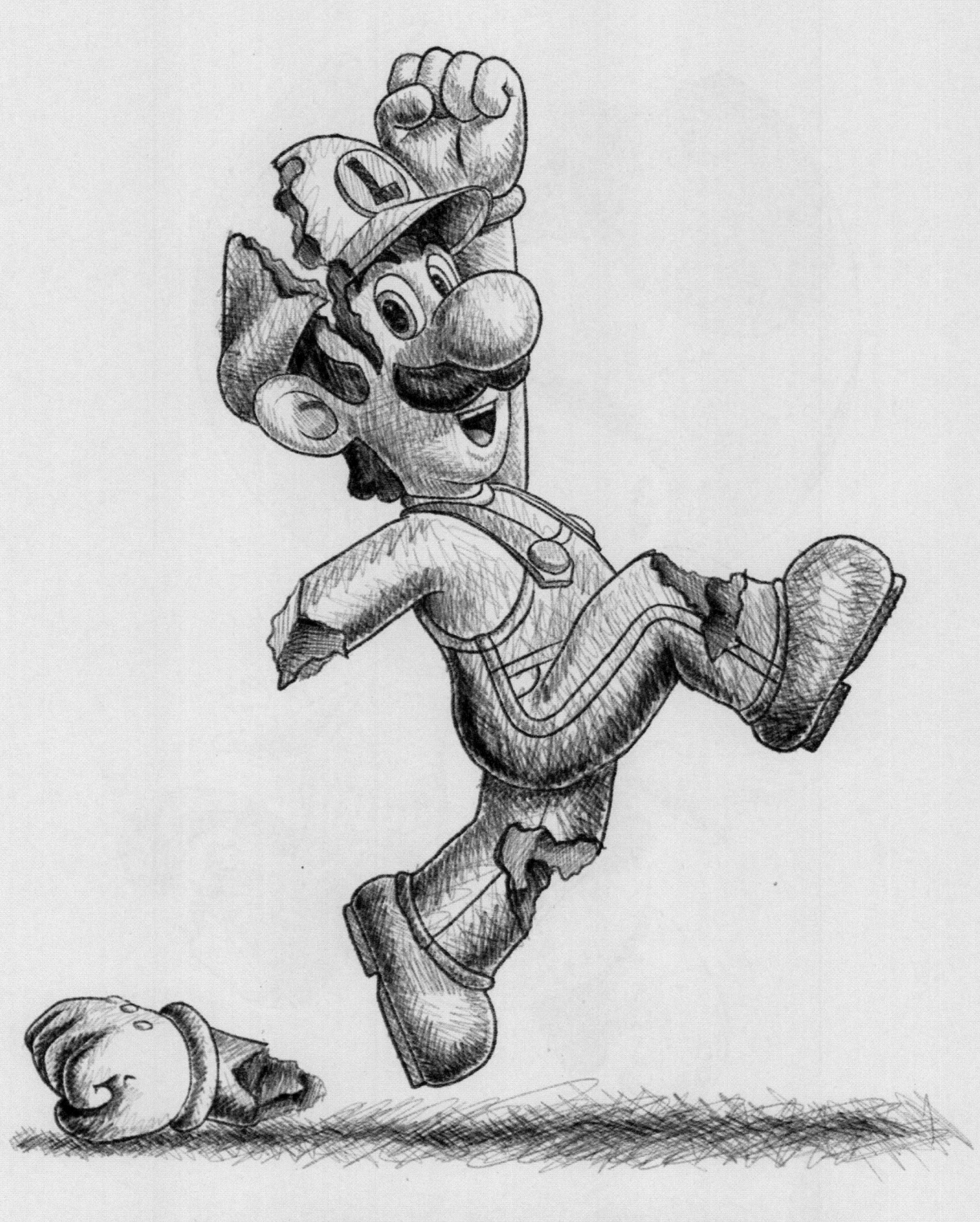

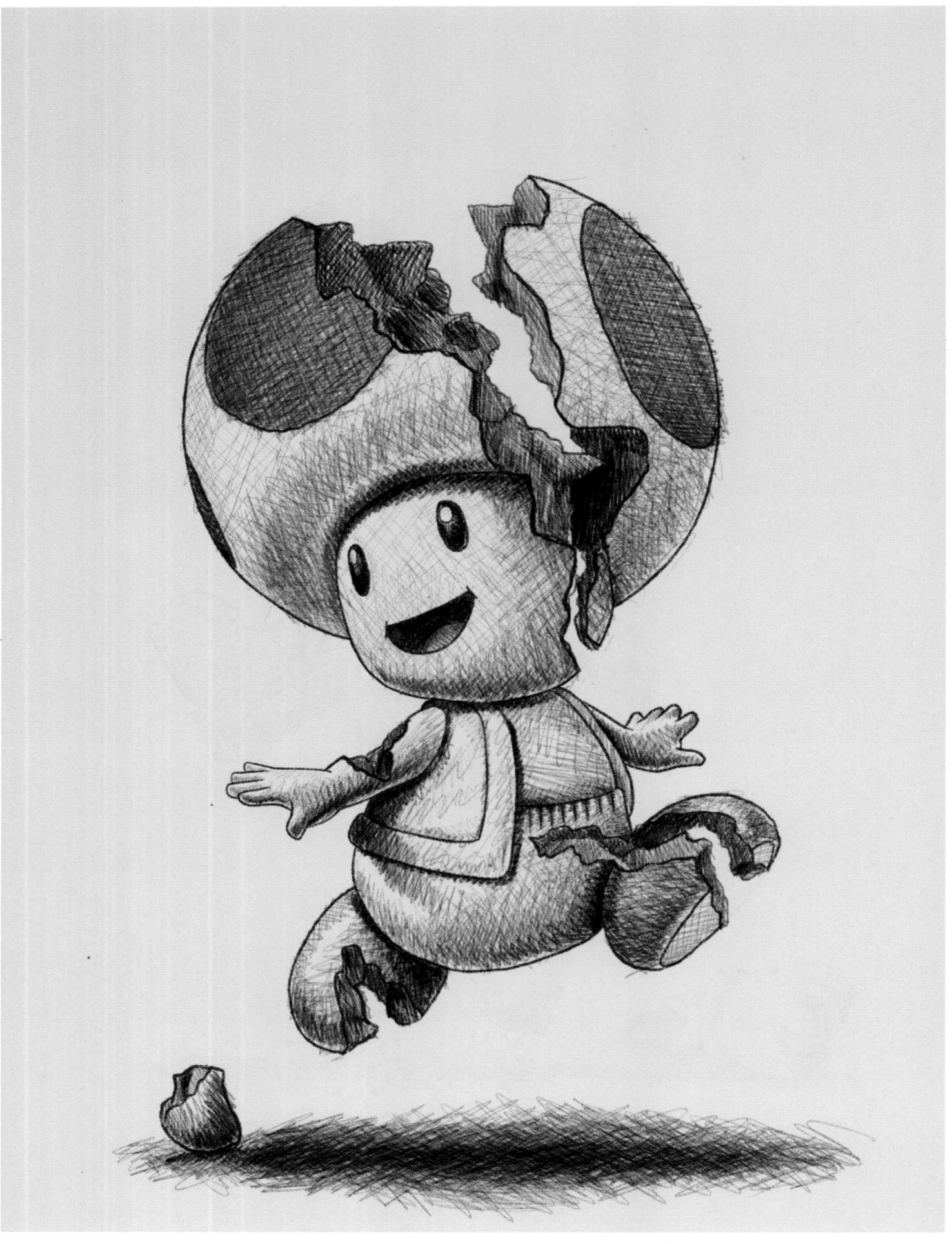

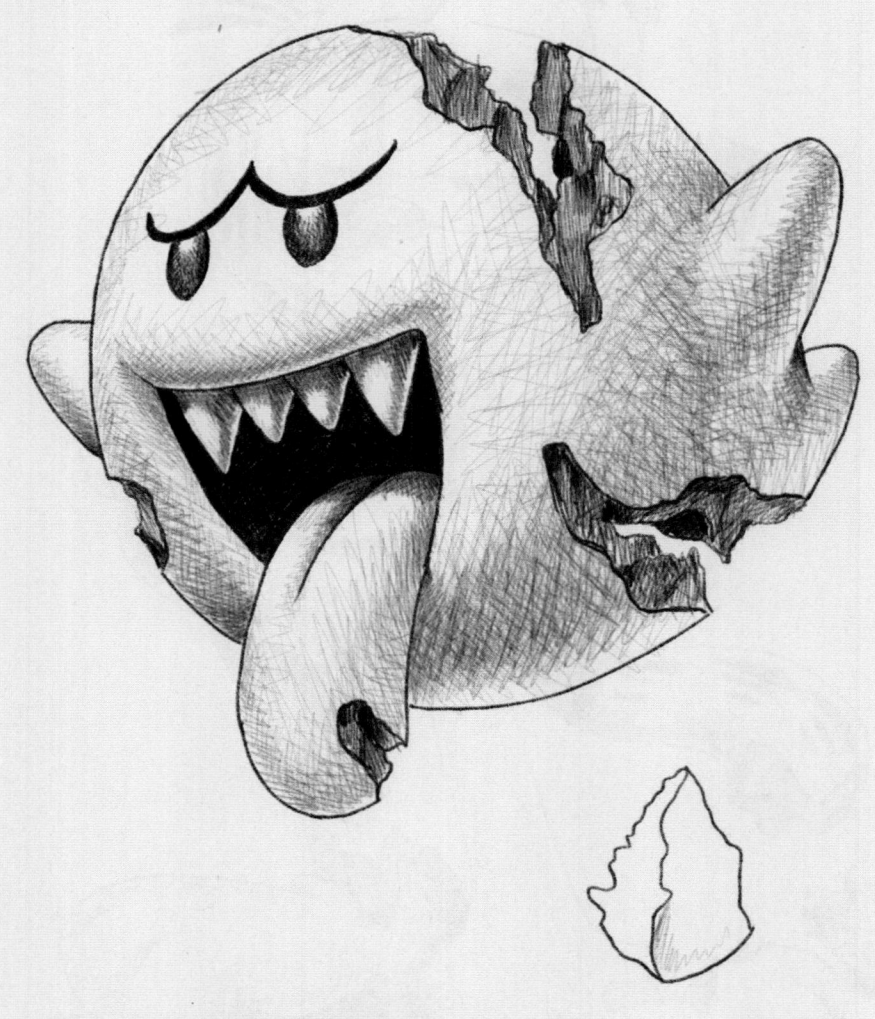

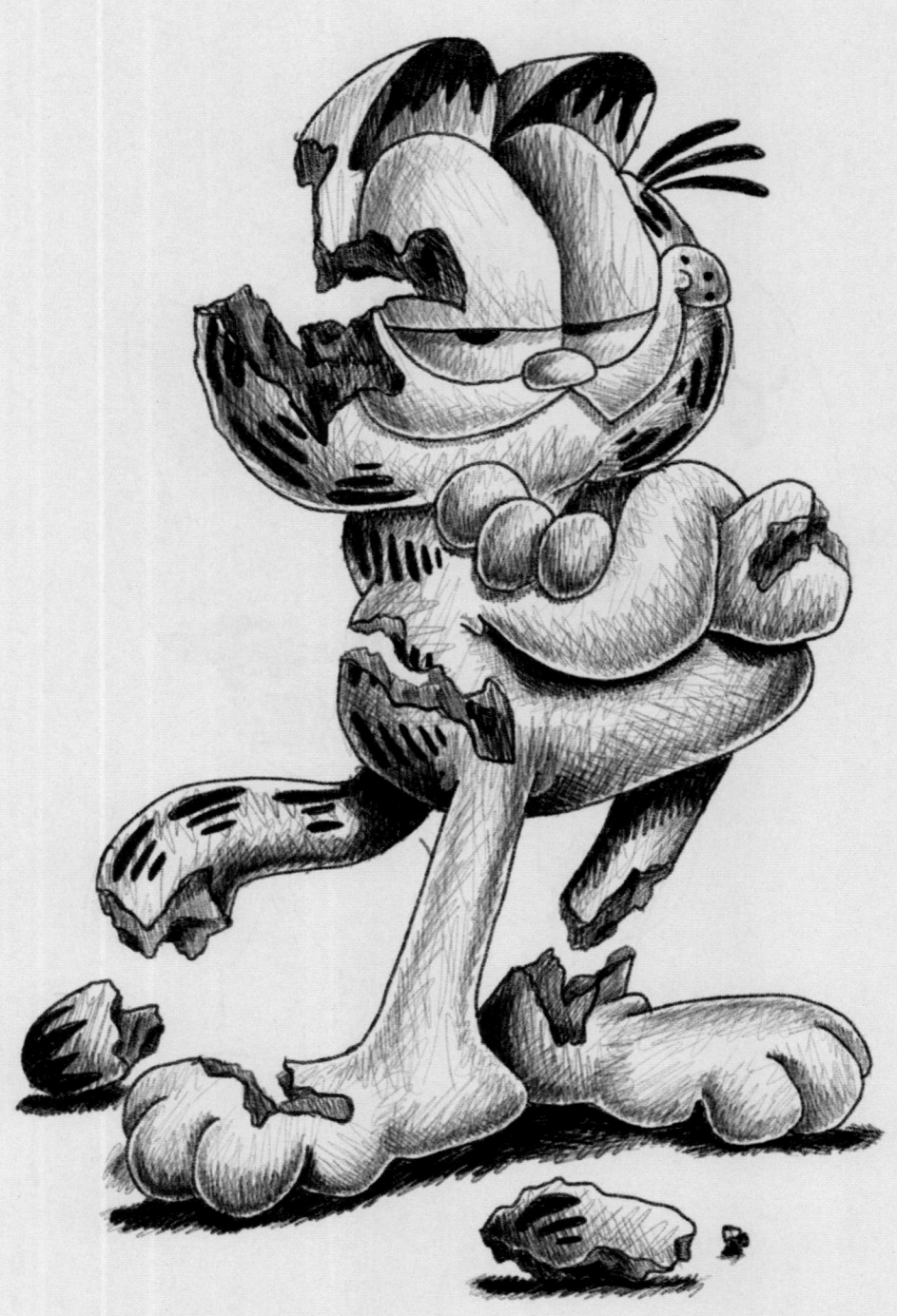

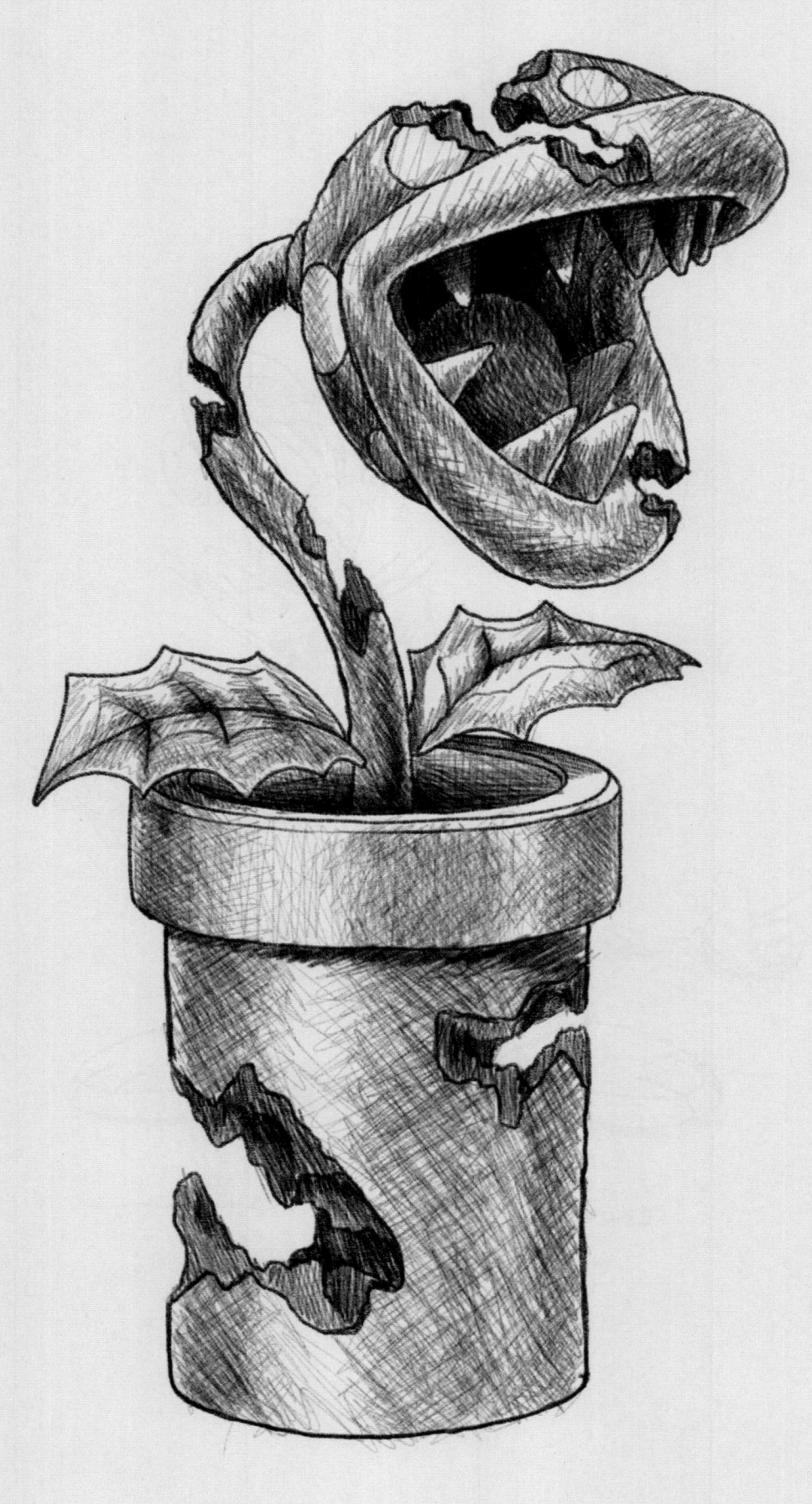

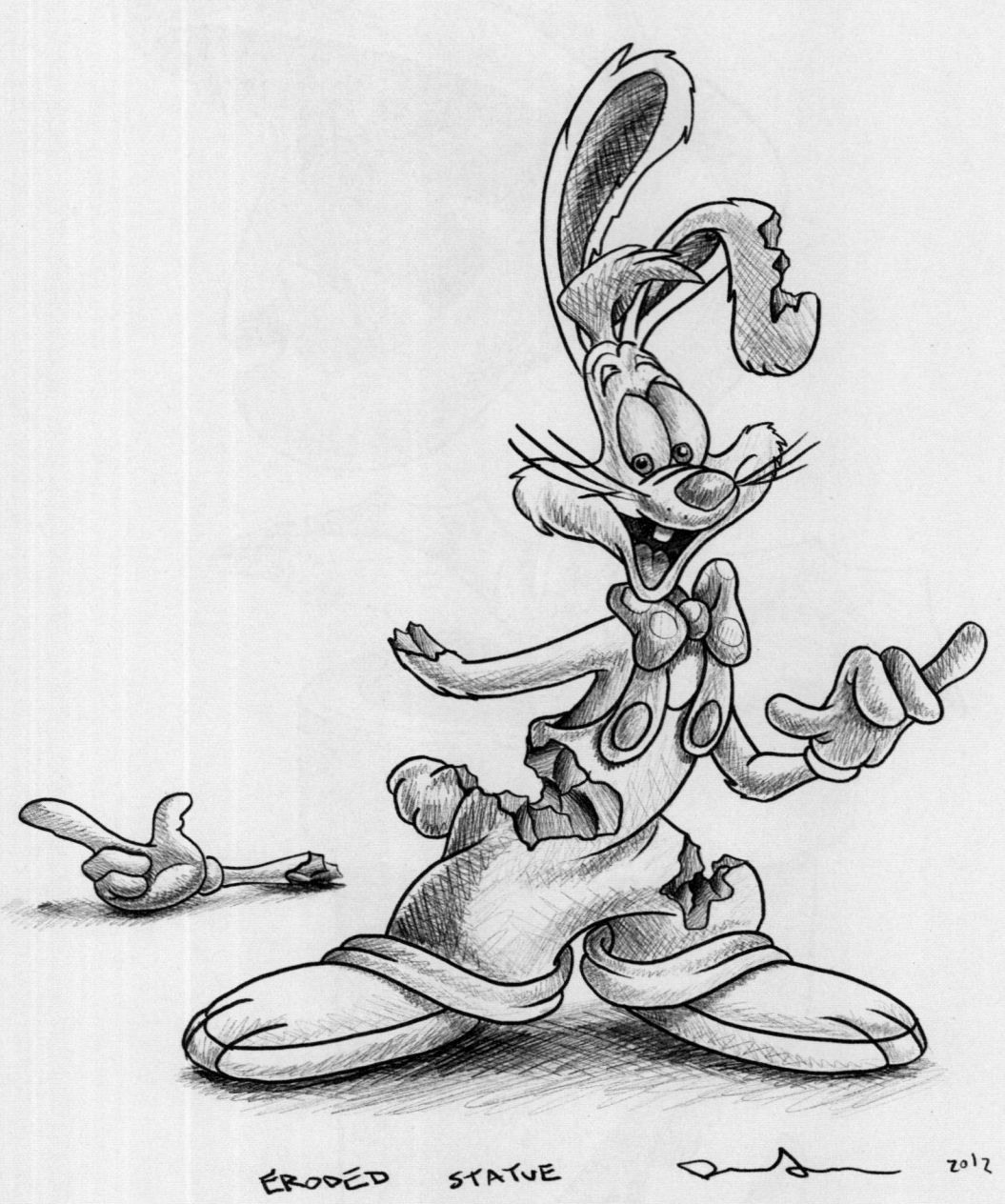

ERODED STATUE

2012

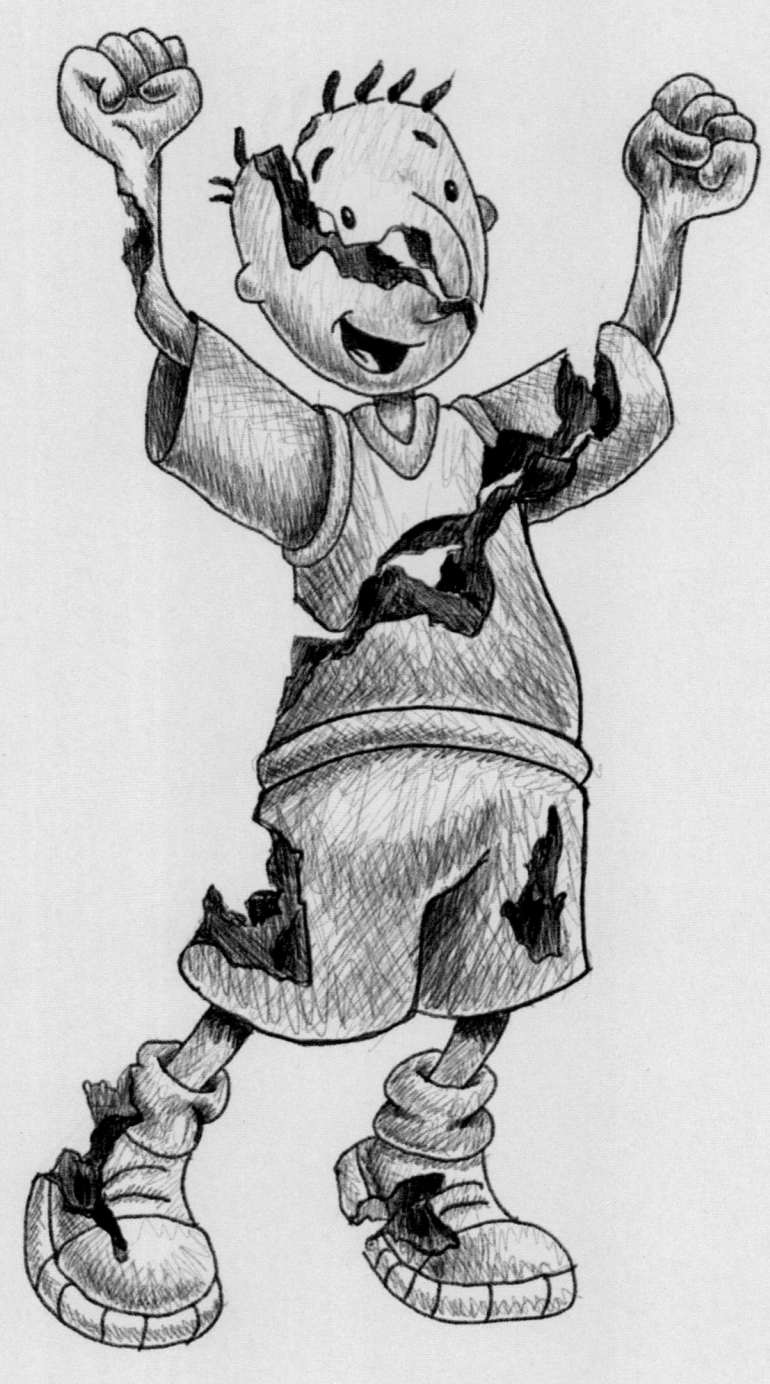

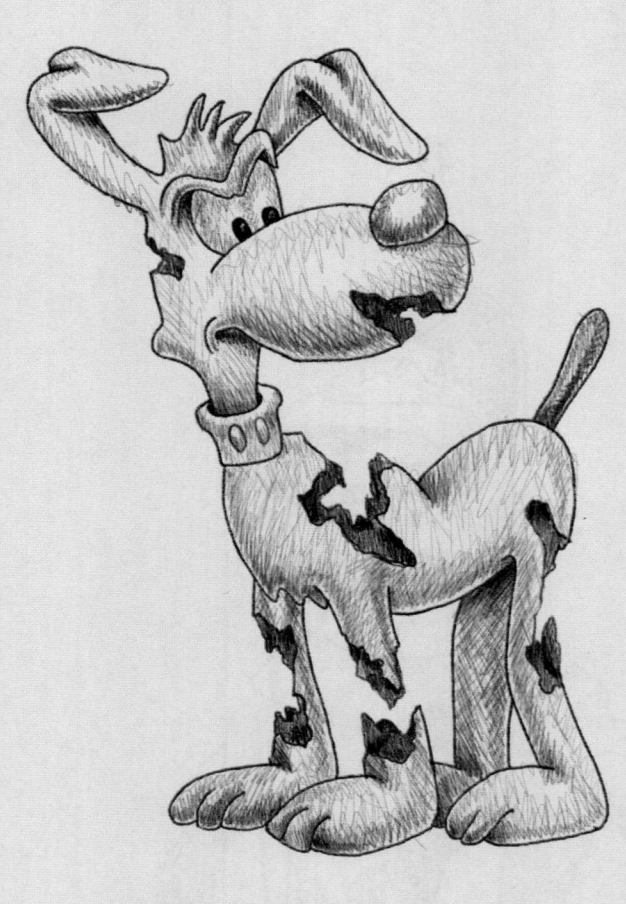

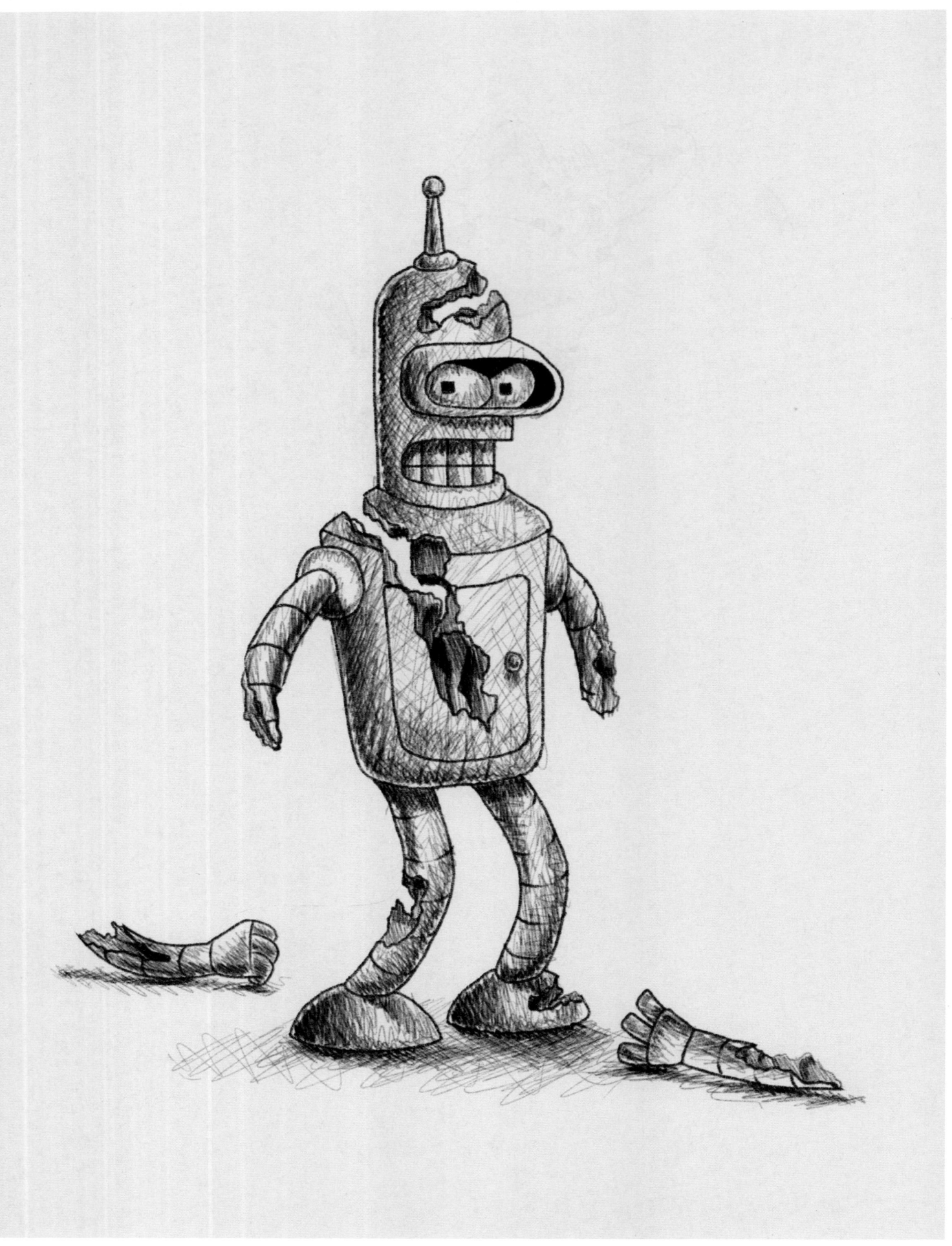

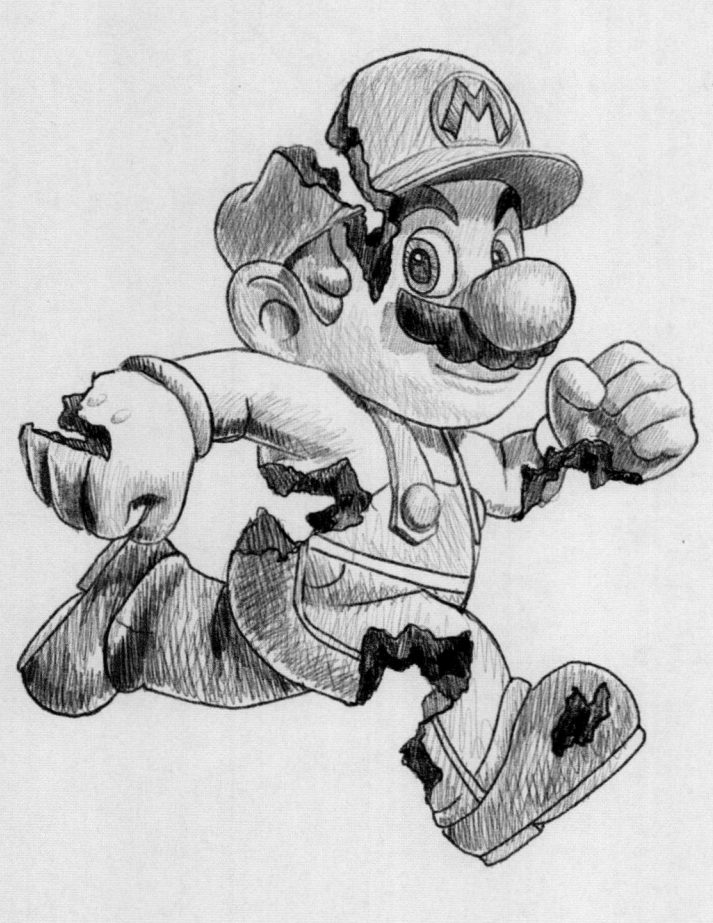

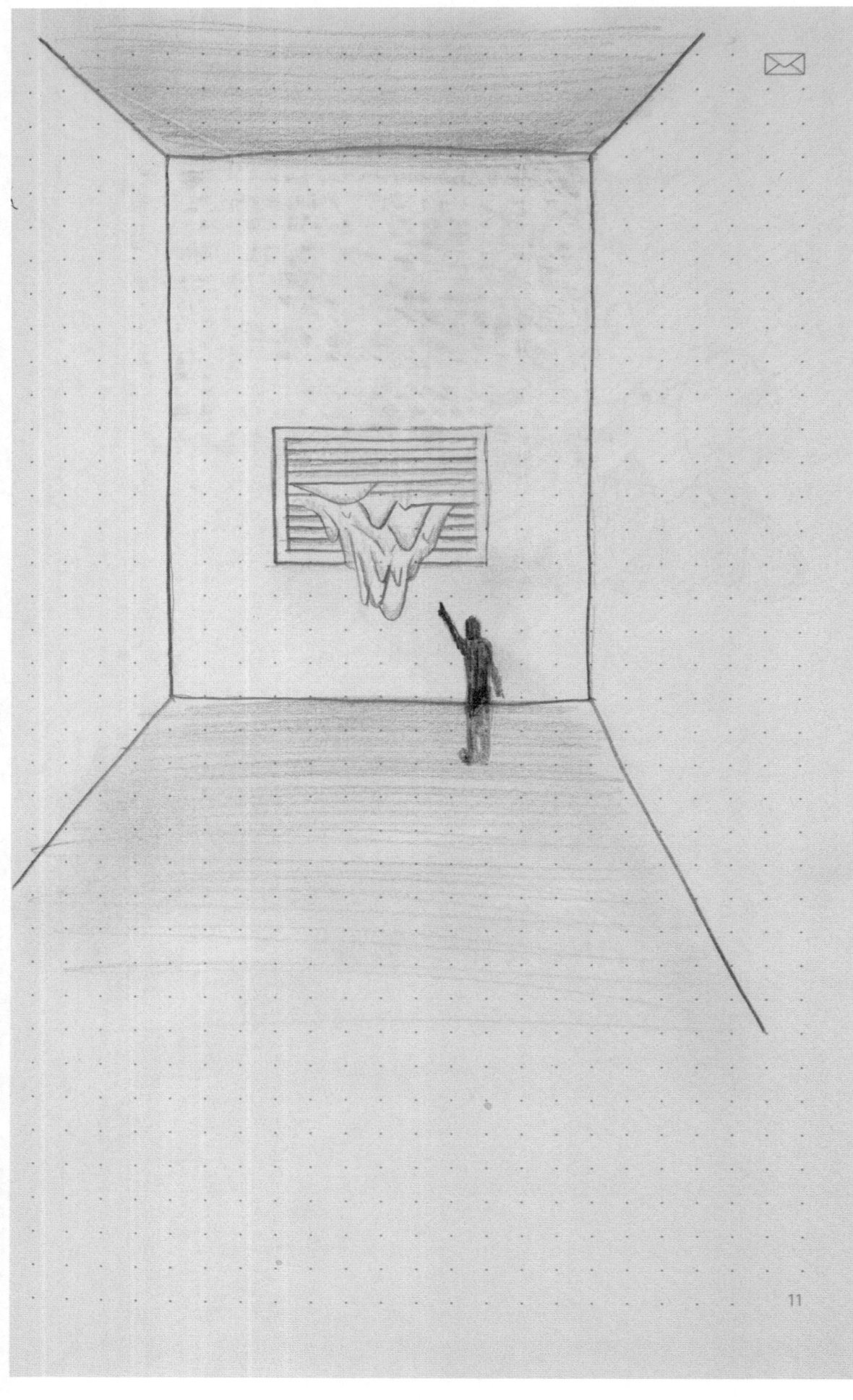

172    Daniel Arsham Sketchbook

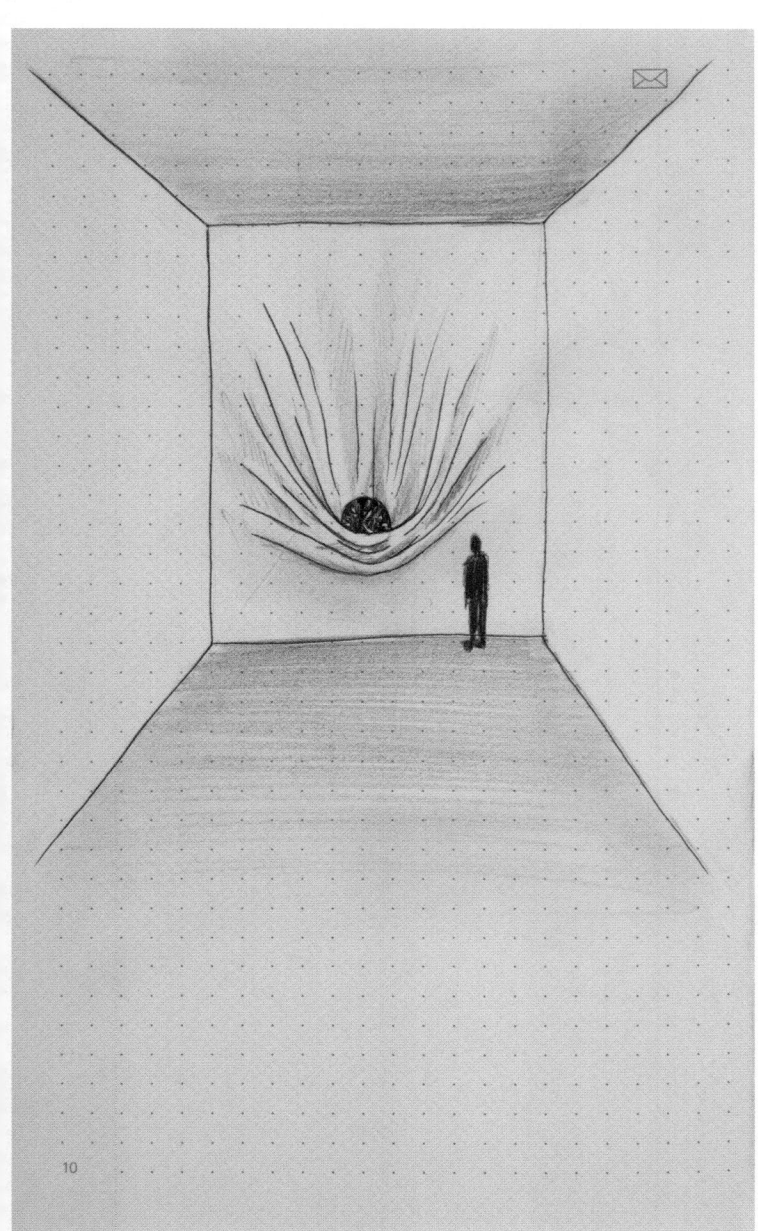

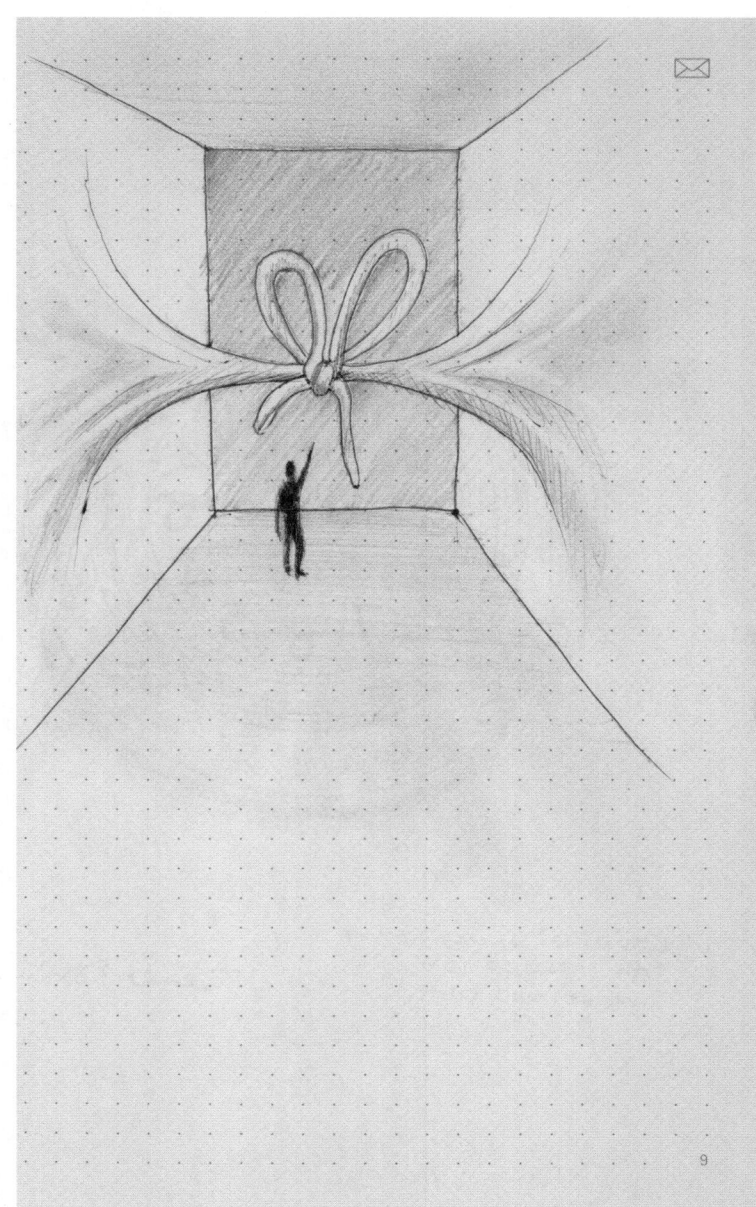

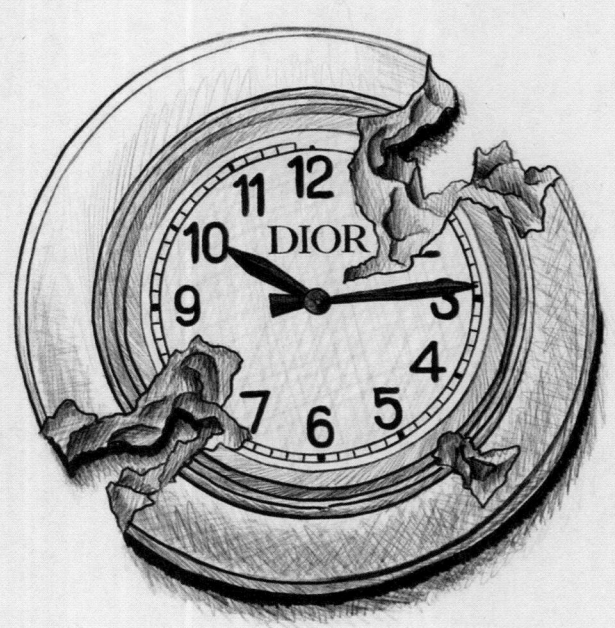

ERODED CLOCK FROM
THE ATELIER OF
CHRISTIAN DIOR

# DIOR x ARSHAM

- ERODED CLOCK FROM DIOR Atelier

- watches

- BAGS WITH Appearance of erosion. w color crystal

- CAST DIOR BOOKS

- CAST Broken and repaired arms for Display of jewelry and watches.

- crates for shipping artwork with Dual lockup.

ERODED WALLS FOR SHOW; gradient of color on walls.

- CASTS of The DIOR PRINT SAMPLES. CRACKED AND PAINTED AS WELL,

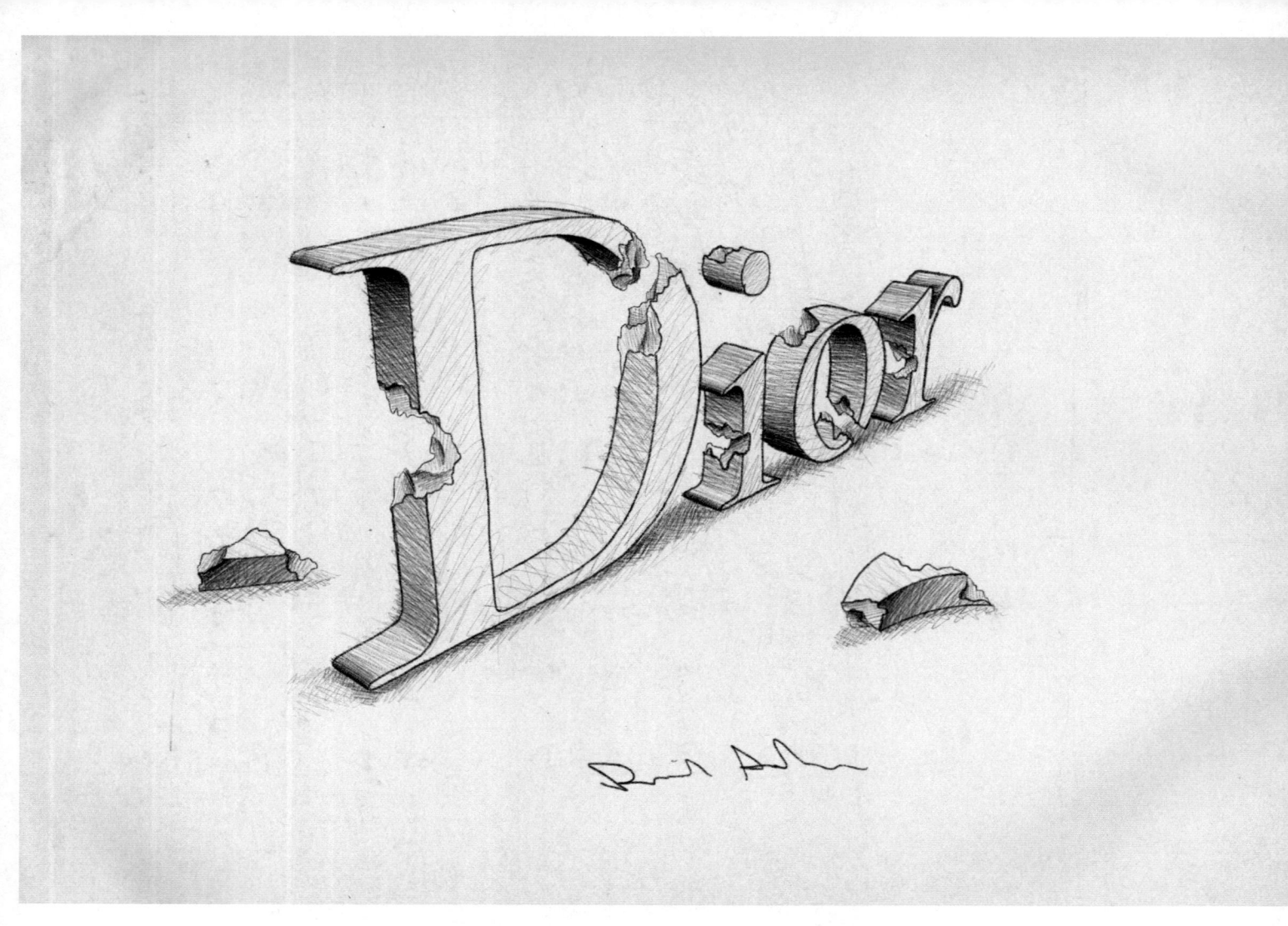

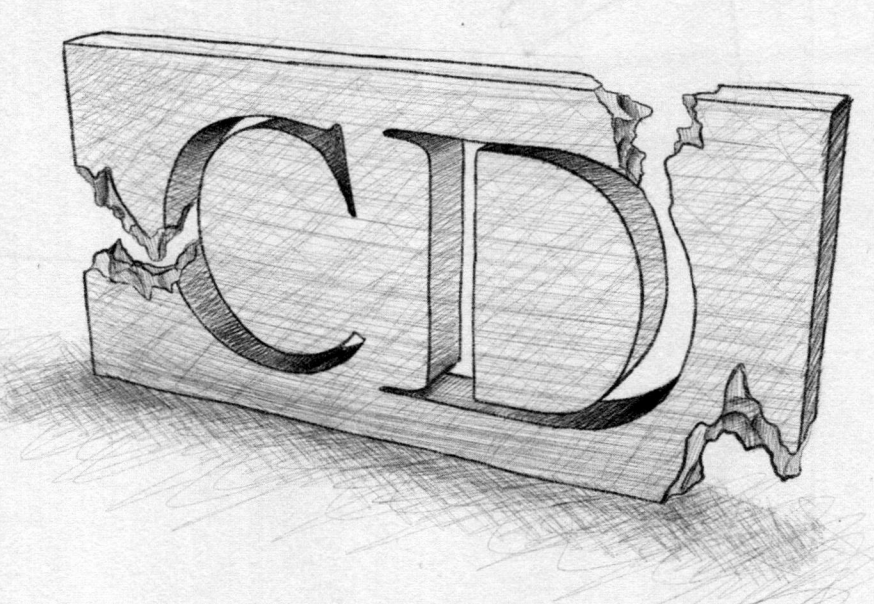

ERODED CHRISTIAN DIOR GRAPHIC
FOR KIM   AUGUST 23 3018

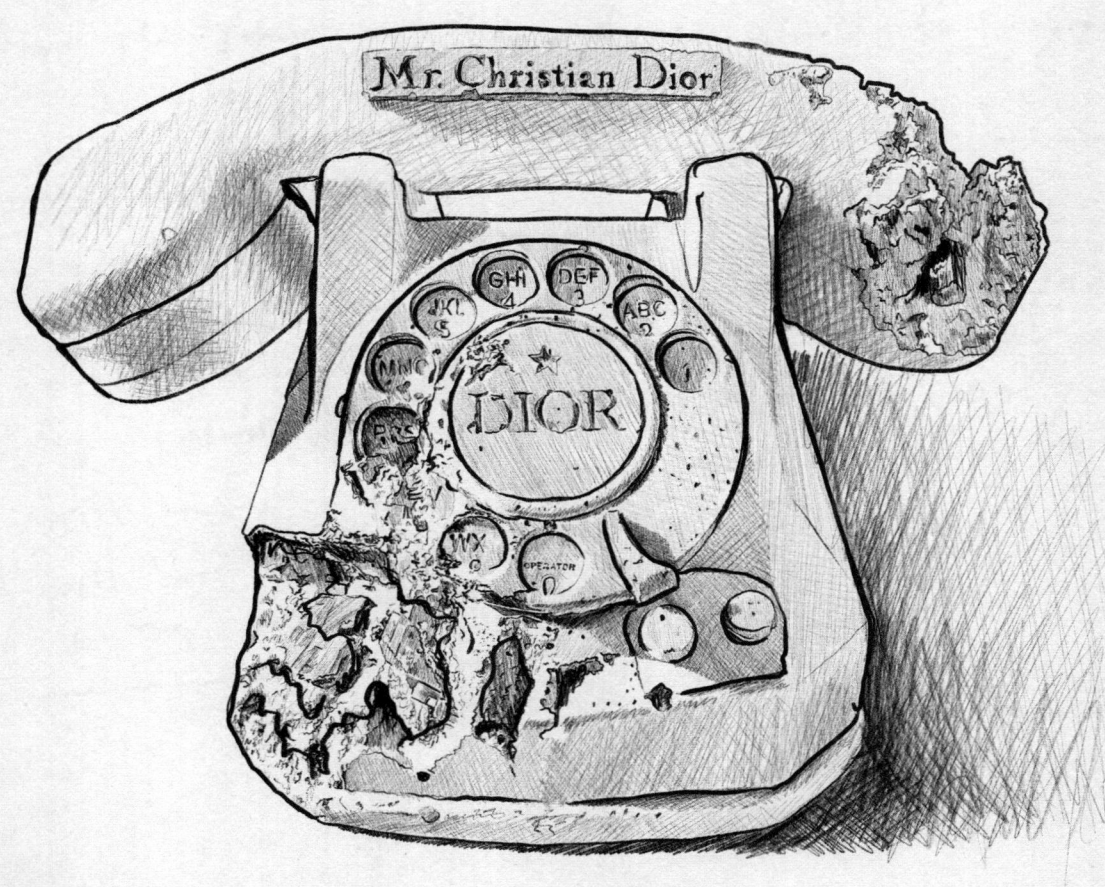

CRYSTAL ERODED PHONE FROM THE DESK OF CHRISTIAN DIOR

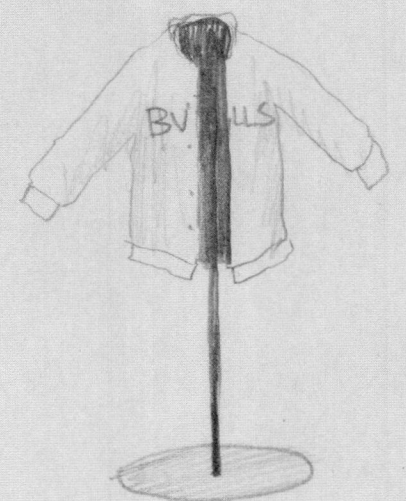

CAST CRYSTAL JACKET

HOLLOW FIGURE
SHEET

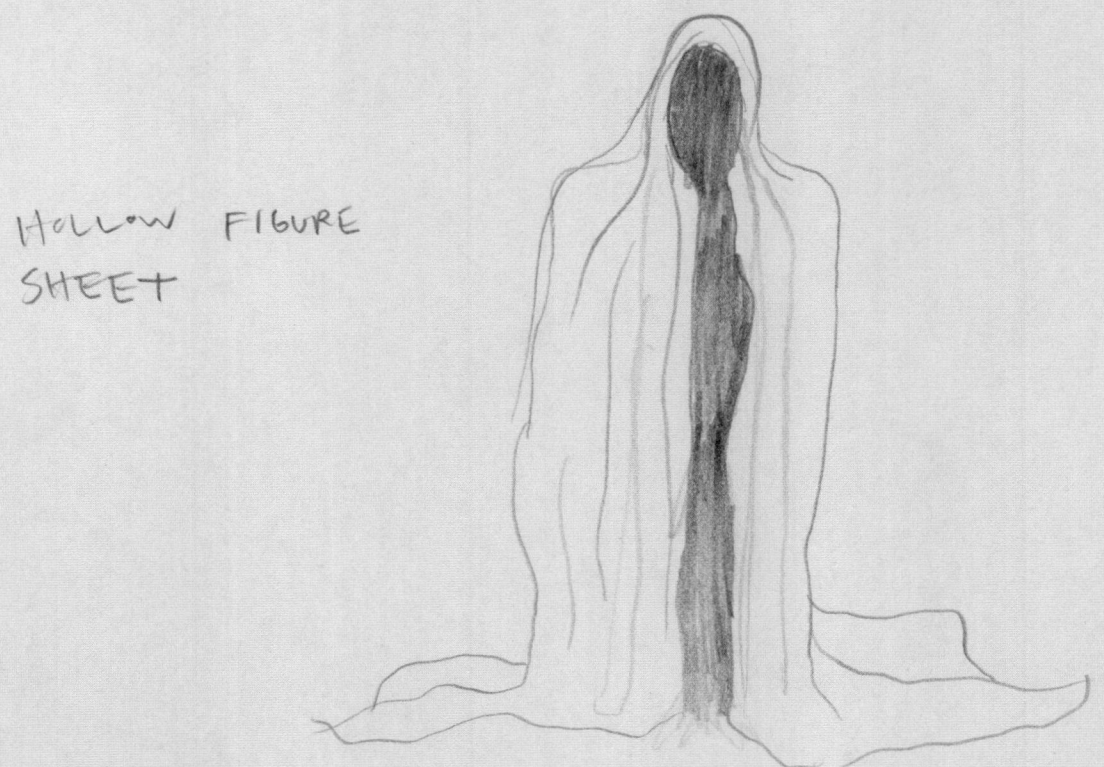

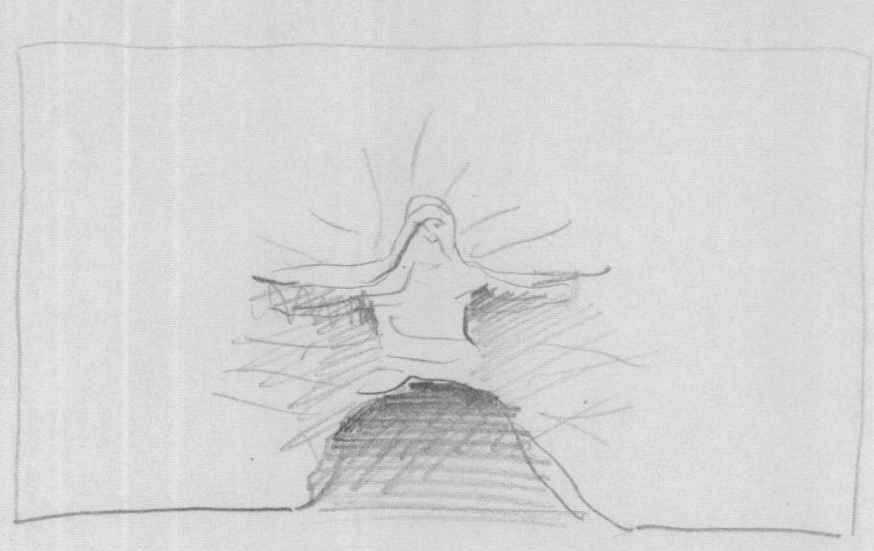

FLOATING FIGURE WITH ARMS OUT

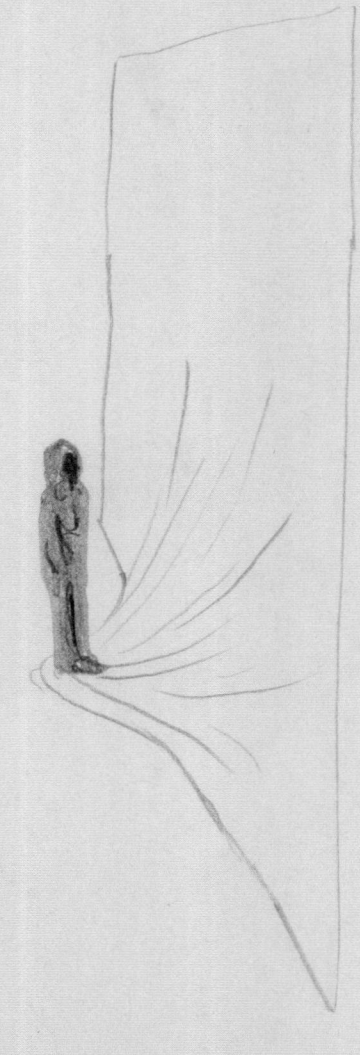

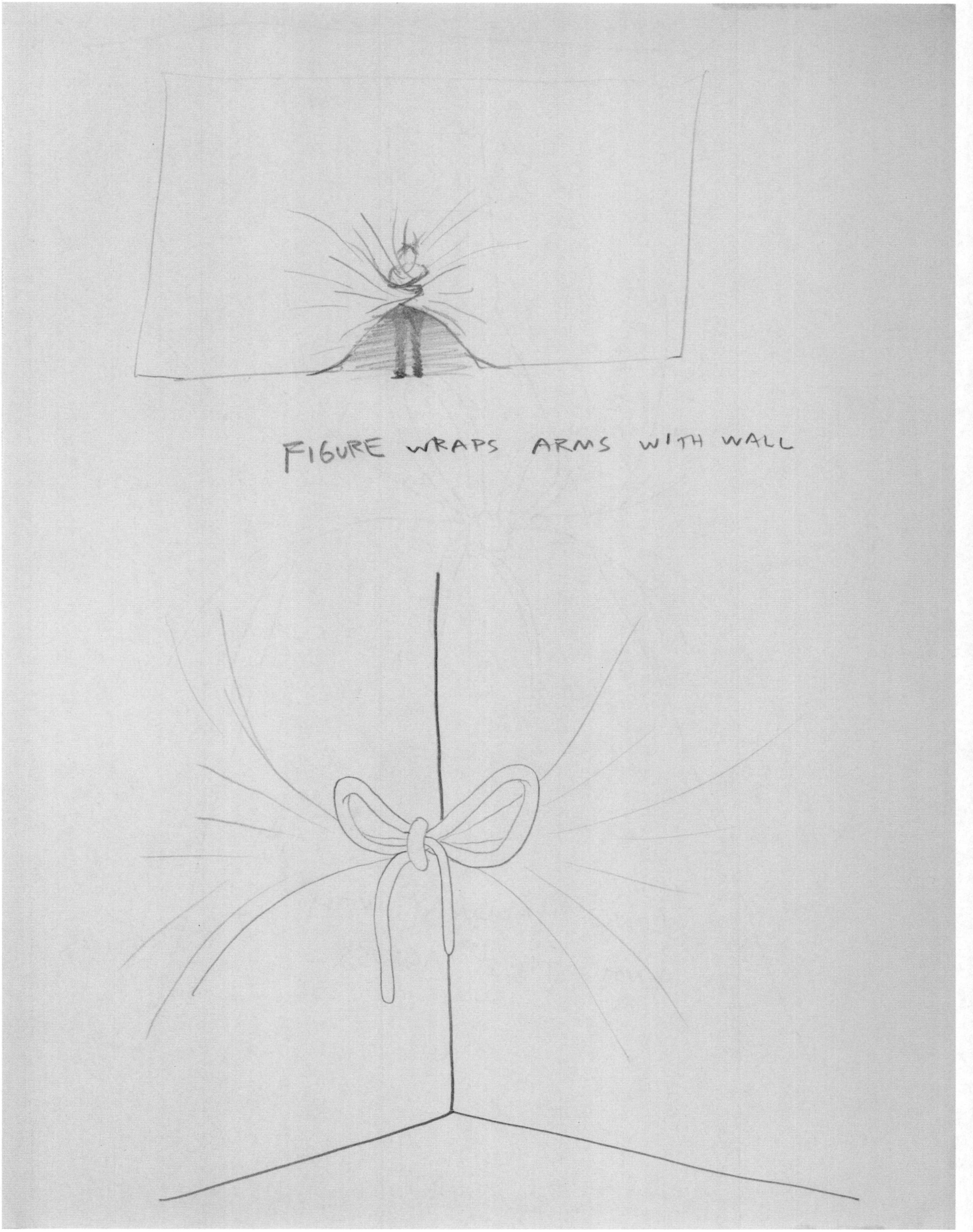

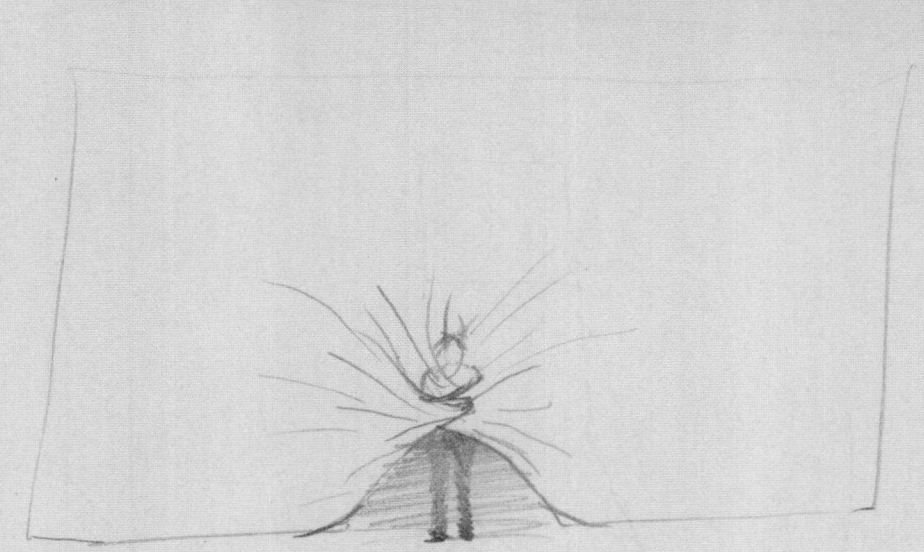

FIGURE WRAPS ARMS WITH WALL

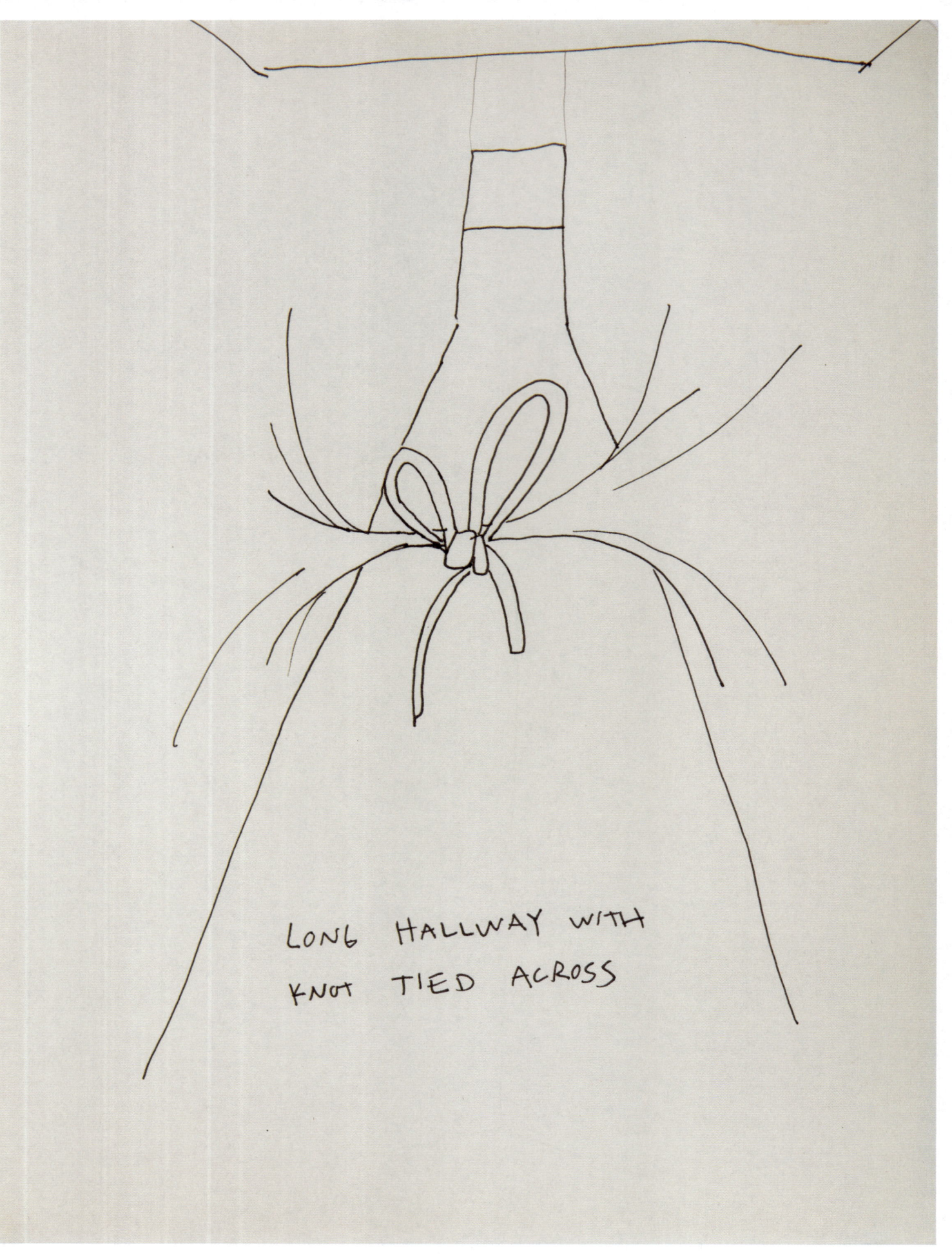

LONG HALLWAY WITH
KNOT TIED ACROSS

confirm works are crated separately.

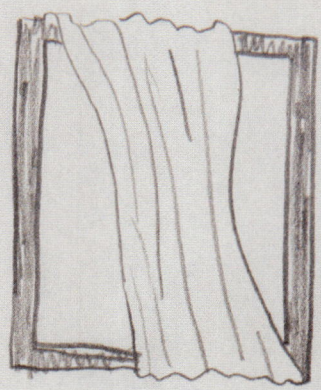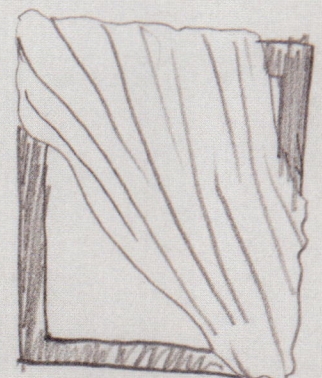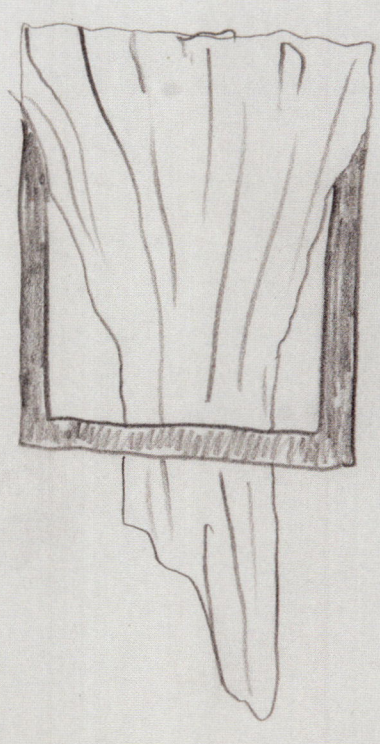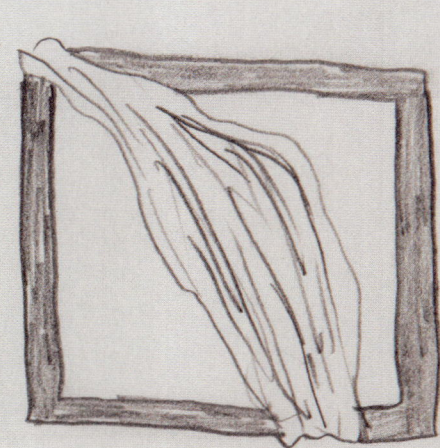

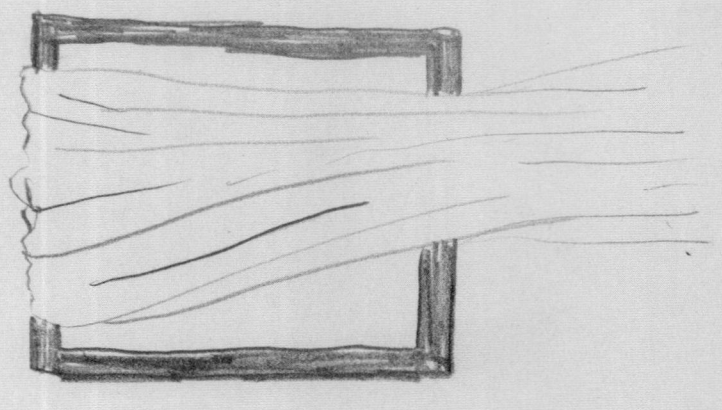

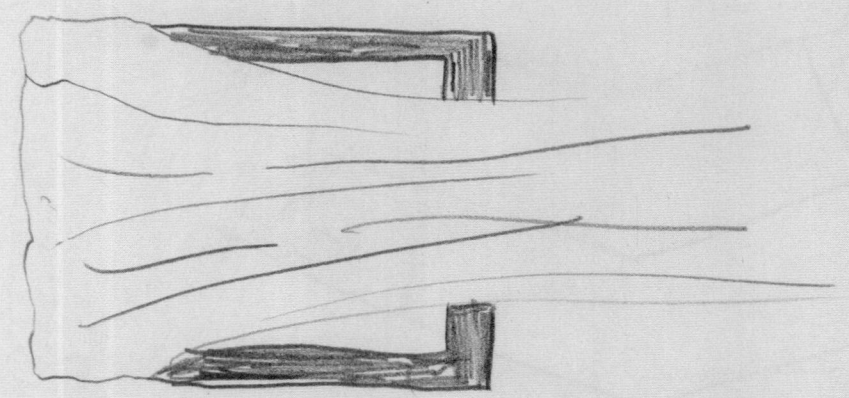

MAYBE FIBERGLASS.?
MAYBE CAST FABRIC

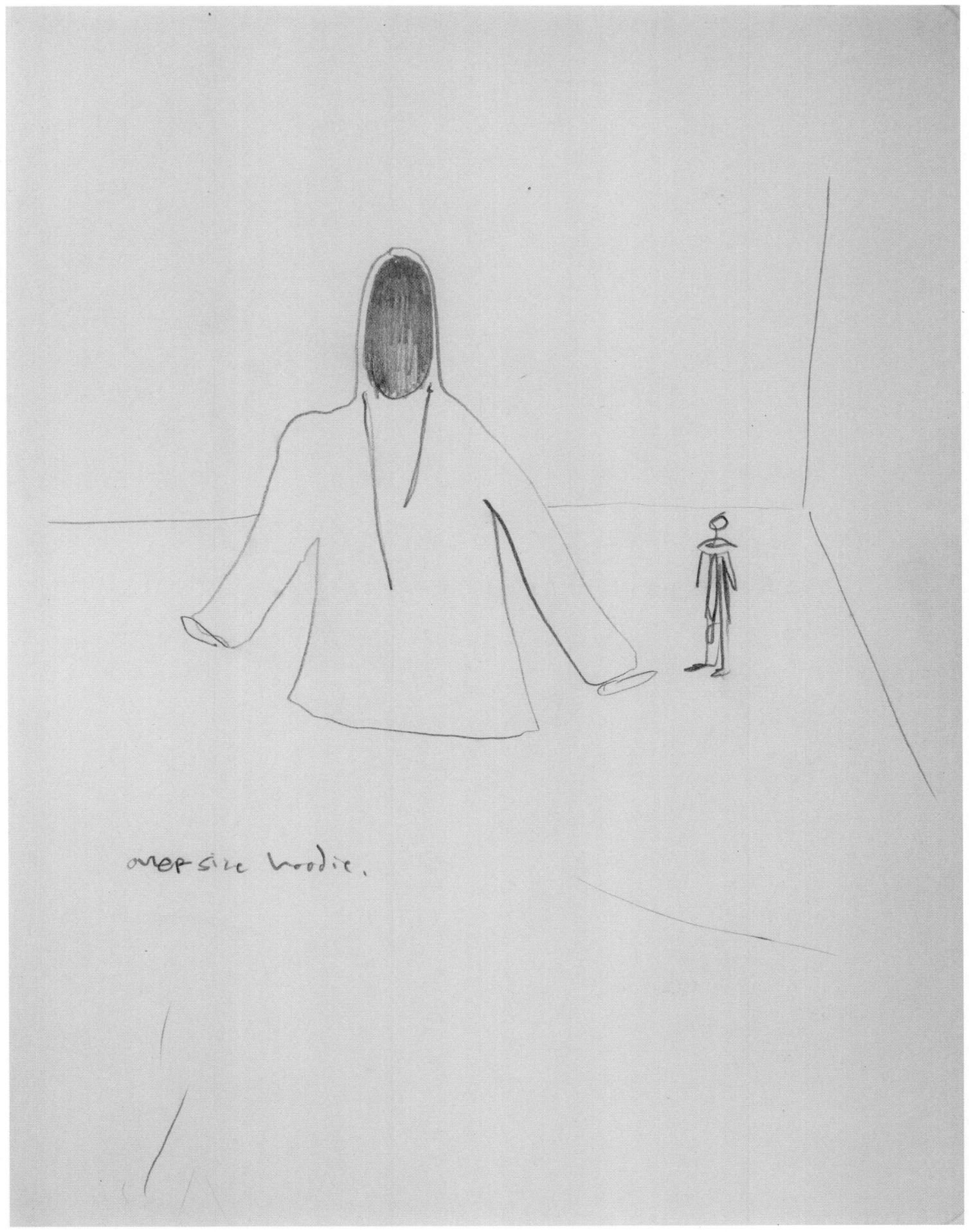

oversize hoodie.

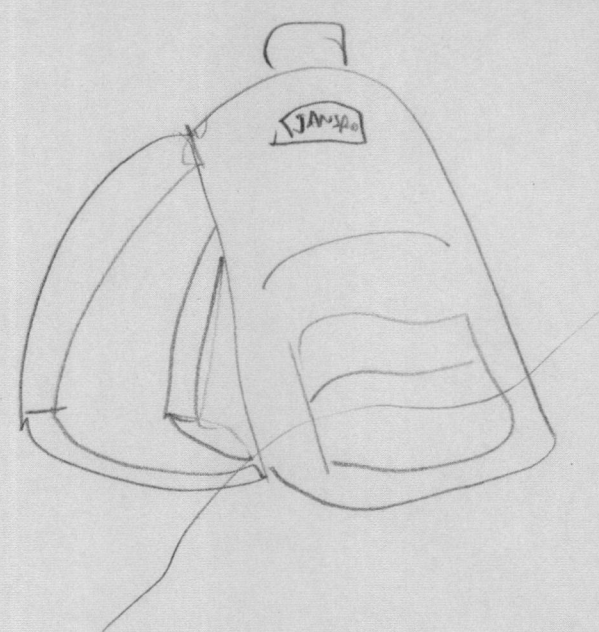

A JANSPORT BACKPACK CAST
IN ASH AND SITTING ON A PEPESTAL

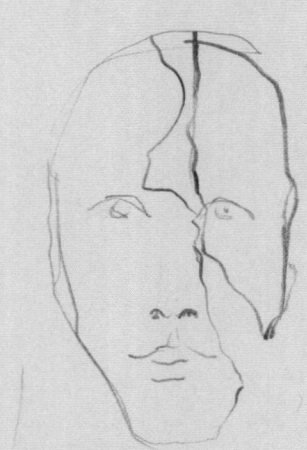

NYC SHOW

- FOOTBALL HELMETS
- HOCKEY MASKS
- FOOTBALL Brancusi style
- BULLS JACKET (HOLLOW)
- DOLPHINS JERSEY (FLAT)

- YANKEES JERSEY (HOLLOW)

- BASKETBALL JERSEY (HOLLOW)

- BASEBALL HAT

- BOXING UNIFORM

- ARMS AND BALLS.

- ARMS IN CORNERS

- DROP ON WALL LARGE

- FREE STANDING DROP ON floor

- LARGE PILE DOWN STAIRS

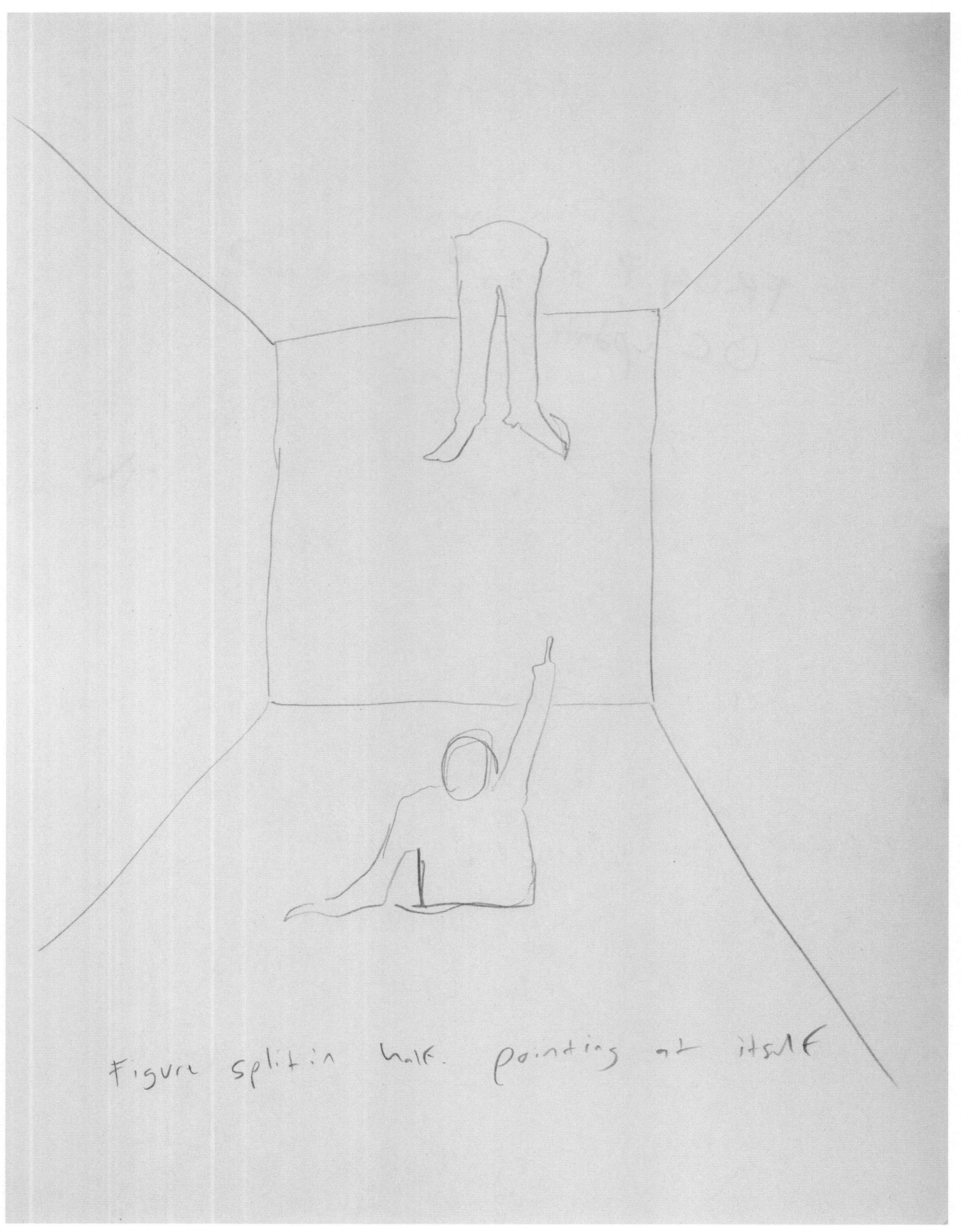

Figure split in half. pointing at itself

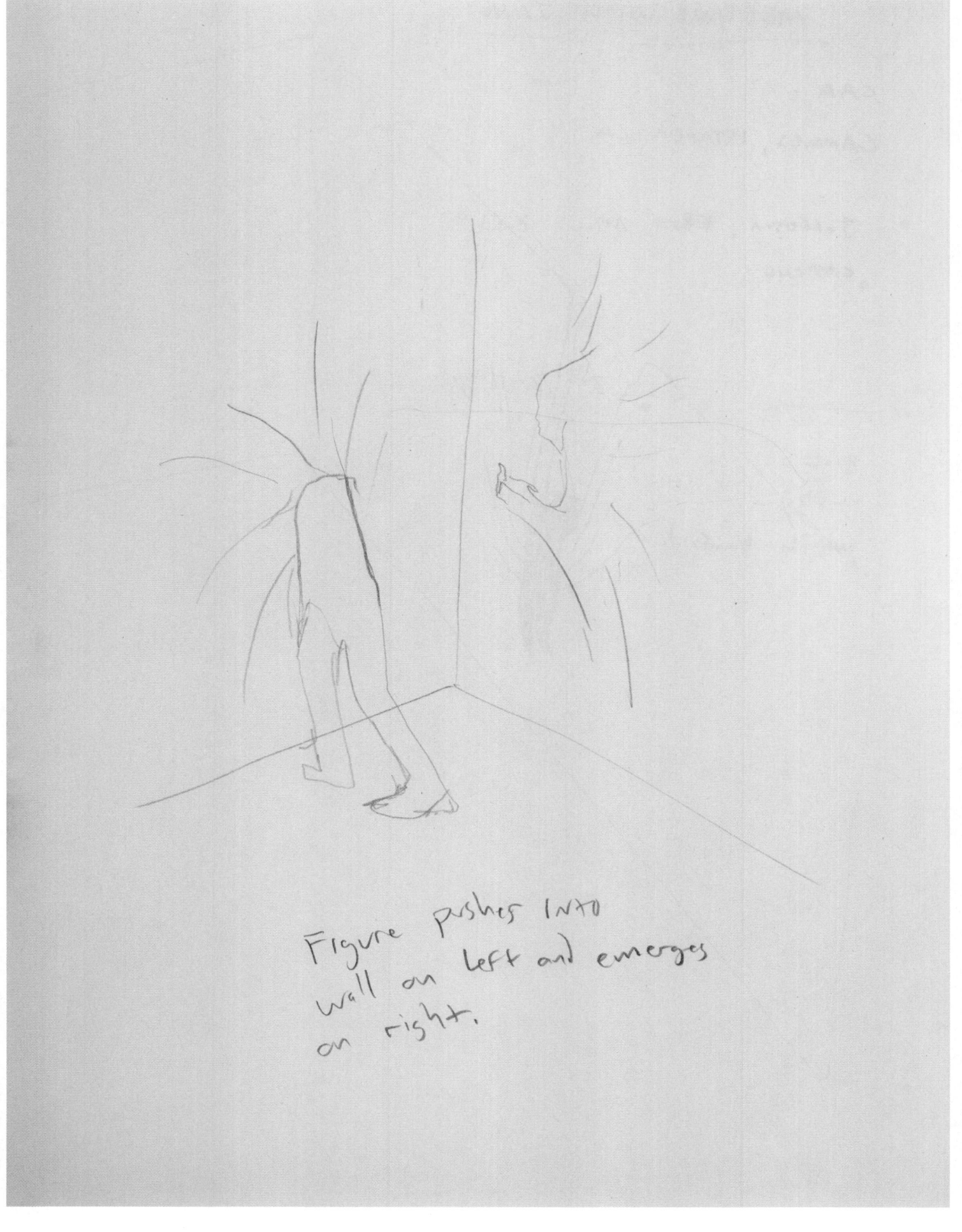

Figure pushes into
wall on left and emerges
on right.

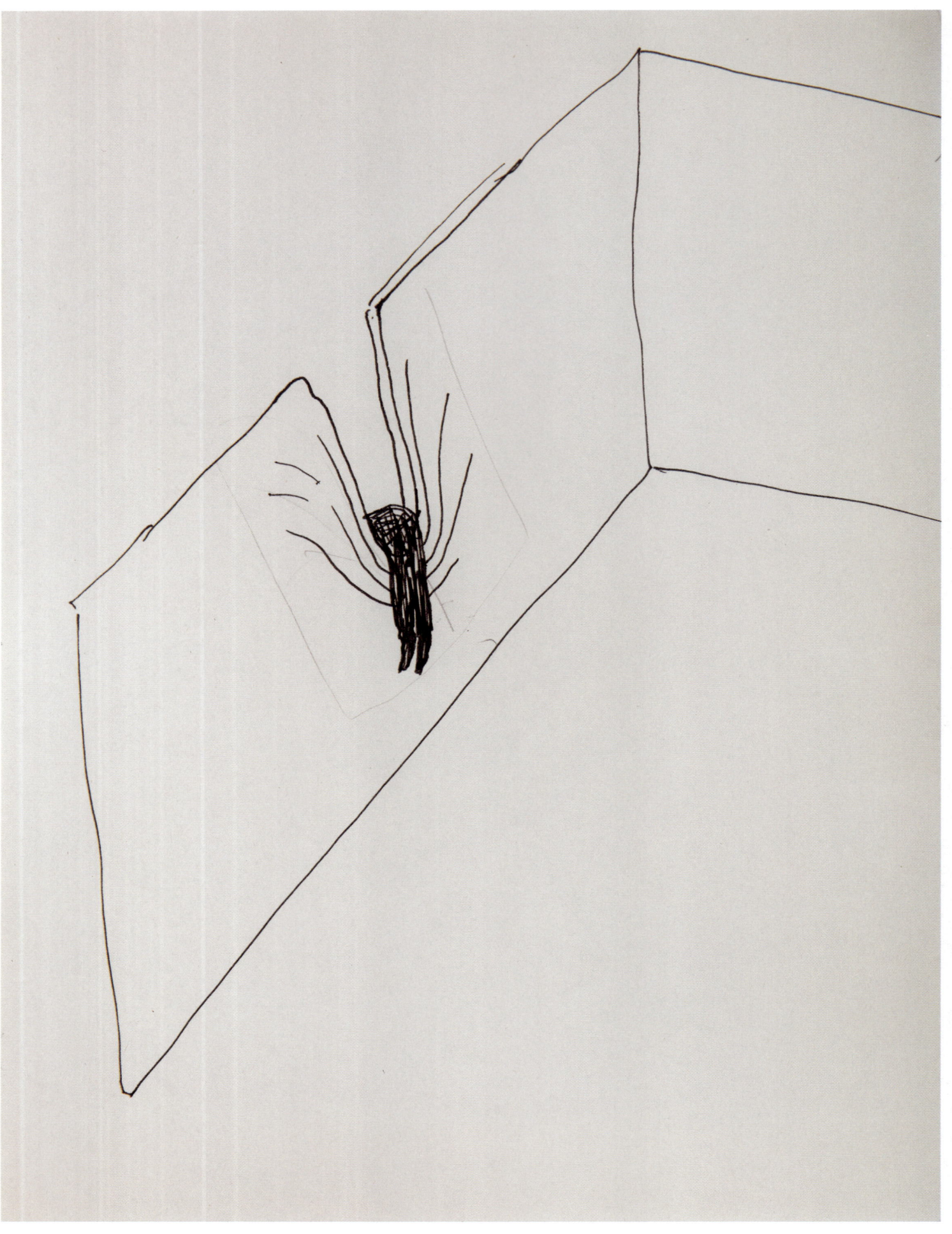

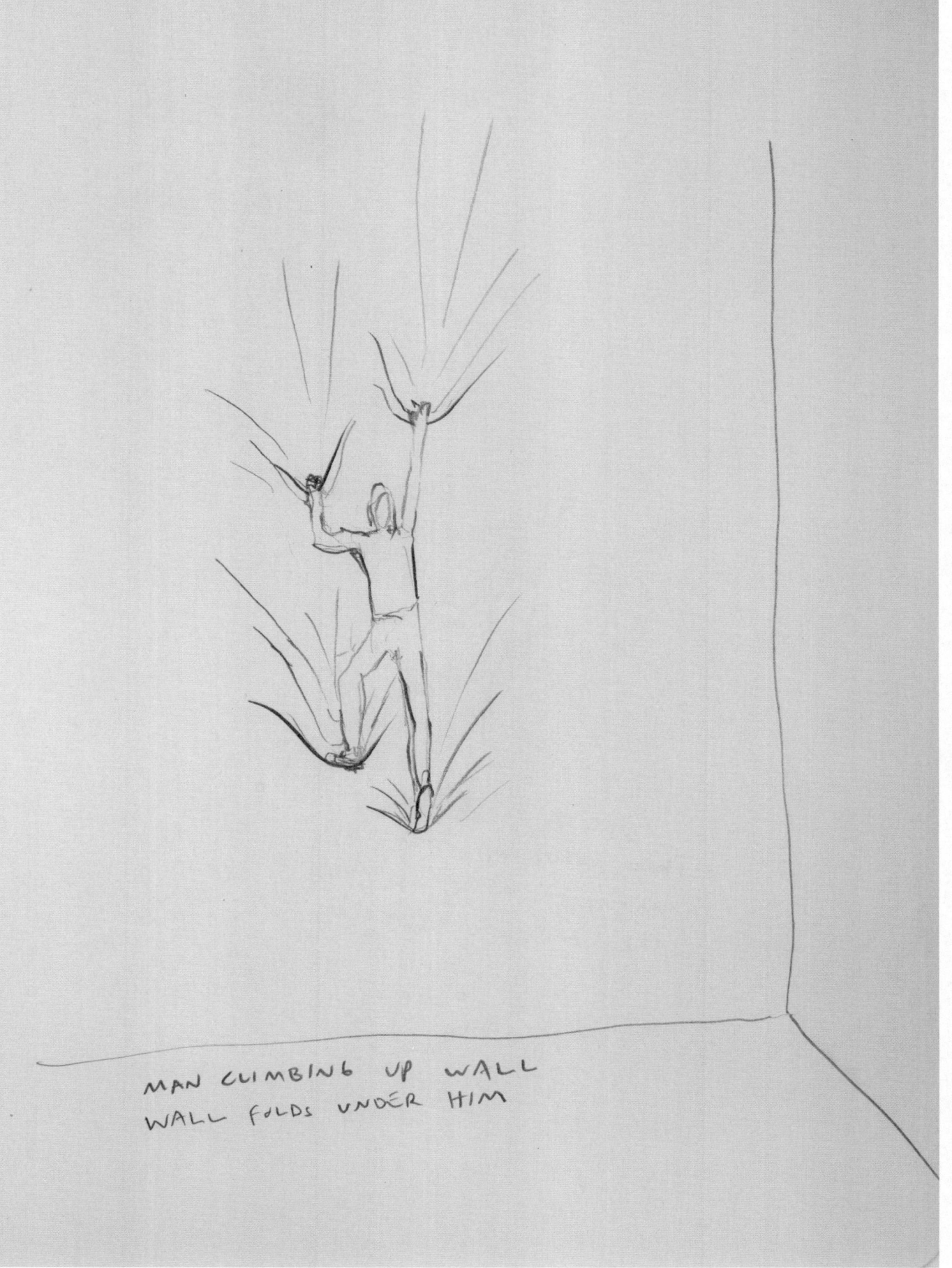

MAN CLIMBING UP WALL
WALL FOLDS UNDER HIM

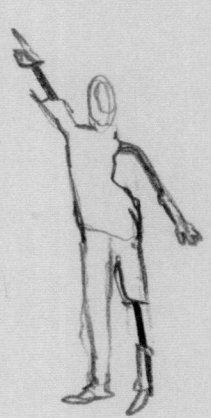

LIKE A MARBLE FIGURE
FROM ANTIQUITY THAT HAS
STAINLESS PIPE COMPLETING
THE MISSING SECTIONS.

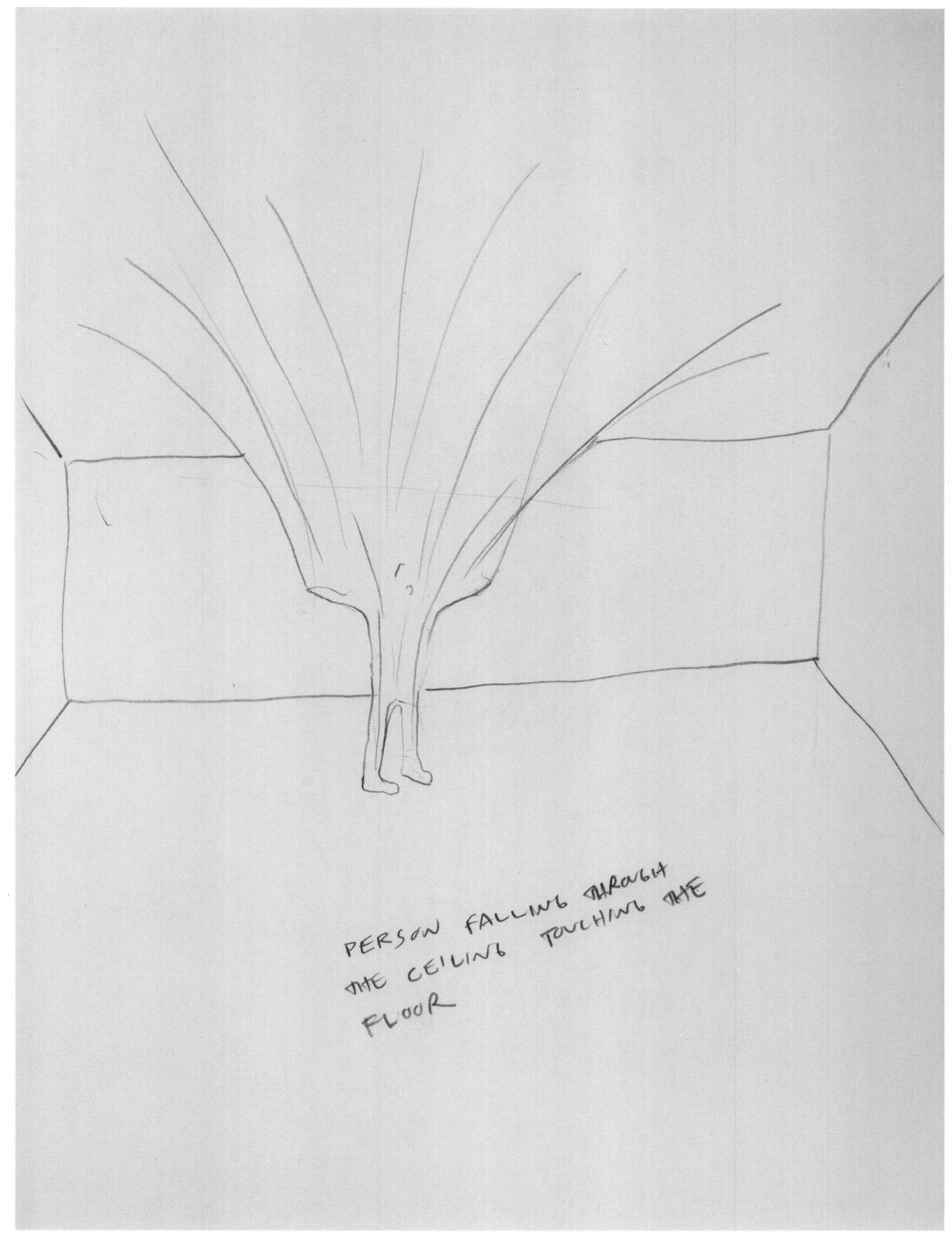

PERSON FALLING THROUGH
THE CEILING TOUCHING THE
FLOOR

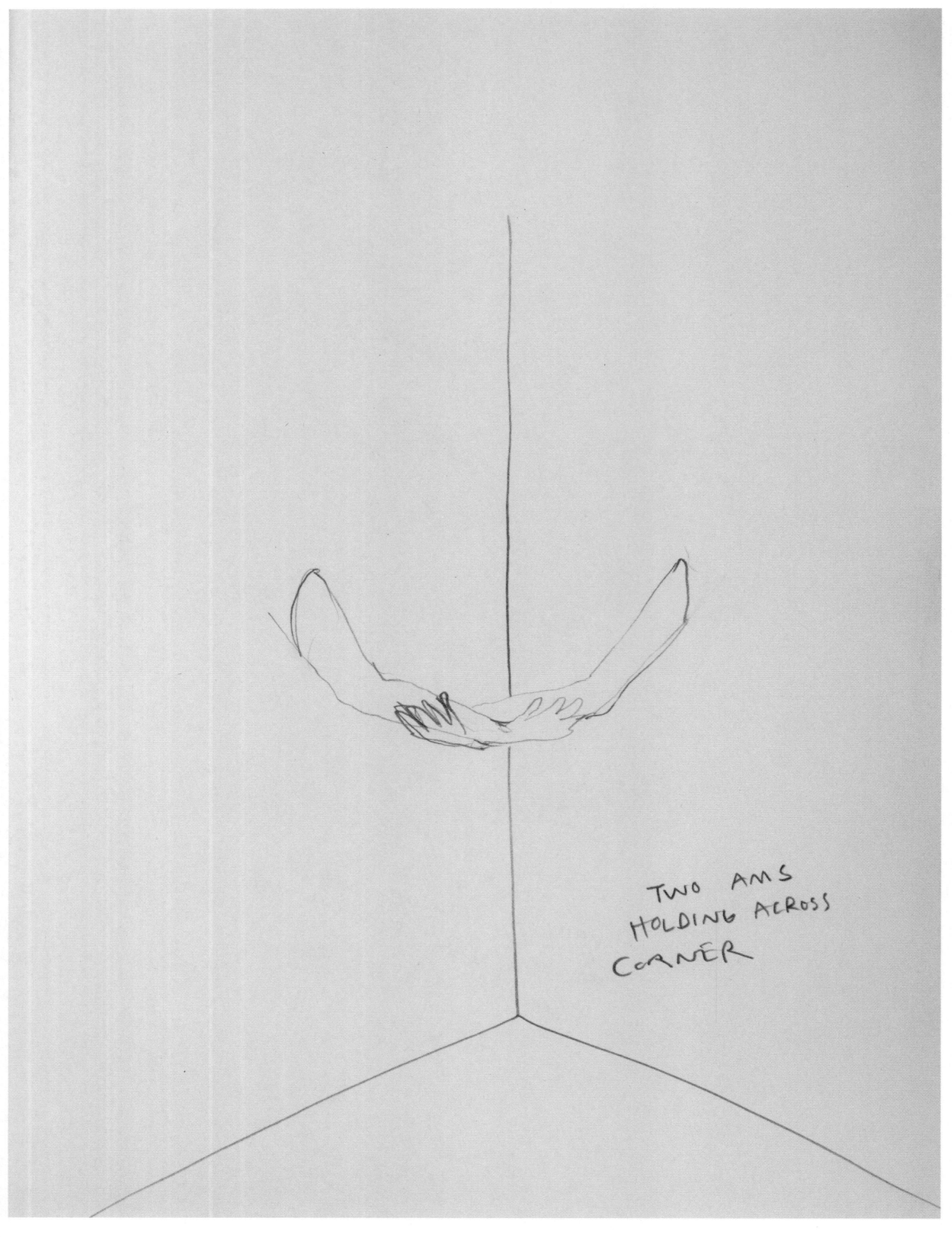

TWO AMS
HOLDING ACROSS
CORNER

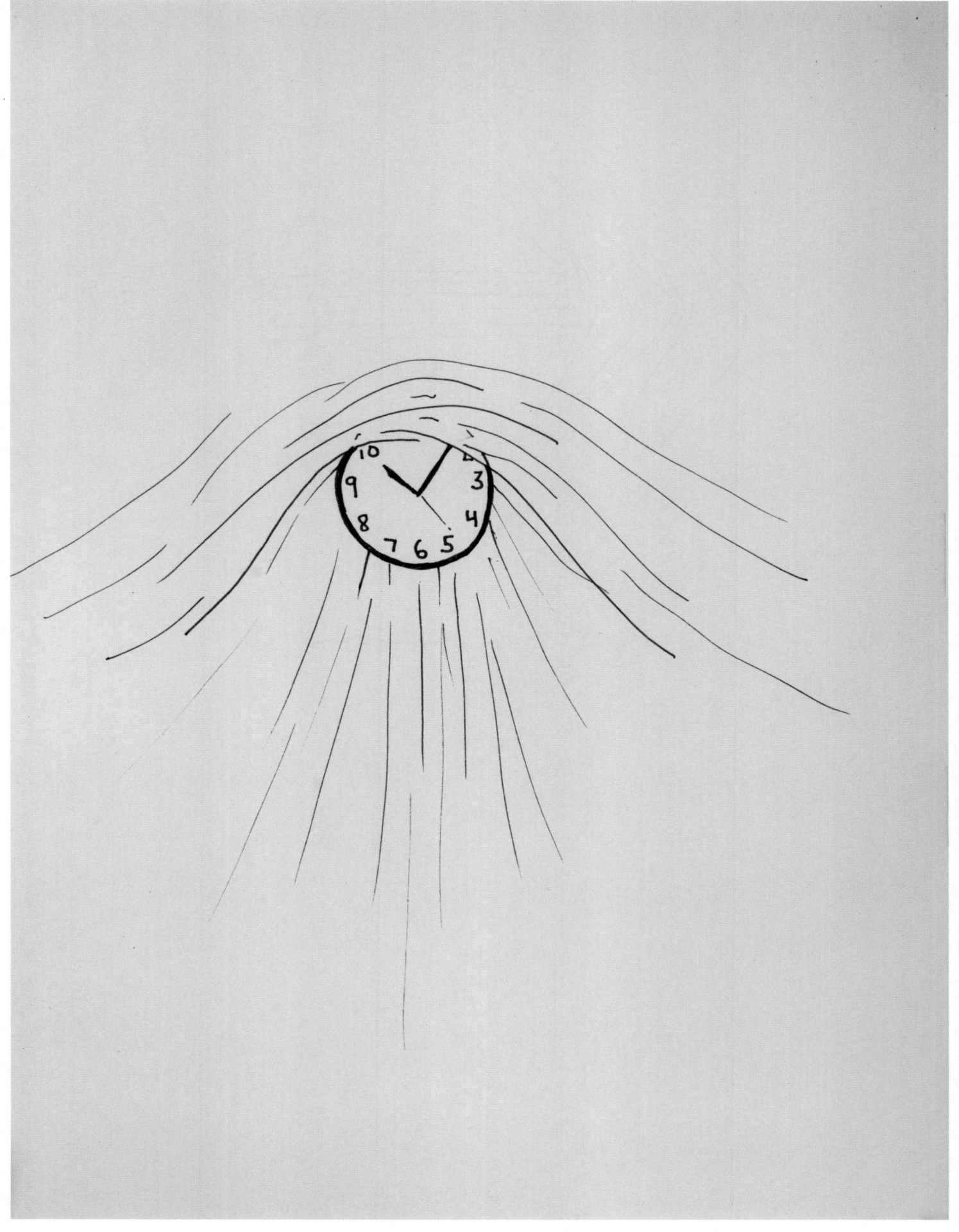

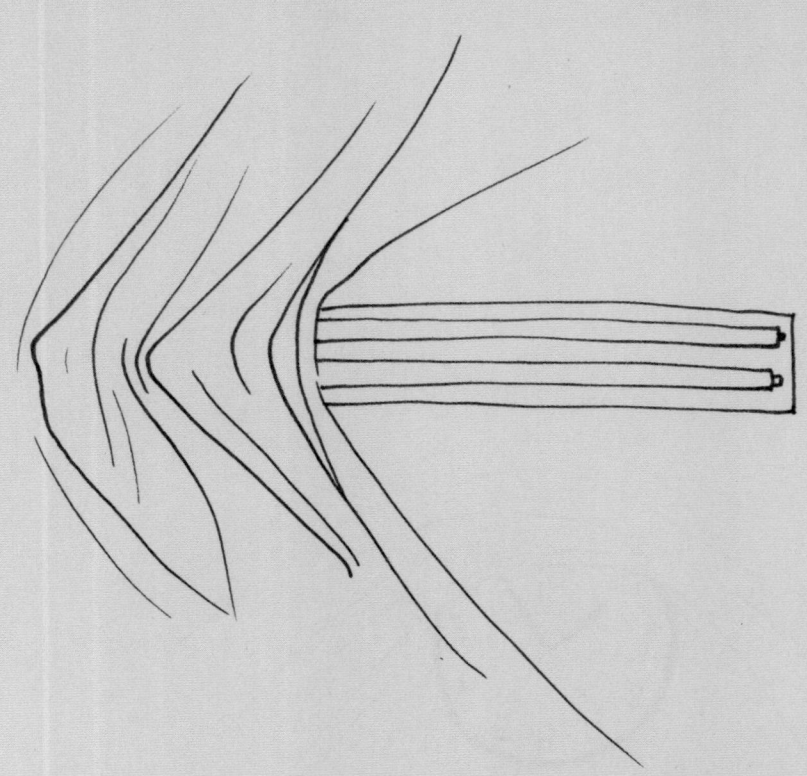

Fluoresent light fixture ~~pushed into~~ sliding on wall.

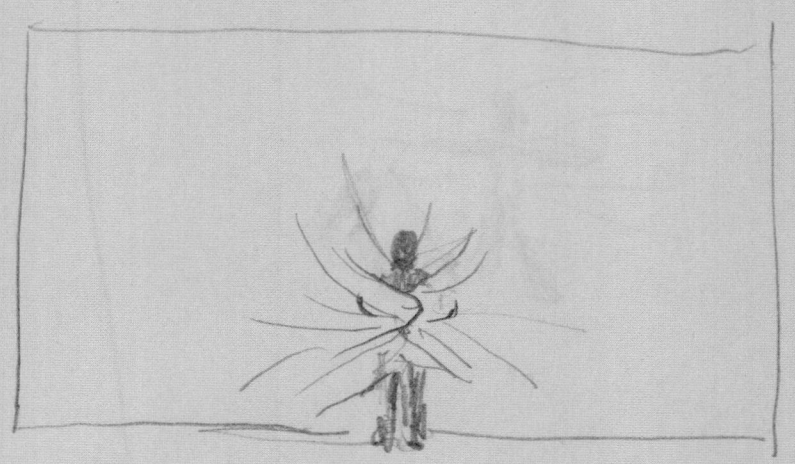

FIGURE PULLING FABRIC OVER.

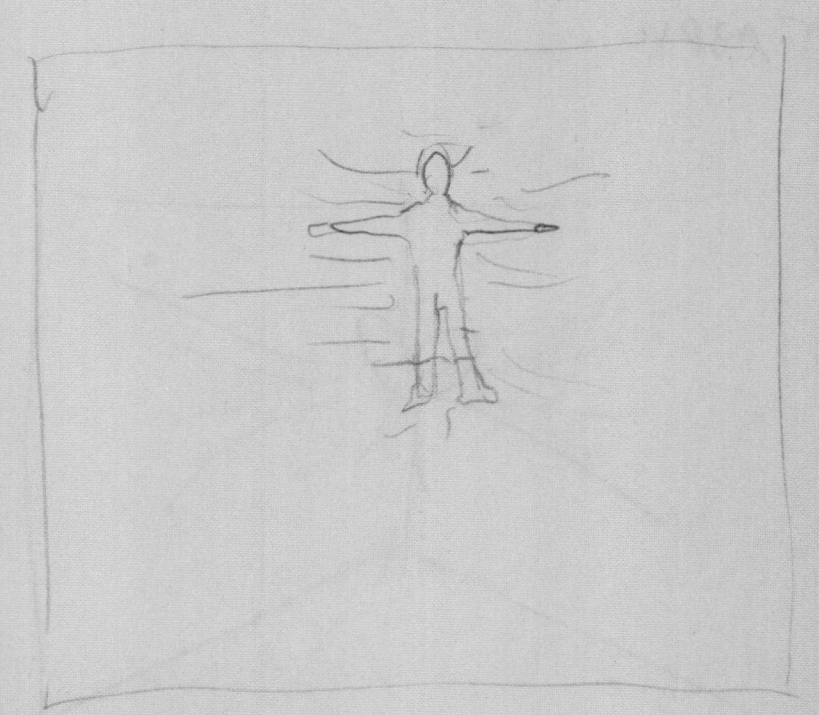

FIGURE BEHIND WALL, ELEVATED
ON THE WALL

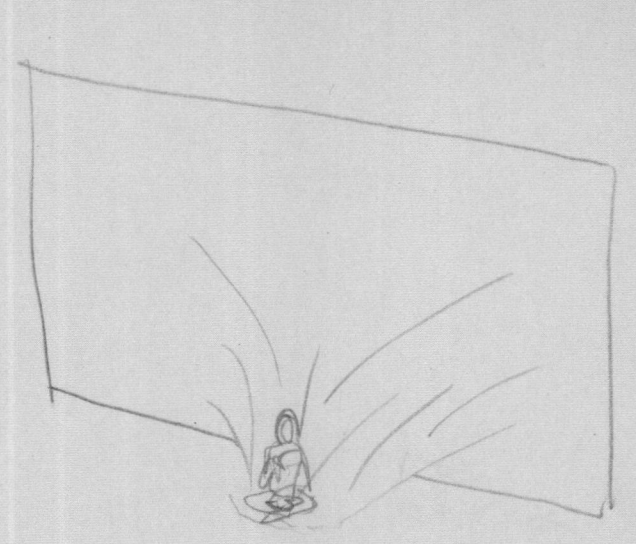

FIGURE SITTING ON WALL

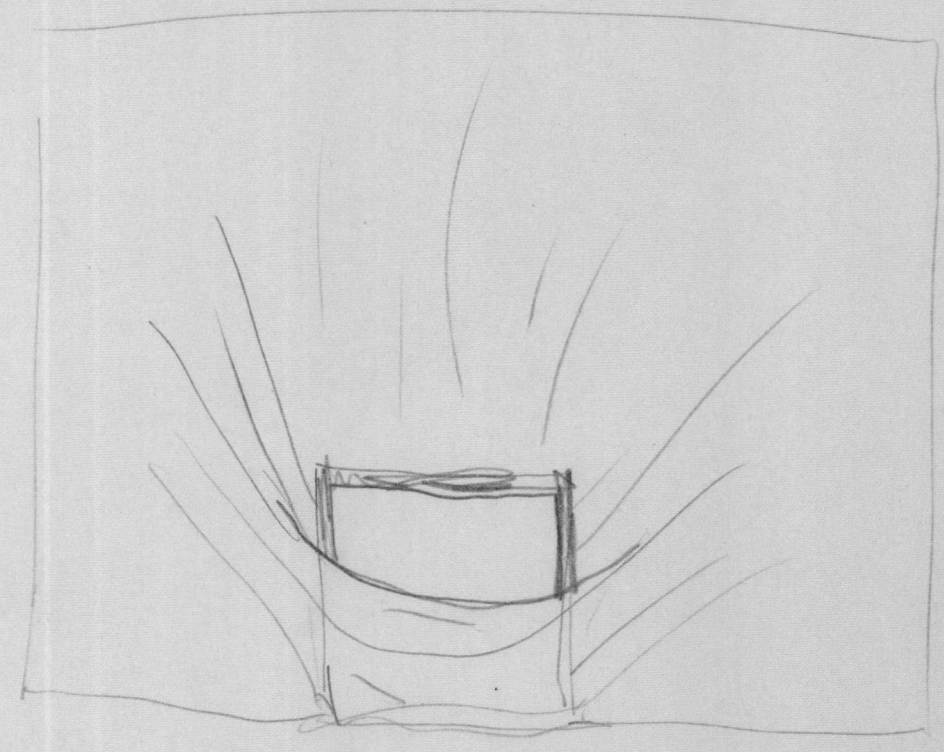

MIRROR SLIDING DOWN THE WALL

NYC 2016 - September.

-oversize Forms.
- Baseball Hat
- Basketballs
- Hands

- WORD FORMS

- GRADIENT COLOR INSTALL DOWN STAIRS?


- Hands stretching from wall.


- WORD FORMS.

syt -tys

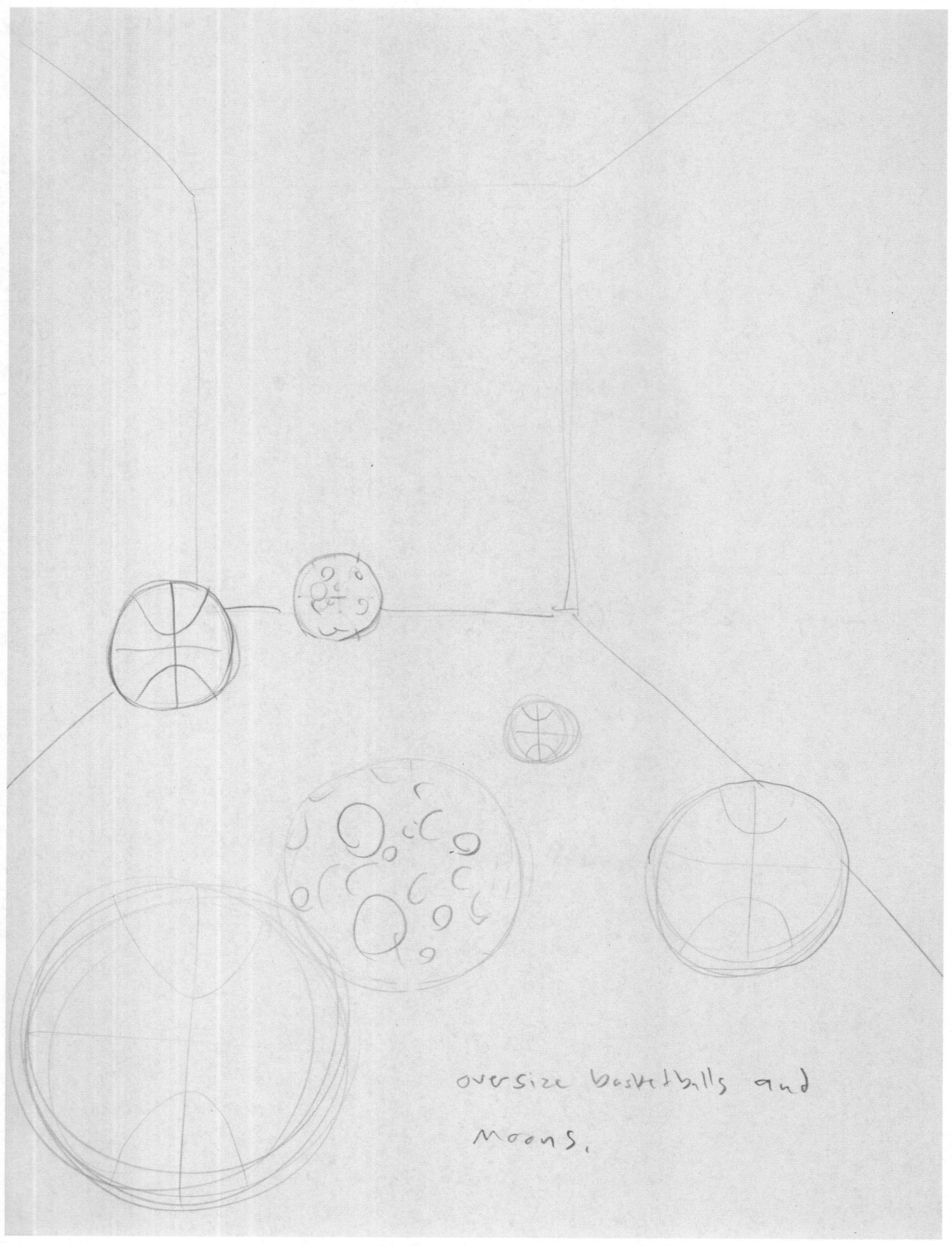

oversize basketballs and
moons,

CAST BOOKS ENLARGED.

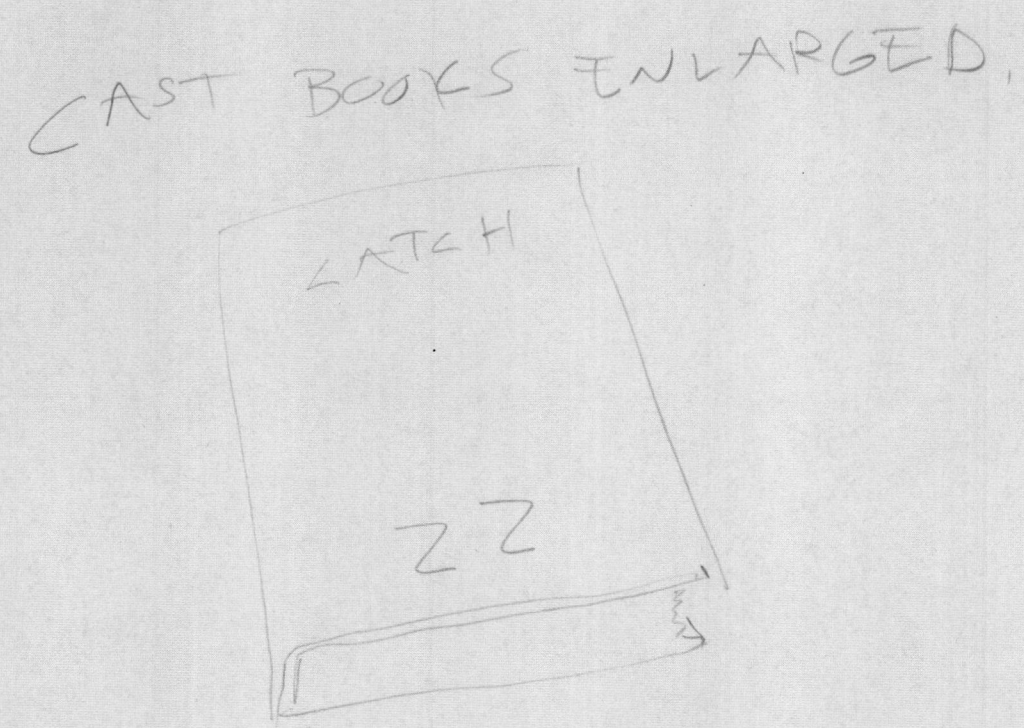

LATCH

ZZ

Rocks or Crystals
cast in color.

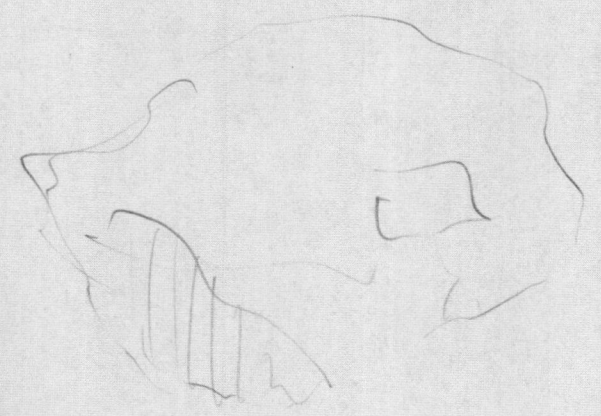

# STUFFED ANIMALS

CAST IN ASH.

## LARGE PAINTINGS

- cut into foam
dense foam.
- corlon?

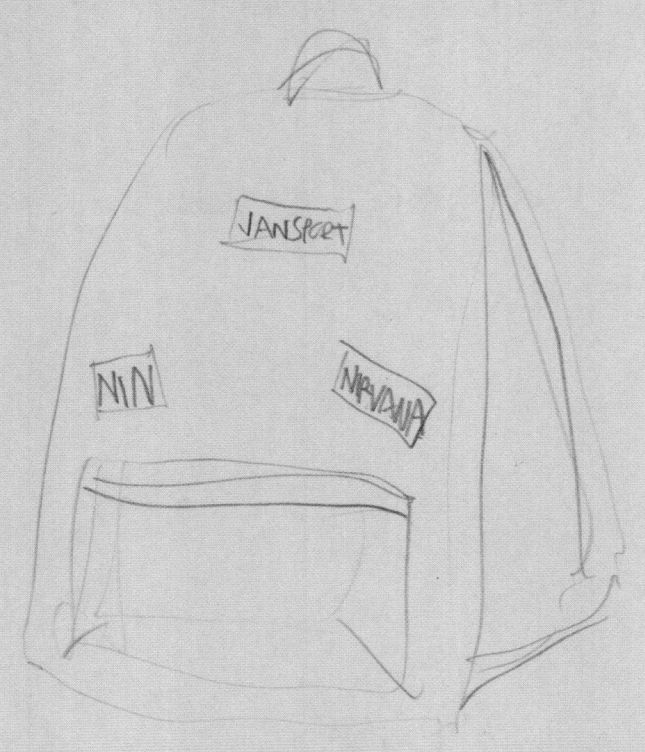

90's JANSPORT BACKPACK
WITH VARIOUS PATCHES.

# THINGS TO START

- HANDS STRETCHING FROM WALL
- BASEBALL HAT
- OVERSIZE BASKETBALL
- STUFFED ANIMALS CAST

PERROTIN NYC
SHOW
SEPTEMBER
2016

GIANT
ROCK GARDEN
IN COLOR.
ONE COLOR

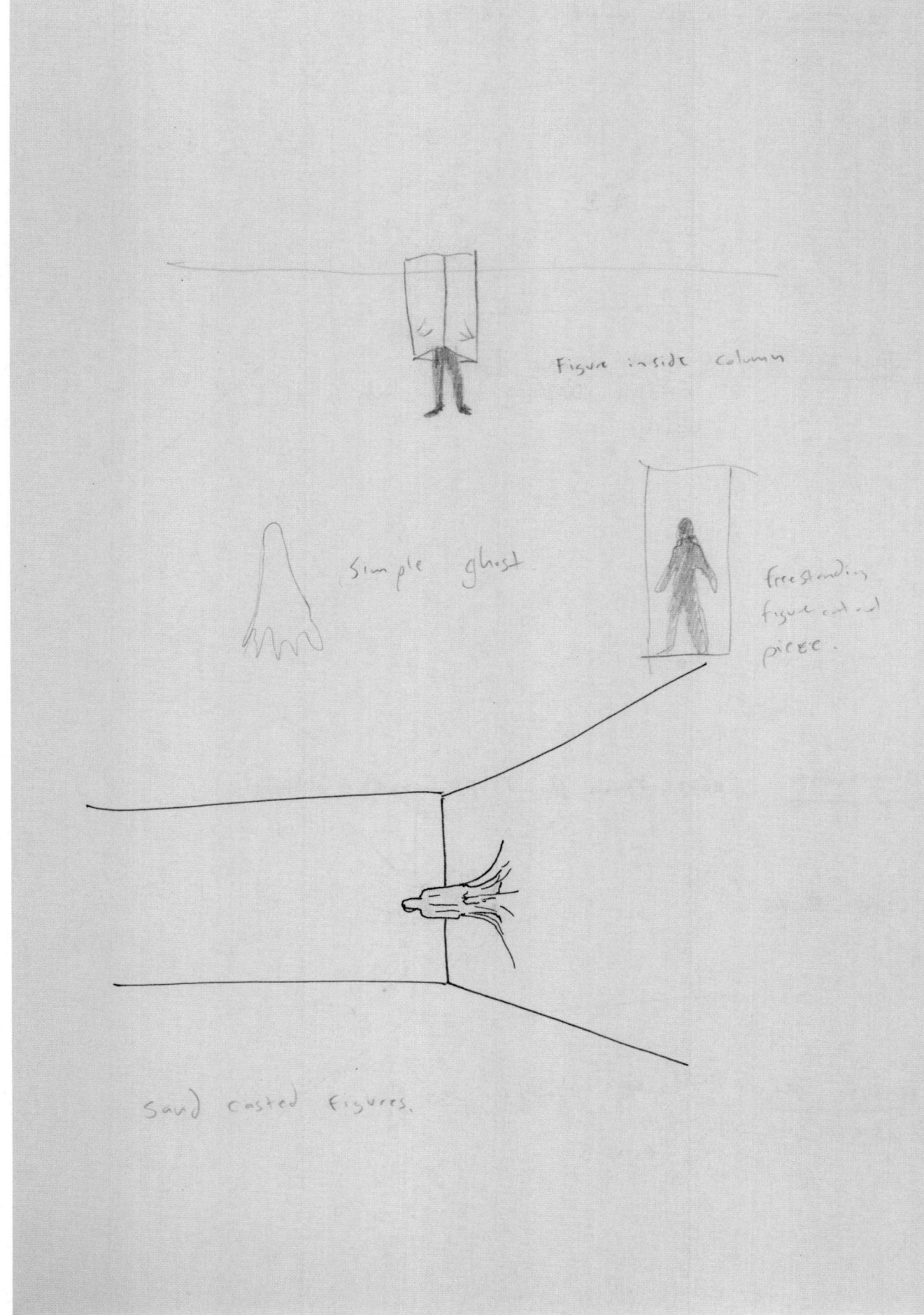

Figure inside column

Simple ghost

Freestanding figure and piece.

Sand casted figures.

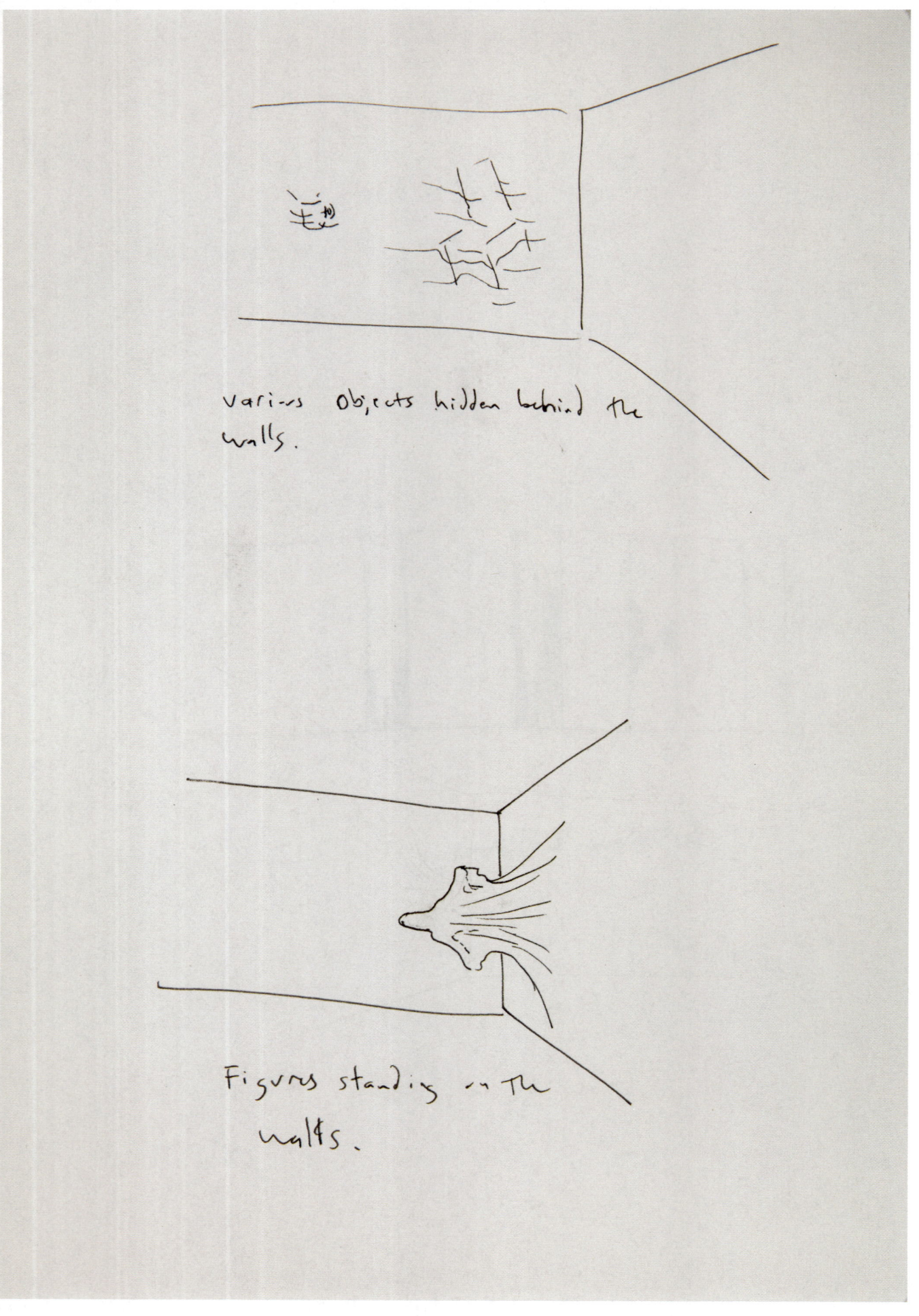

various objects hidden behind the walls.

Figures standing on the walls.

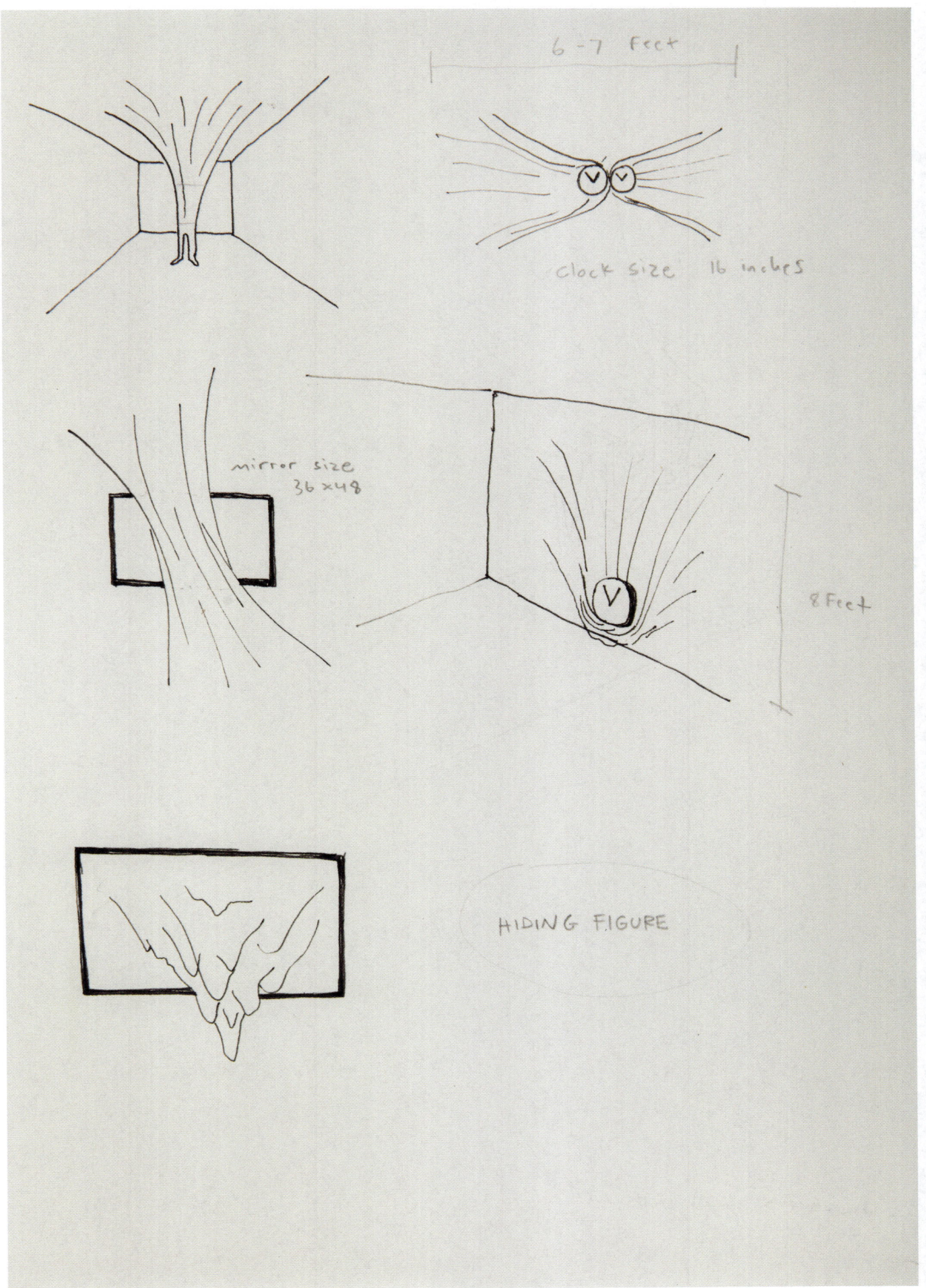

6-7 Feet

Clock size 16 inches

mirror size
36 x 48

8 Feet

HIDING FIGURE

211

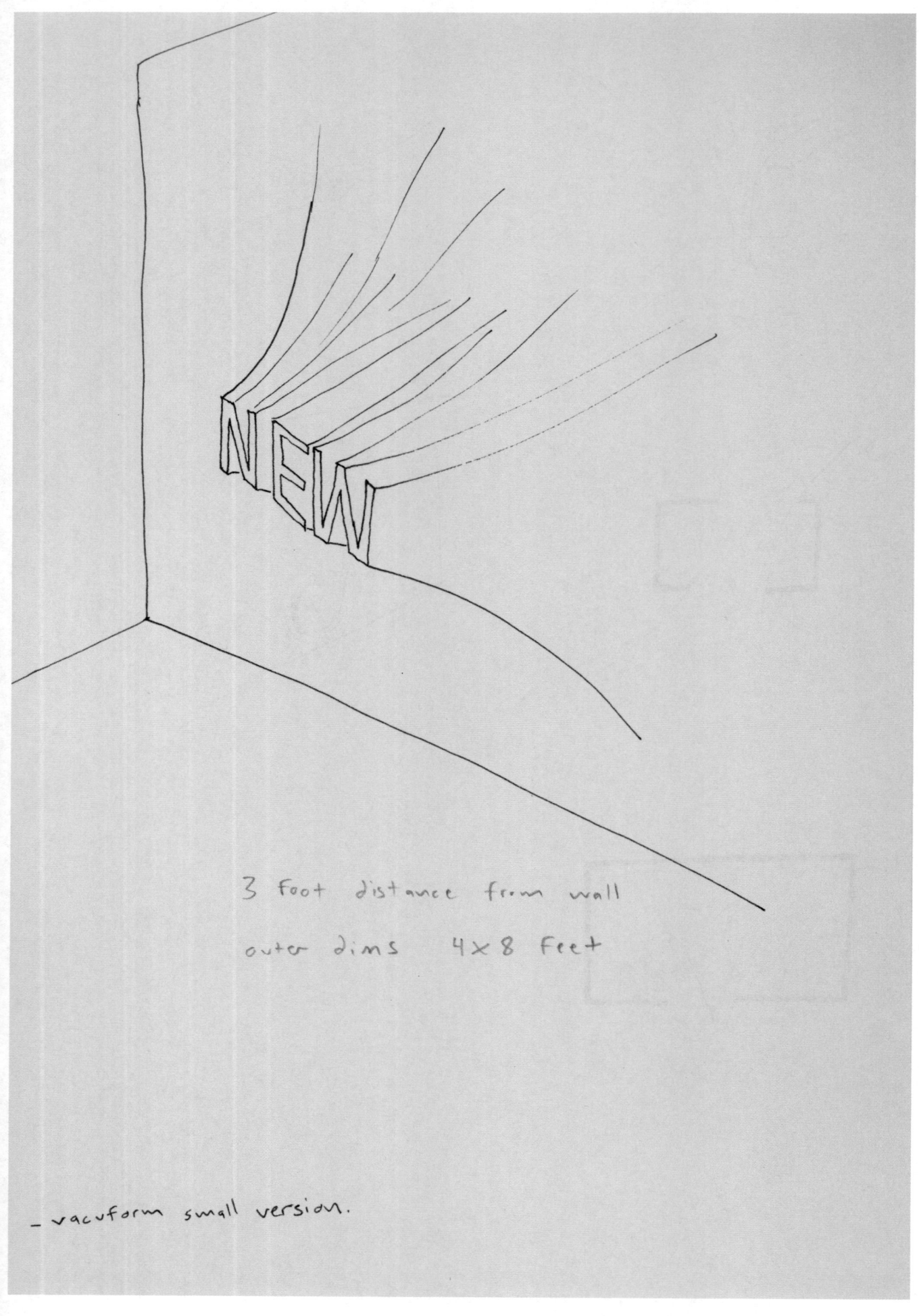

3 foot distance from wall

outer dims 4x8 feet

- vacuform small version.

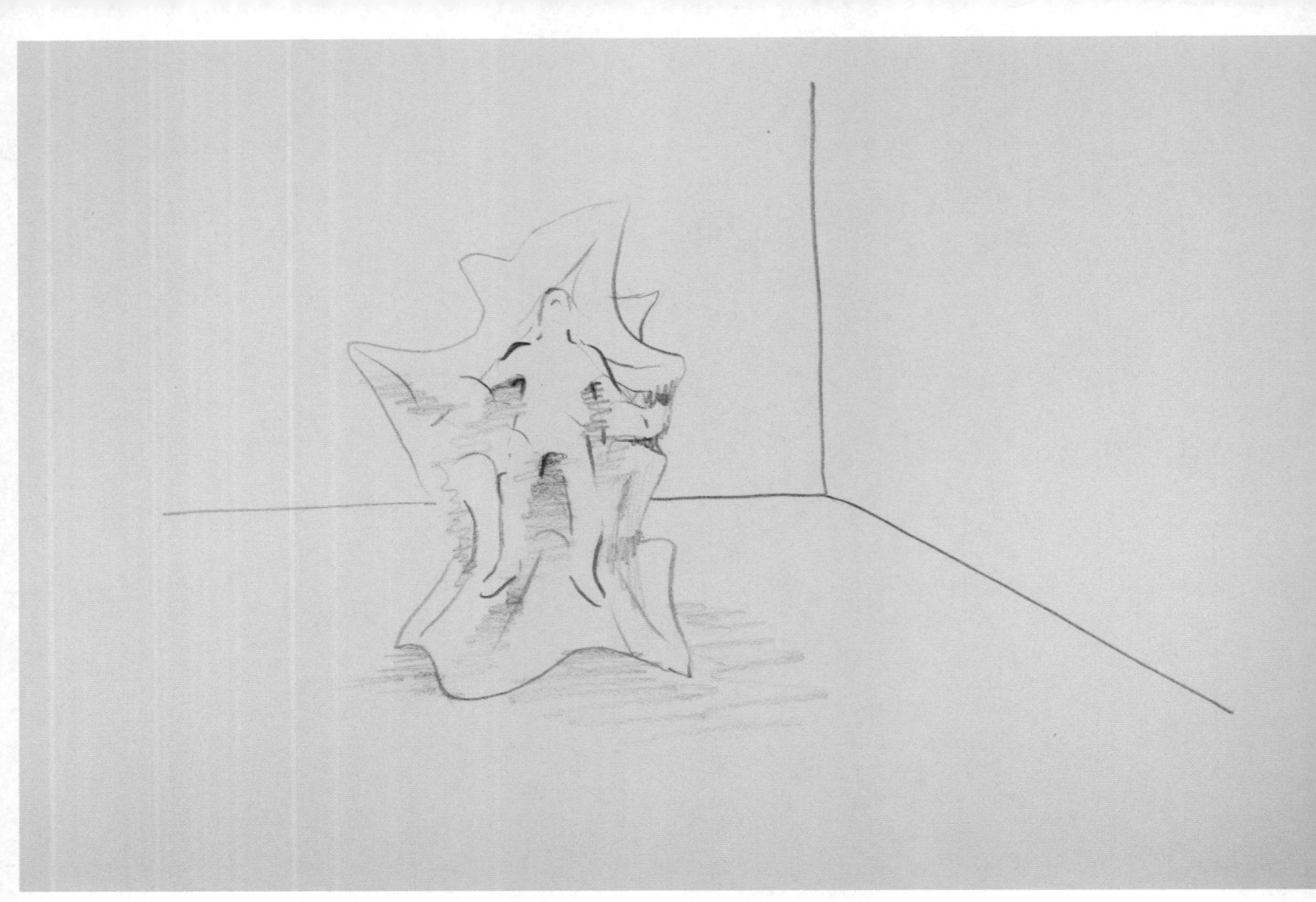

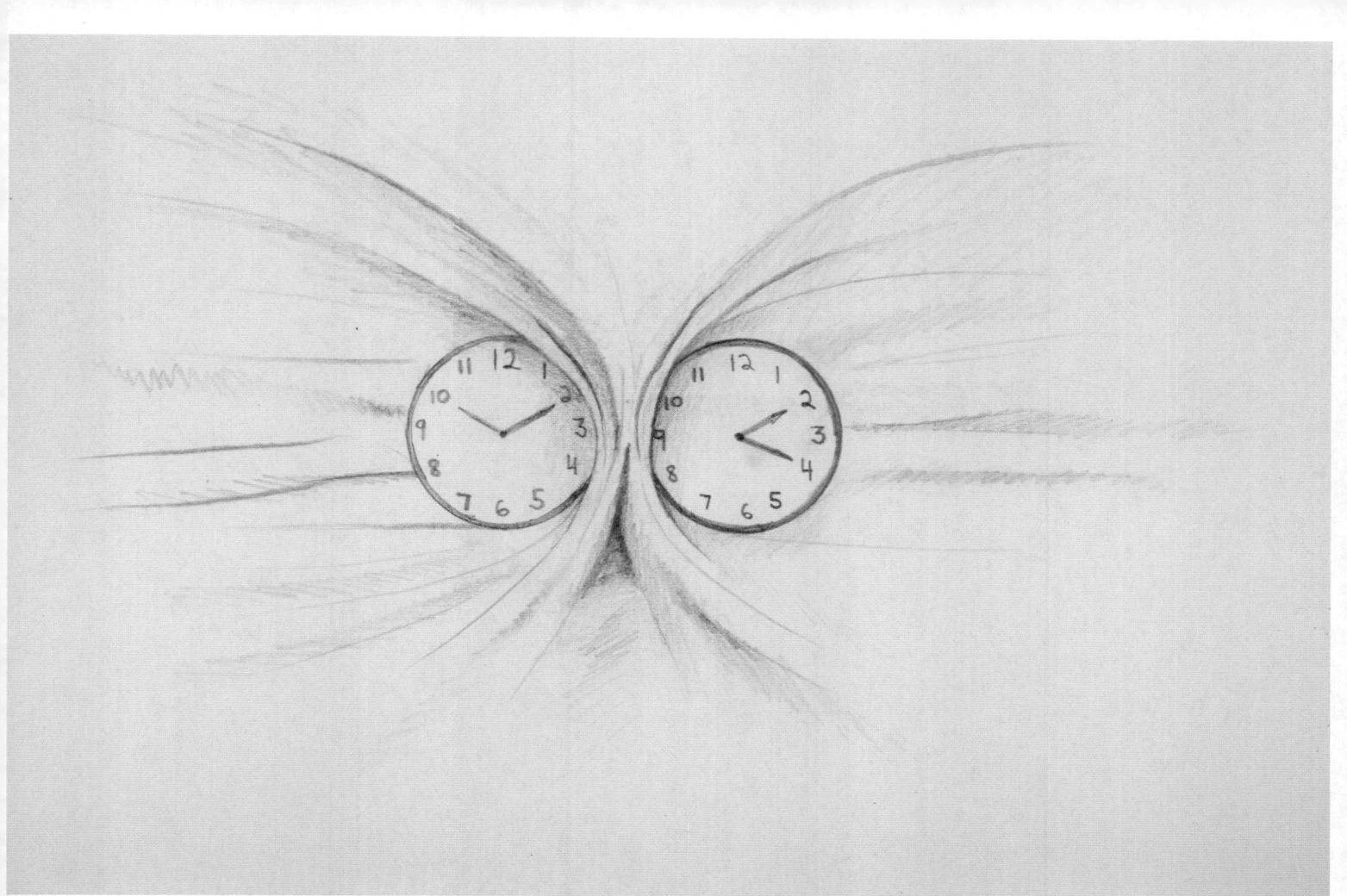

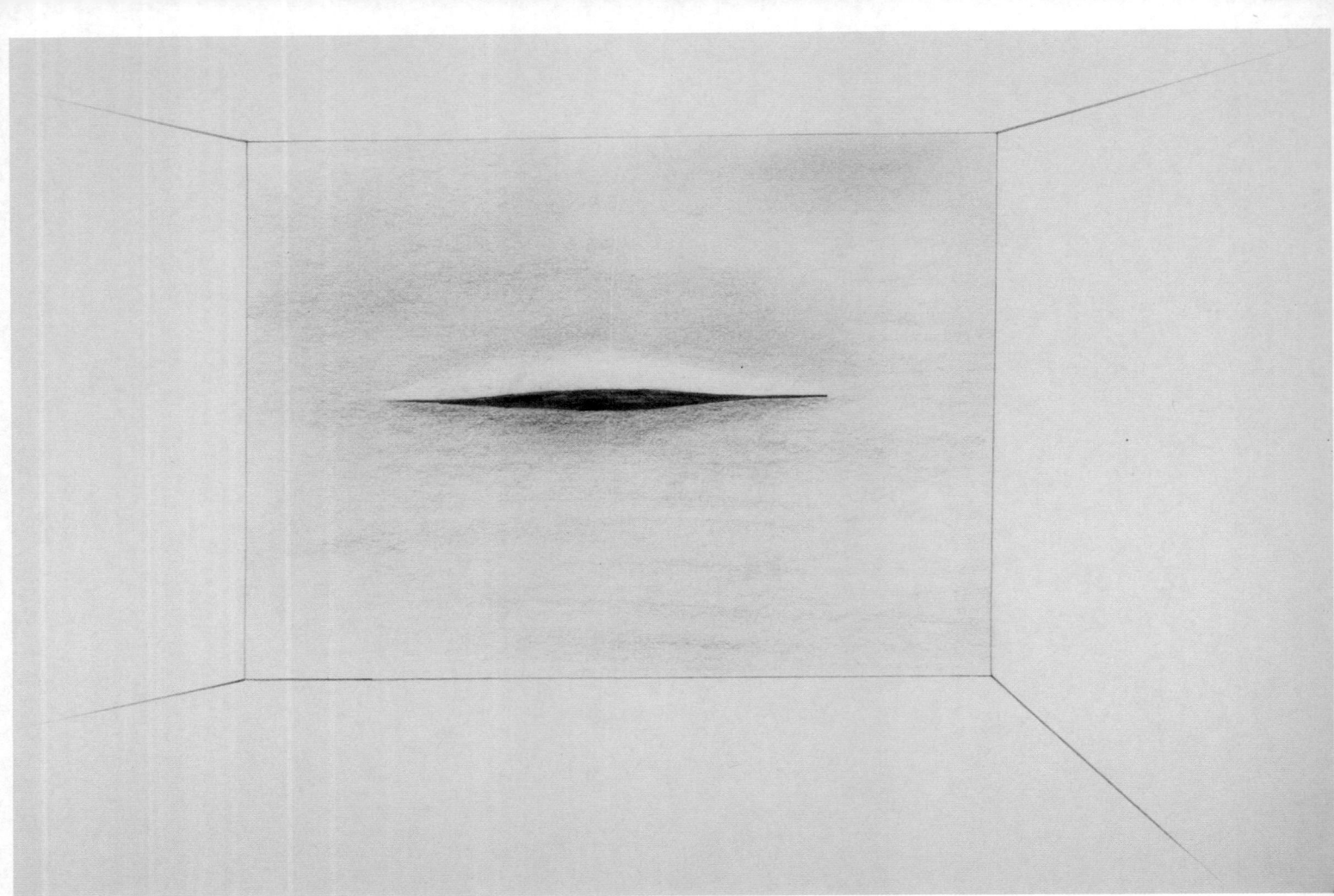

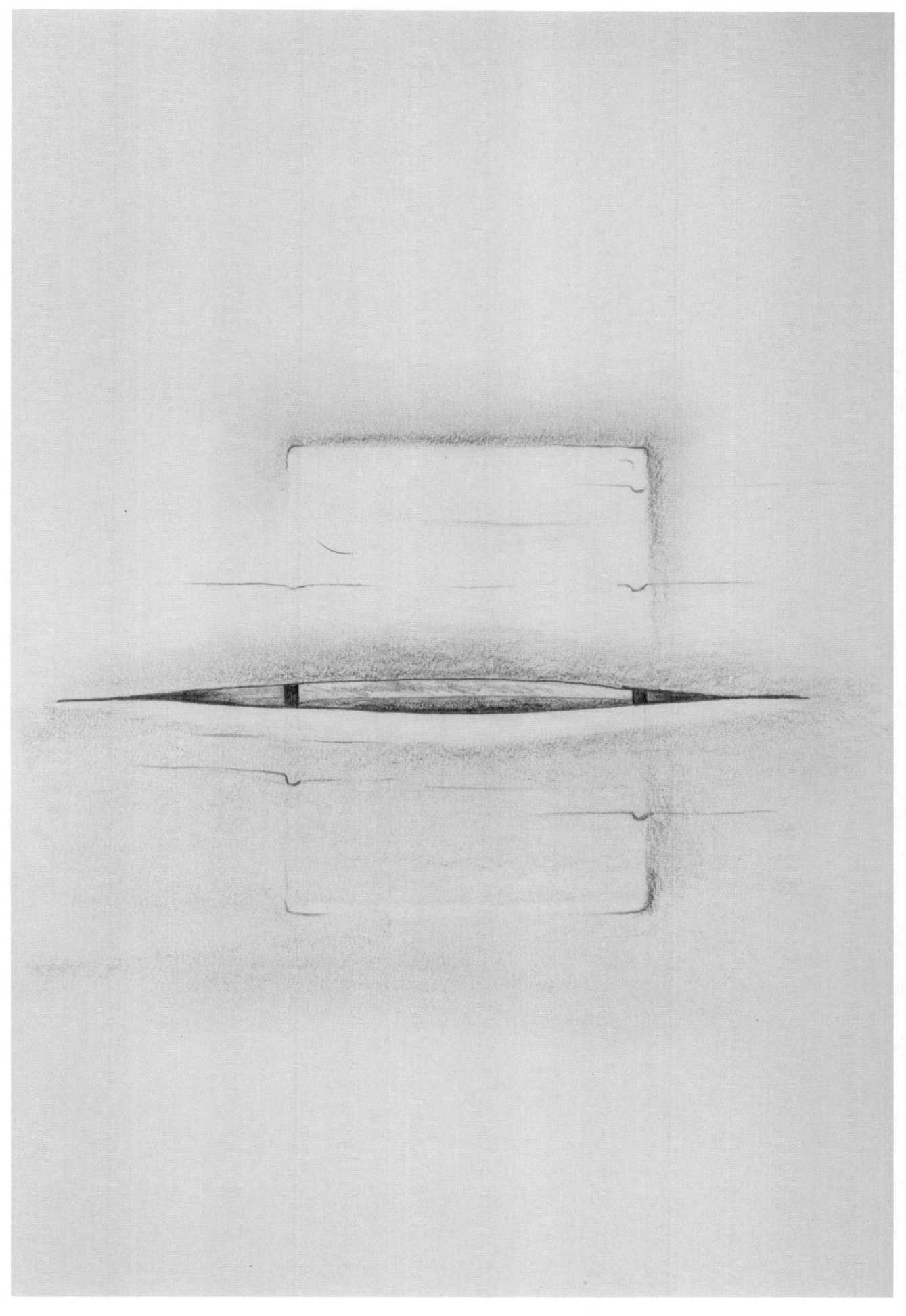

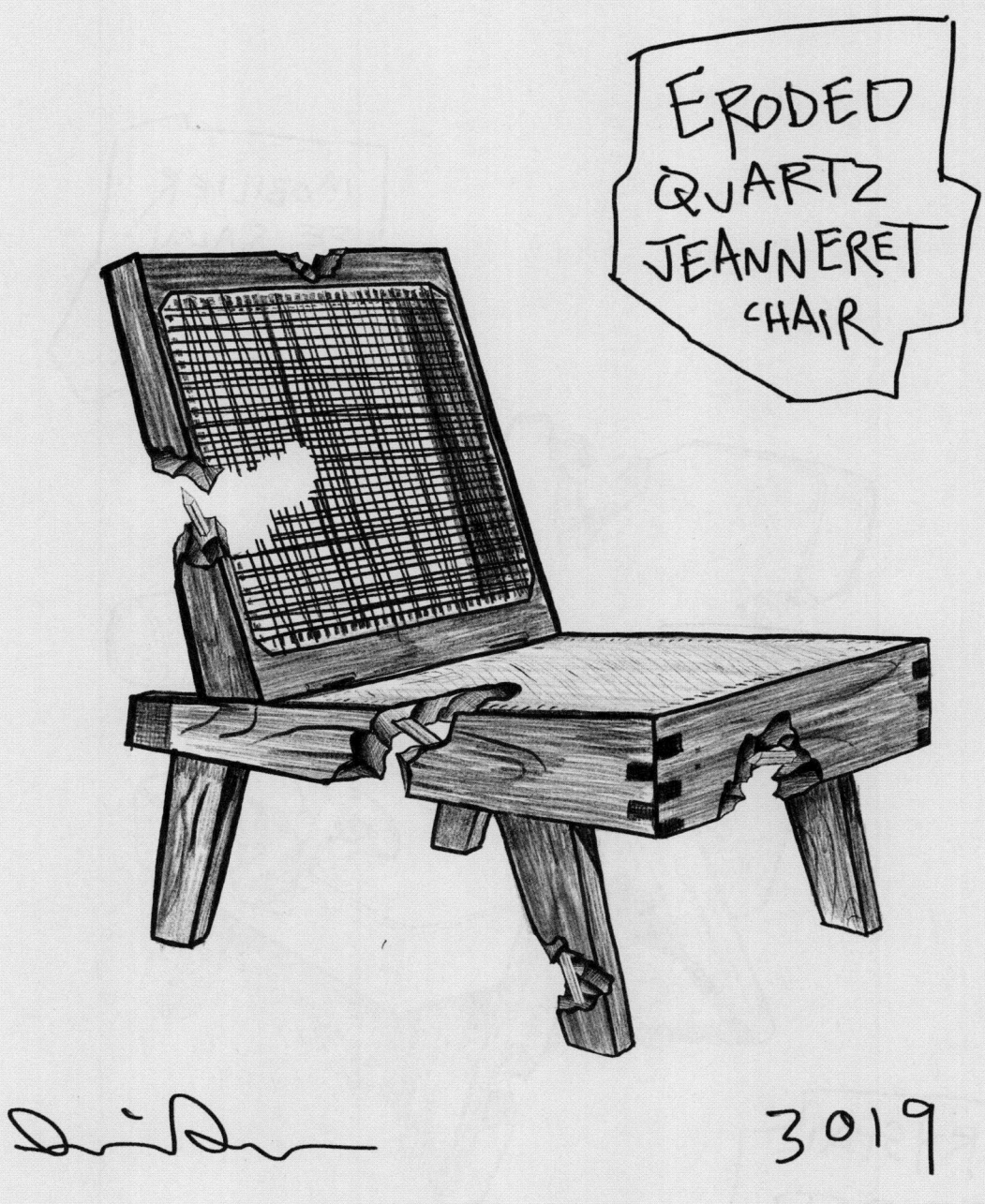

ERODED QUARTZ JEANNERET CHAIR

3019

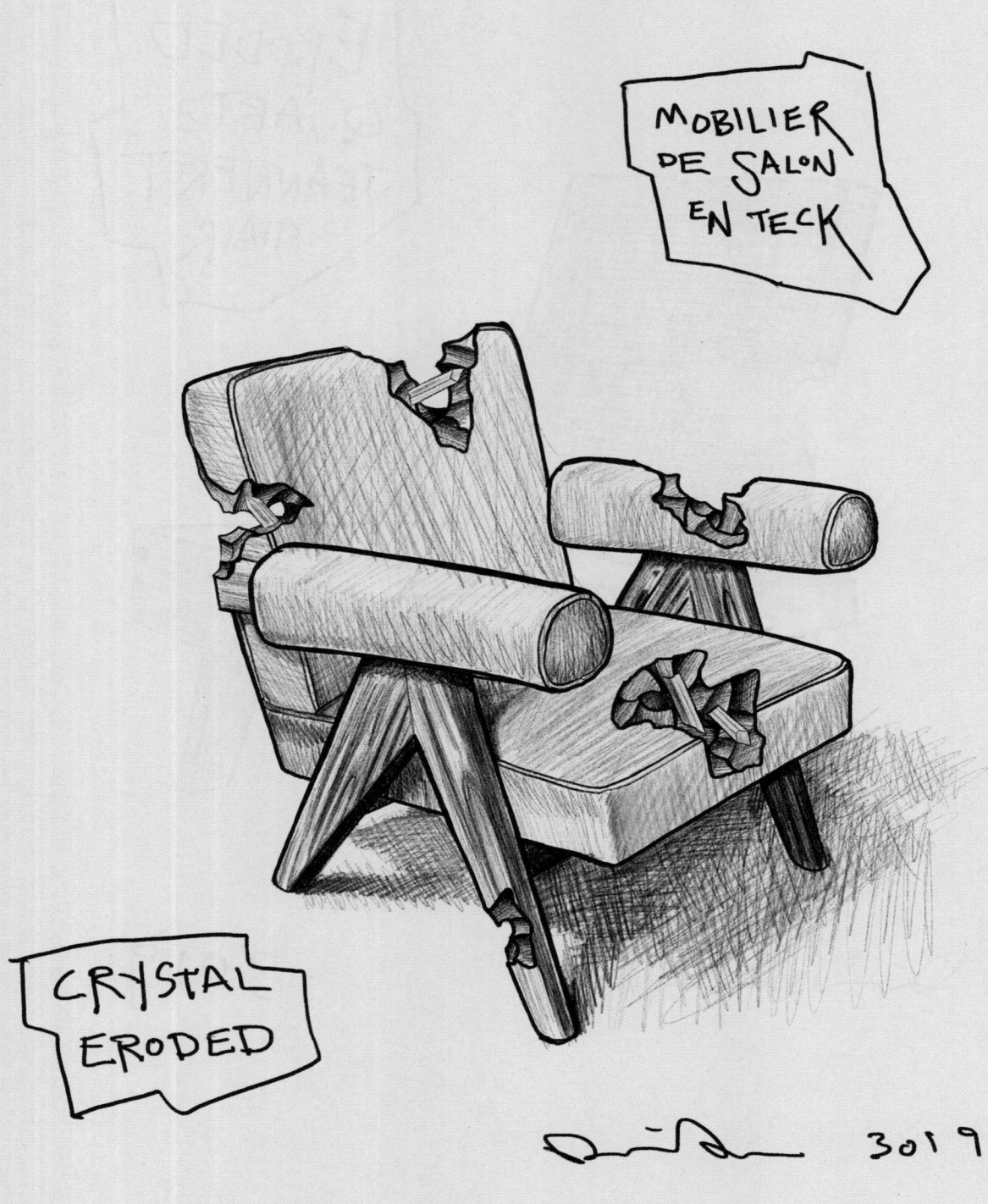

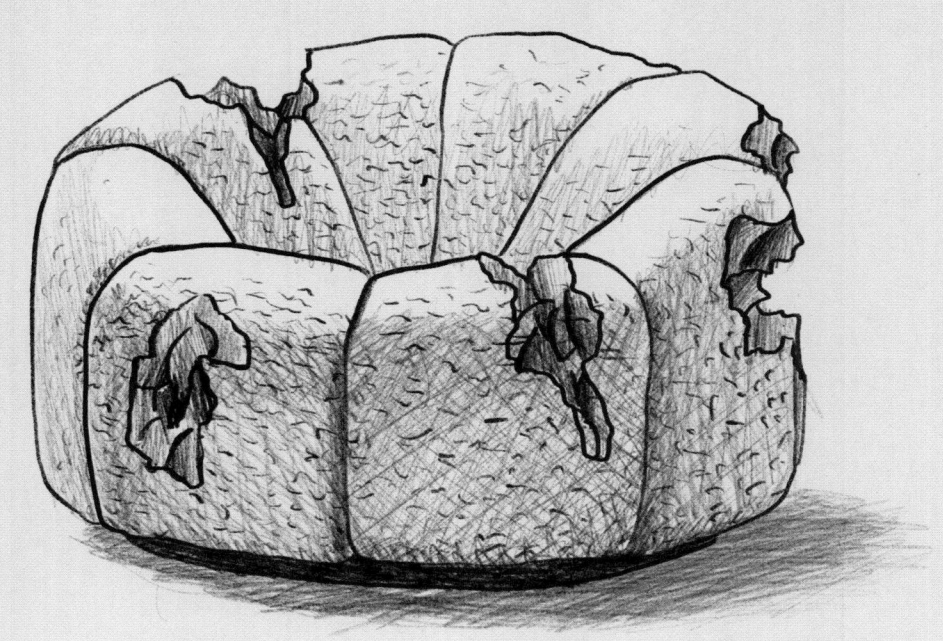

ERODED PIERRE PAULIN
ELYSÉE CHAIR

2009

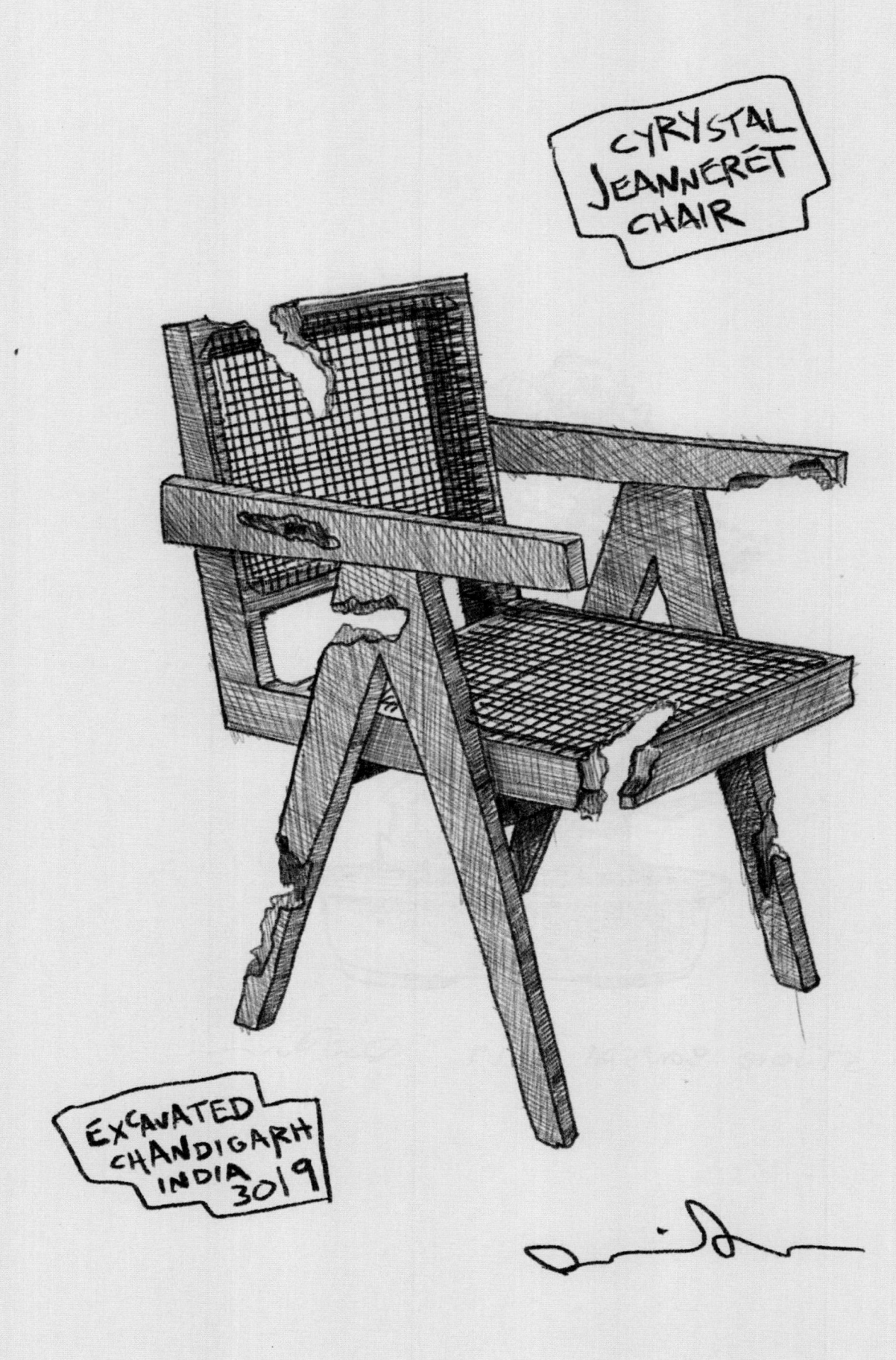

CYRYSTAL
JEANNCRÉT
CHAIR

EXCAVATED
CHANDIGARH
INDIA
3019

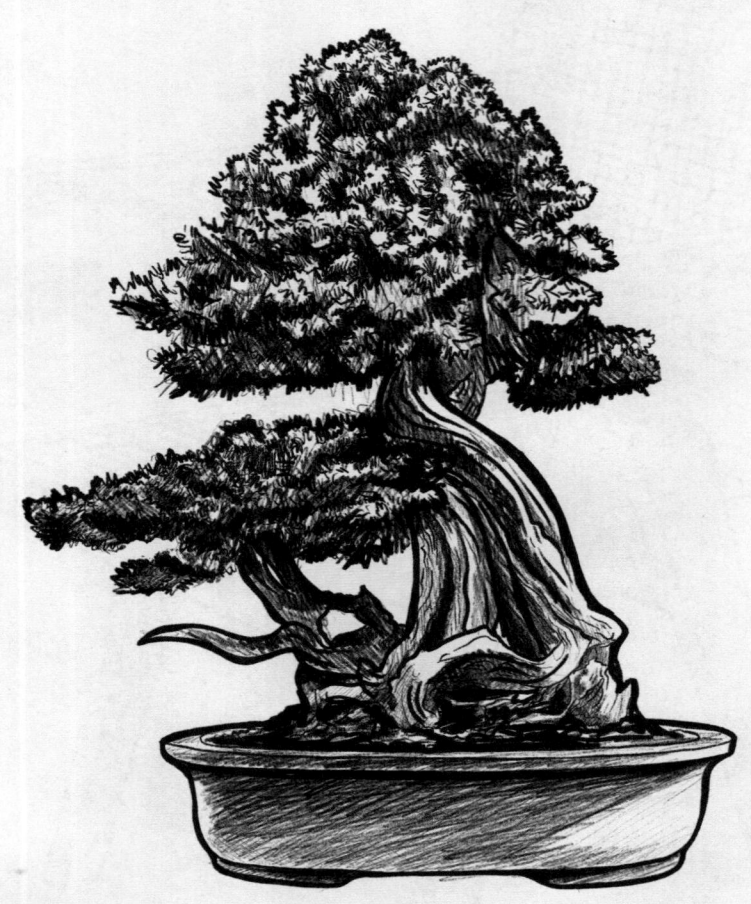

STUDIO BONSAI 3019

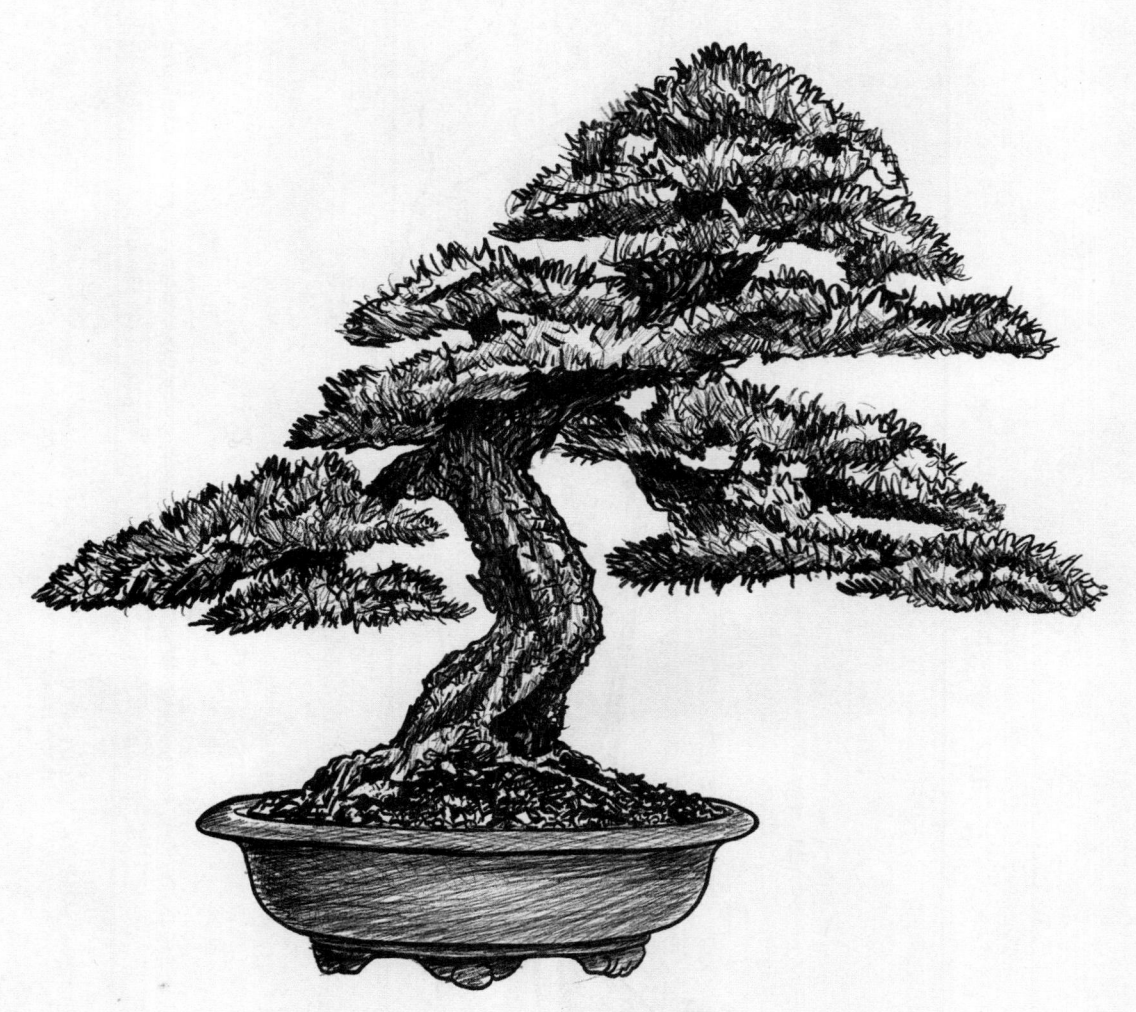

STUDIO BONSAI 3059

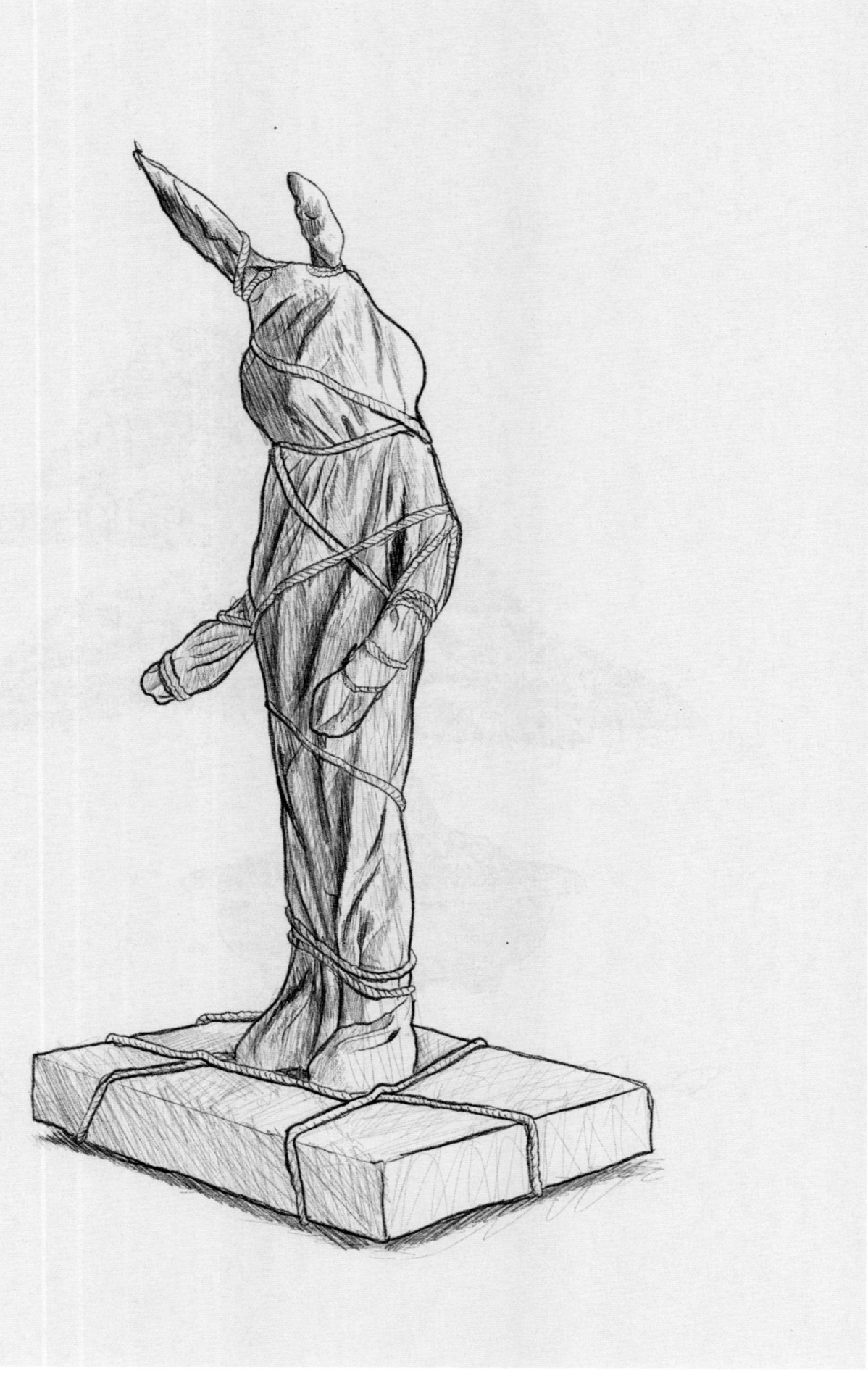

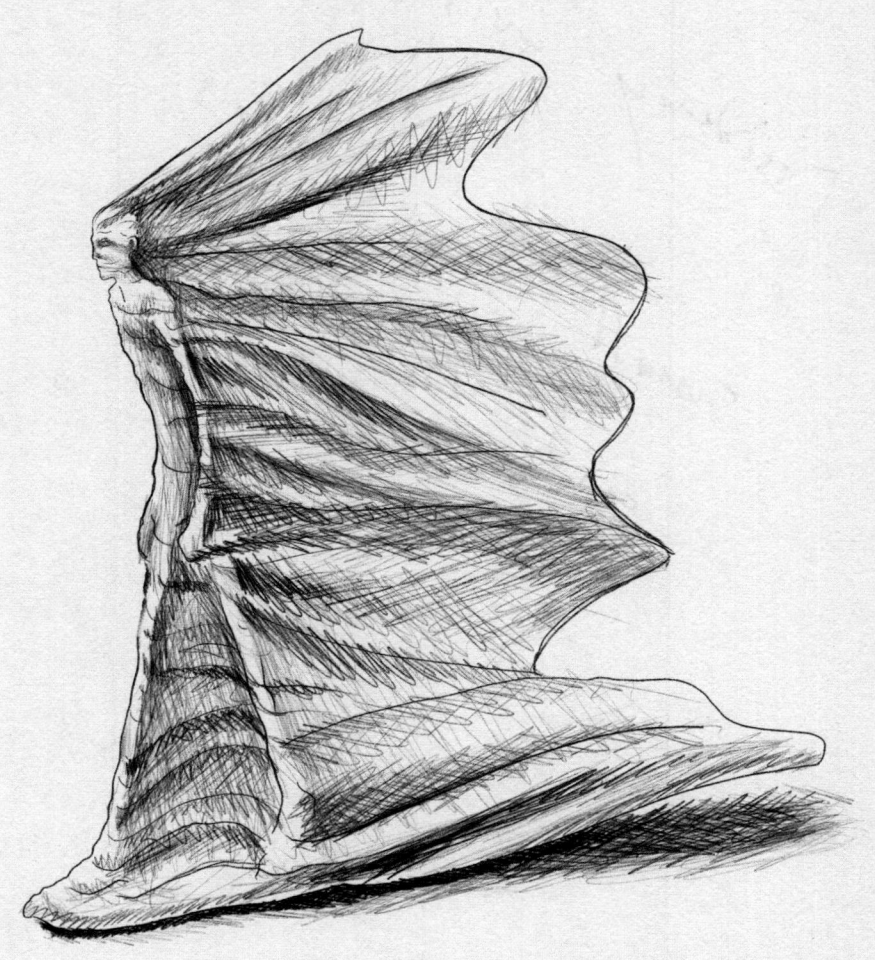

HIDING
GIACOMETTI

2018

- ACROBRANCH

    - CREATE AN AN EXPERIENCE
    OF TRAVERSING THE MUSEUM
    COLLECTION THROUGH AN
    ACROBRANCH OBSTACLE
    COURSE, WITH LADDERS
    AND ZIP LINES.

    - THE OBJECTS IN THE
    MUSEUM WOULD BE
    REPLICATED IN STONE
    AND USED AS HAND HOLDS
    FOR THE SHOW.

    - THE STRAPS AND ALL
    HARDWARE WOULD BE
    MADE BY THE STUDIO
    AND BRANDED
                    ARSHAM
                    STUDIO
                    STANDARD
                    ISSUE.

    - VIEWERS WILL ENGAGE
    WITH THE WORK ON A NEW
    LEVEL.

TUESDAY

—ADIDAS ROLL OUT PLAN
MEETING

—REVIEW MOSCOW
—REVIEW PARIS
—

—DESIGN EXHIBITION
FOR BRAZIL
    ~check in on Tea house

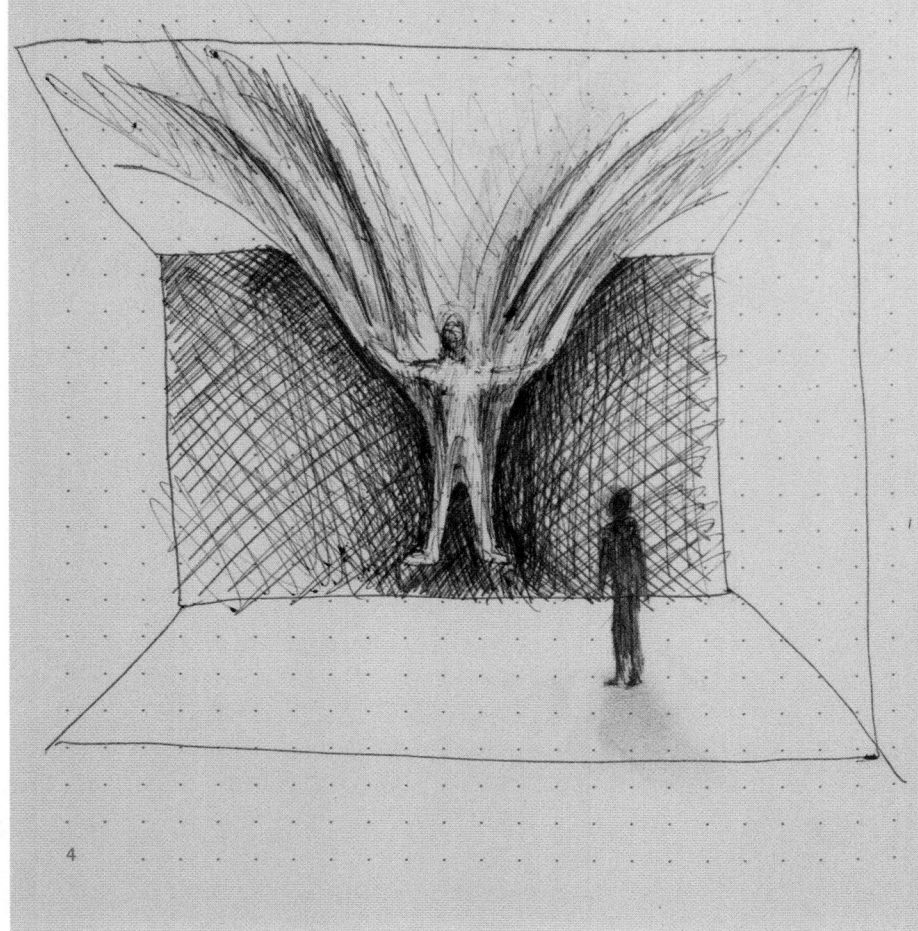

4

ARSHAM
STUDIO
EXCAVATION
CREW

IN-CIRCULATION

ARCHIVED
DO NOT REMOVE
ONCE ARCHIVED

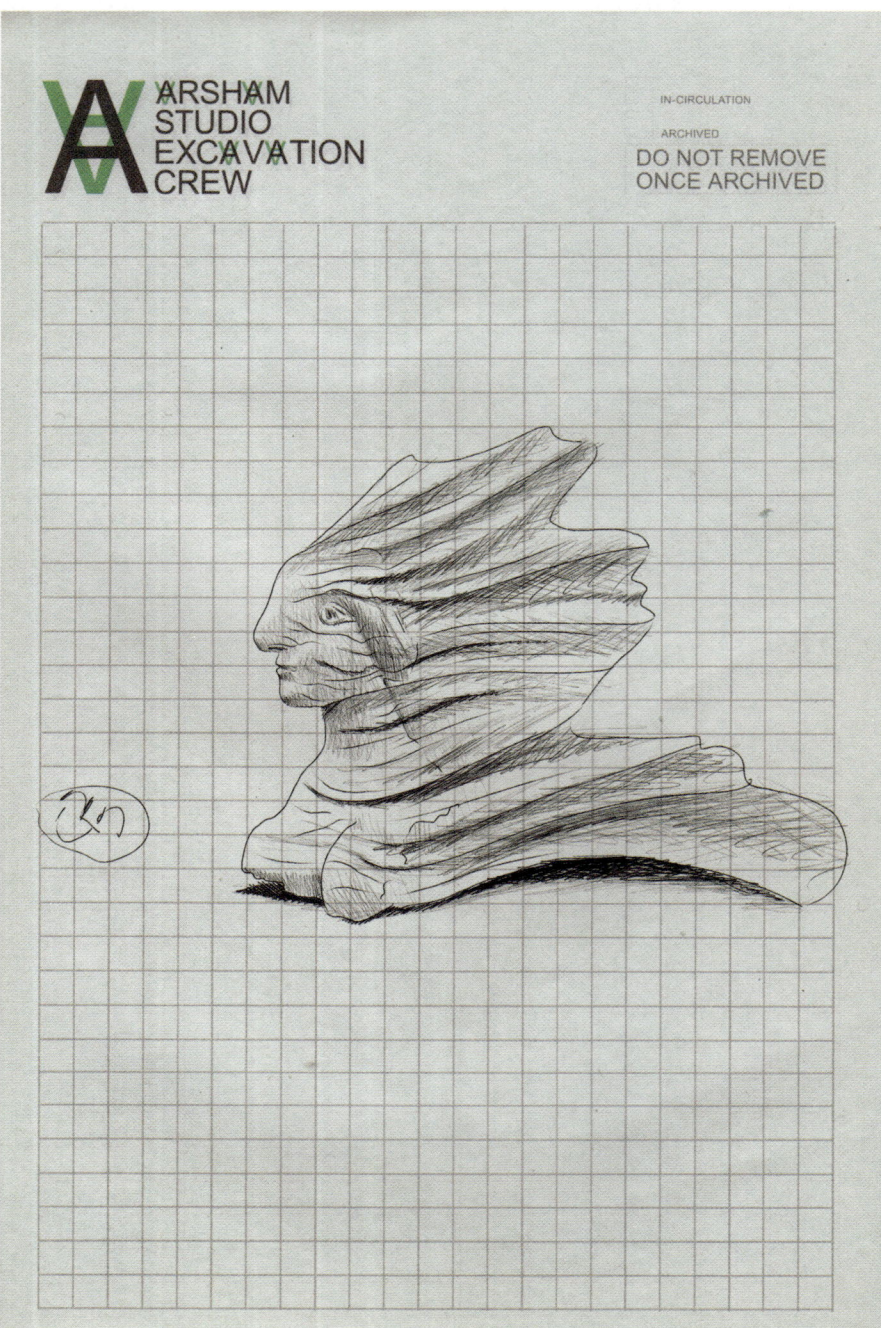

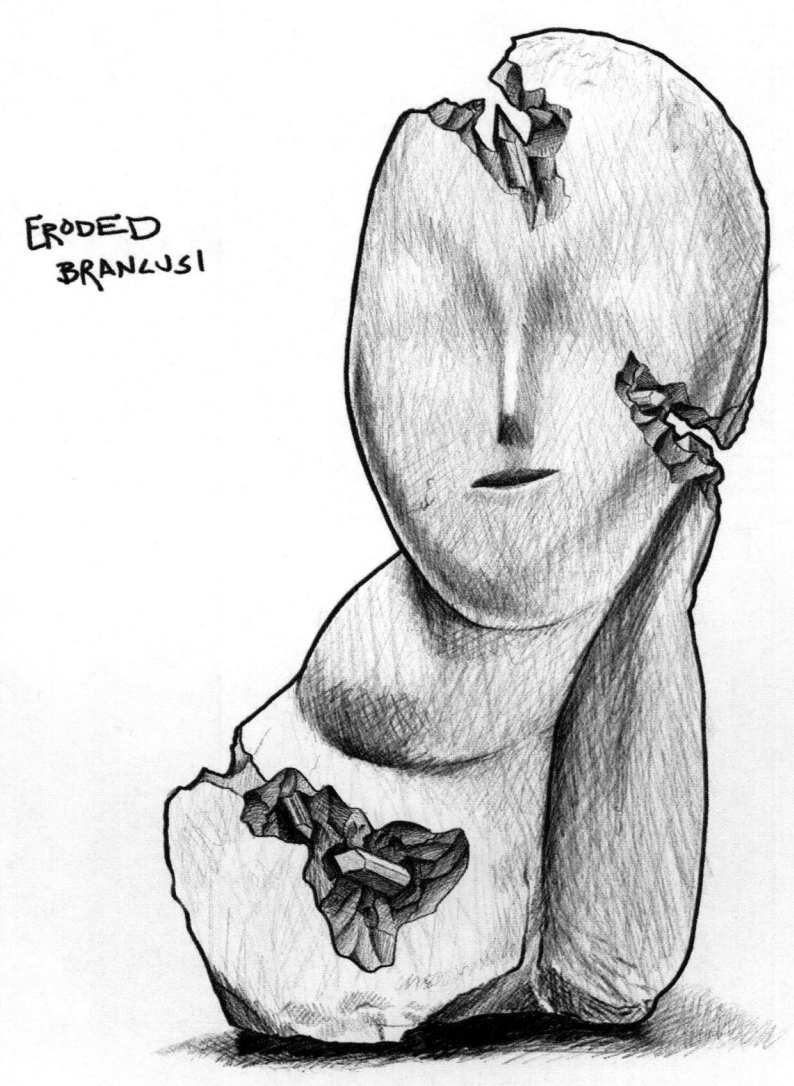

ERODED
BRANCUSI

2014

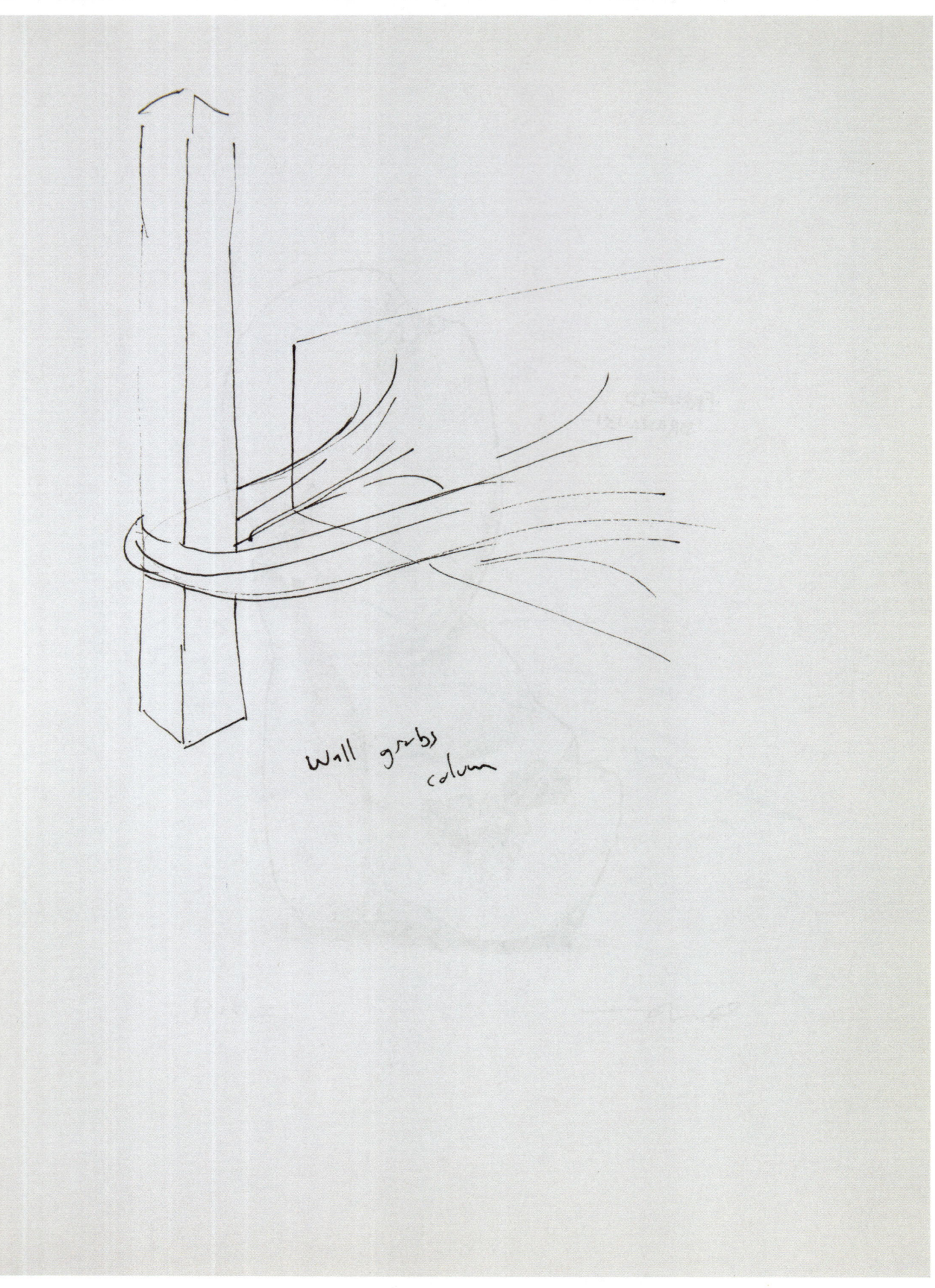

Wall grabs
colum

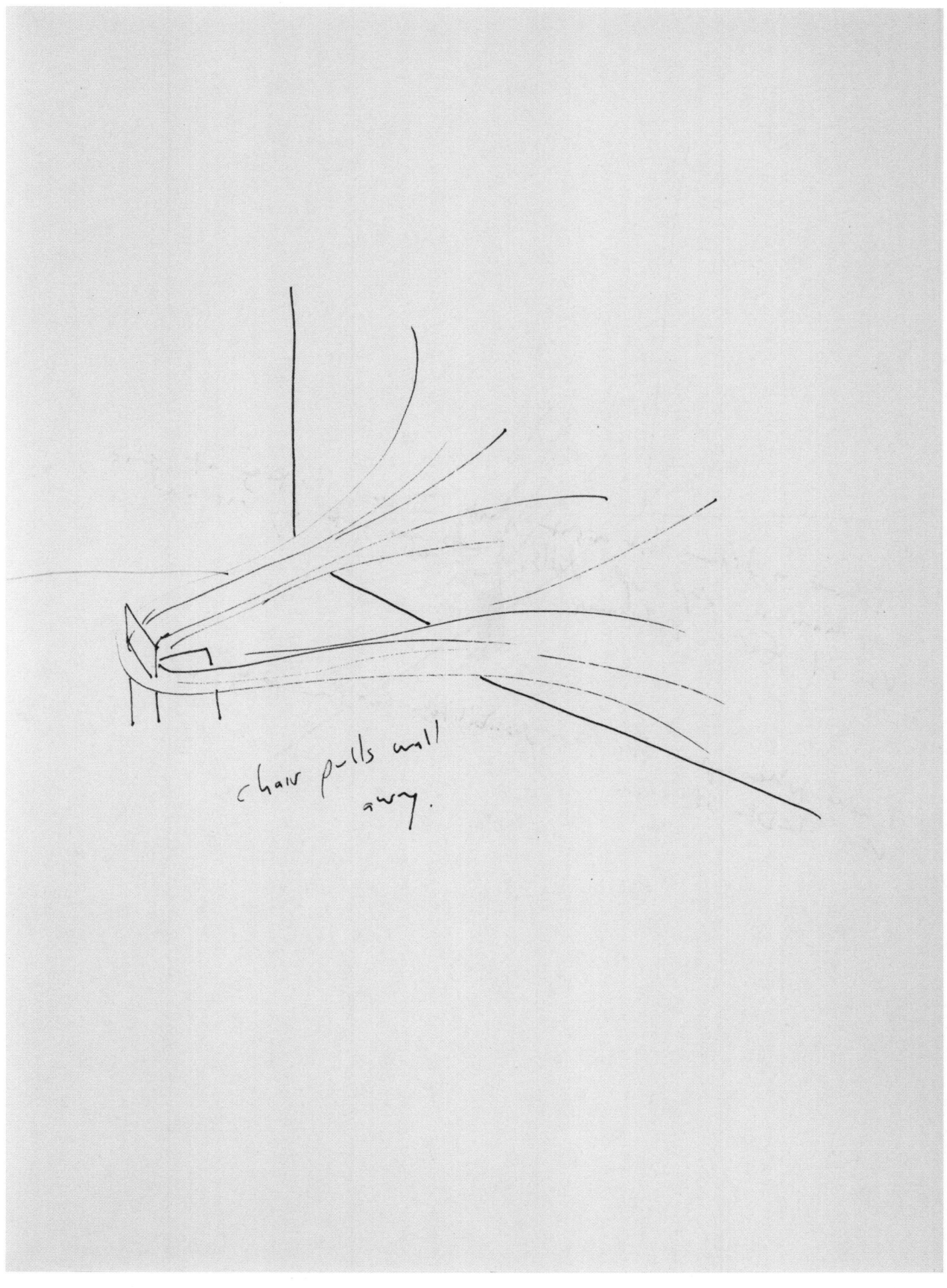

chair pulls wall
away.

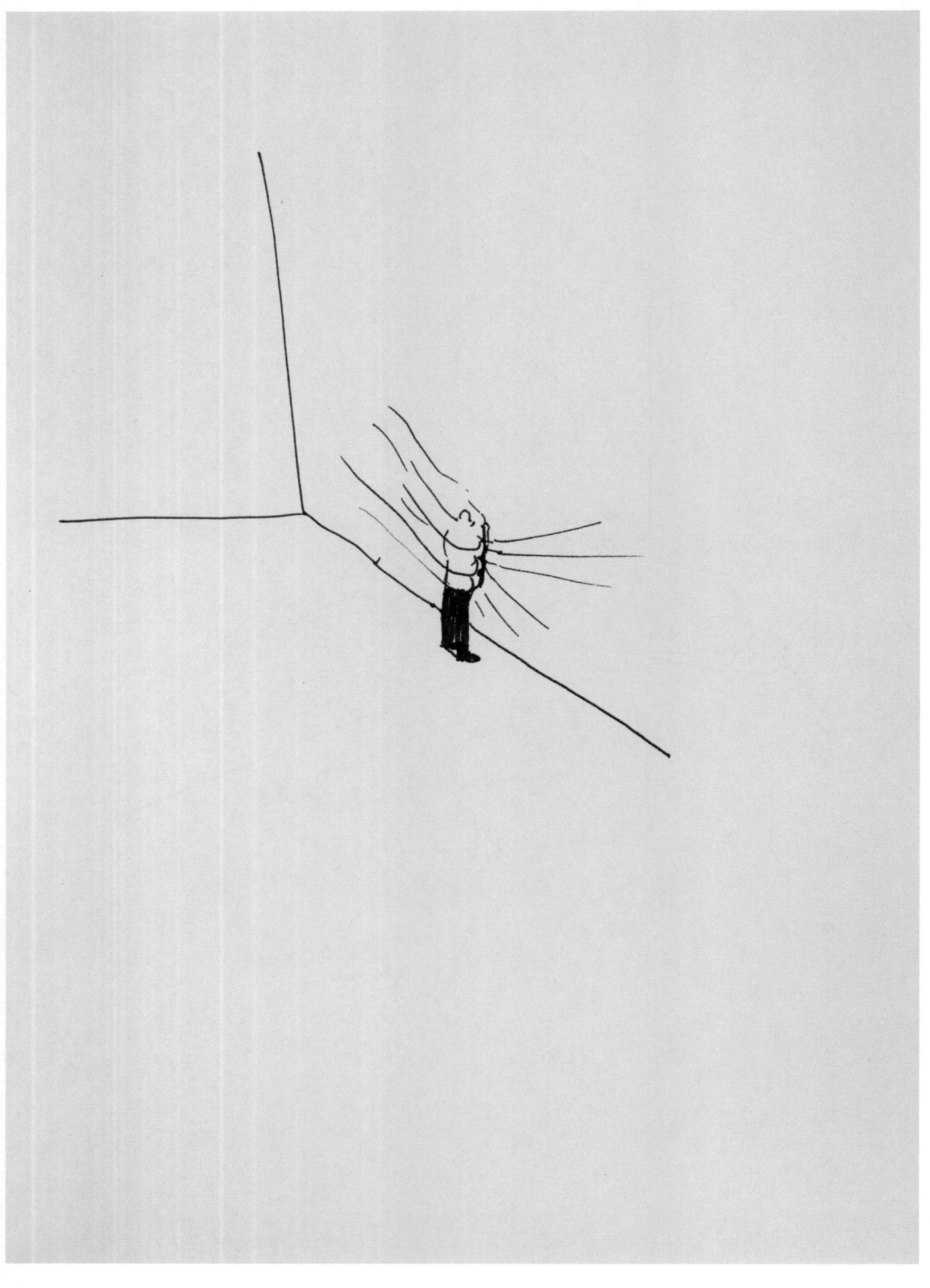

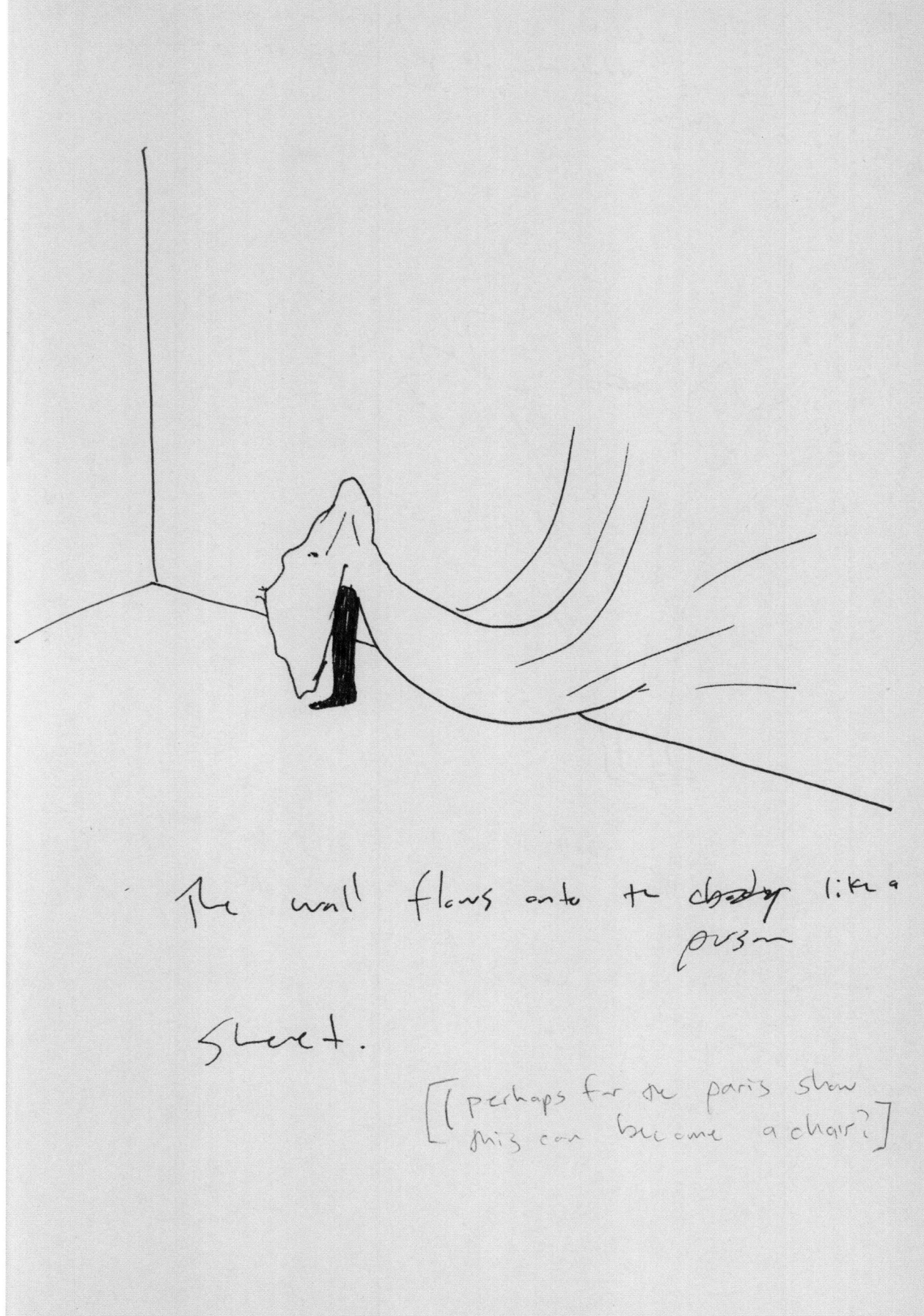

The wall flows onto the *chair* like a
prism
sheet.

[[perhaps for the paris show
this can become a chair?]]

The project at MoDC should be a three night
event that has on performance designe day for dance
students and art students from Cooper Union.

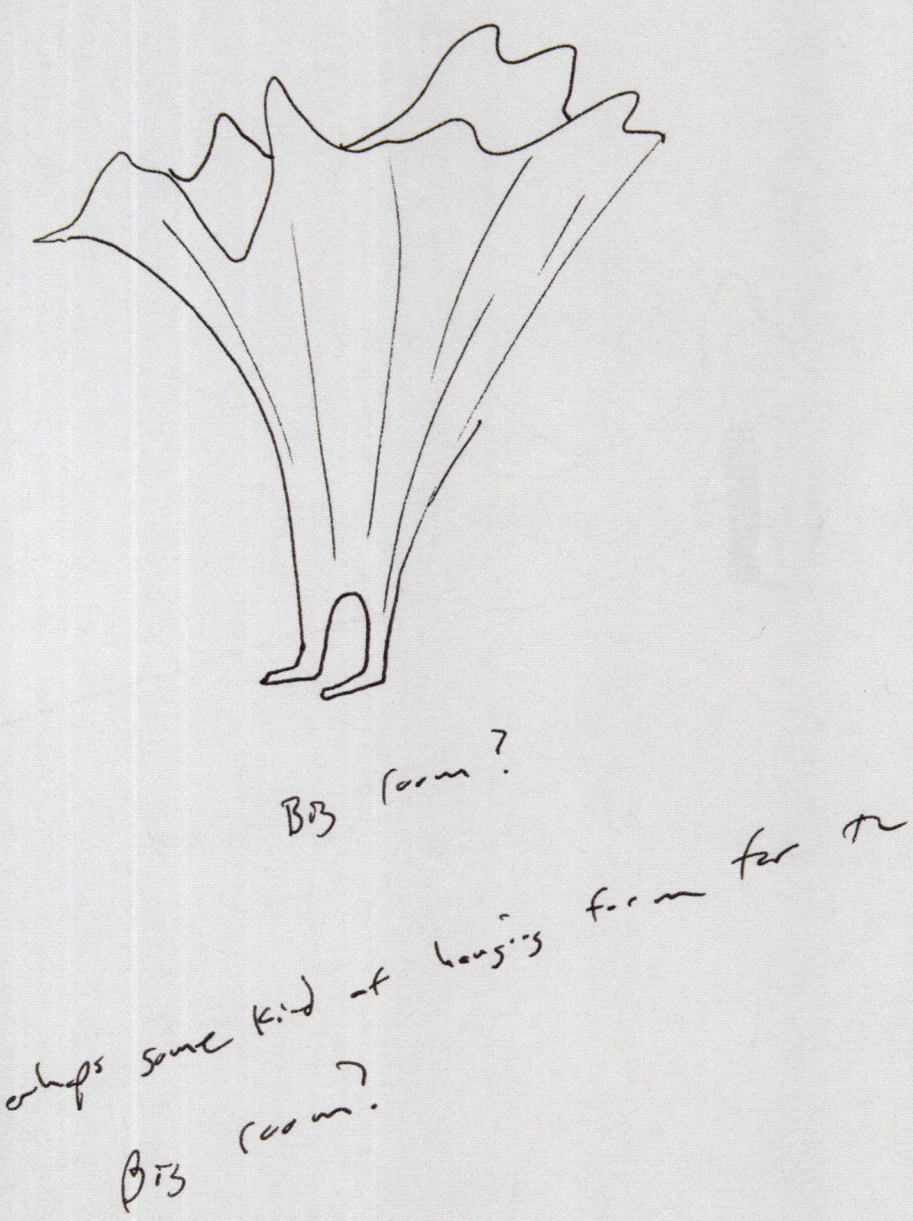

BB room?

perhaps some kind of housing form for the
BB room?

etched walls for Miami.

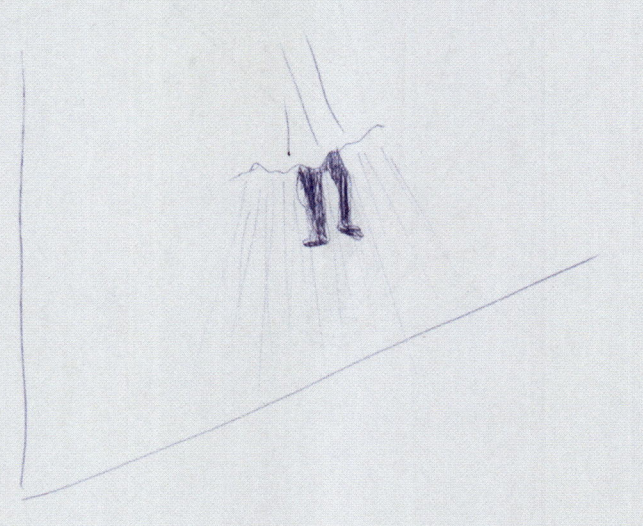

Super bright light emanating
from where the figure is crawling
into the wall
perhaps this is a female? with
a skirt?. the light is so
bright you can't see if
it?

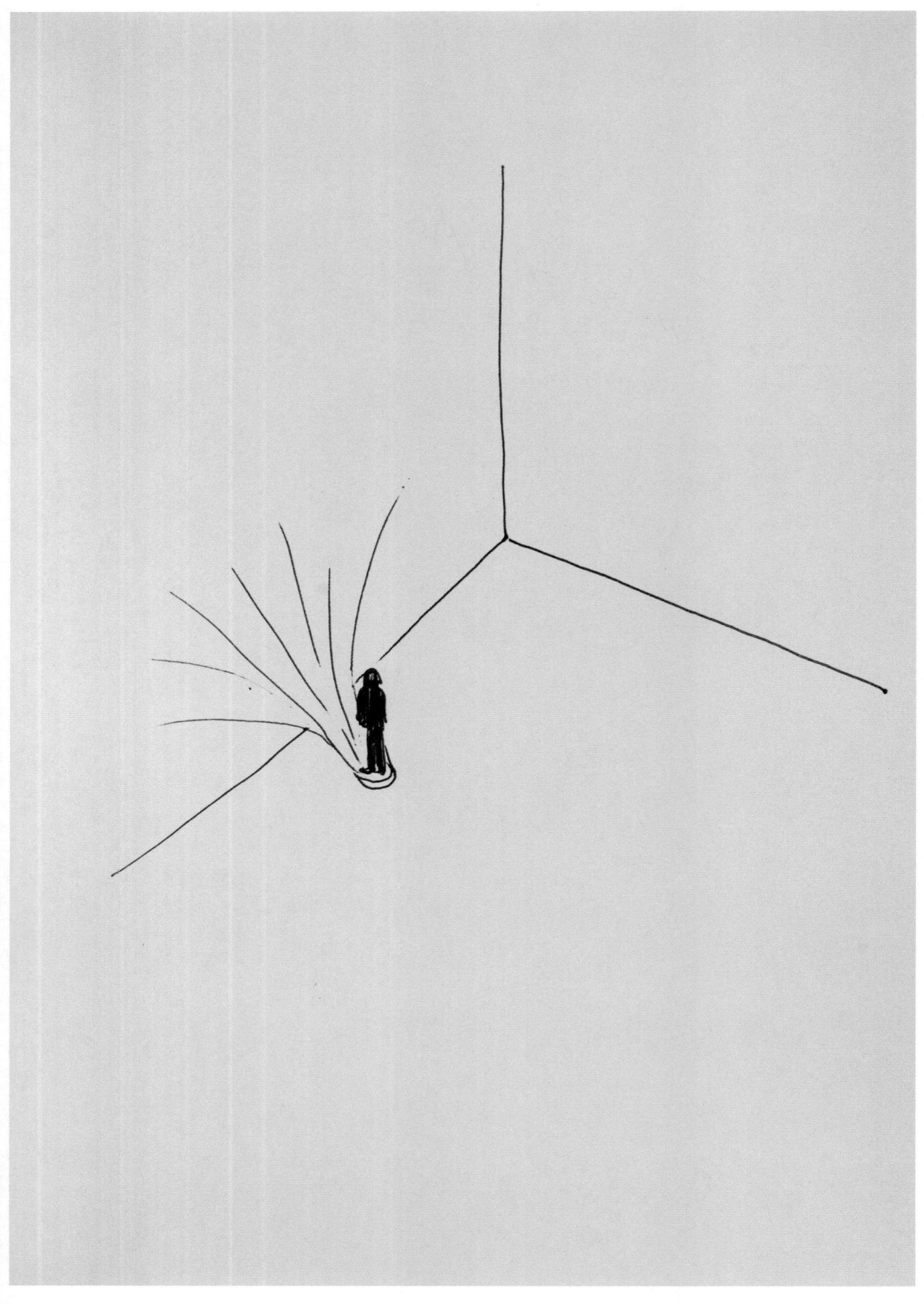

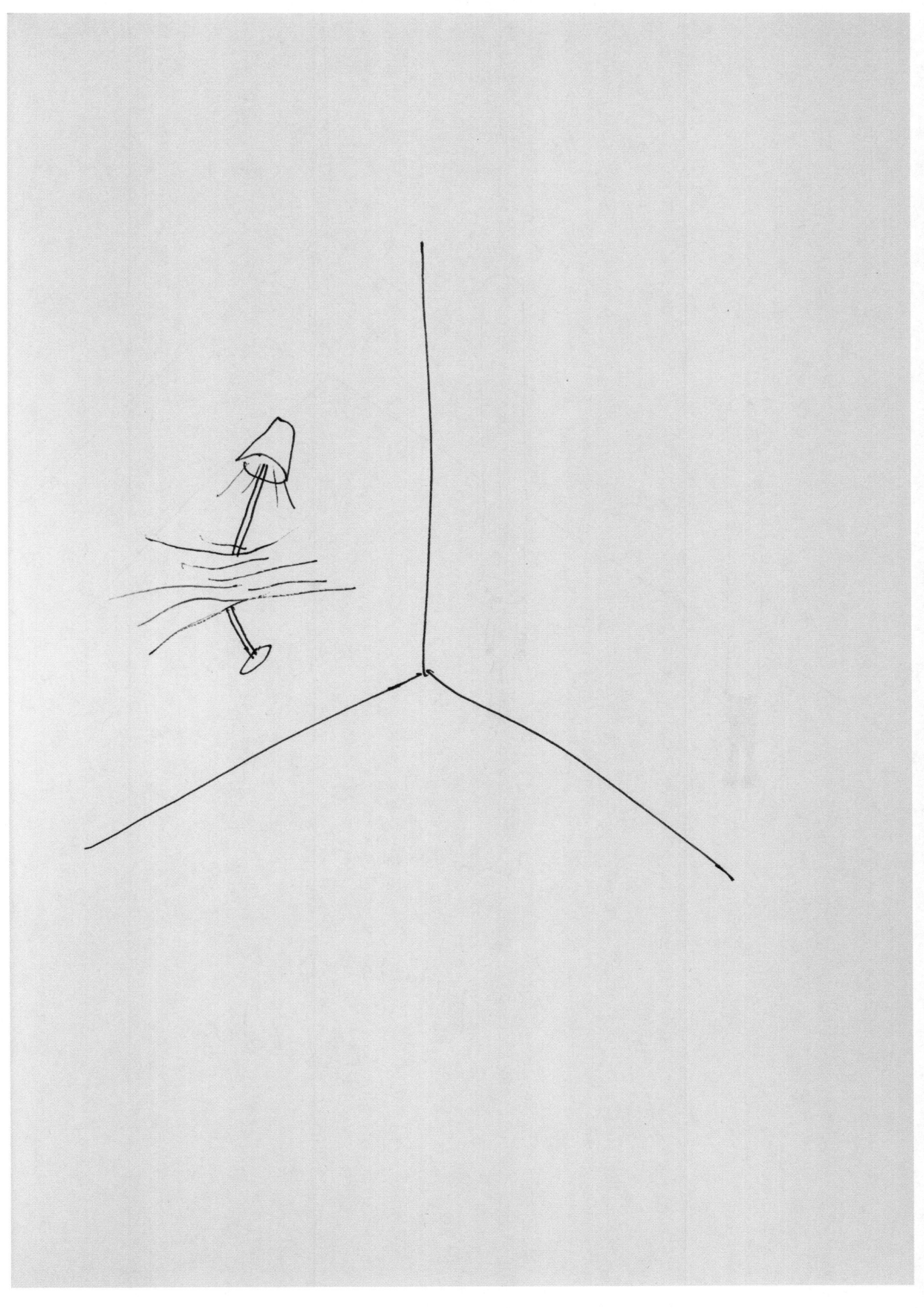

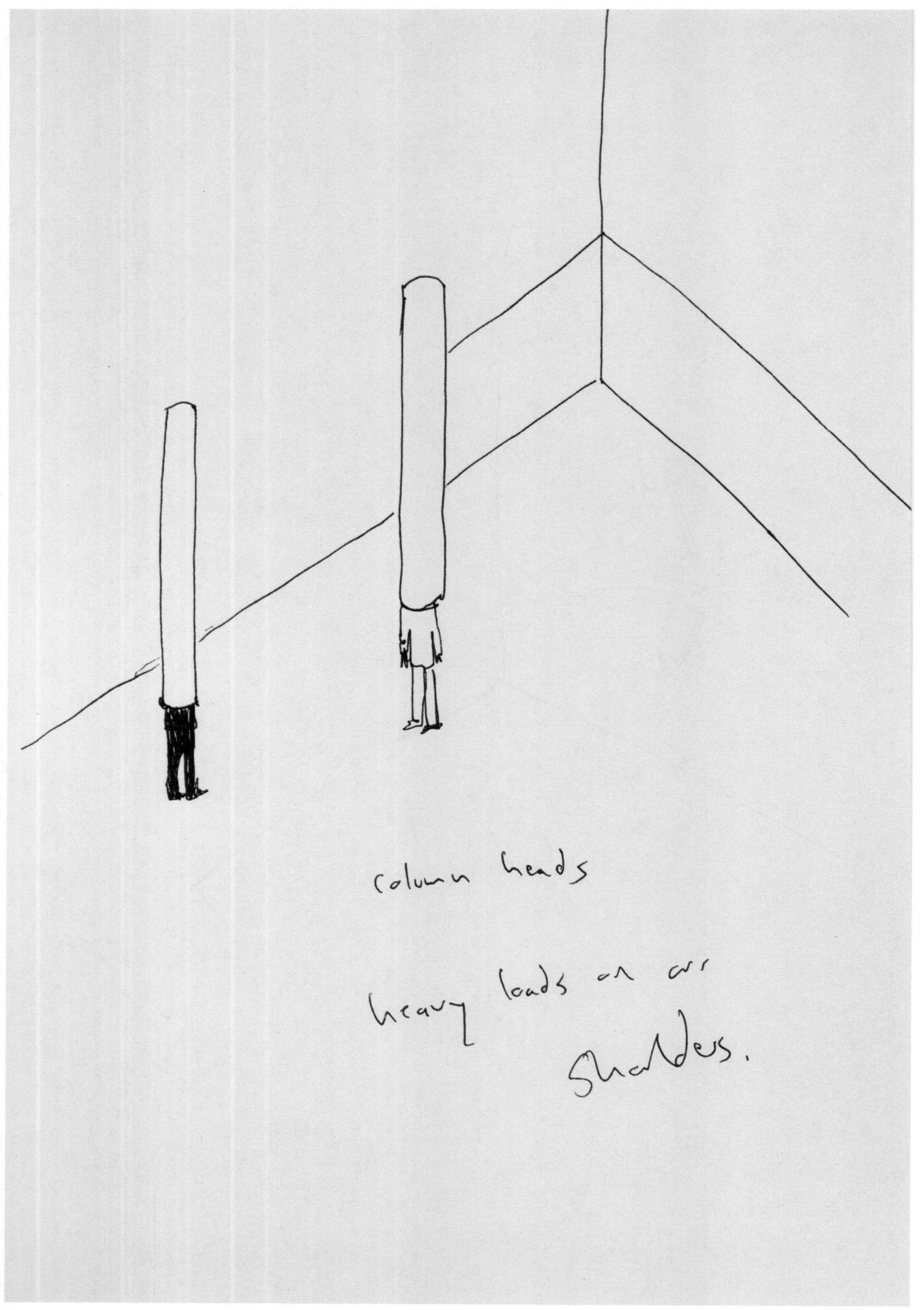

column heads

heavy loads on our

shoulders.

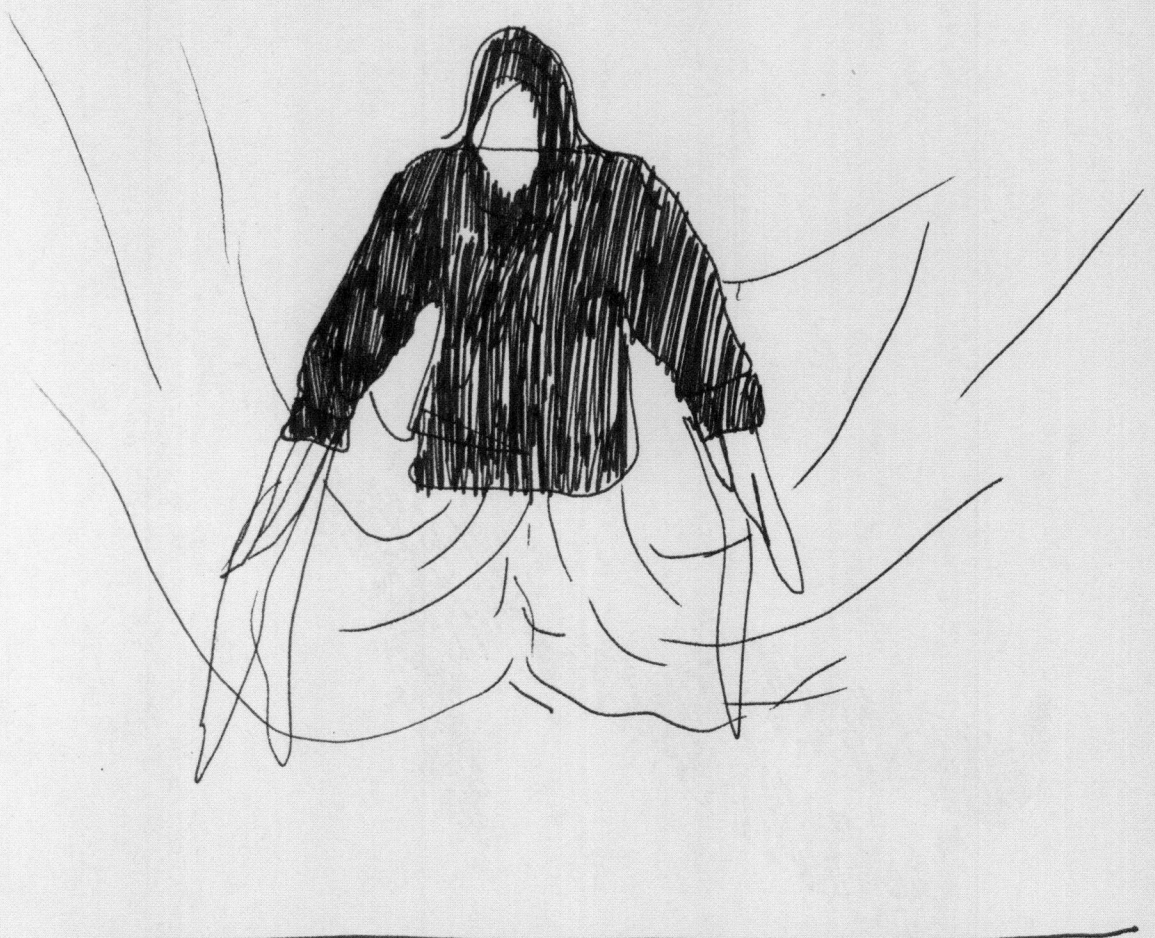

wall forms body over which hoodie
is draped.

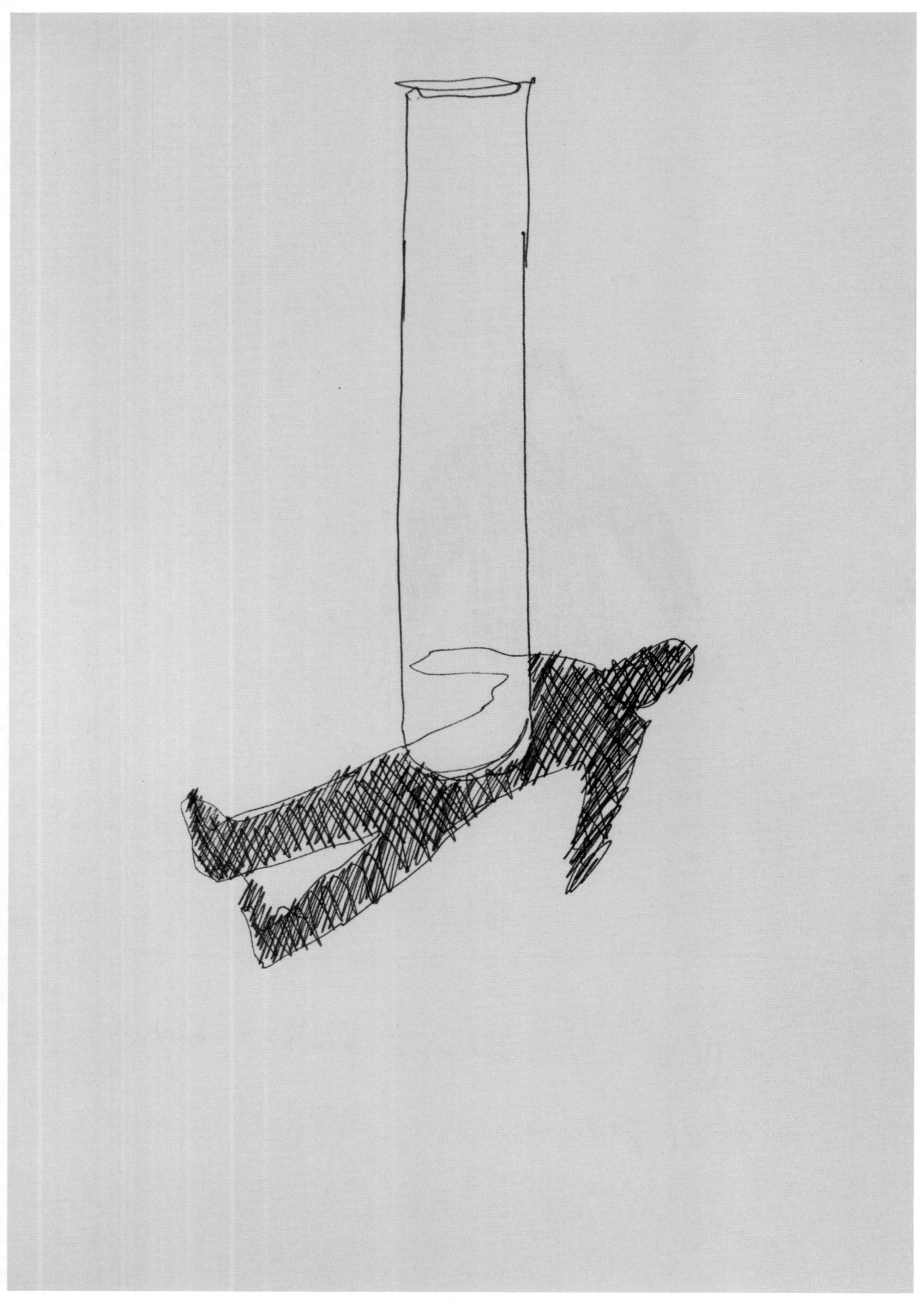

Colum hugger.

This work could have a various height
depending on the space.

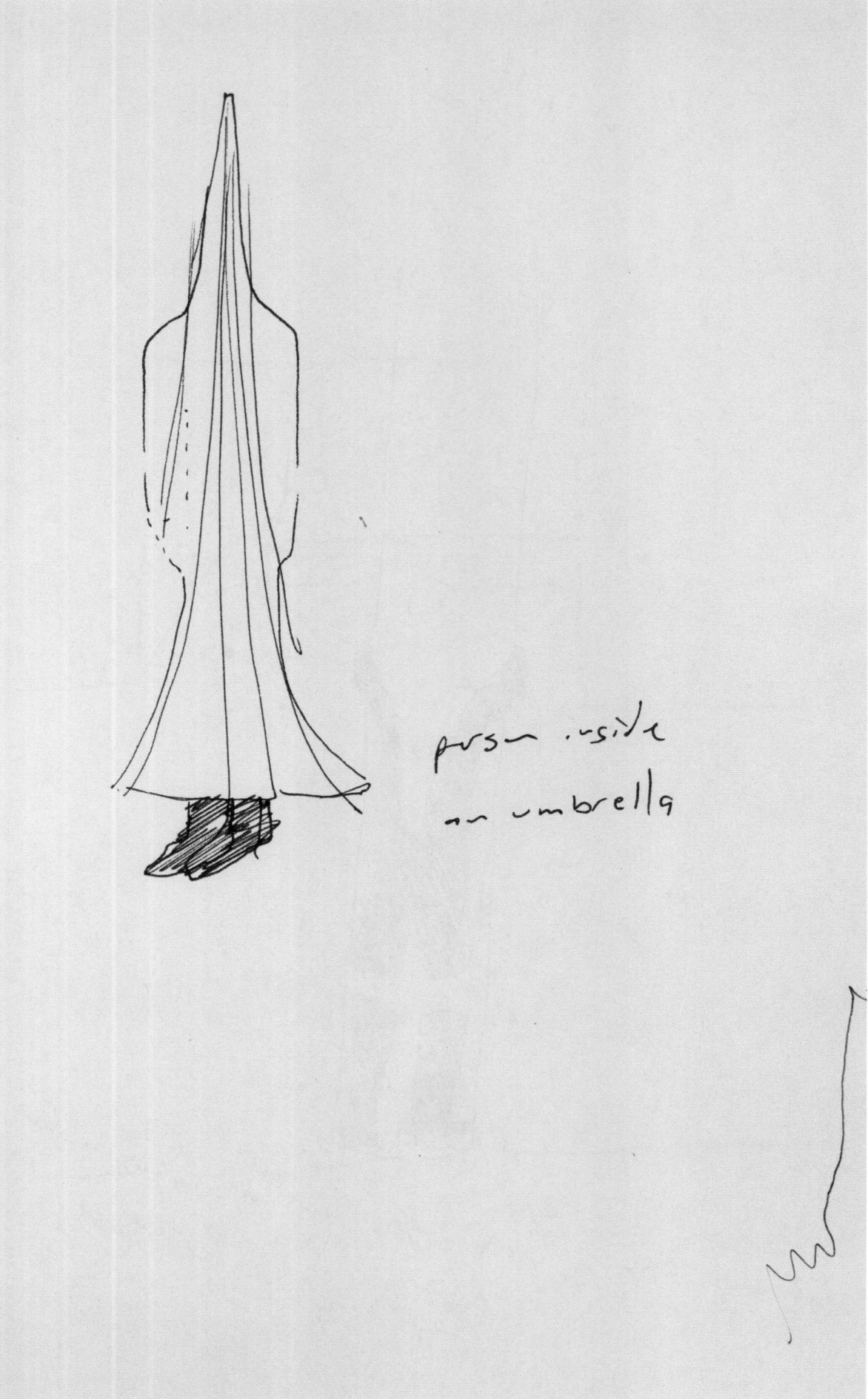

person inside
an umbrella

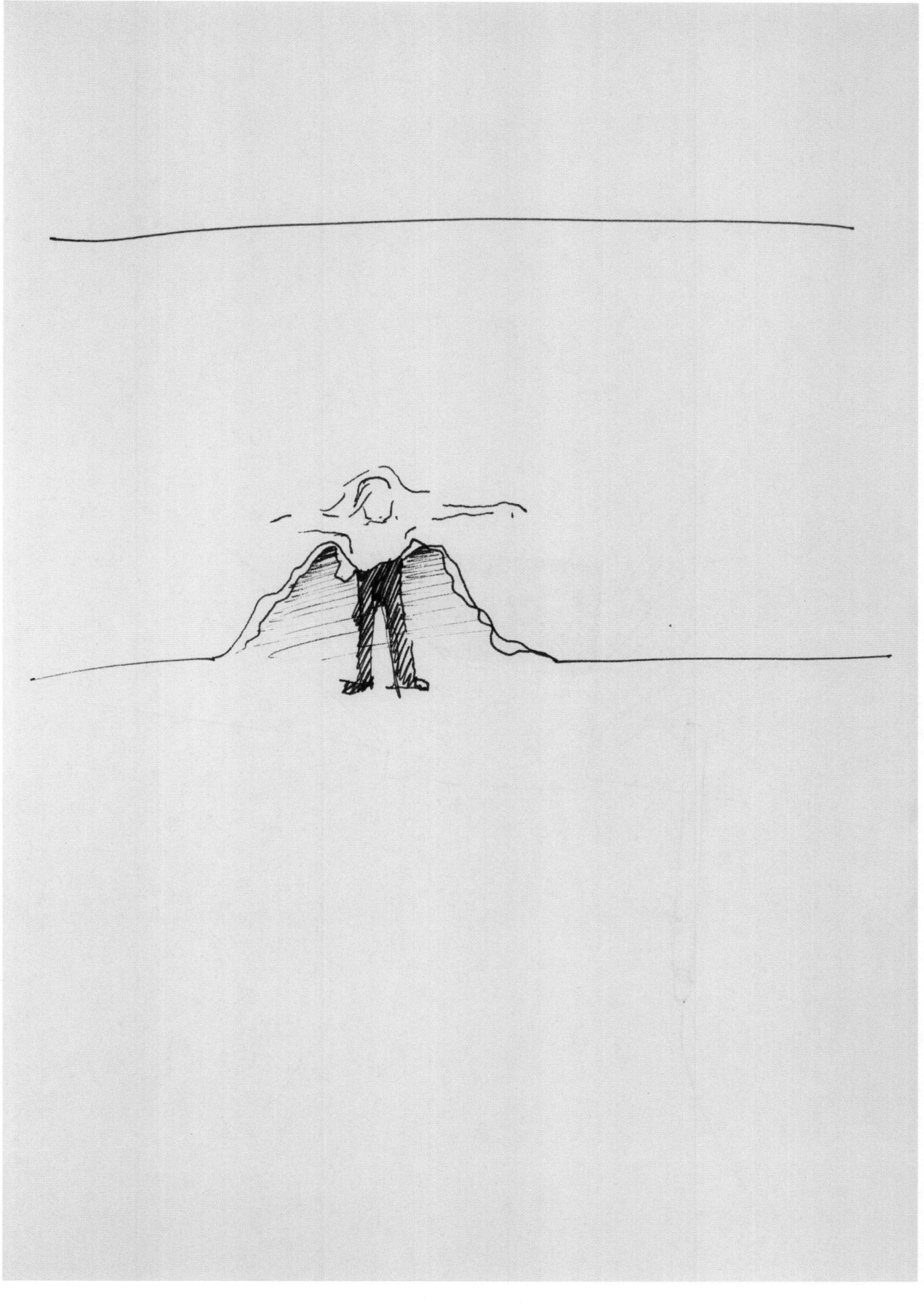

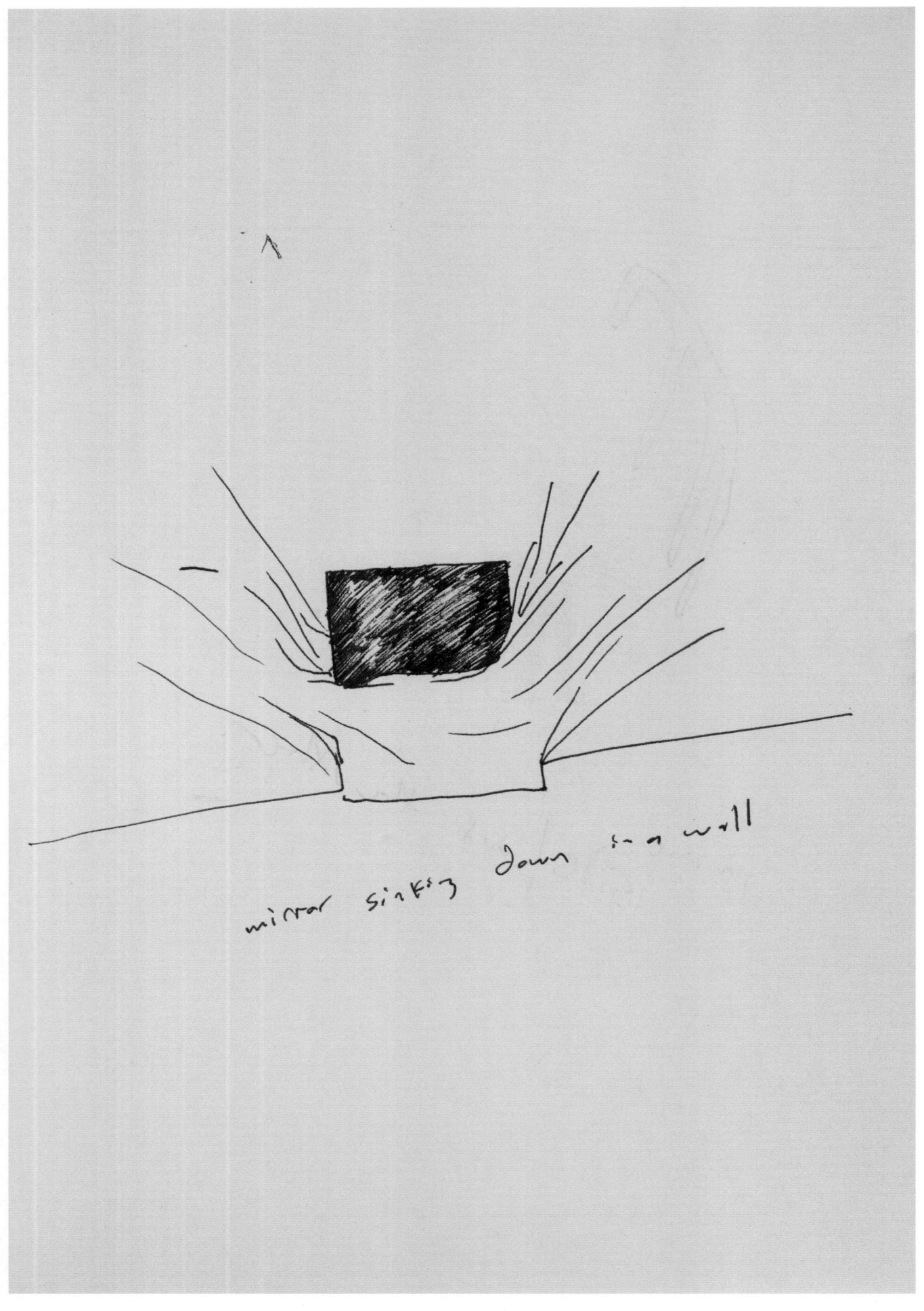

mirror sinking down into wall

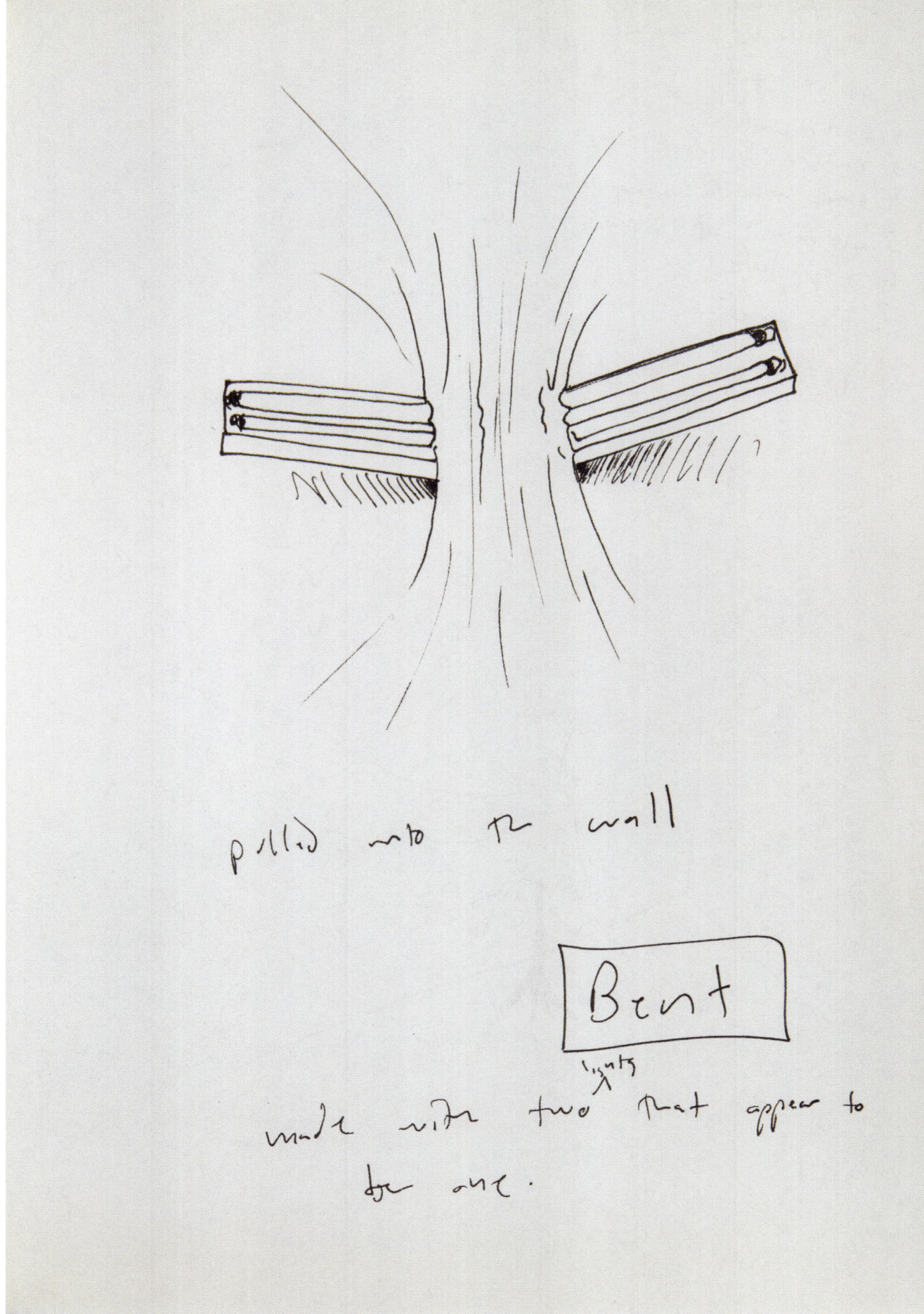

pulled into the wall

Bent

made with two lights that appear to be one.

possible works for mia
(works on my mind)

1. up skirt
2. etched walls
3. burned walls
4. small articles wrapped in the wall
5. elevator call button
6. key hole
7. Big erosion in left hand wall...
8. postage slot..

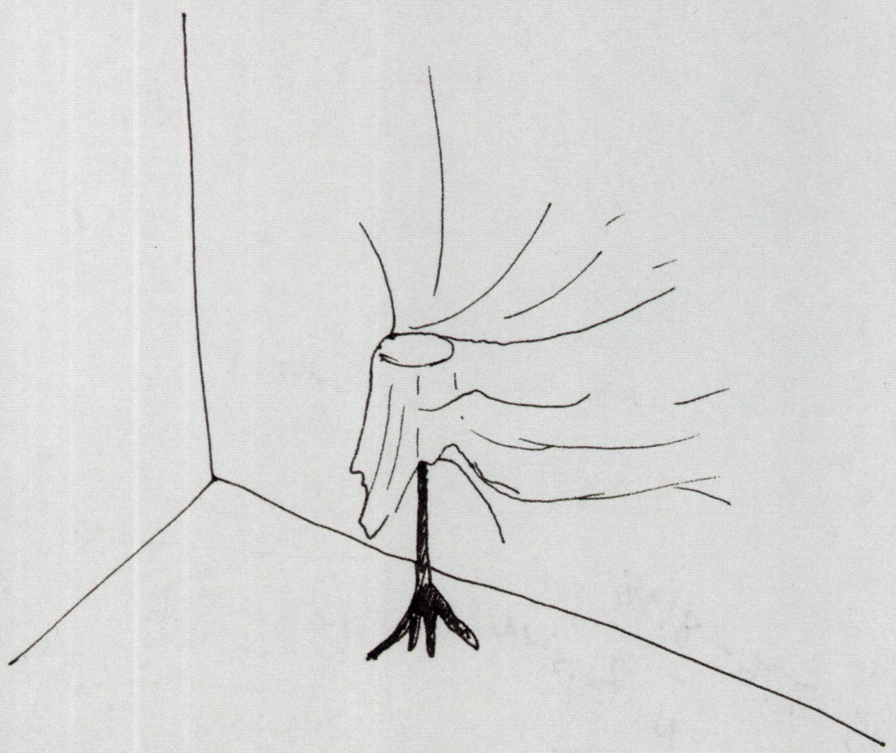

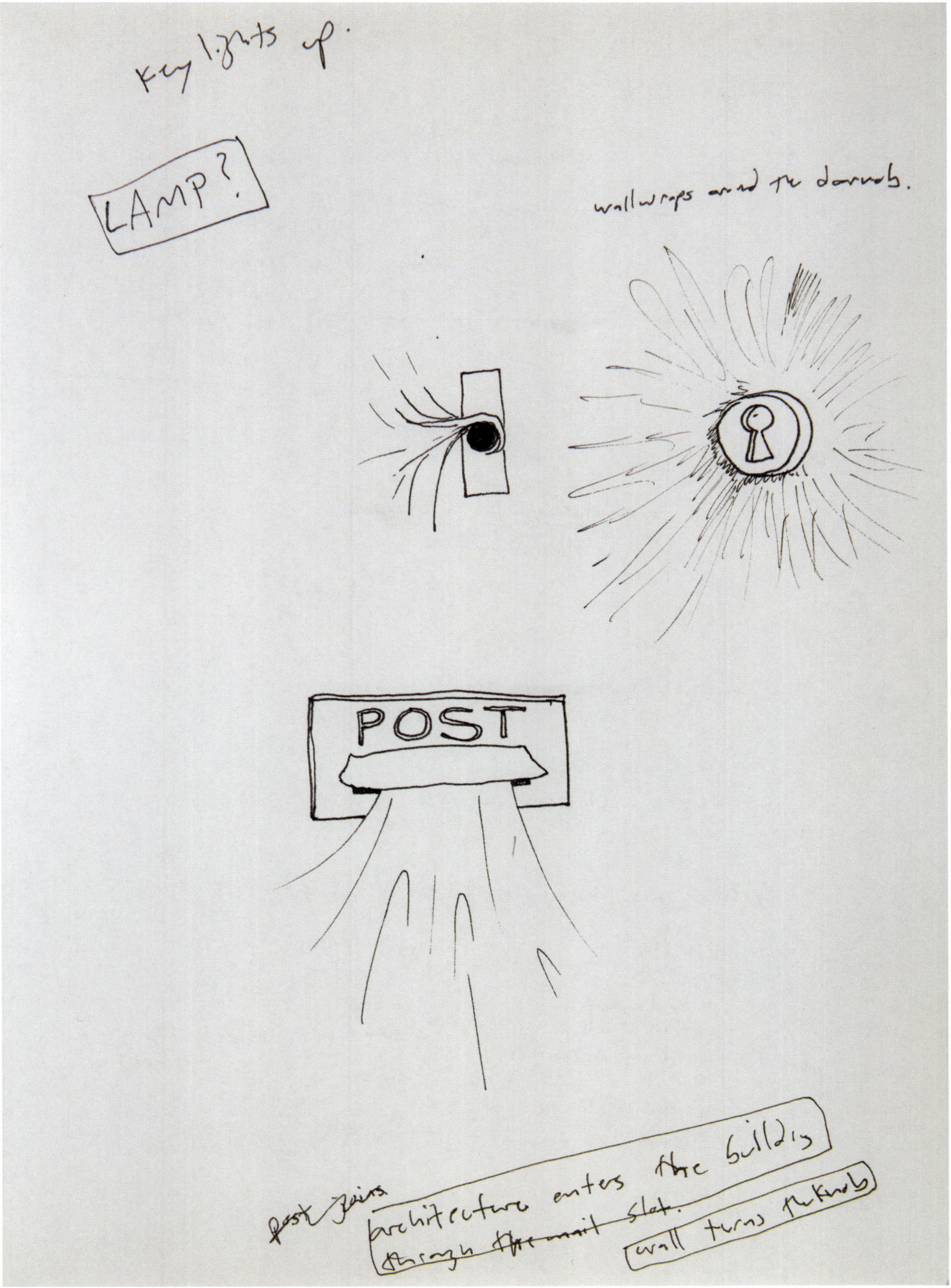

key lights up.

LAMP?

wall wraps around the doorknob.

POST

post skirs

architecture enters the building
through the mail slot.

wall turns the knob

251

should the mail slot and doorknob be
vintage. reproduced? ...

Maybe no doorknob

is there a way
to reconcile the
word drawings
with Another
light drawings )

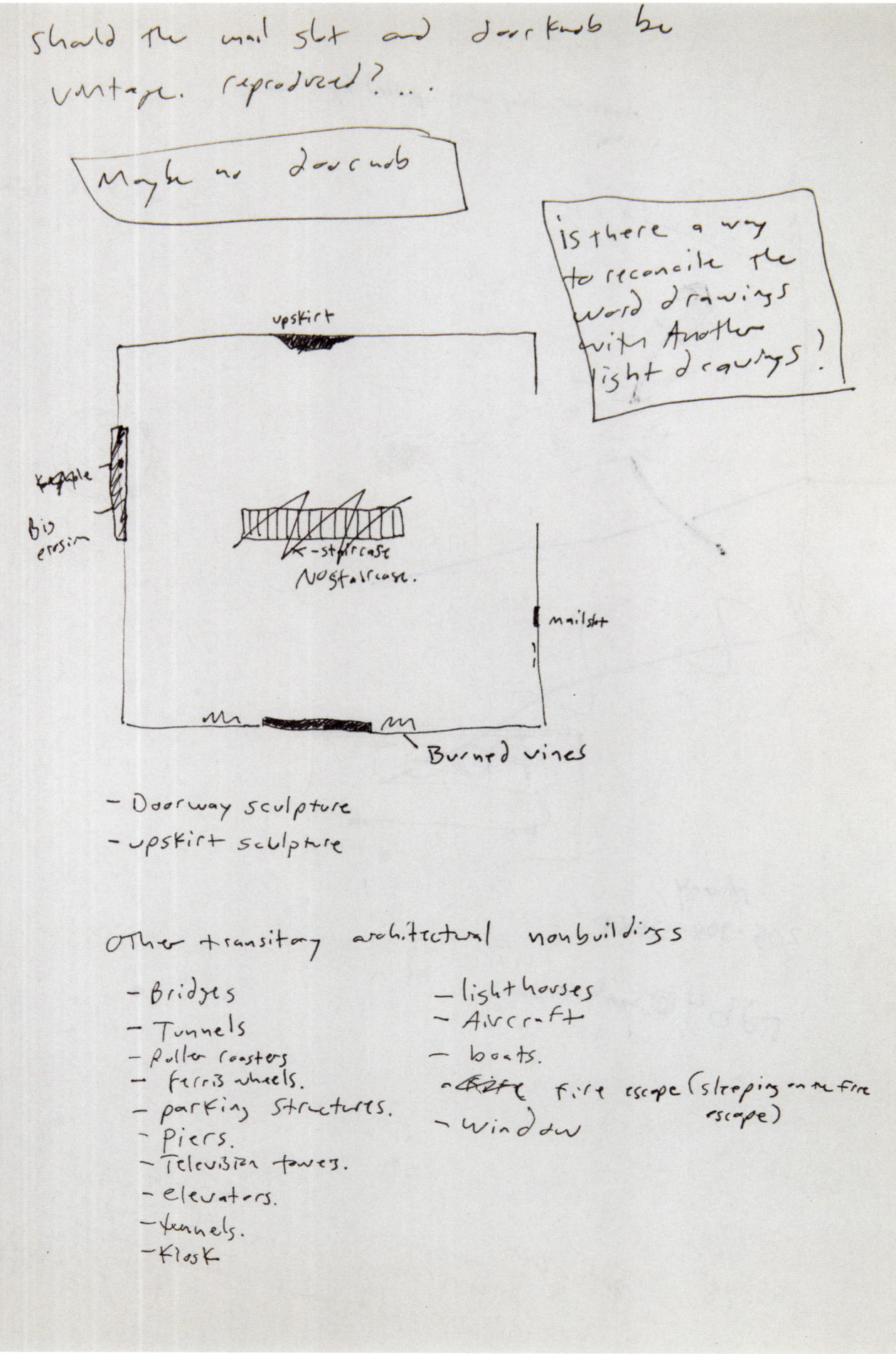

upskirt

keyhole
too
big
erosion

-staircase
Nostalrcase.

mailslot

Burned vines

- Doorway sculpture
- upskirt sculpture

Other transitory architectural nonbuildings

- Bridges
- Tunnels
- Roller coasters
- Ferris wheels.
- parking Structures.
- Piers.
- Television towers.
- elevators.
- tunnels.
- Kiosk

- lighthouses
- Aircraft
- boats.
- fire escape (sleeping on the fire escape)
- Window

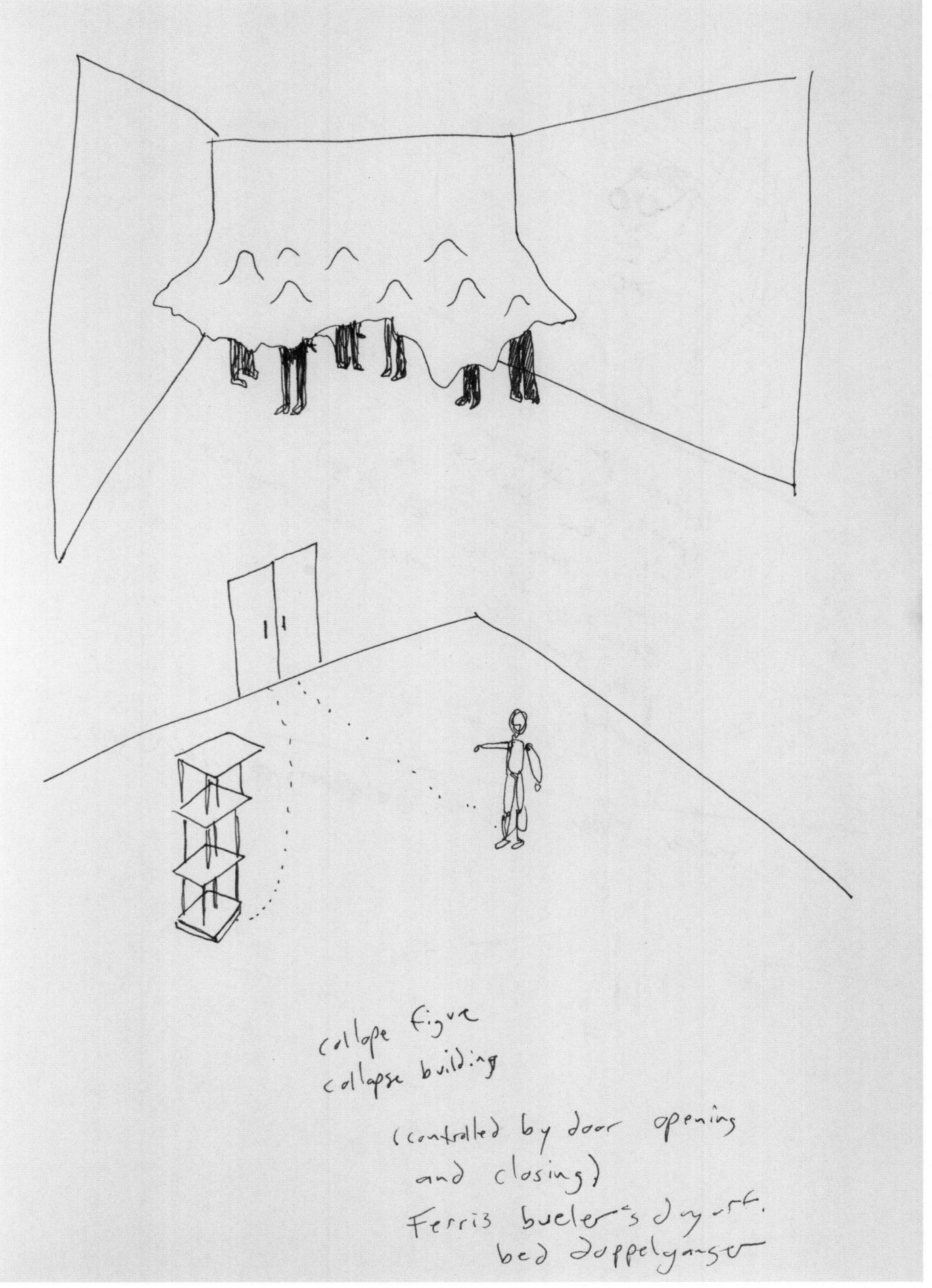

collape figure
collapse building

(controlled by door opening
and closing)
Ferris bueler's day-off.
bed doppelganger

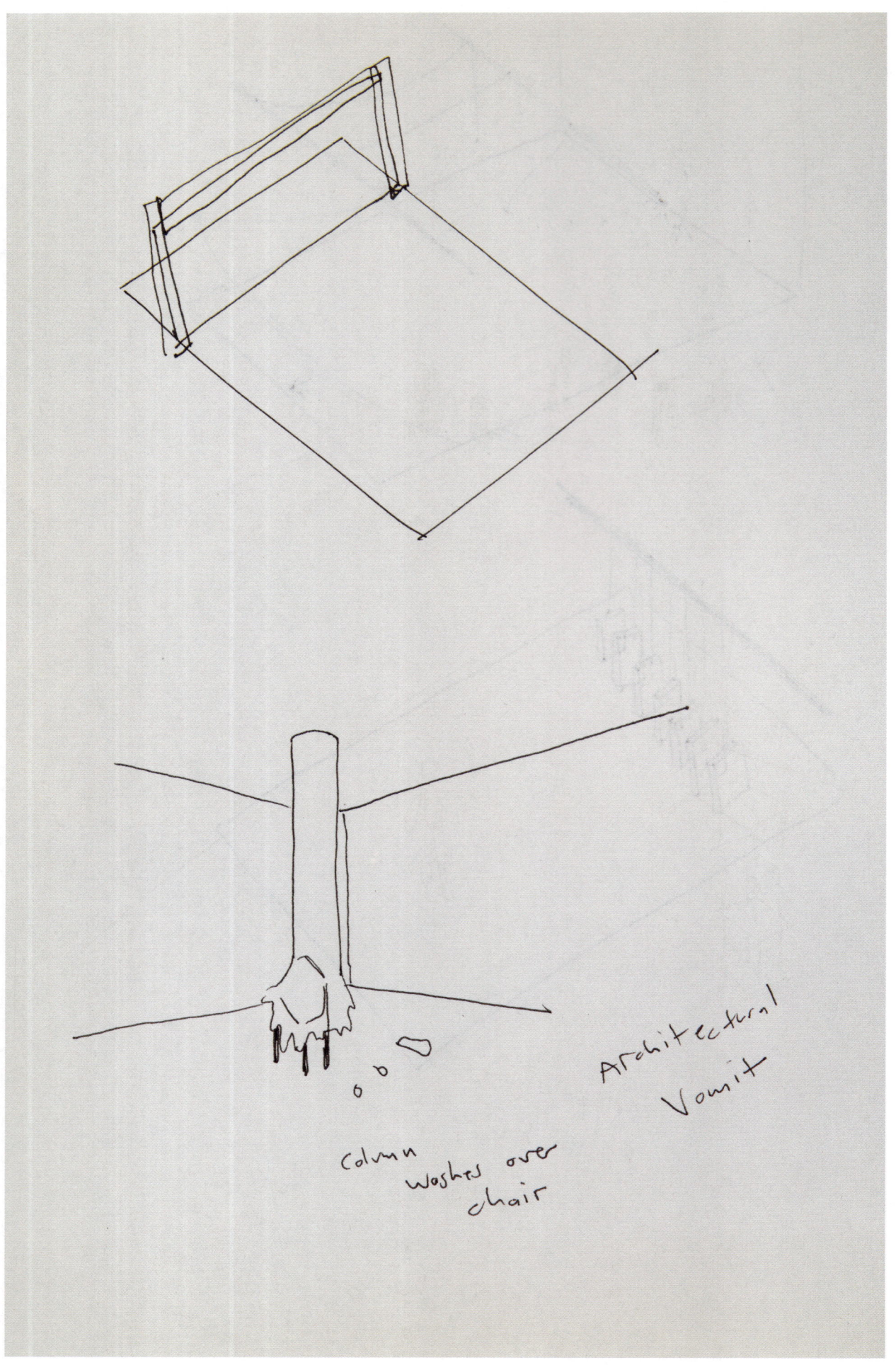

Column
Washes over
chair

Architectural
Vomit

Perhaps for seattle I could make a much larger.
iceberg form with,

or inside the museum though art there could be
errosions into the walls.
        ˅
       and
      growths,

a Sculpture pulled from form could be displayed
and the negative cavities created from making it
could be inserted into the walls and ceilings.

Dear LA.
    the walls could be flowing over the
chair. and the mirror could be somesimilarly
covered by the wall.

What is the relationship between smithson
and arts and crafts. The integration of the
natural and the manmade?

Also - Grotto / white walls,

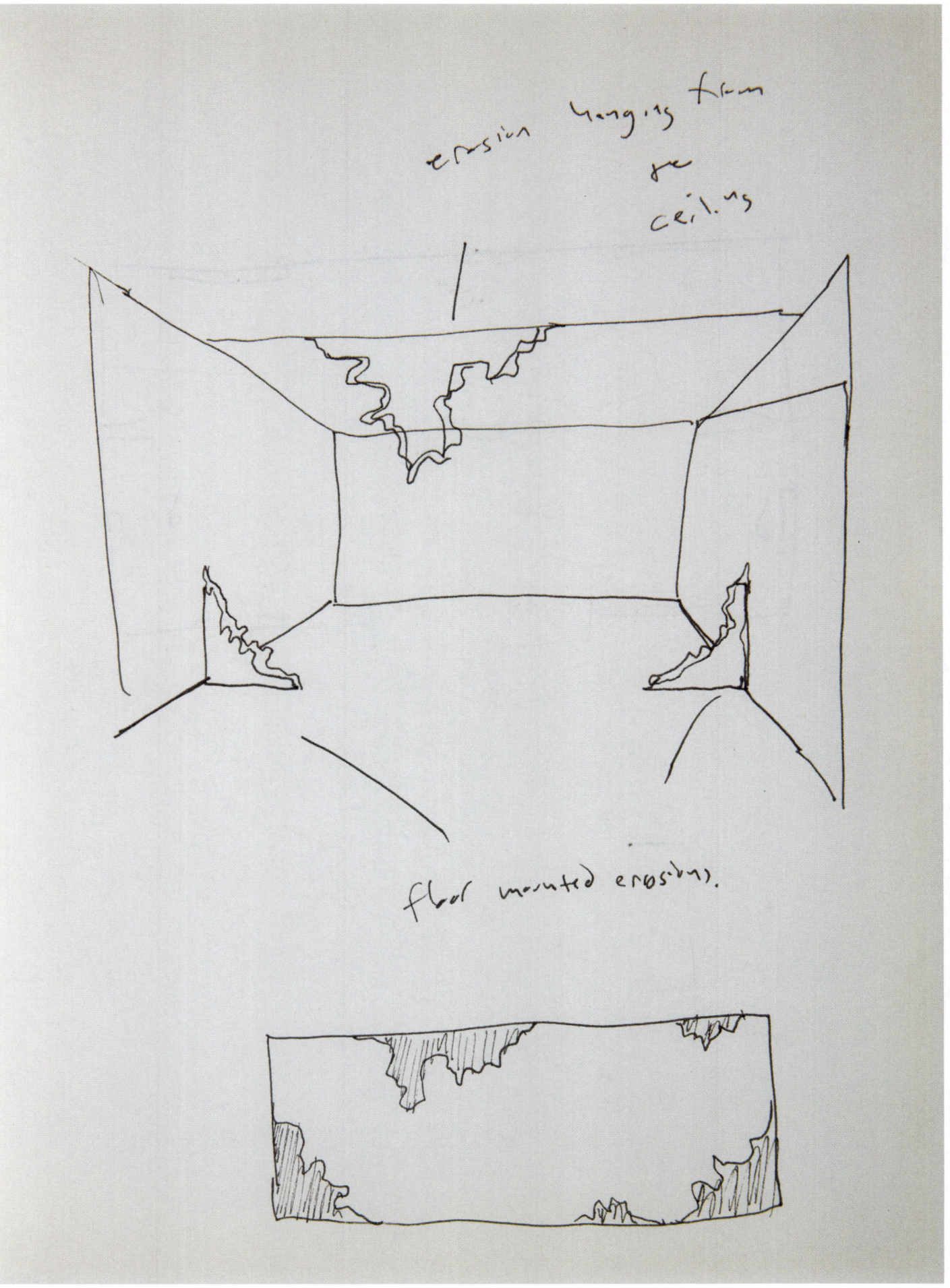

erosion hanging from
the
ceiling

floor mounted erosions.

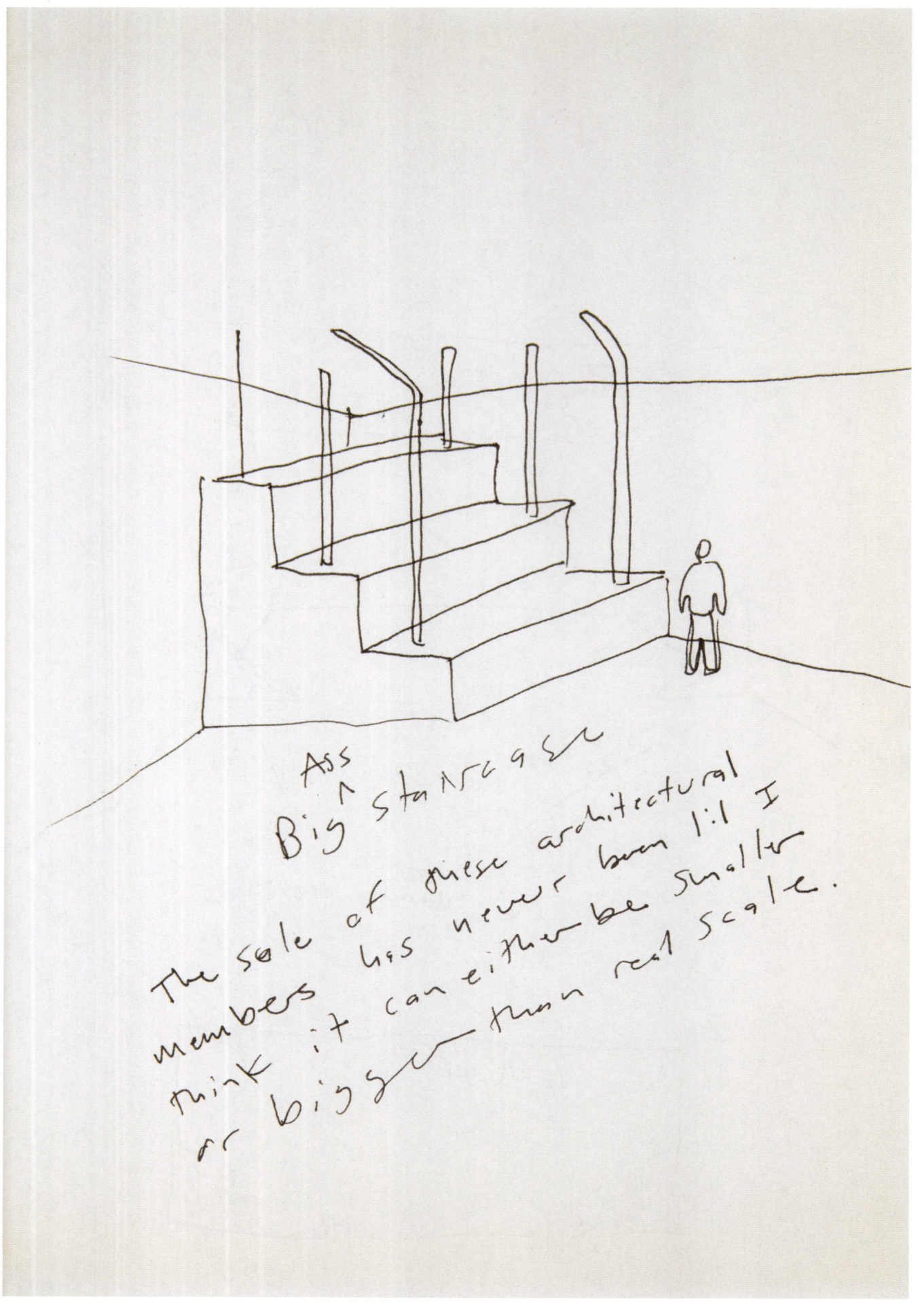

Ass

Big staircase

The sale of these architectural members has never been 1:1 I think it can either be smaller or bigger than real scale.

Should I die away I should be cremated and the ashes should be dispersed among the people I know. Those who want some. The The preferred use of the ashes is that they should be mixed with joint compound and should be used in the first coat of joint compound to fill the seam between two sheets of drywall, It must be used in the first coat because the last coat will be sanded and I do not wish to end up in a shop vac. The other use which could be permitted is if someone owns a large building (not a skyscraper) maybe not more than 10 - 15 stories (Cooper Union is a proper size) They may take the ashes to the ventilation system of the building and allow the ashes to be sucked into and dispersed throughout the building (yes I am aware that this has been done before)

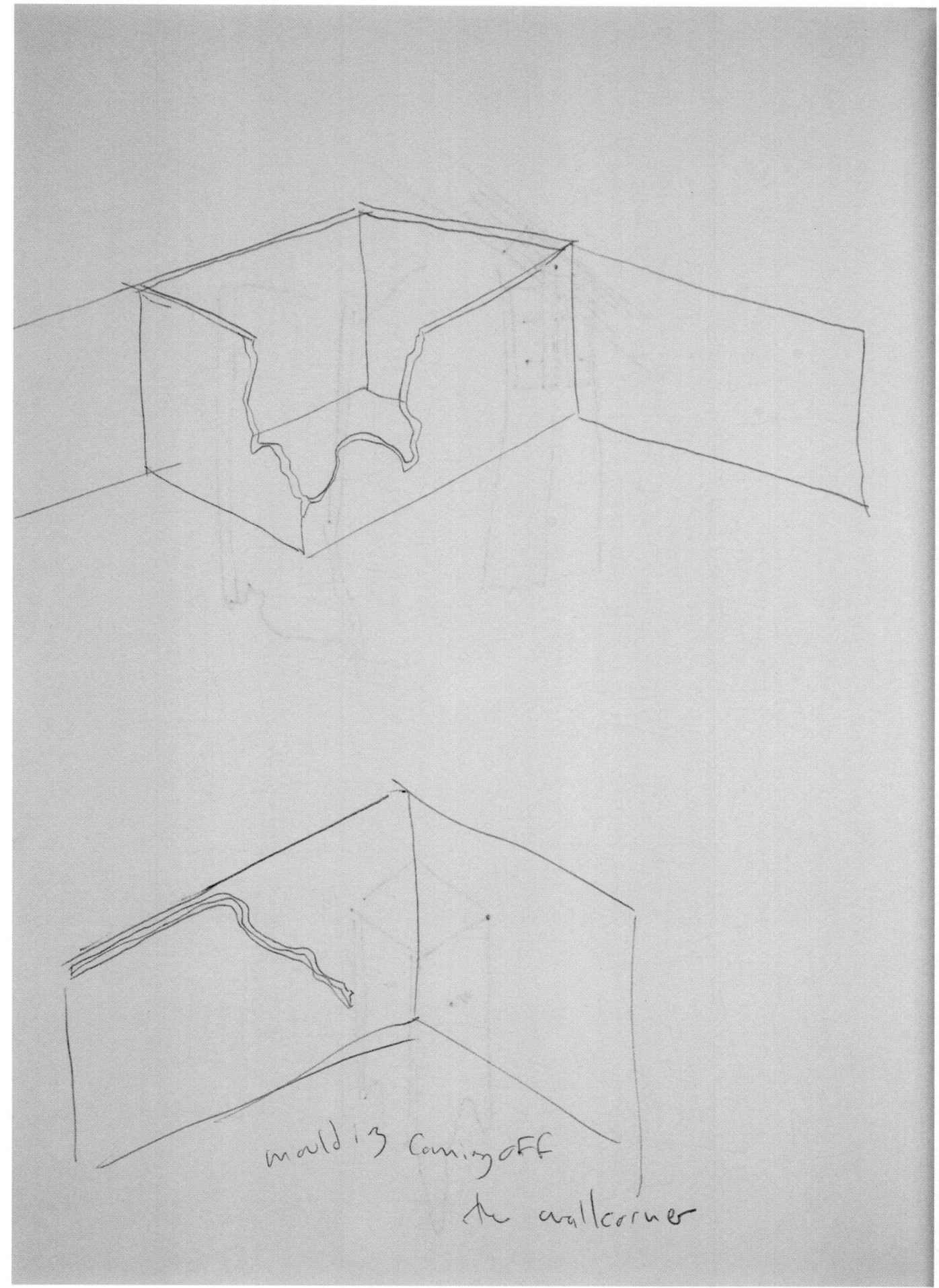

mould is coming off

the wallcorner

Aventura.

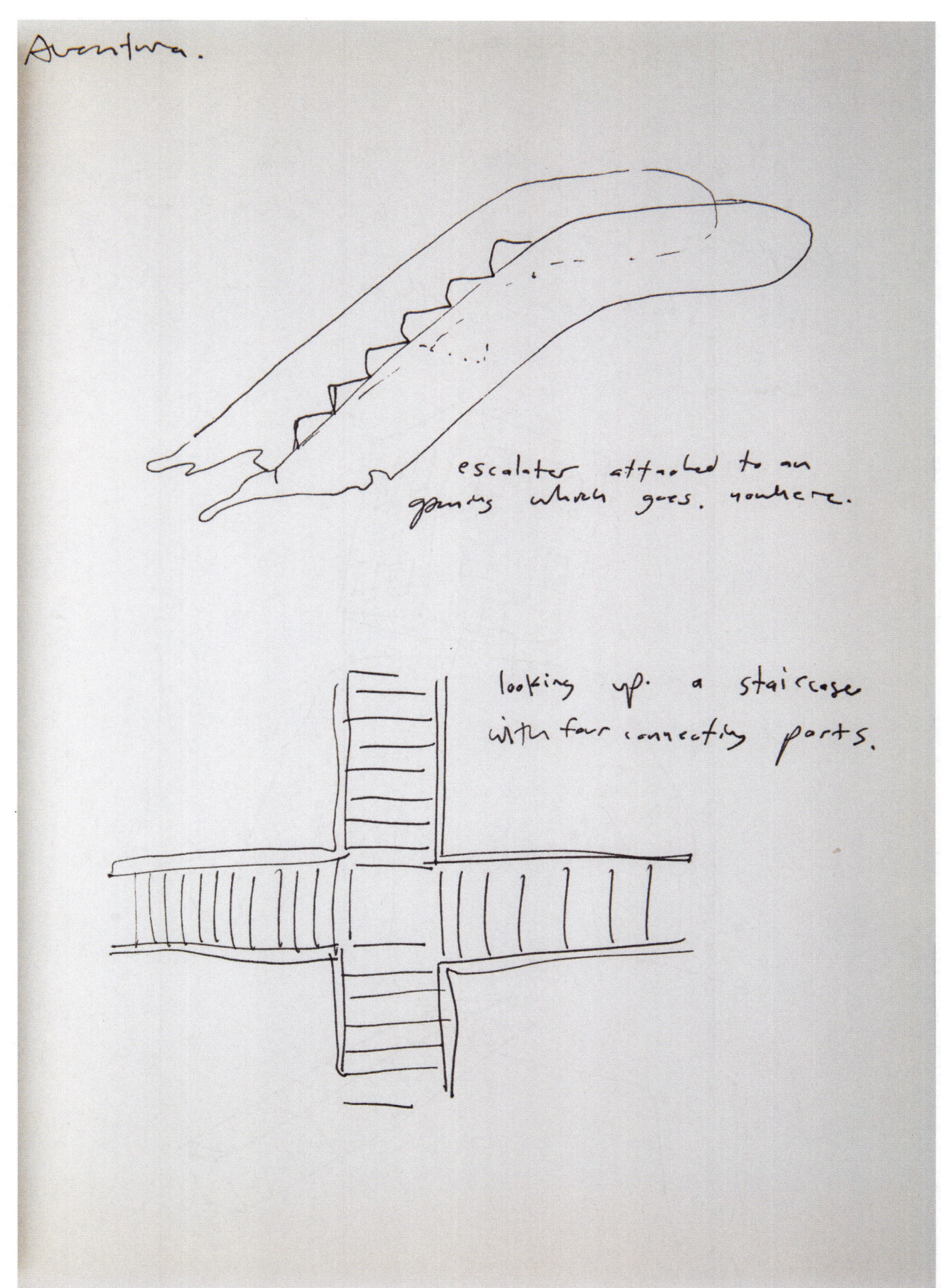

escalater attached to an opening which goes. nowhere.

looking up. a staircase with four connecting ports.

Fucking Architecture.

Play with the forms in the computer. Go and take photos at rails staircases, other architectural elements.

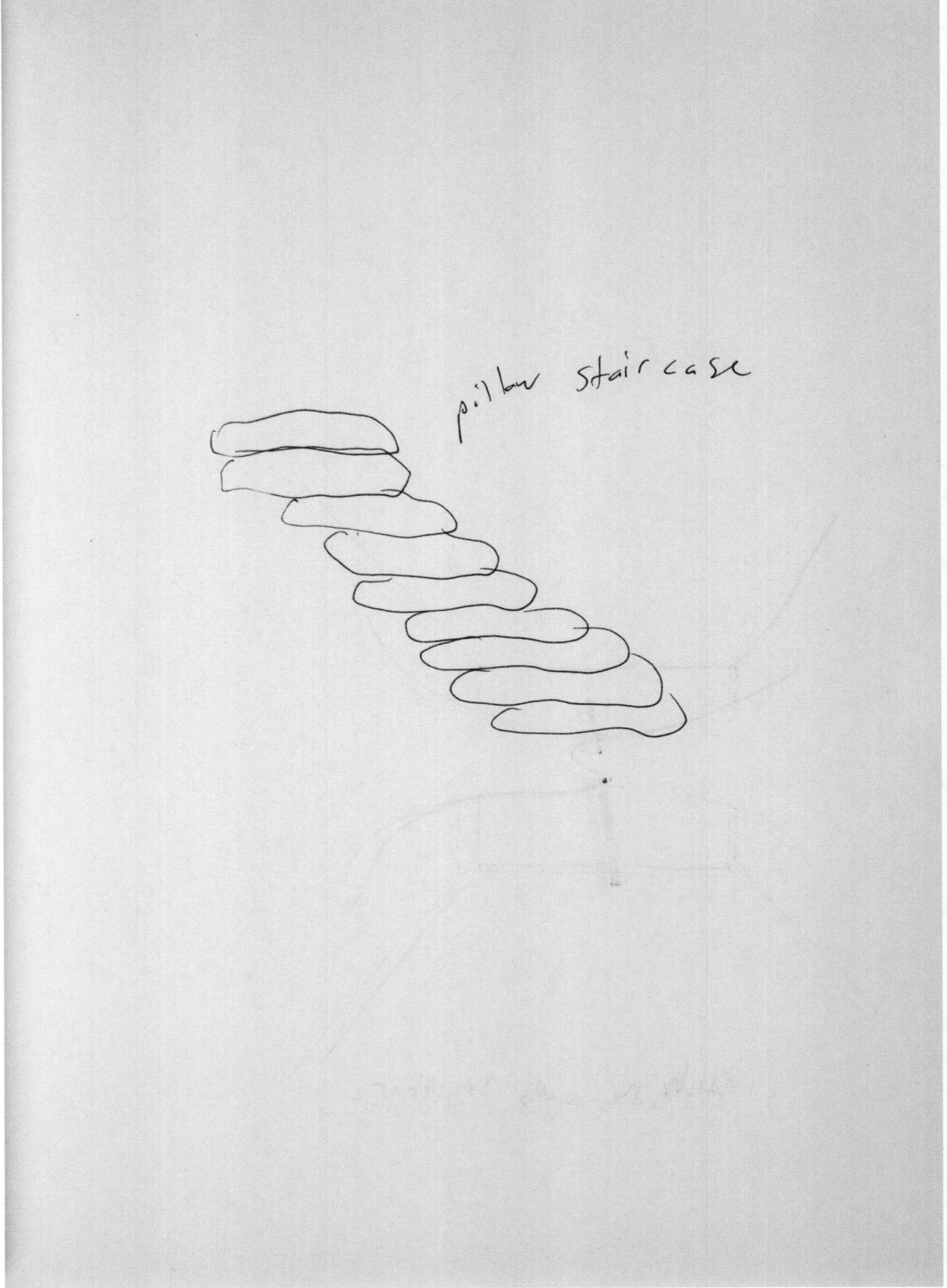

pillow staircase

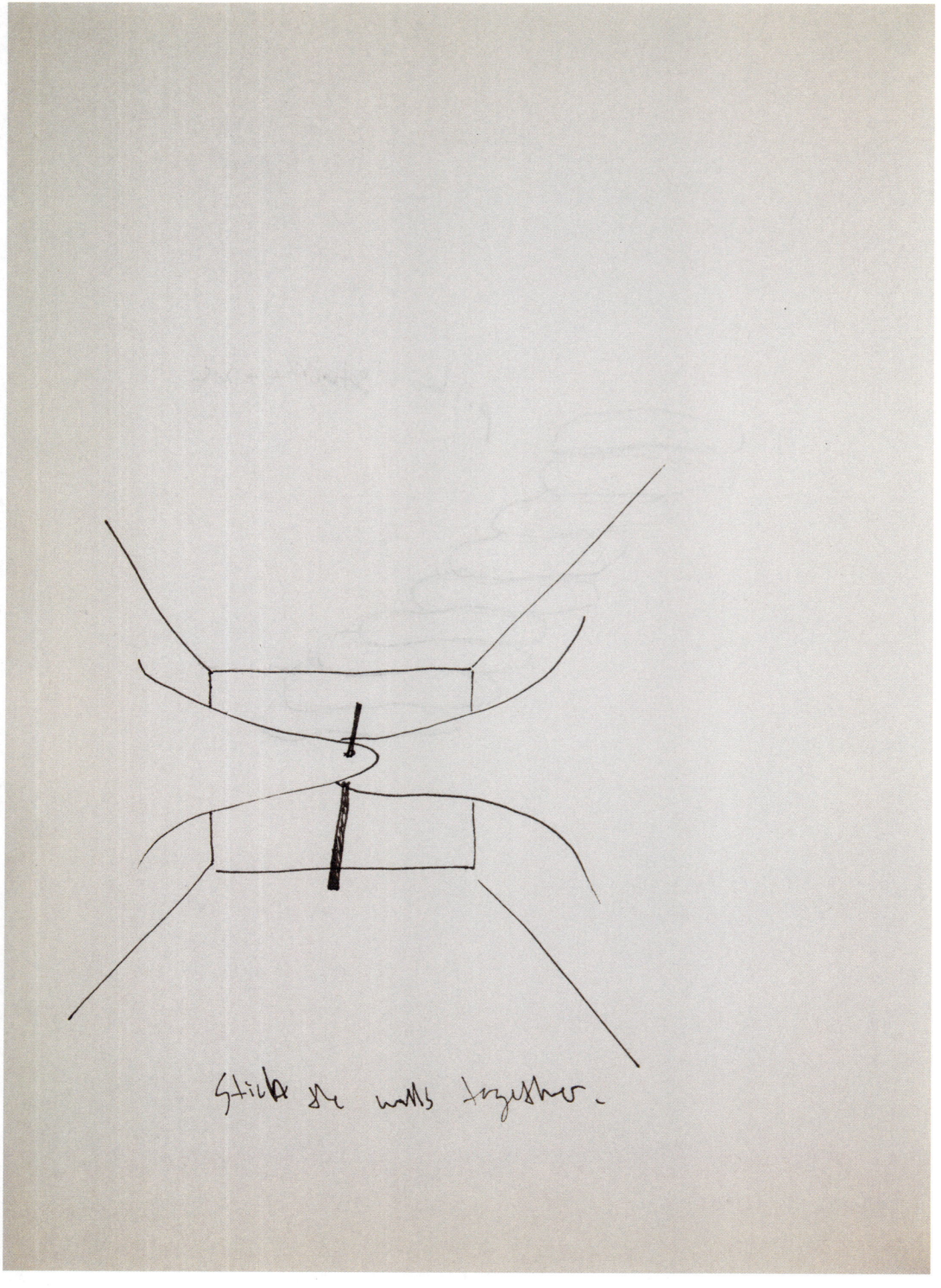

Stick the walls together.

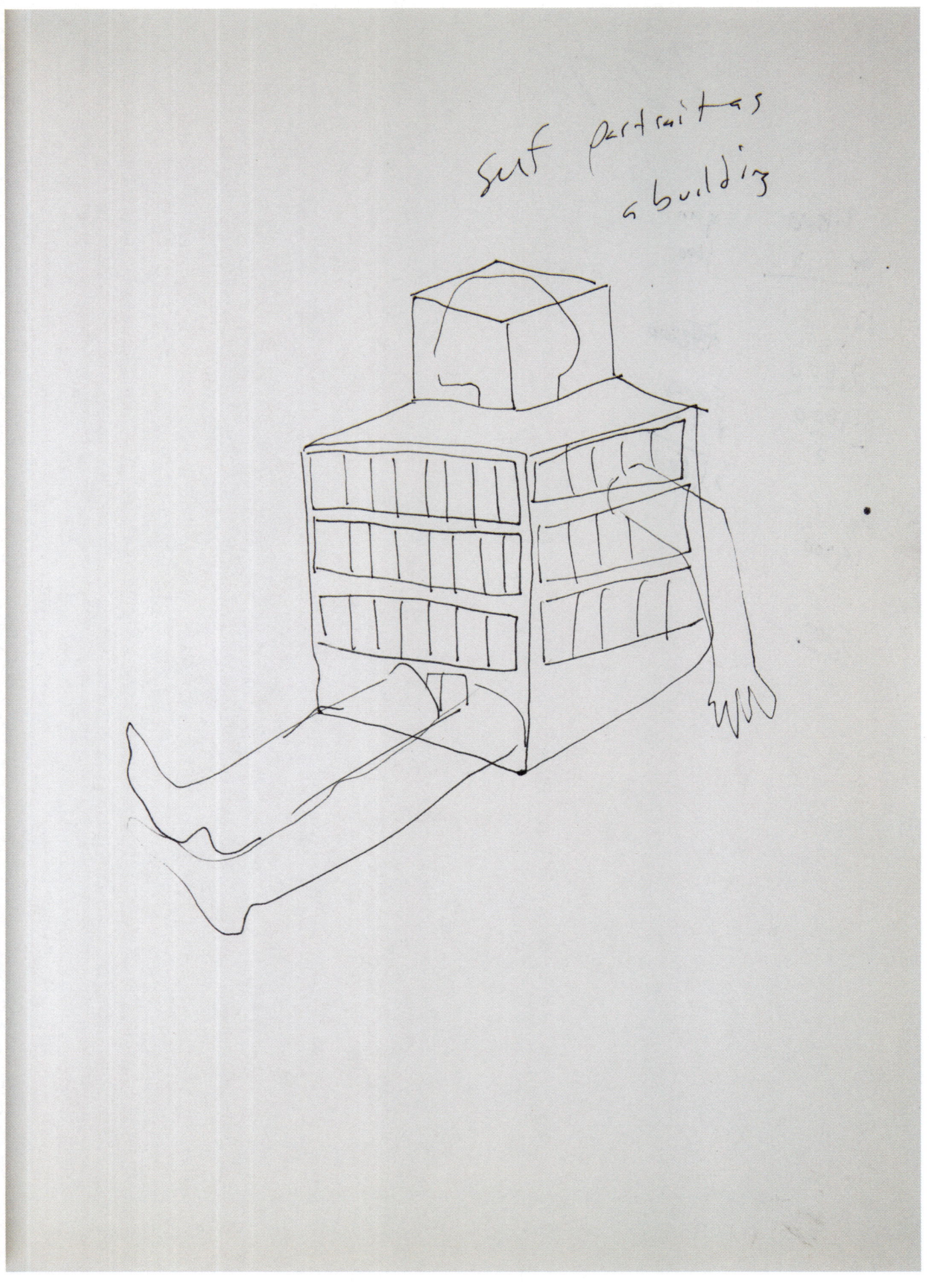

self portrait as
a building

Self portrait as

a building

Soft porcelin
staircase.

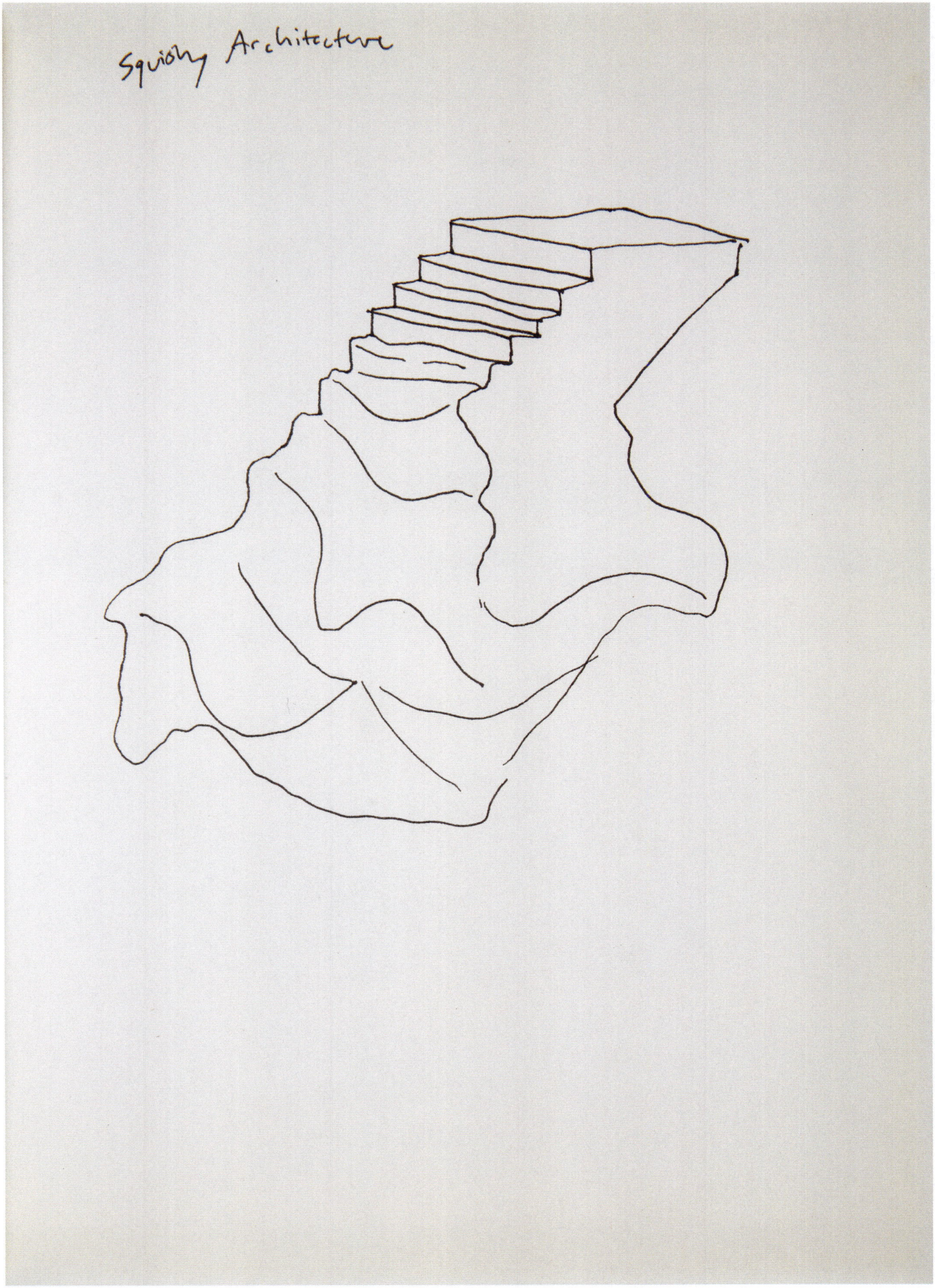
Squishy Architecture

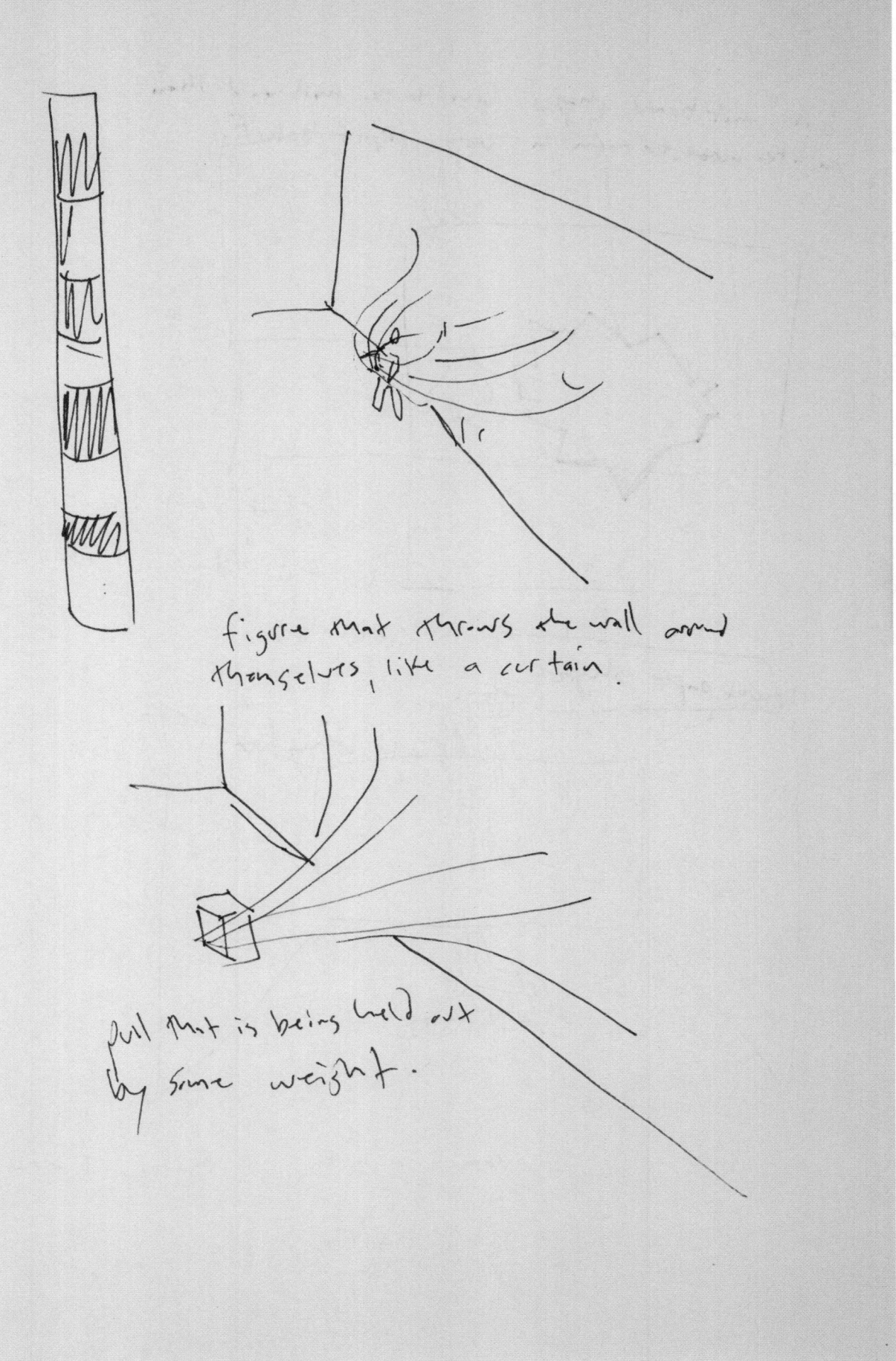

figure that throws the wall around themselves, like a curtain.

pull that is being held out by some weight.

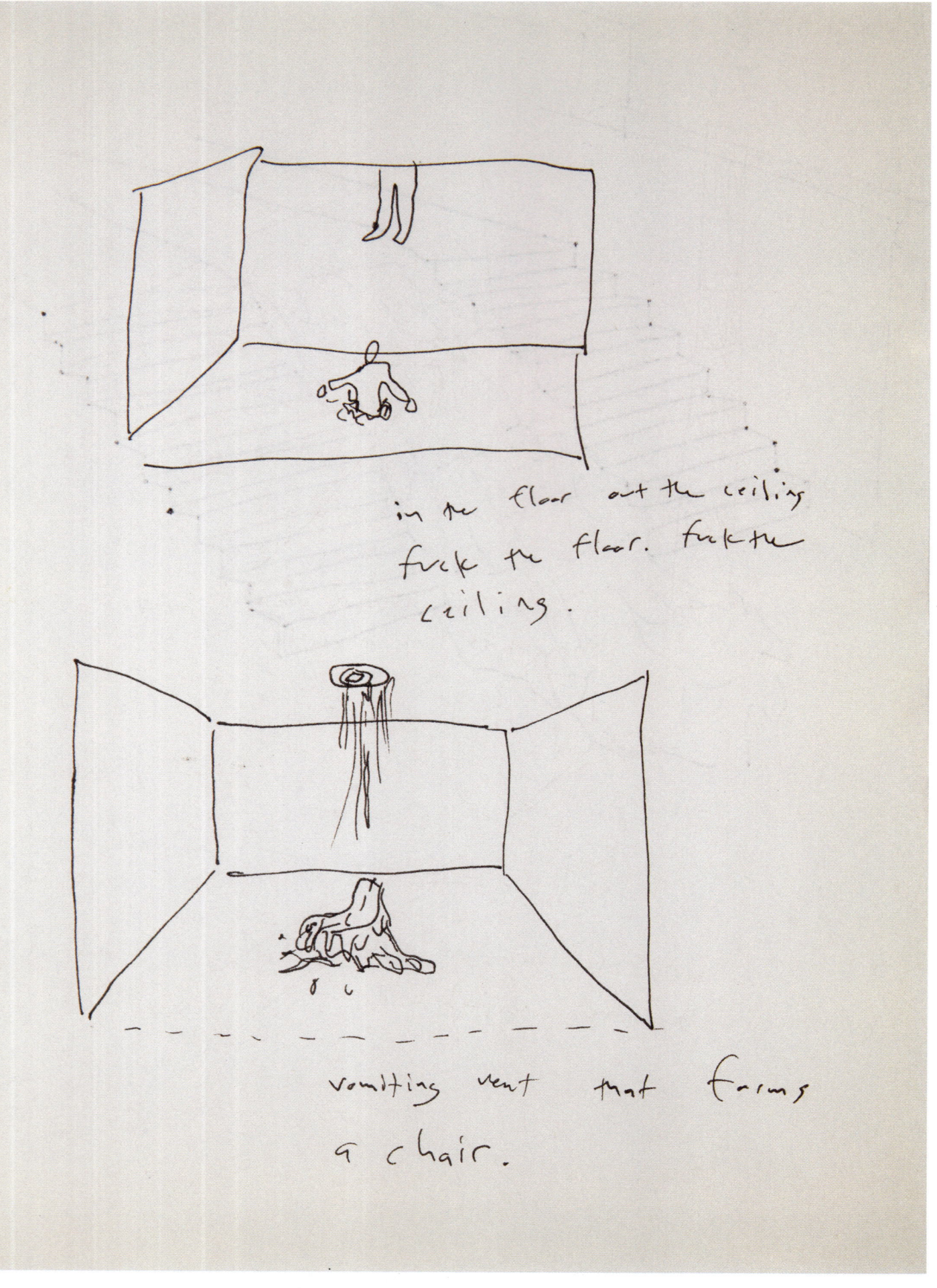

in the floor out the ceiling
fuck the floor. fuck the
ceiling.

vaulting vent that forms
a chair.

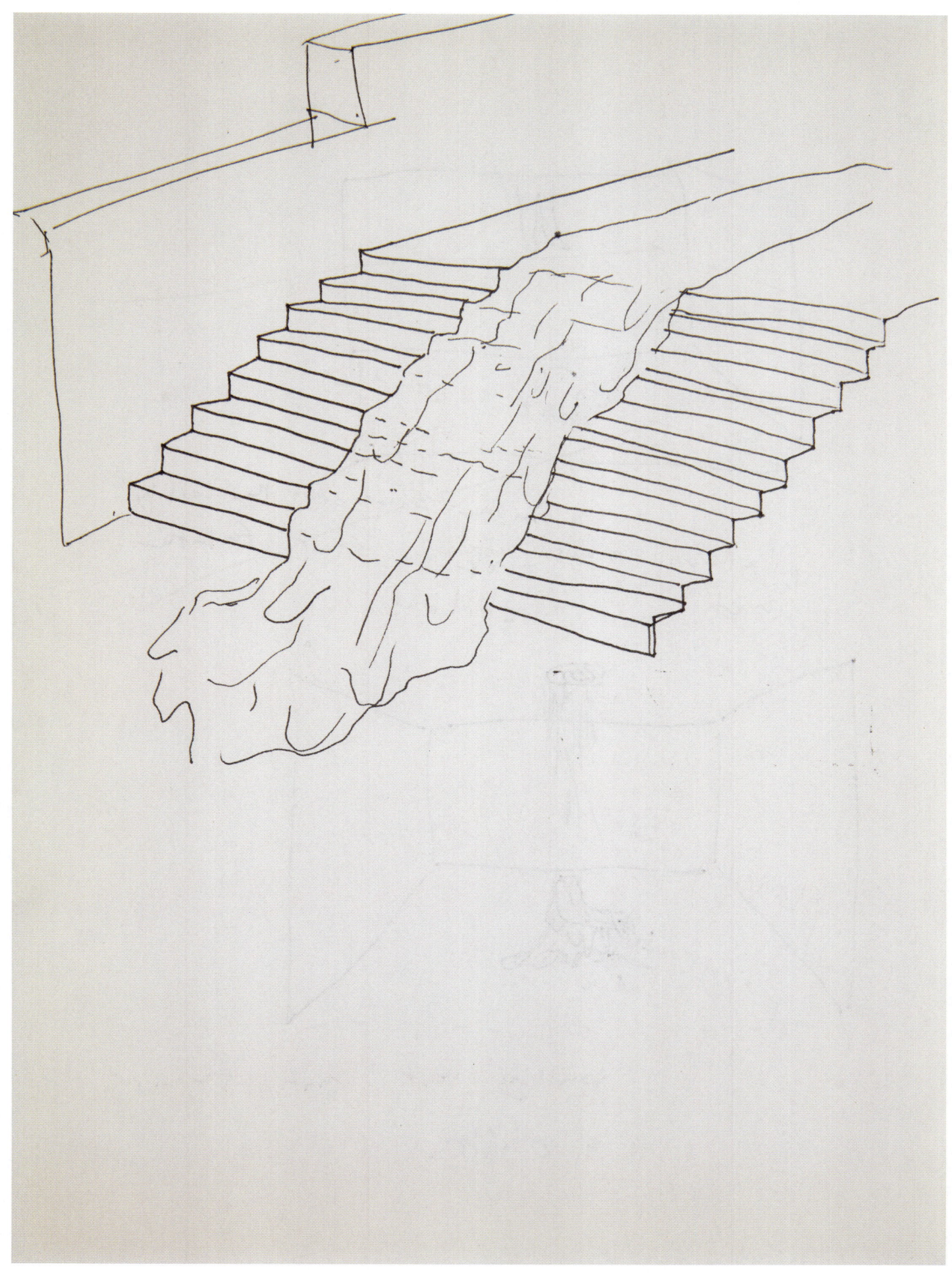

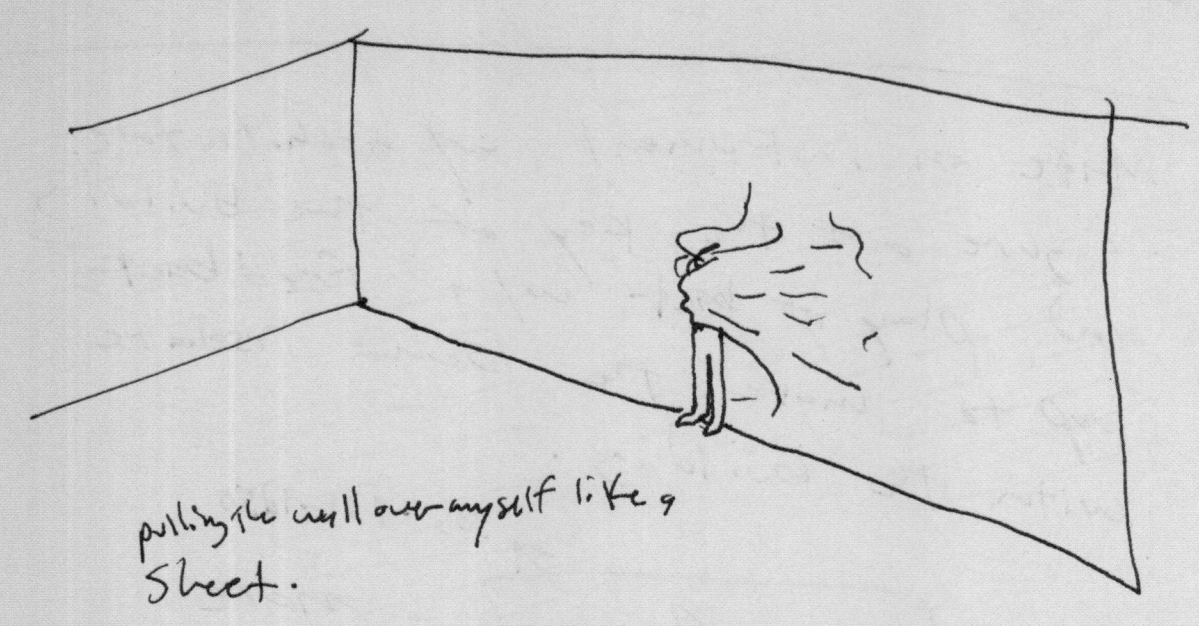

pulling the wall over myself like a
sheet.

plane/ground

playground

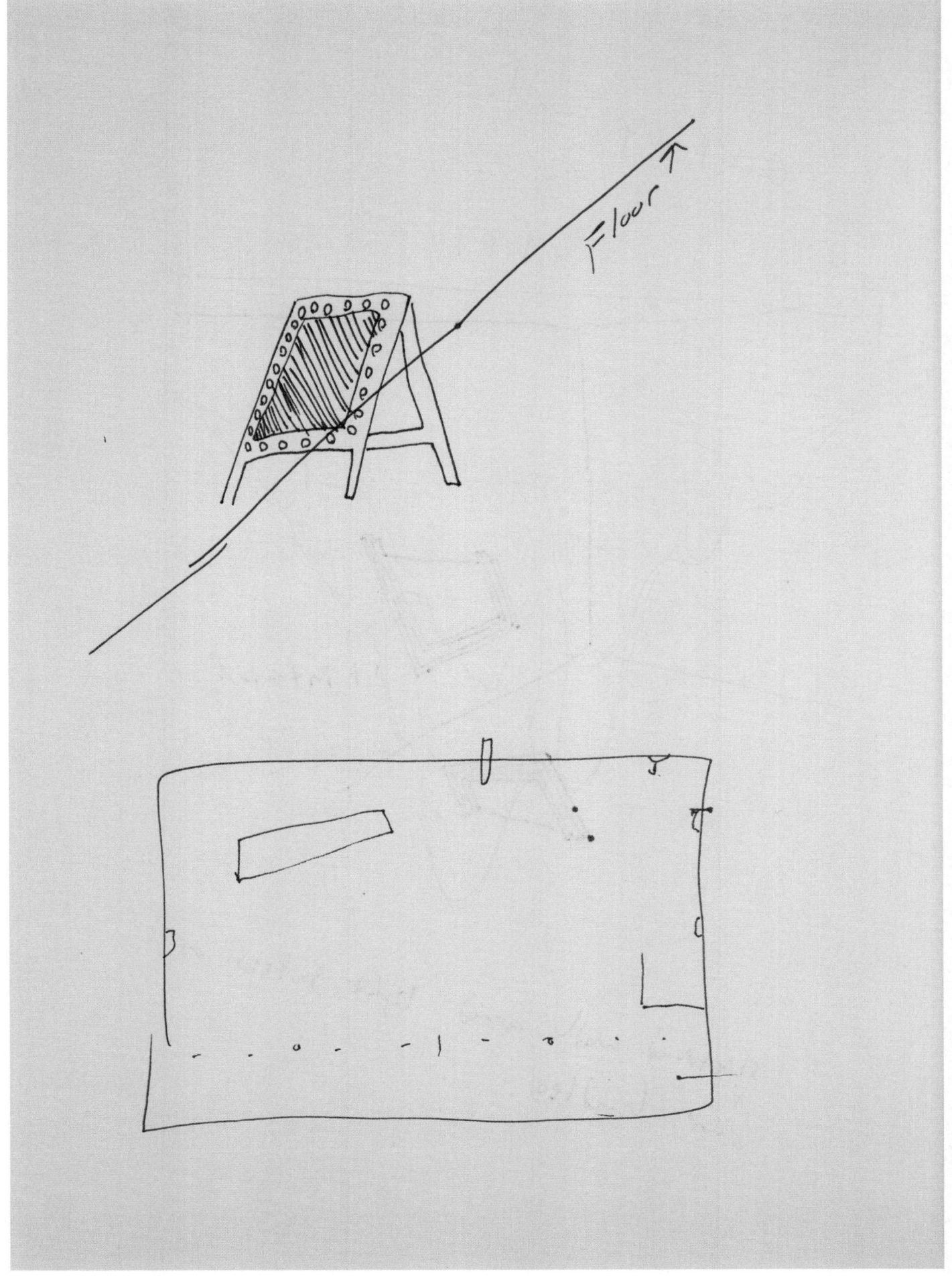

Floor ↑

Giant drip wall.

4 ft.

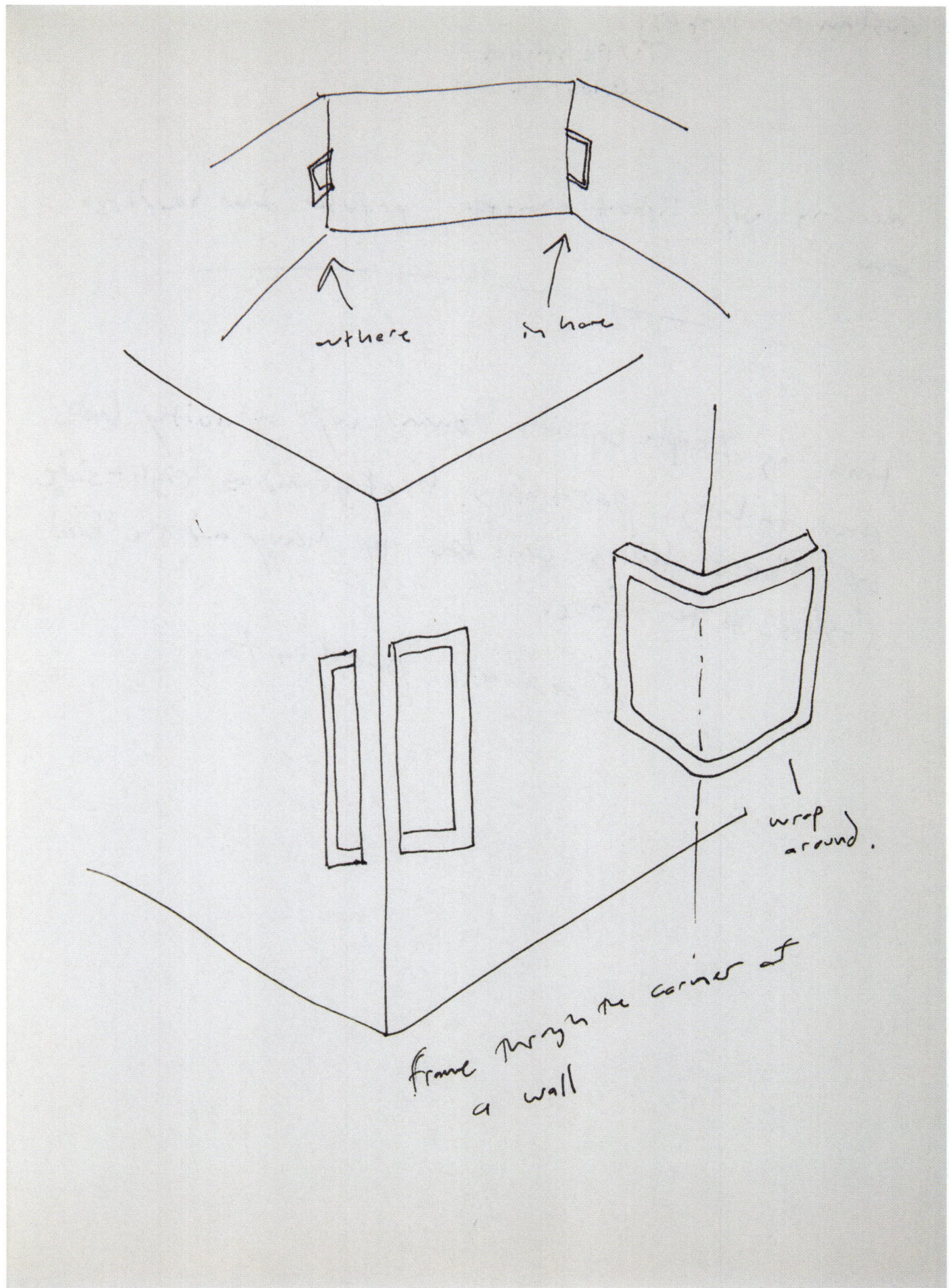

out here       in here

wrap
around.

frame through the corner of
a wall

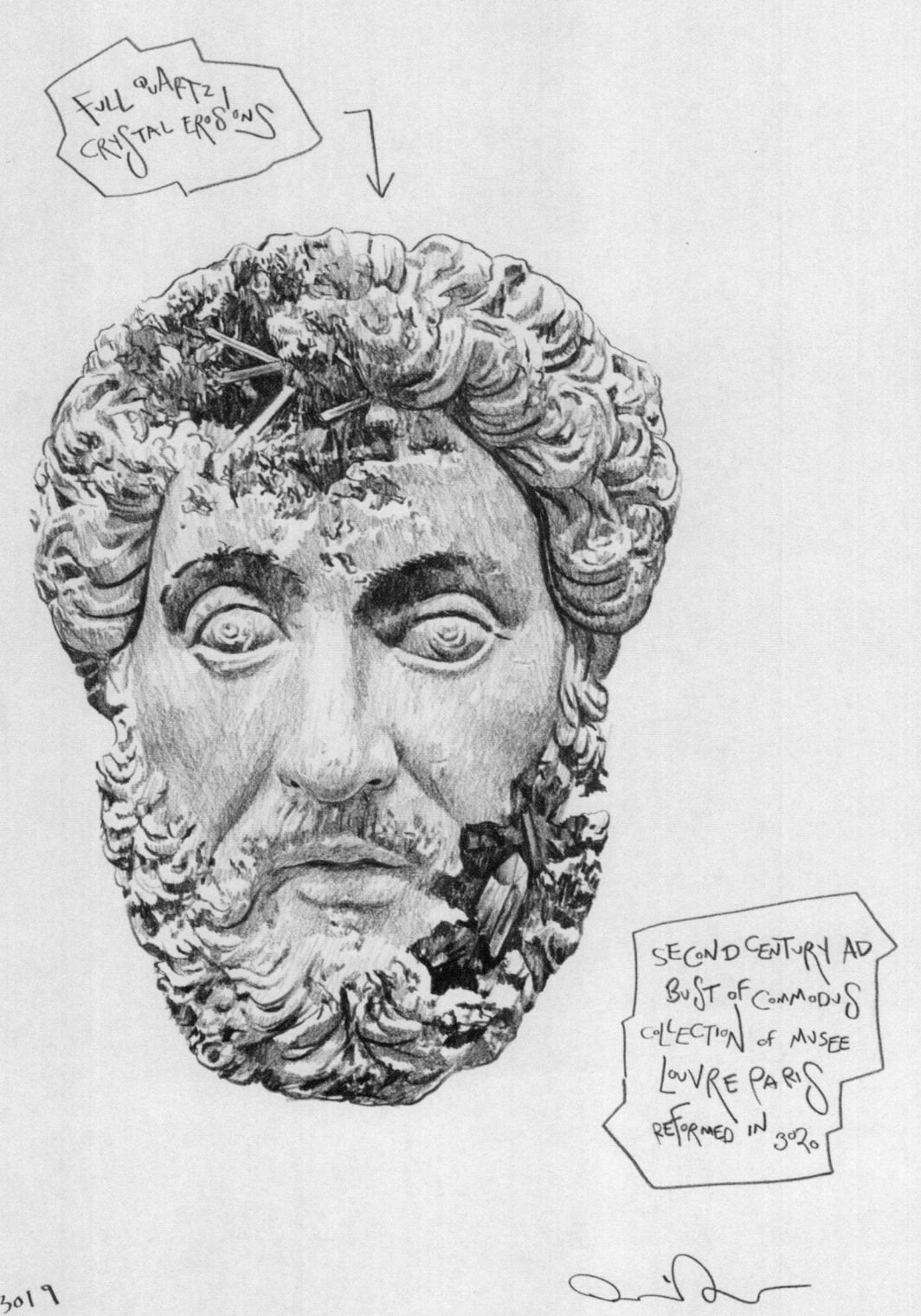

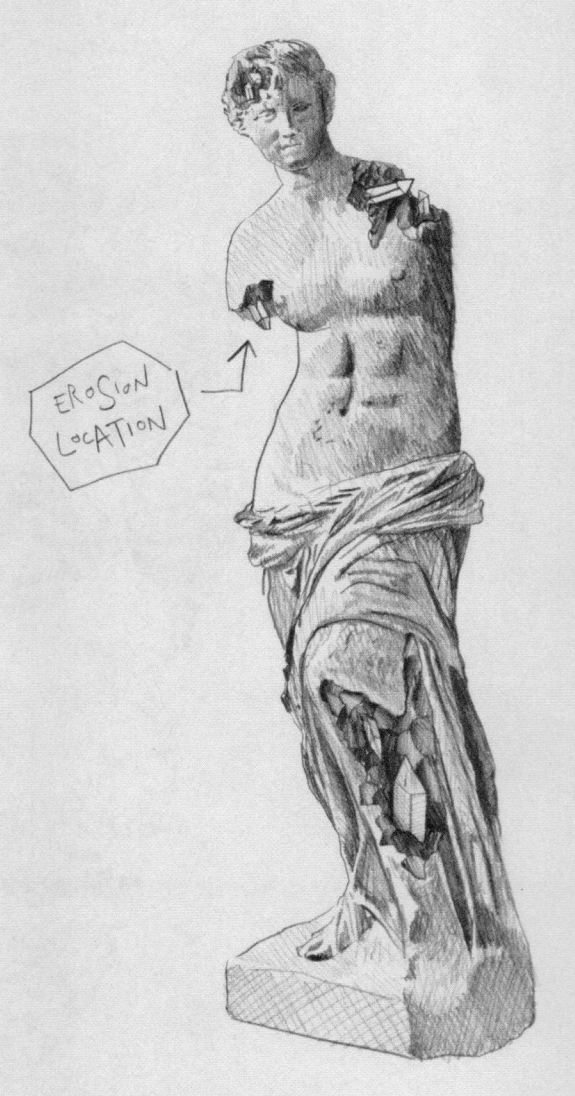

EROSION LOCATION

3019

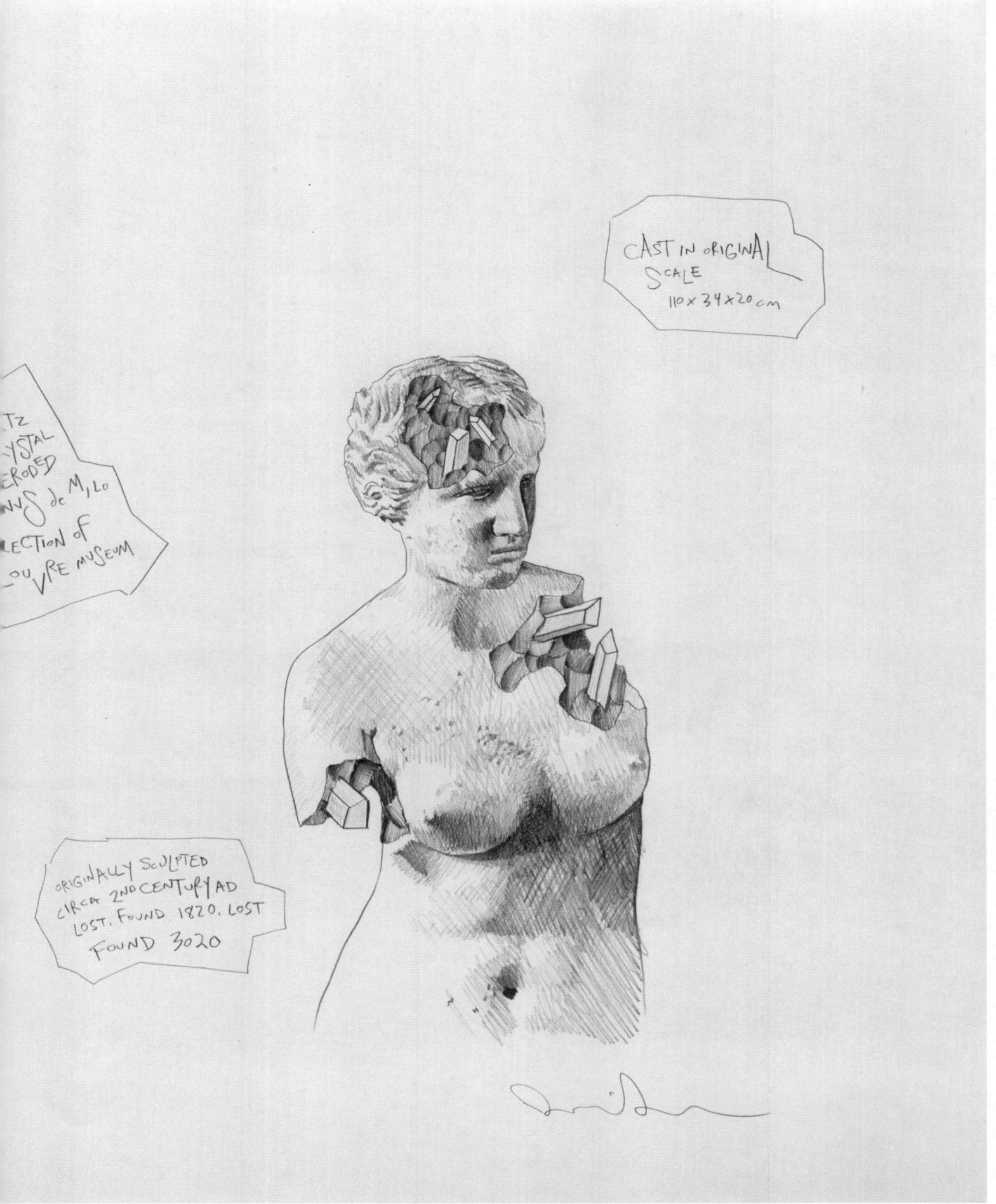

CAST IN ORIGINAL
SCALE
110 x 34 x 20 cm

...TZ
...YSTAL
...ERODED
...NS de MILO
...ECTION OF
...OUVRE MUSEUM

ORIGINALLY SCULPTED
CIRCA 2ND CENTURY AD
LOST, FOUND 1820, LOST
FOUND 3020

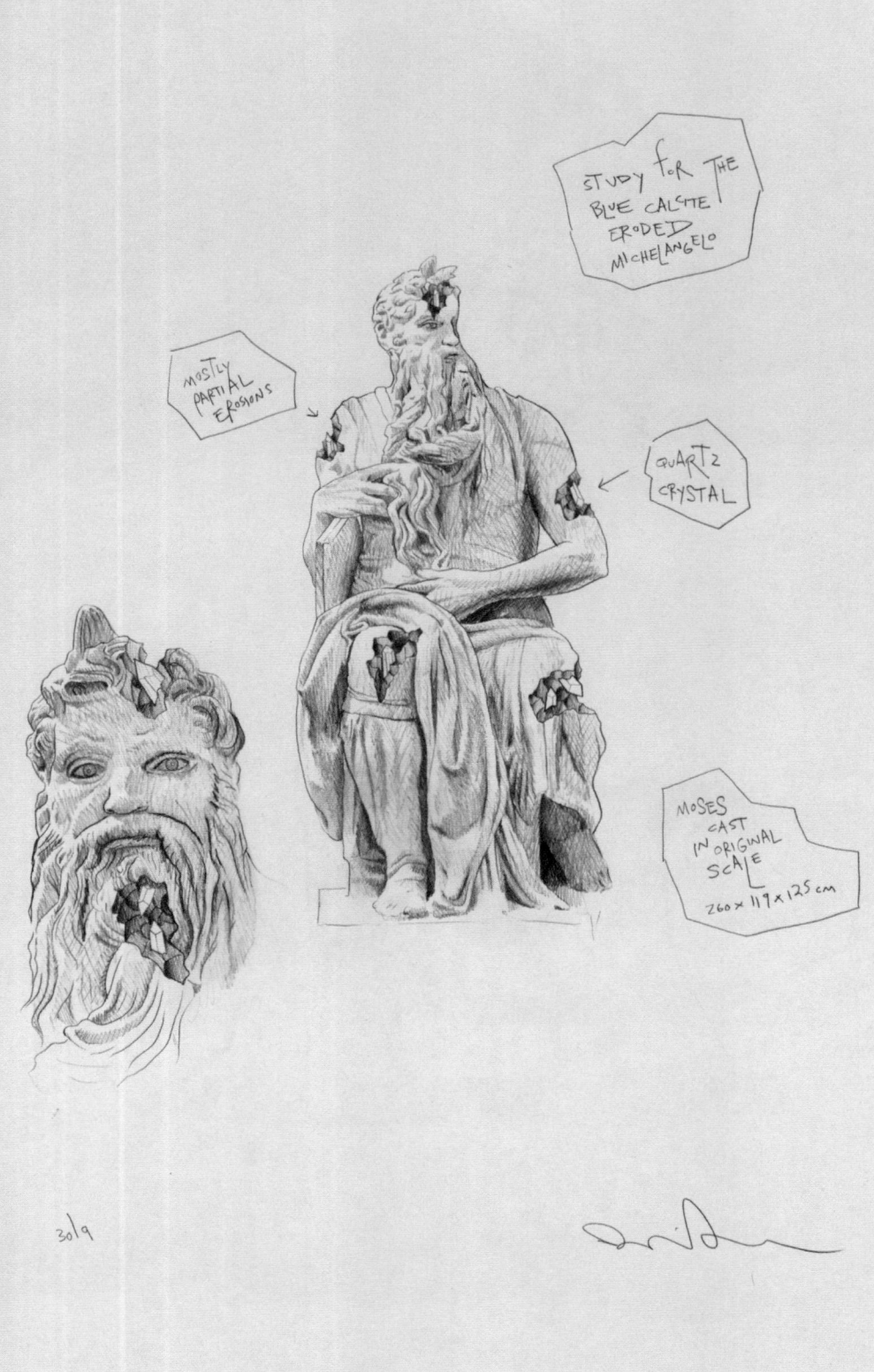

STUDY FOR THE
BLUE CALCITE
ERODED
MICHELANGELO

MOSTLY
PARTIAL
EROSIONS

QUARTZ
CRYSTAL

MOSES
CAST
IN ORIGINAL
SCALE
260 x 119 x 125 cm

30/9

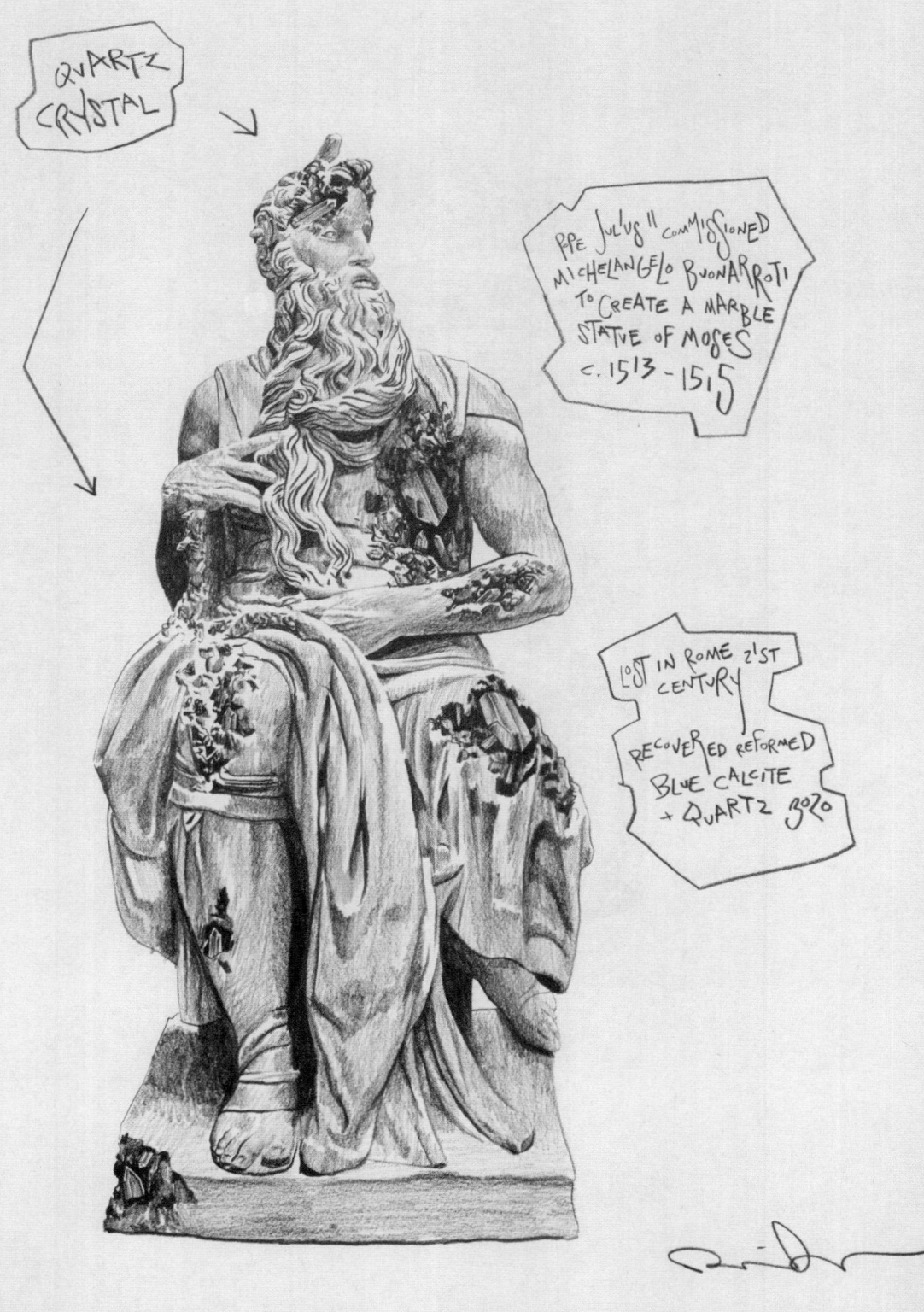

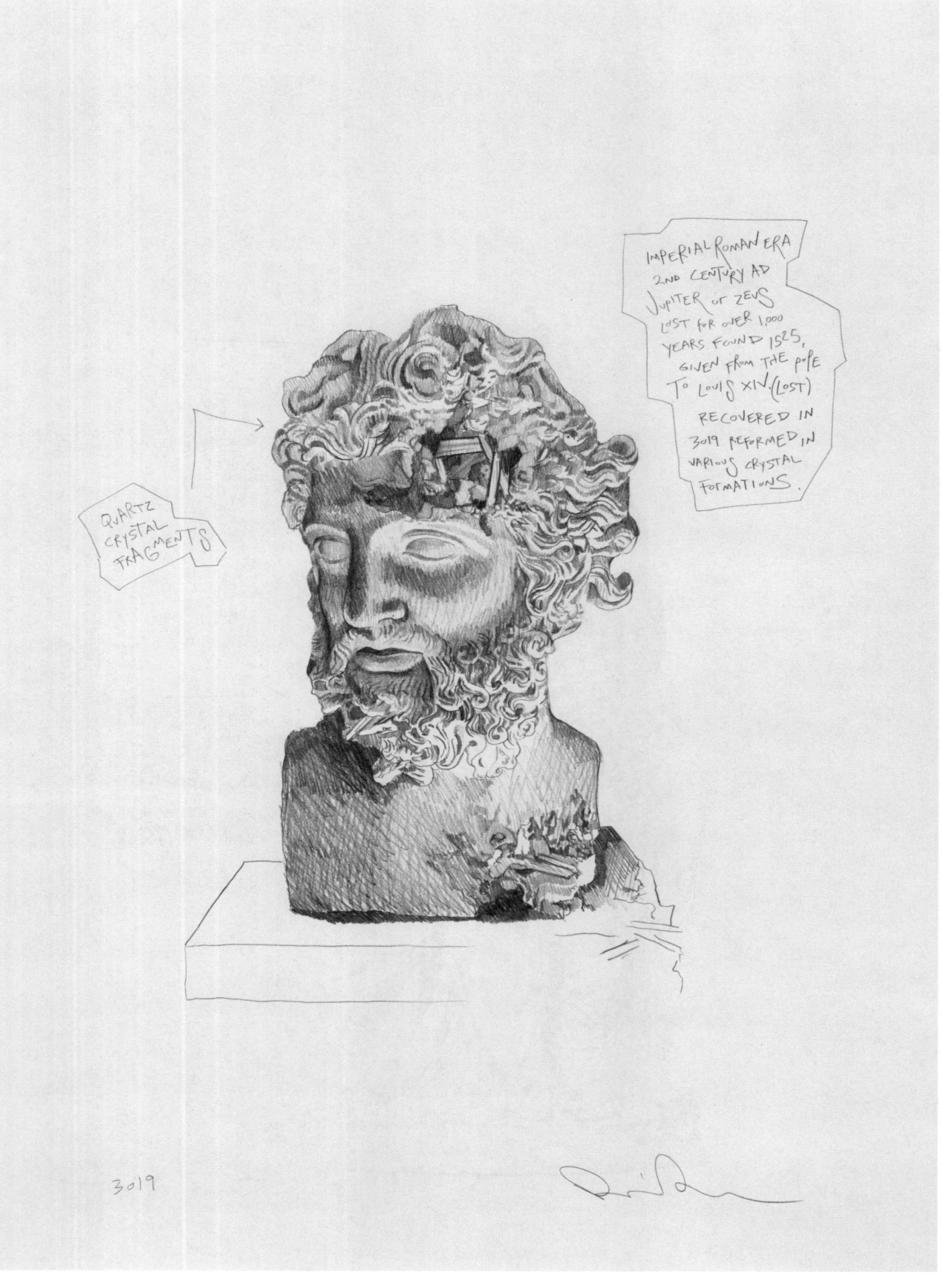

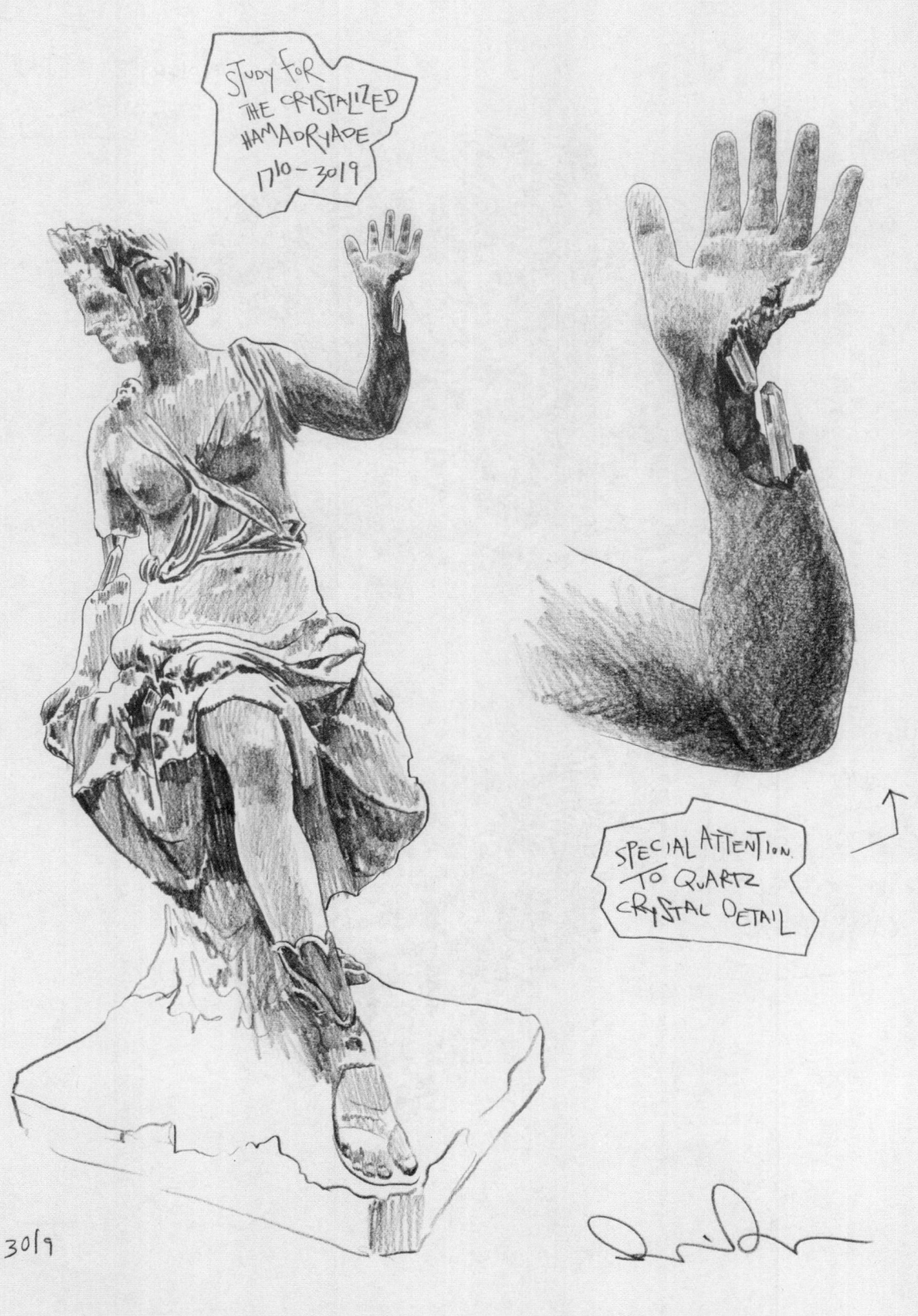

STUDY FOR
THE CRYSTALIZED
HAMADRYADE
1710 - 3019

SPECIAL ATTENTION
TO QUARTZ
CRYSTAL DETAIL

3019

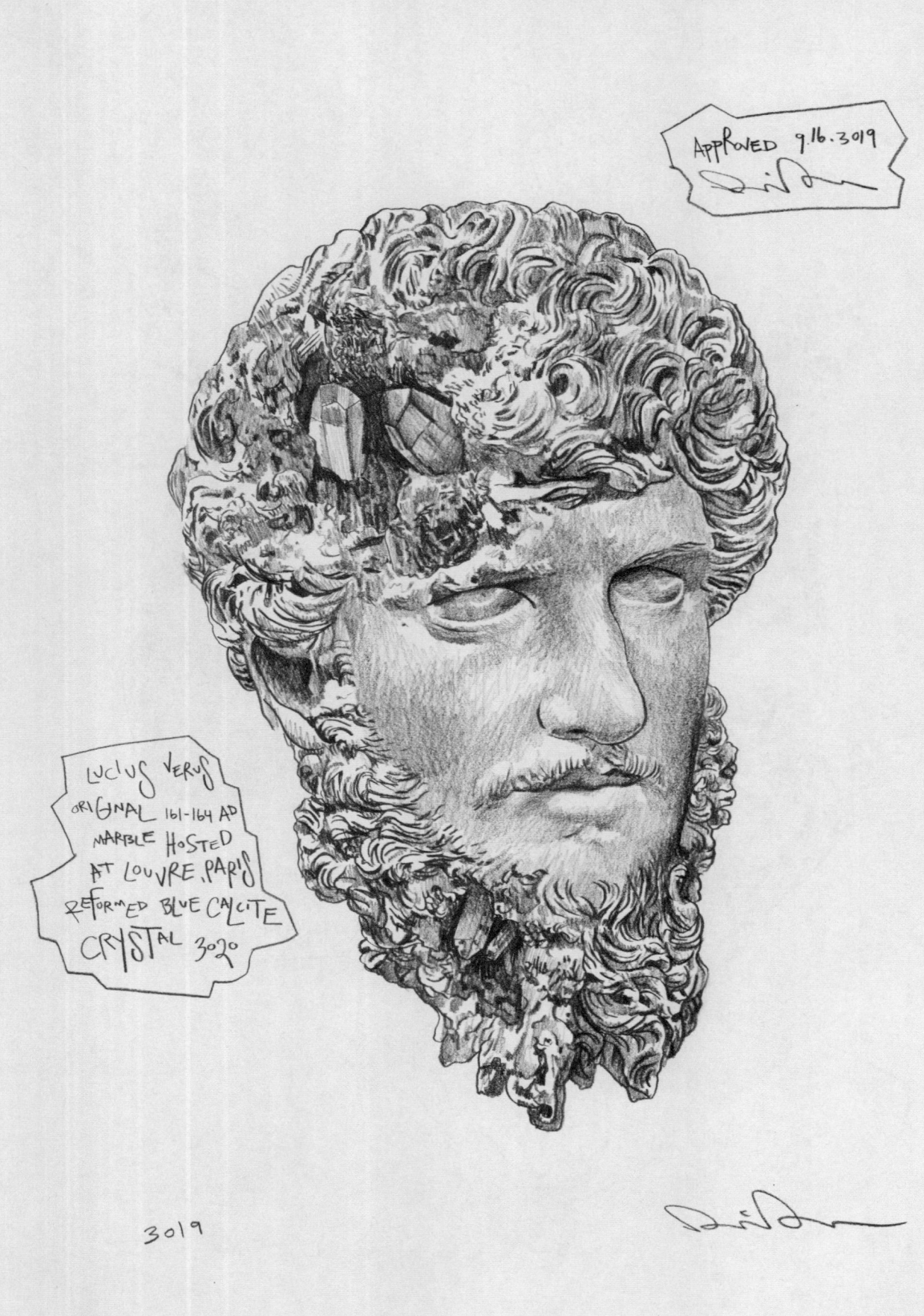

APPROVED 9.16.3019

LUCIUS VERUS
ORIGNAL 161-164 AD
MARBLE HOSTED
AT LOUVRE, PARIS
REFORMED BLUE CALCITE
CRYSTAL 3020

3019

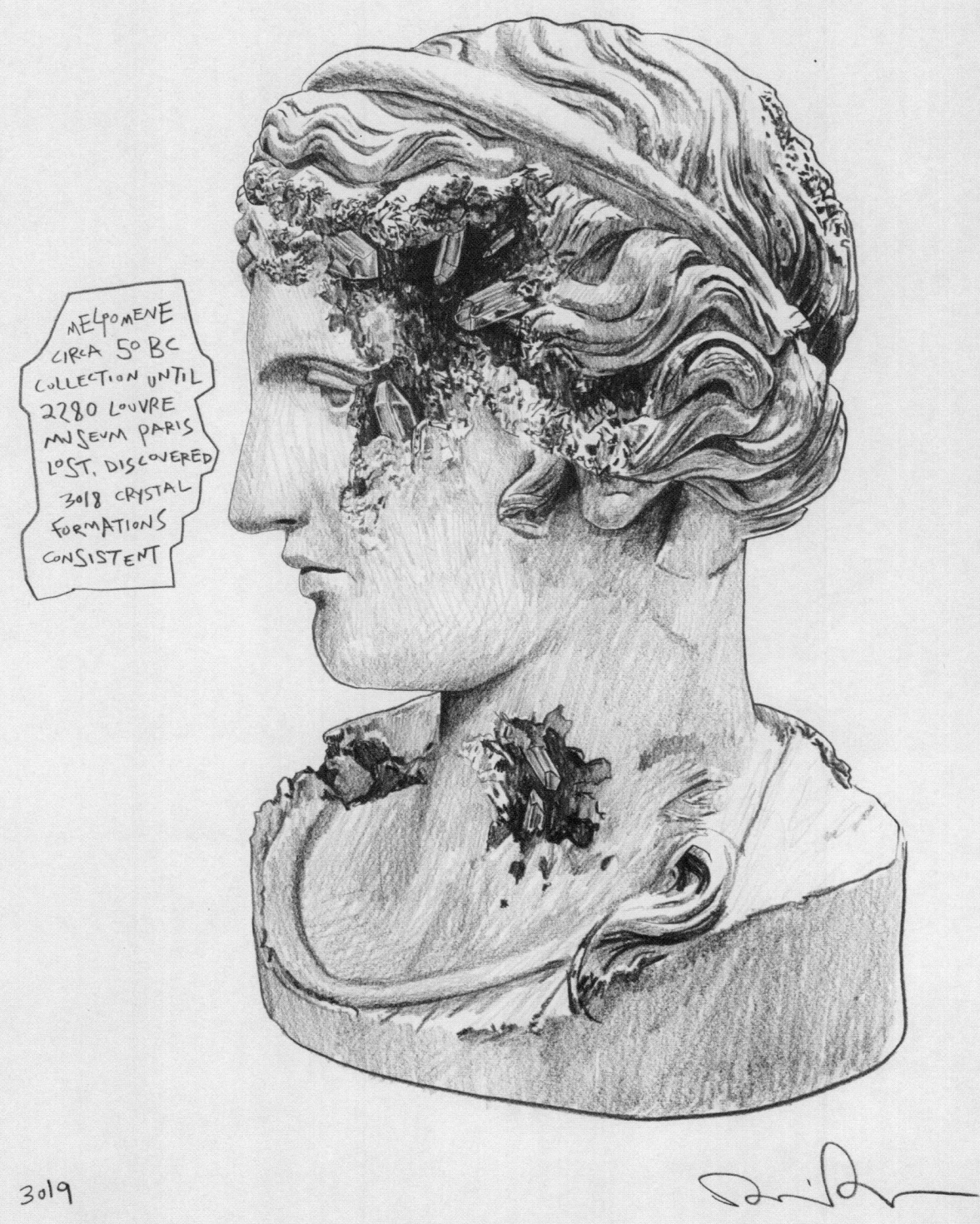

MELPOMENE
CIRCA 50 BC
COLLECTION UNTIL
2280 LOUVRE
MUSEUM PARIS
LOST, DISCOVERED
3018 CRYSTAL
FORMATIONS
CONSISTENT

3019

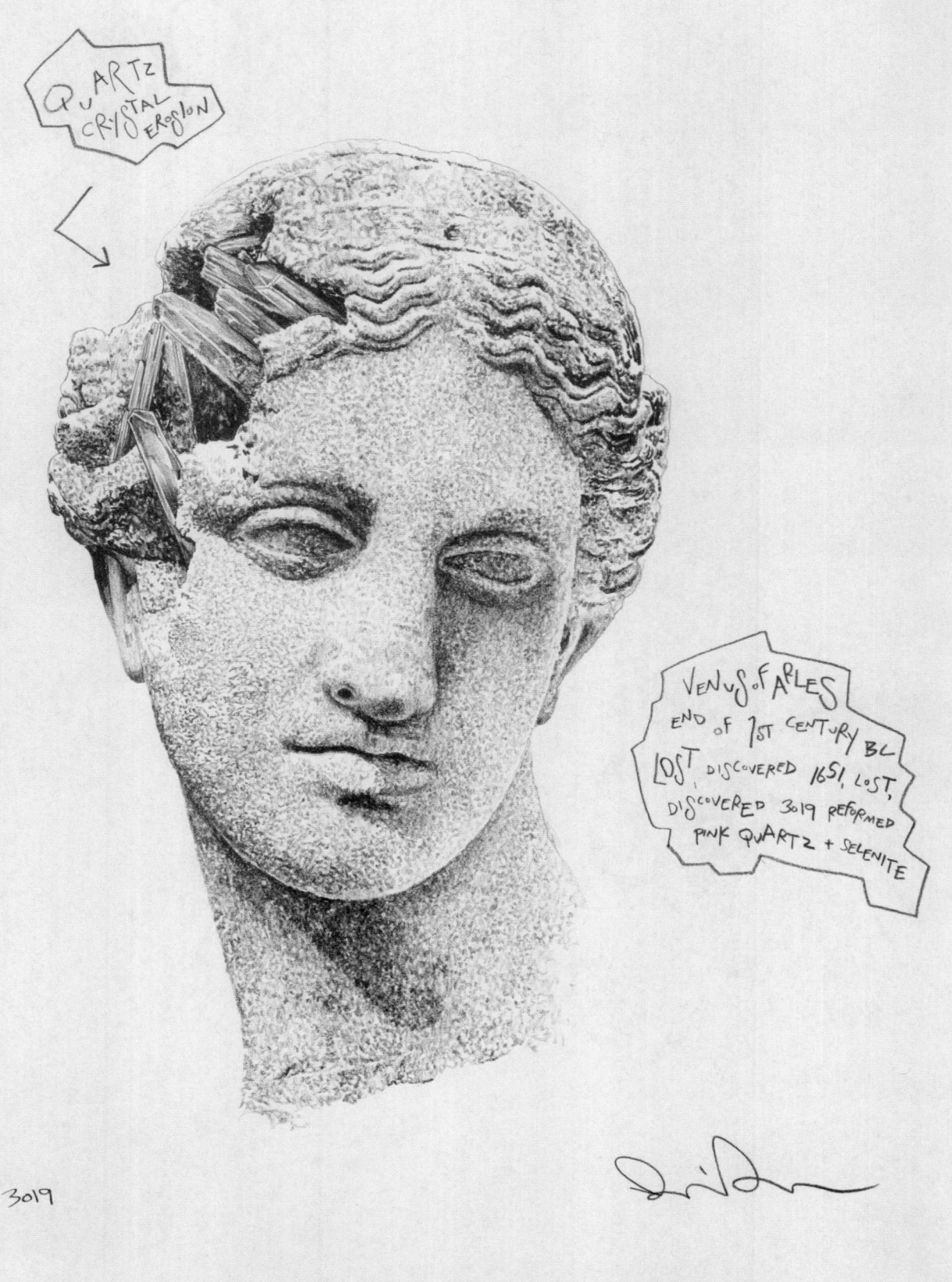

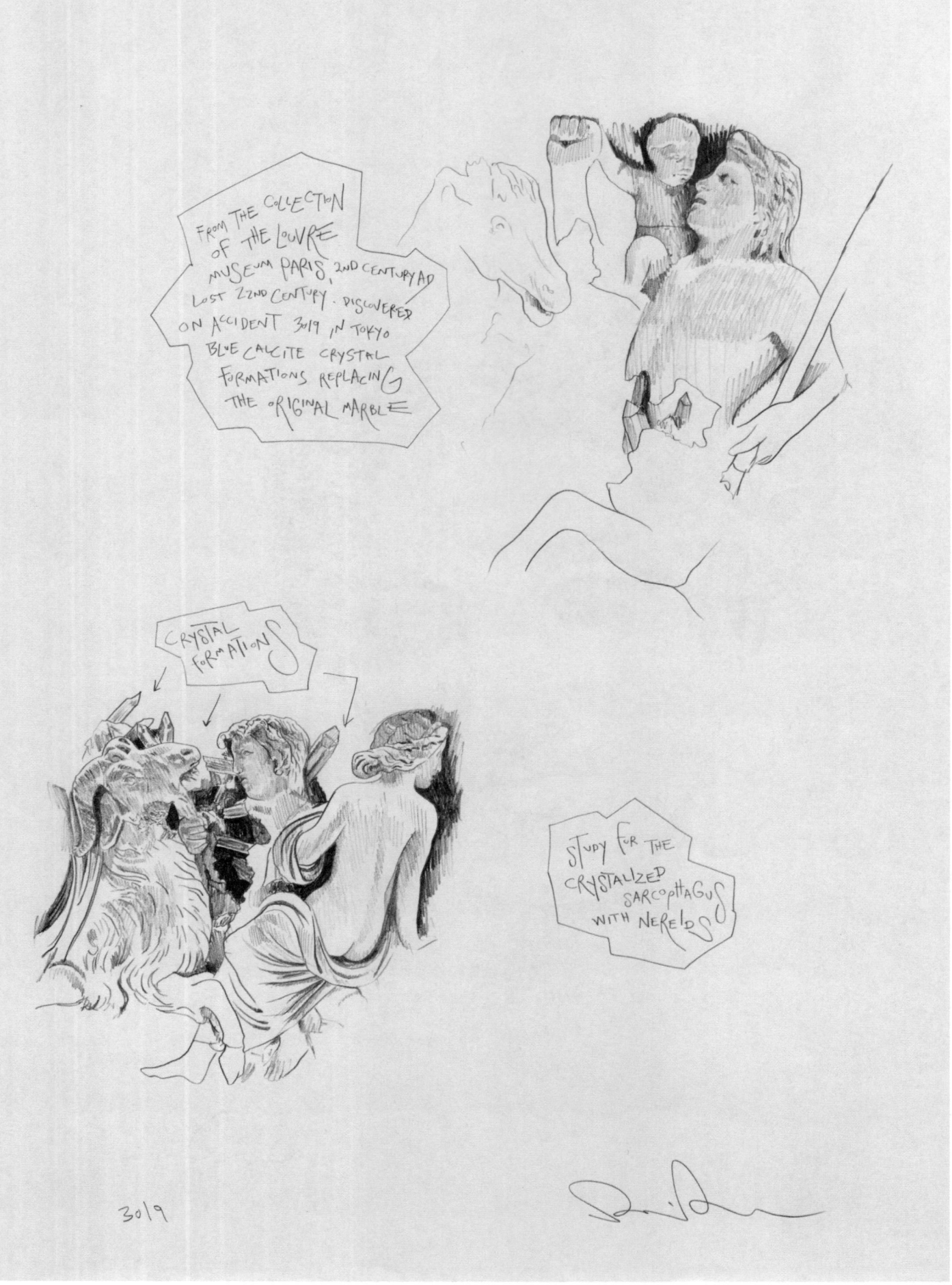

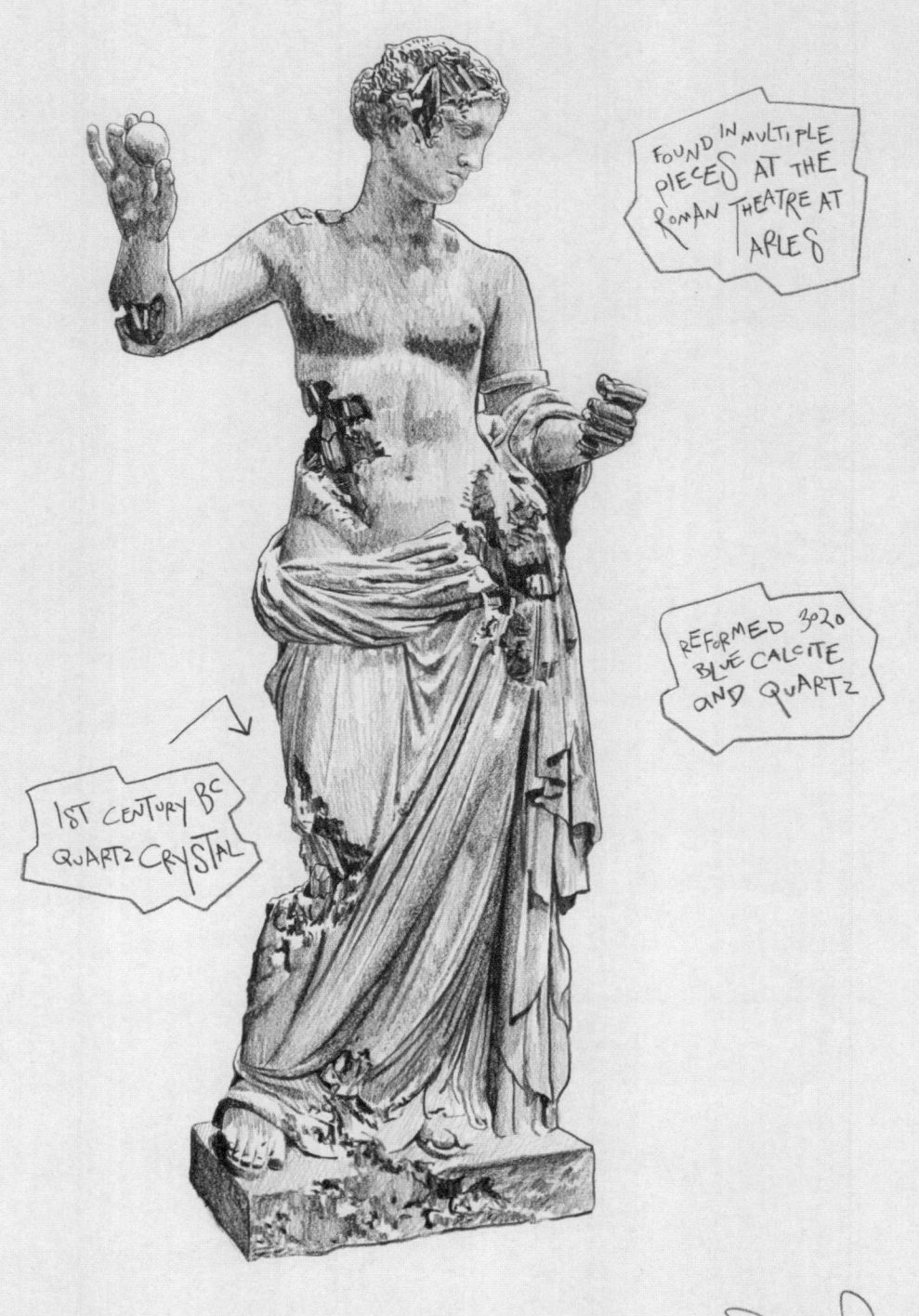

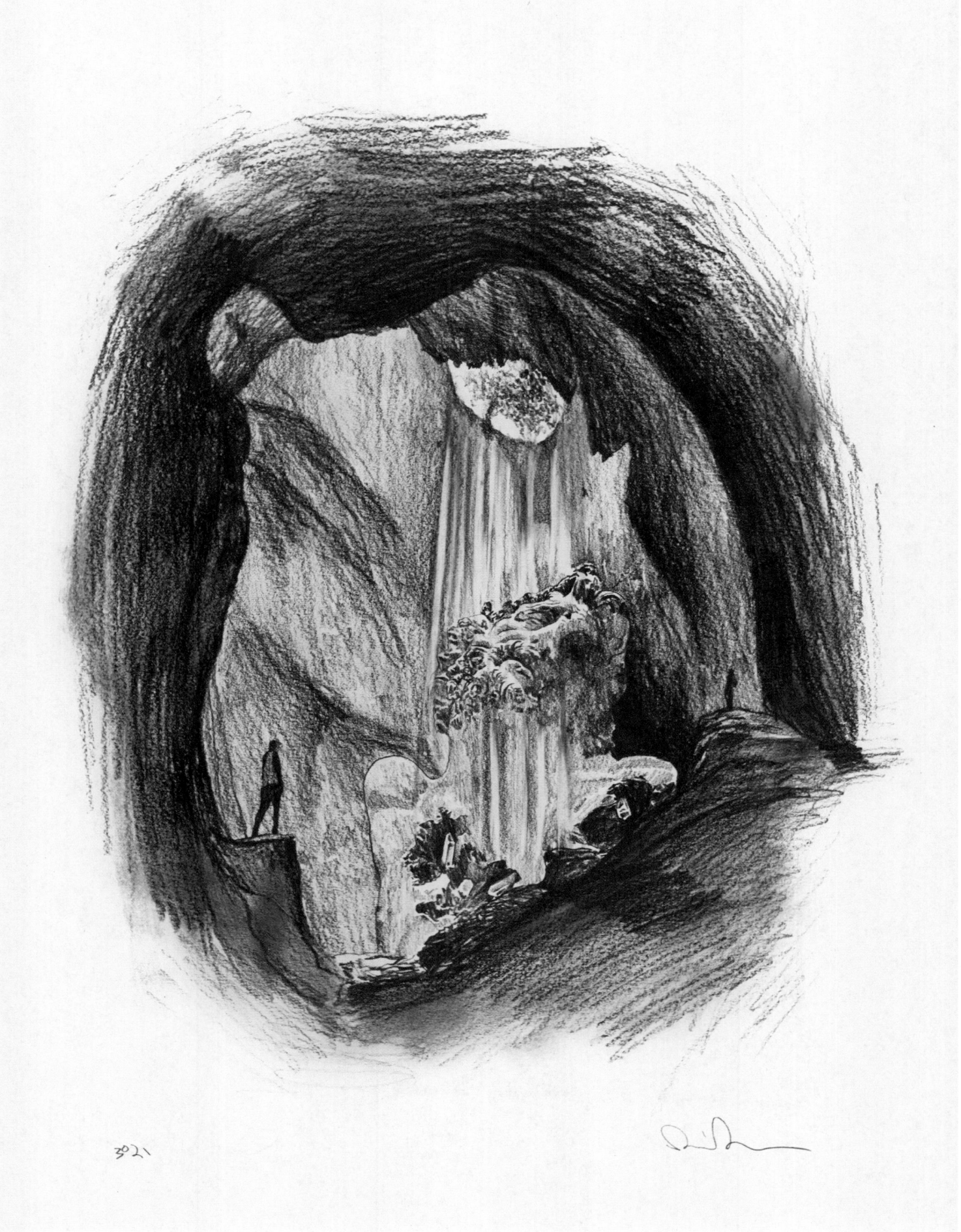

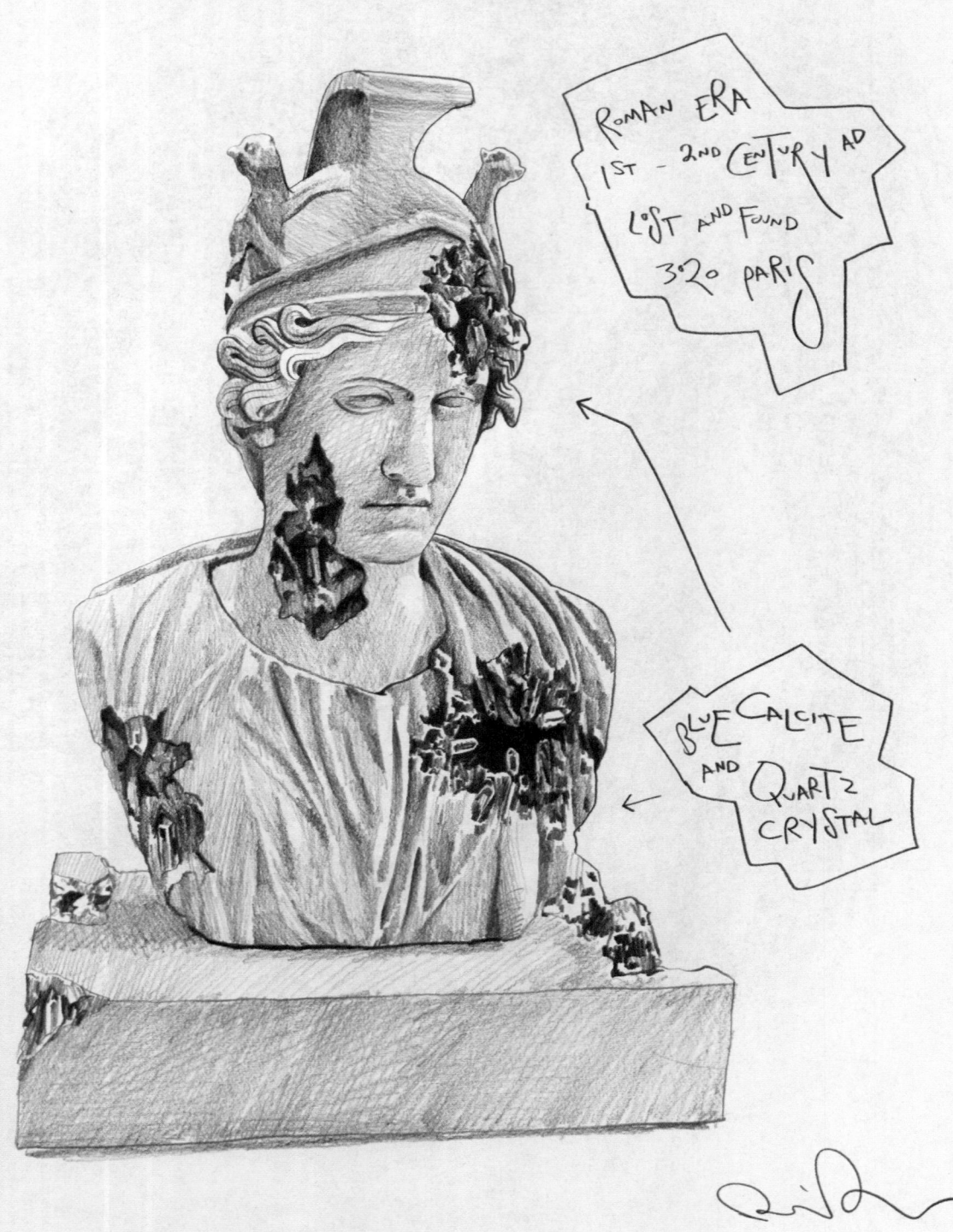

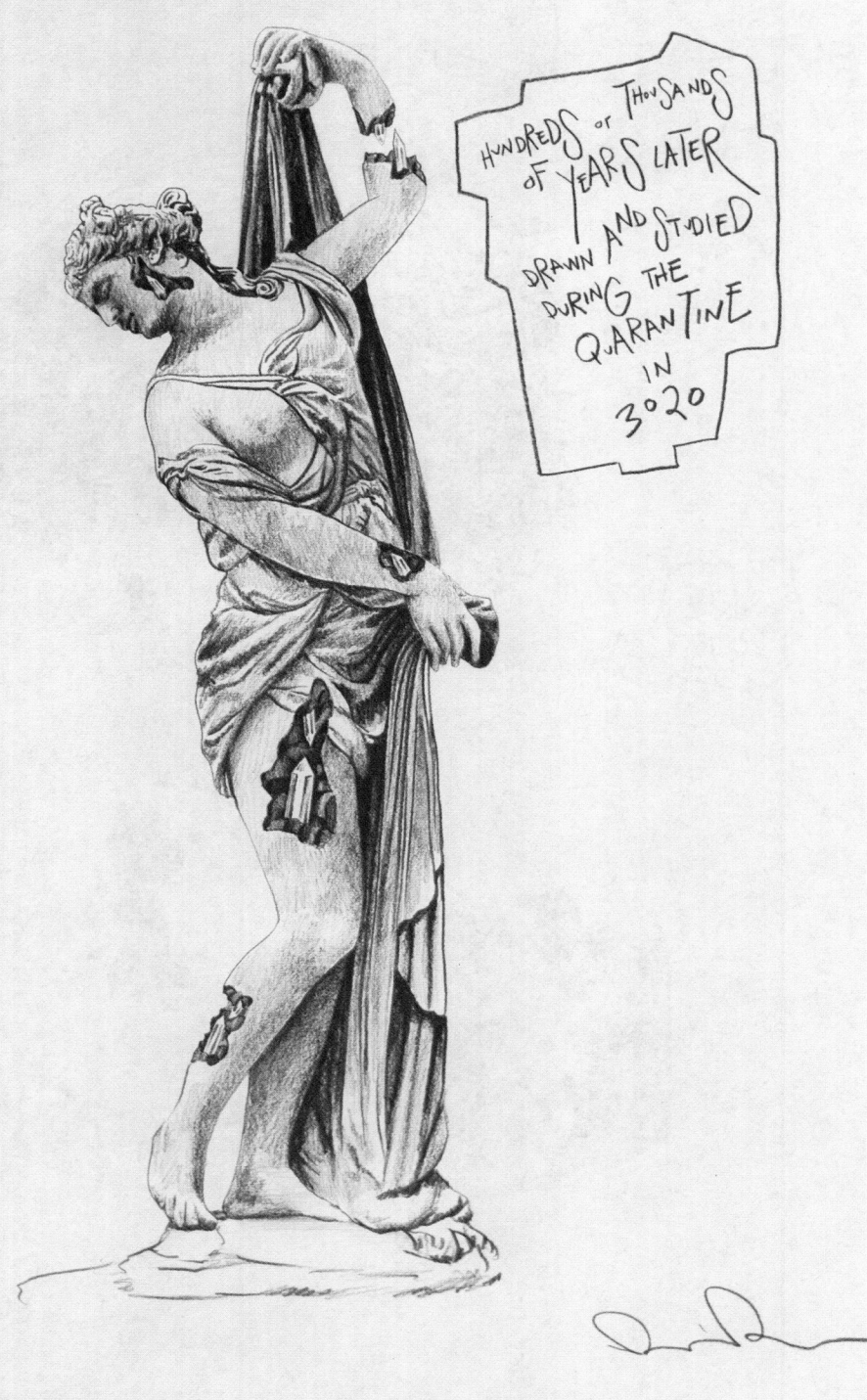

HUNDREDS or THOUSANDS
OF YEARS LATER

DRAWN AND STUDIED
DURING THE
QUARANTINE
IN
3020

3020

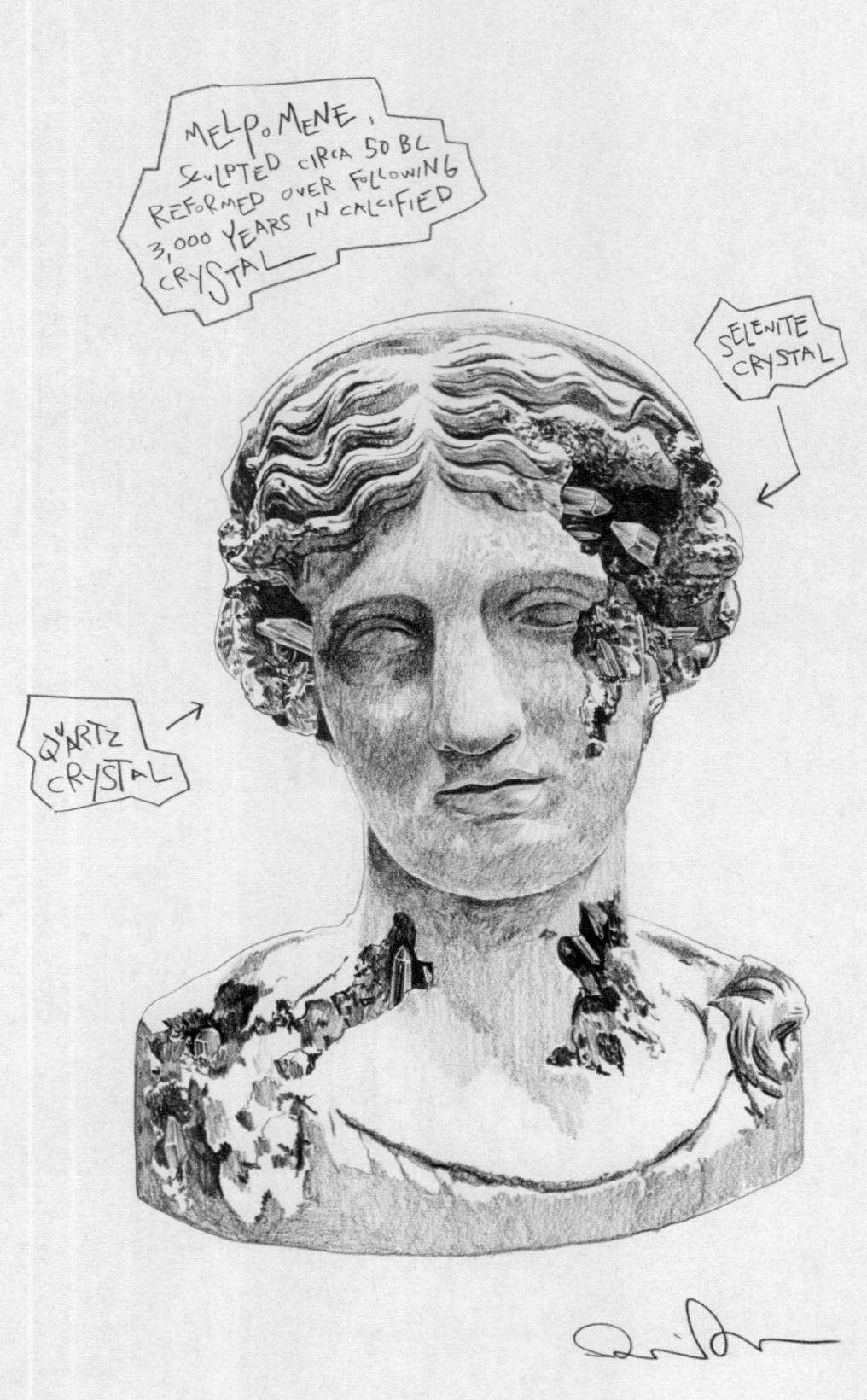

3019

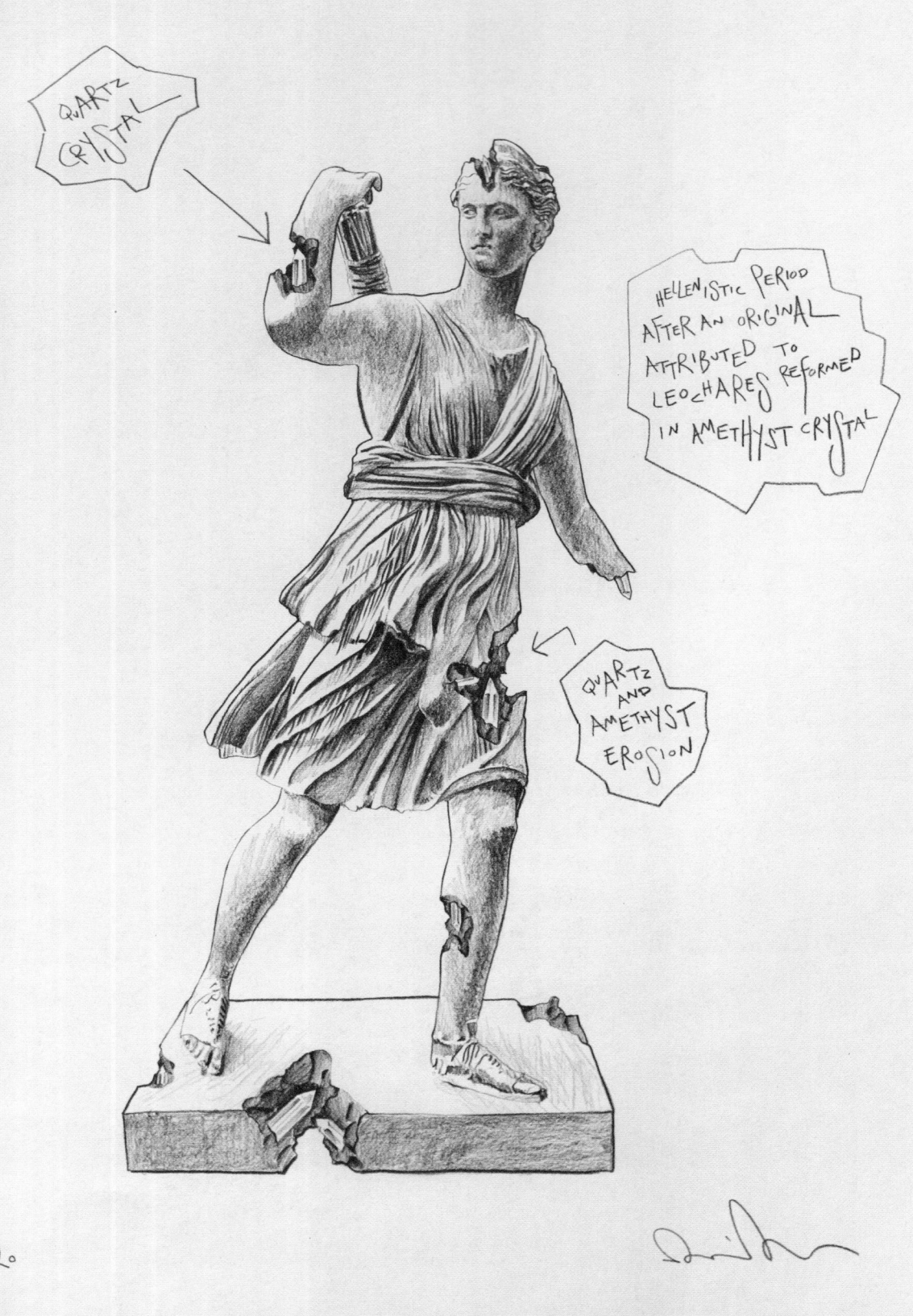

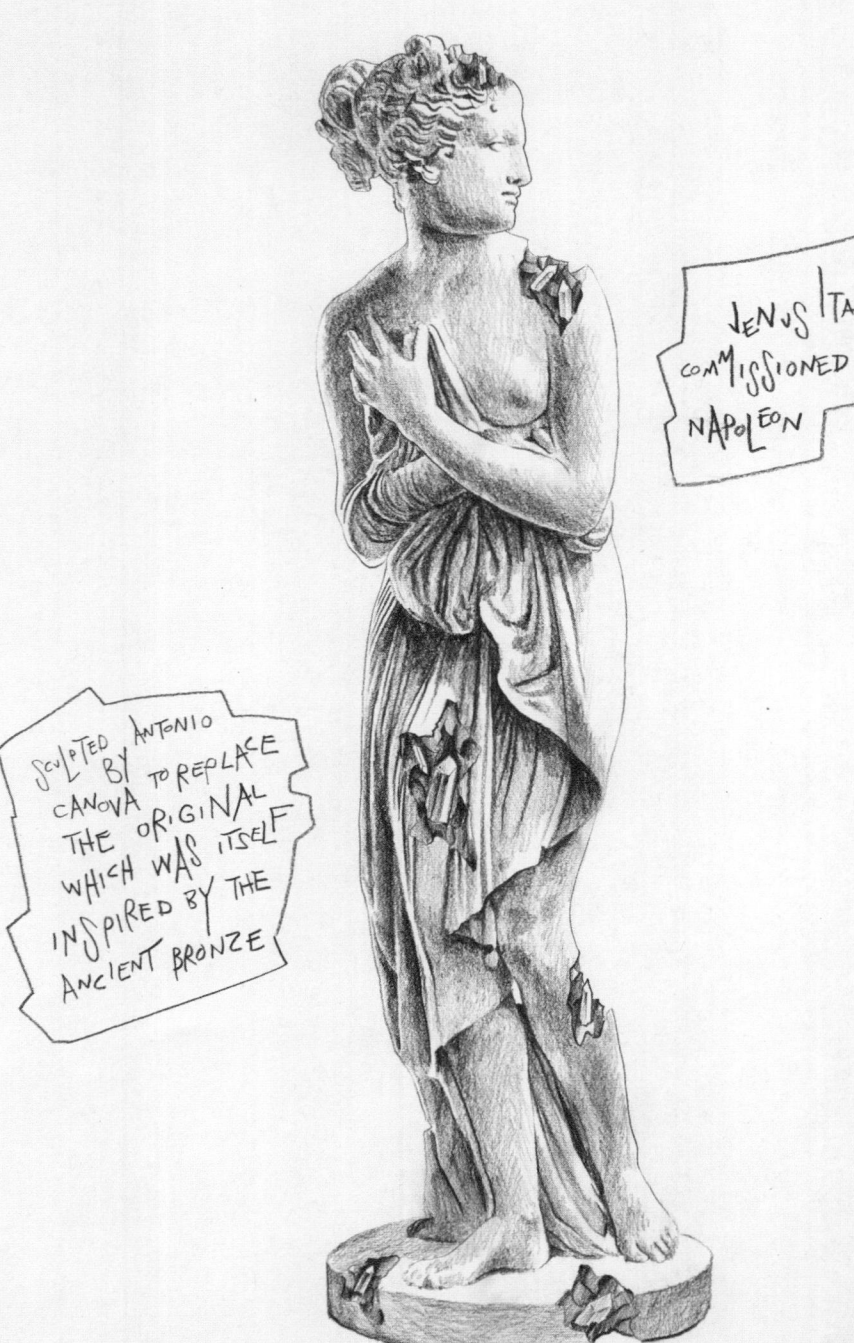

VENUS ITALICA COMMISSIONED BY NAPOLEON

SCULPTED BY ANTONIO CANOVA TO REPLACE THE ORIGINAL WHICH WAS ITSELF INSPIRED BY THE ANCIENT BRONZE

3020

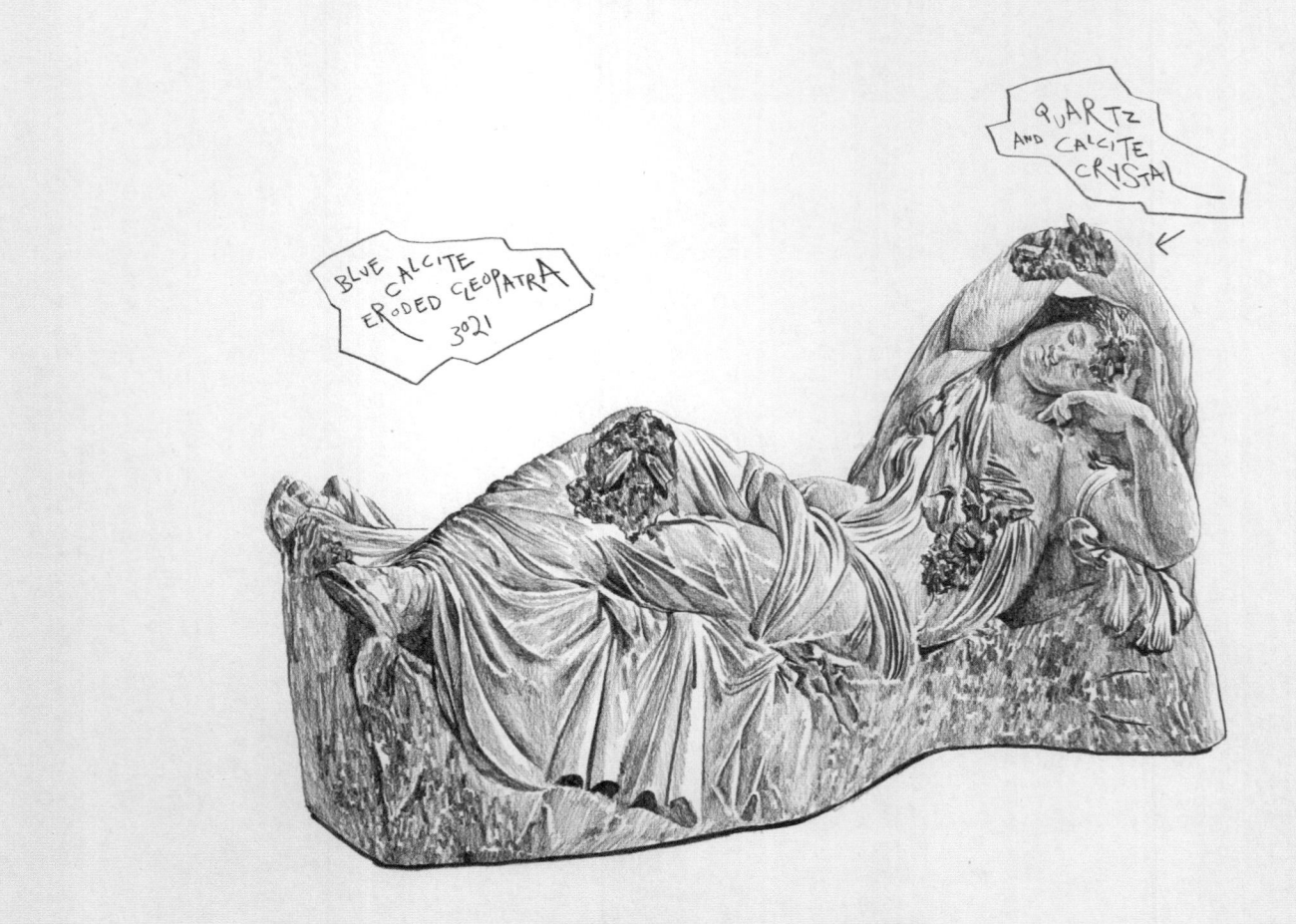

# Index

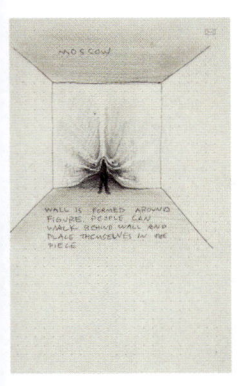
Page 10

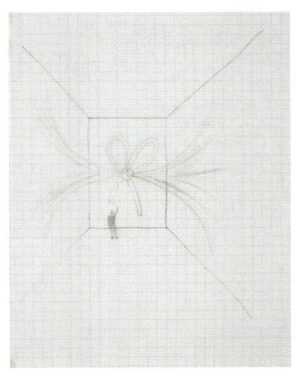
Page 11

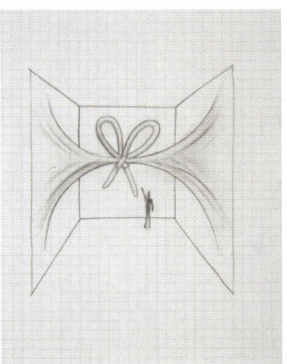
Page 11

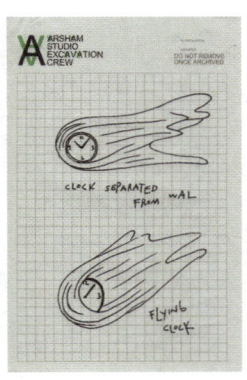
Page 12

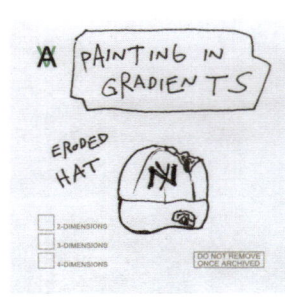
Page 12

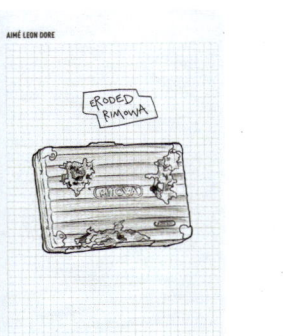
Page 13

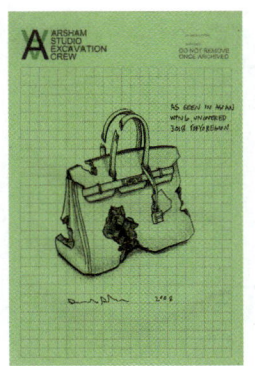
Page 14

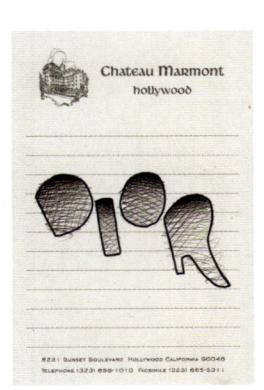
Page 14

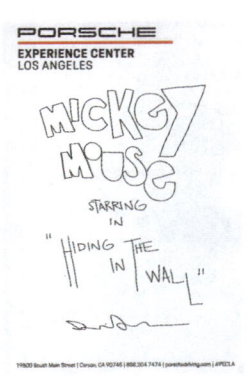
Page 15

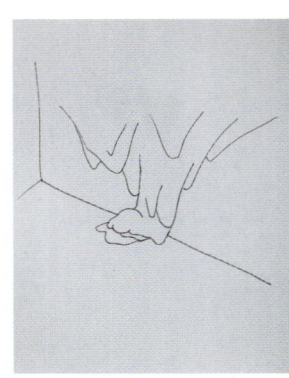
Page 16

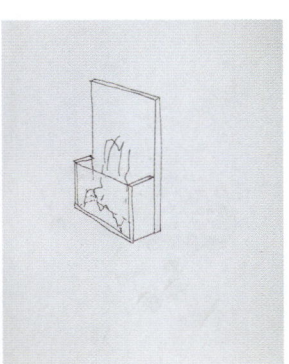
Page 17

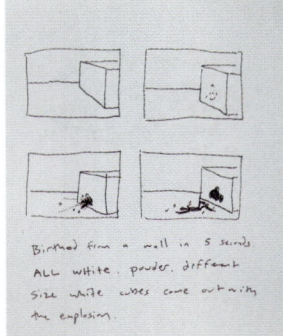
Page 18

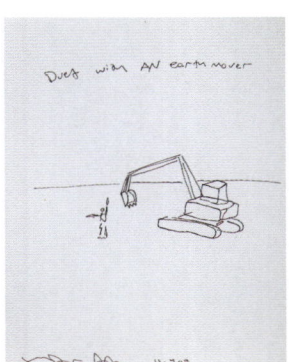
Page 19

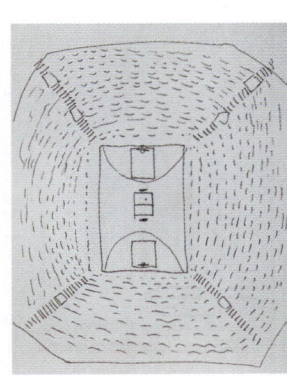
Page 20

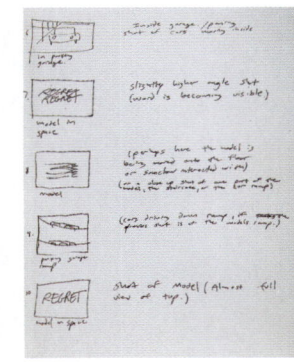
Page 22

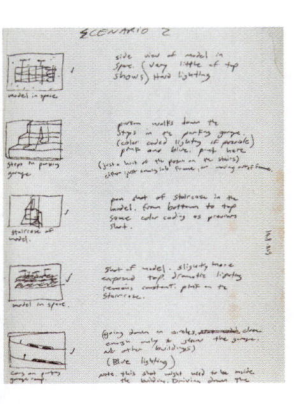
Page 23

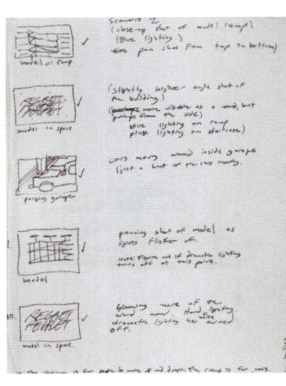
Page 24

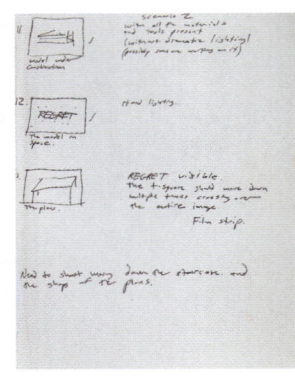
Page 25

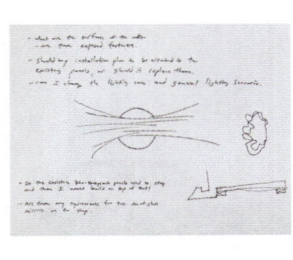
Page 26

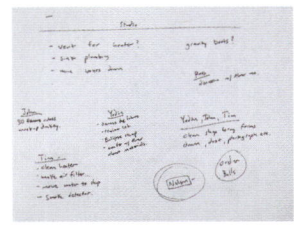
Page 28

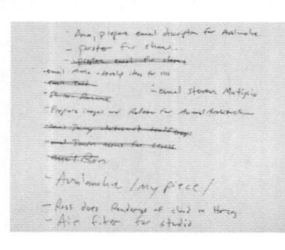

Page 29

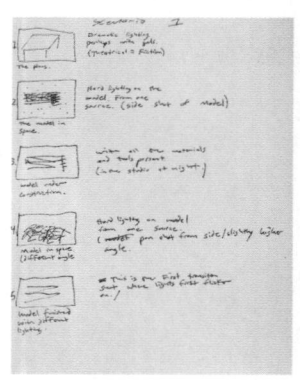

Page 31

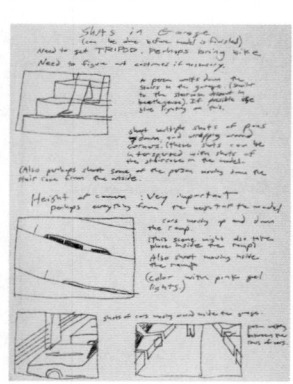

Page 32

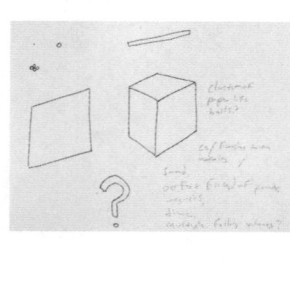

Page 34

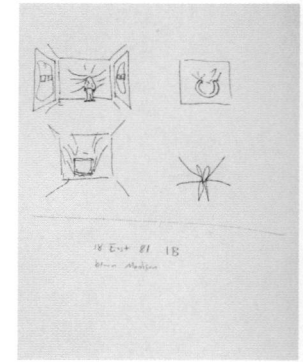

Page 35

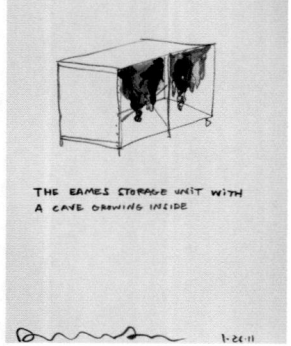

Page 36

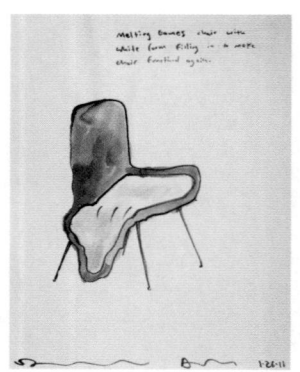

Page 38

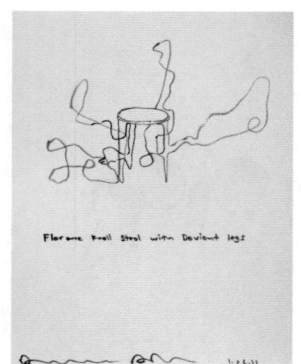

Page 39

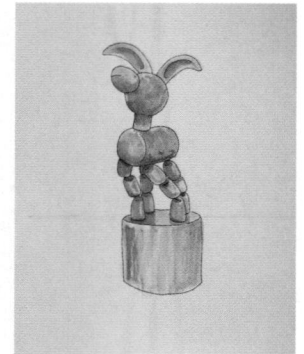

Page 41

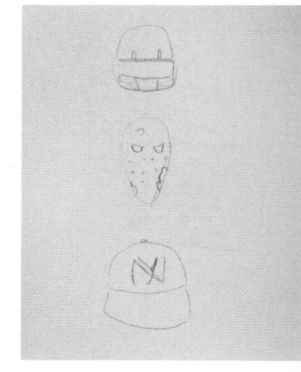

Page 43

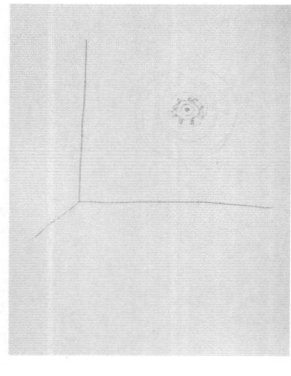

Page 44

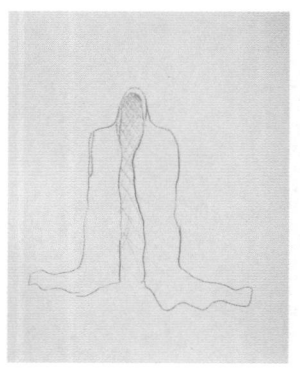

Page 45

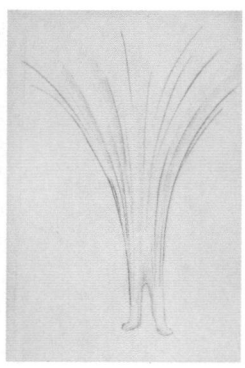

Page 47

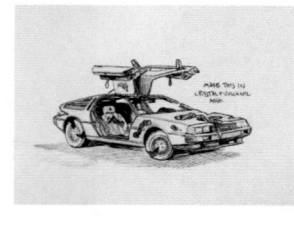

Page 48

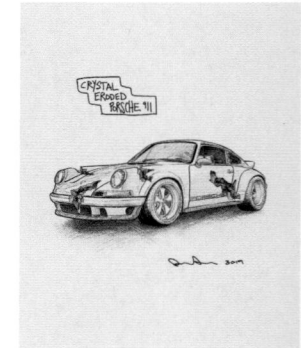

Page 51

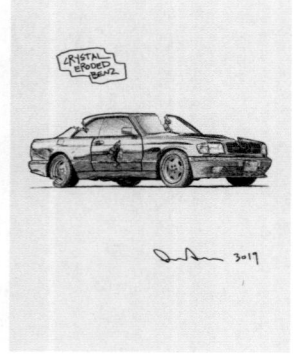

Page 52

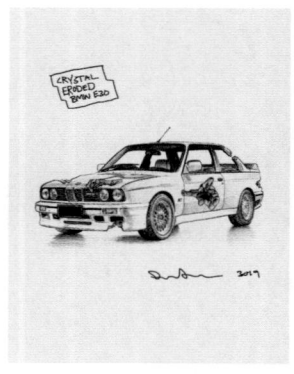

Page 53

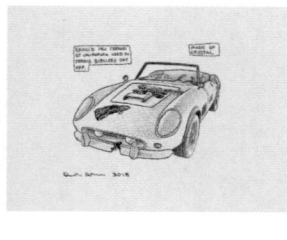

Page 54

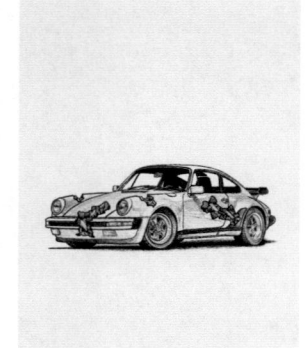

Page 57

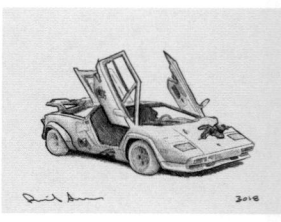

Page 58

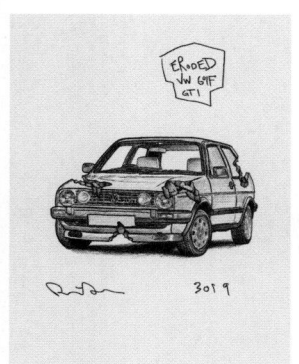

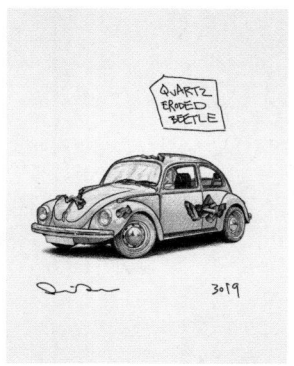

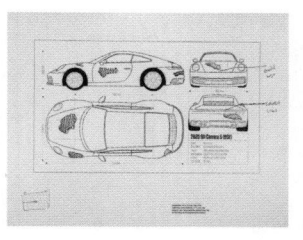

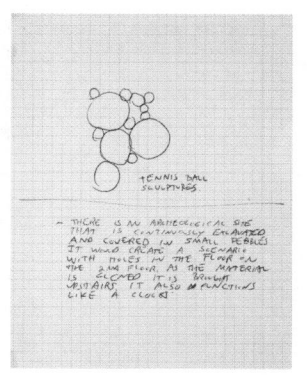

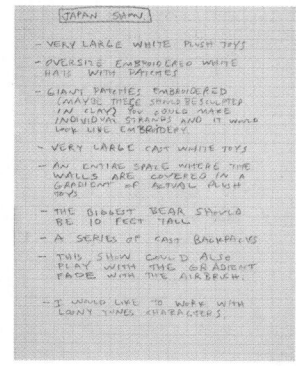

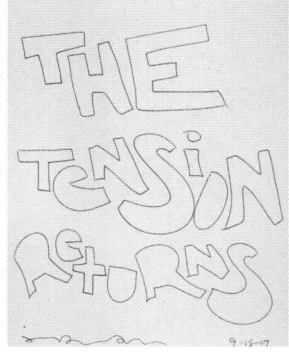

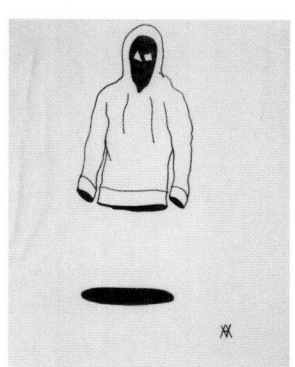

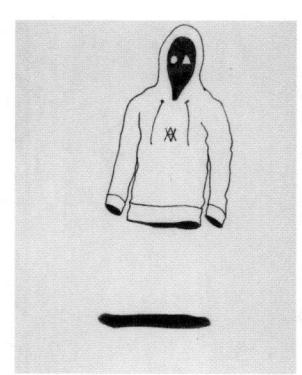

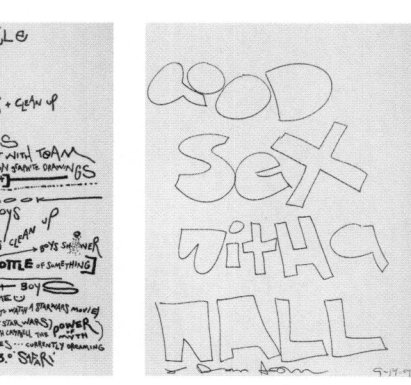

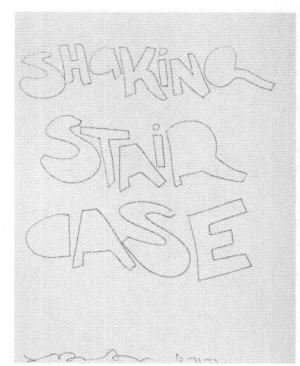

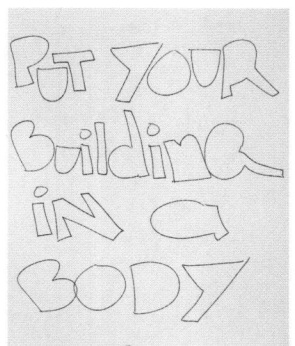

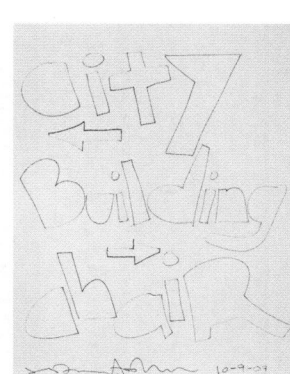

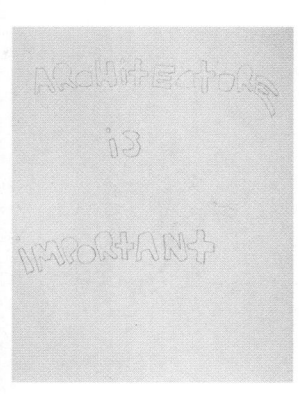

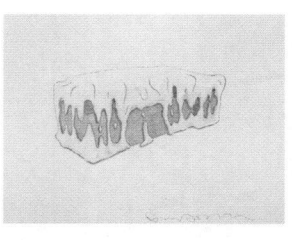

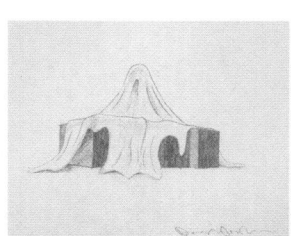

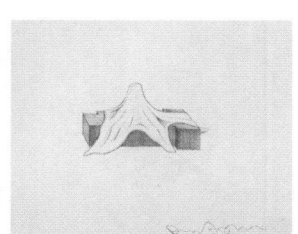

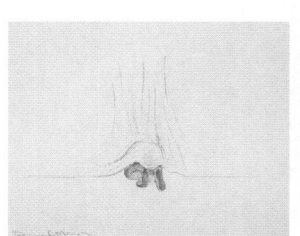

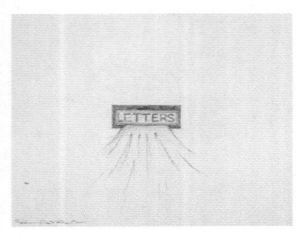

Page 83

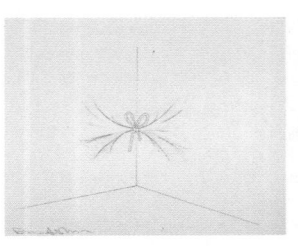

Page 84

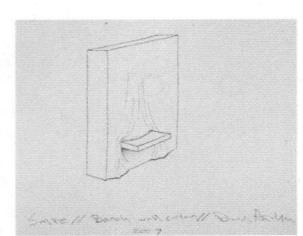

Page 86

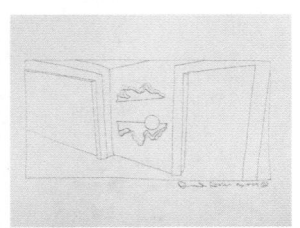

Page 88

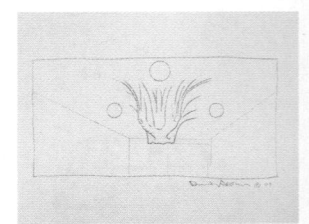

Page 91

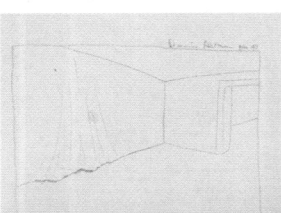

Page 92

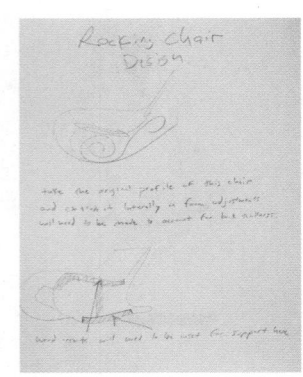

Page 93

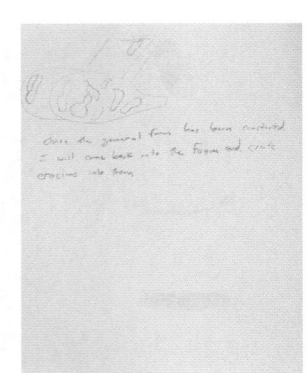

Page 94

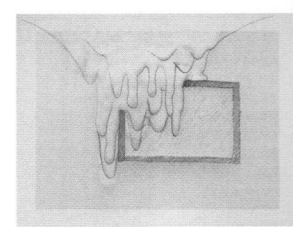

Page 95

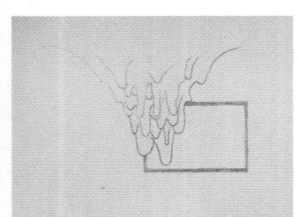

Page 96

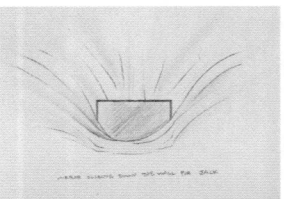

Page 97

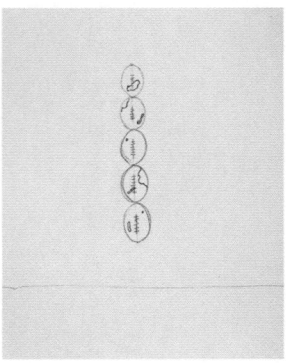

Page 98

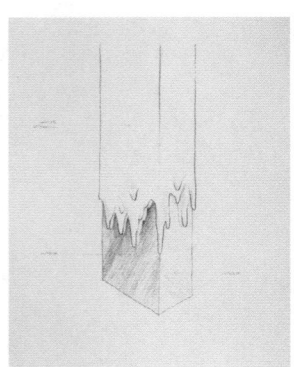

Page 100

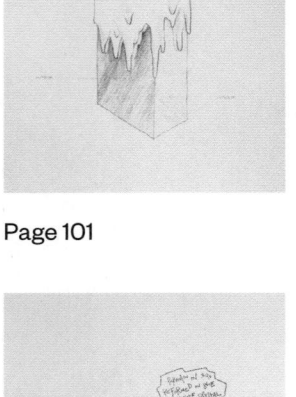

Page 101

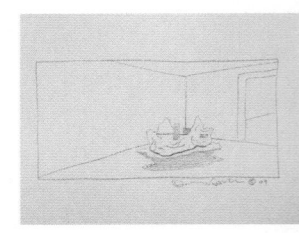

Page 103

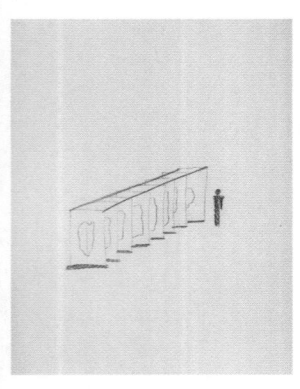

Page 104

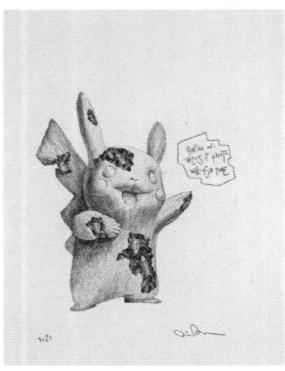

Page 106

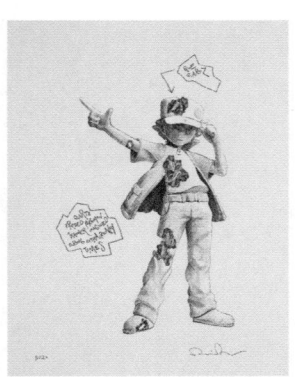

Page 109

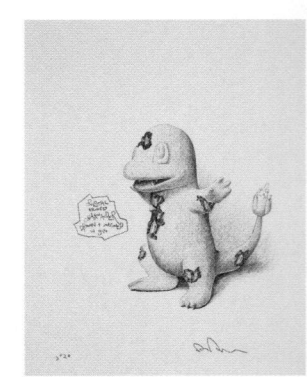

Page 110

Page 111

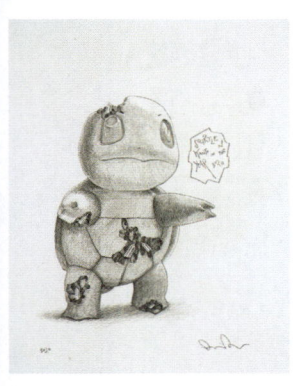

Page 112

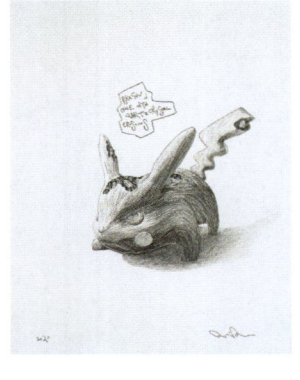

Page 113

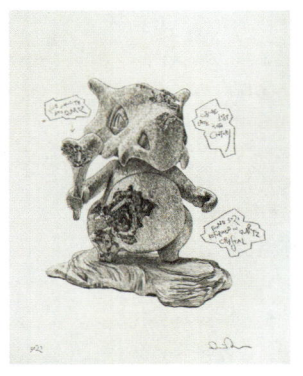

Page 114

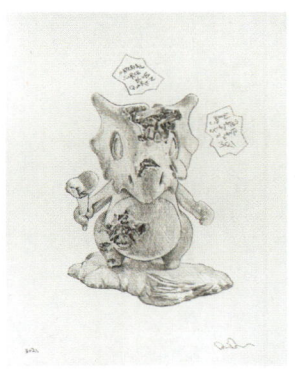

Page 115

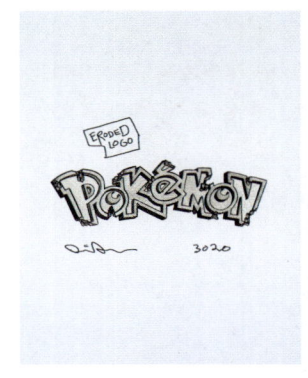

Page 117

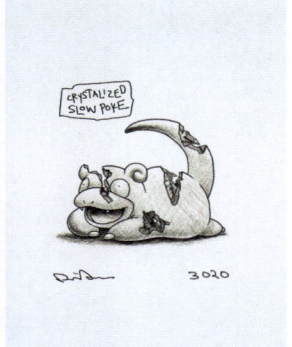

Page 118

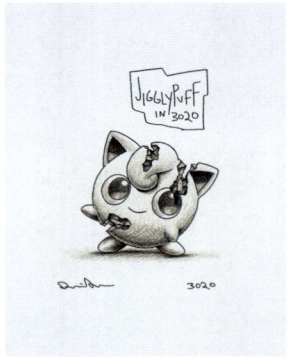

Page 119

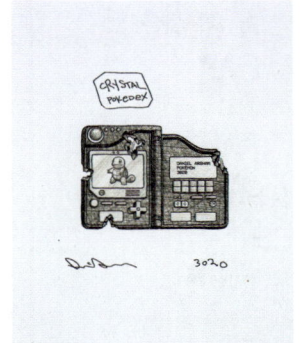

Page 120

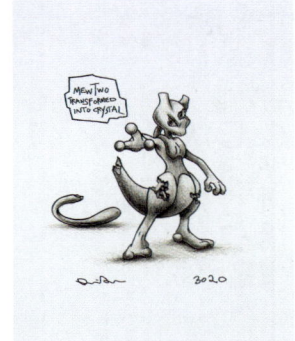

Page 121

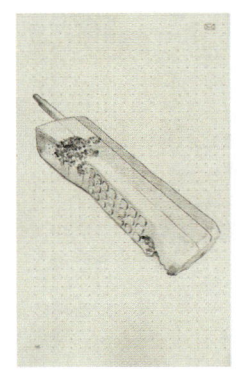

Page 122

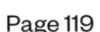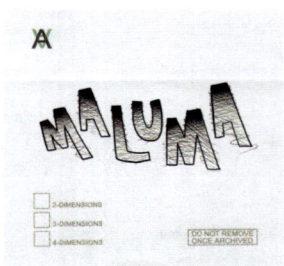

Page 122

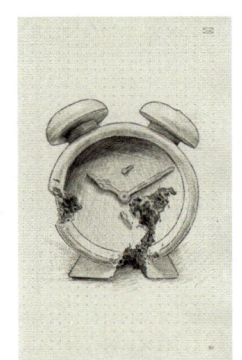

Page 122

Page 123

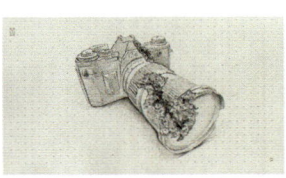

Page 124

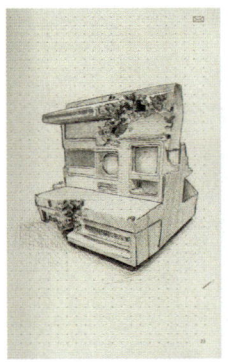

Page 125

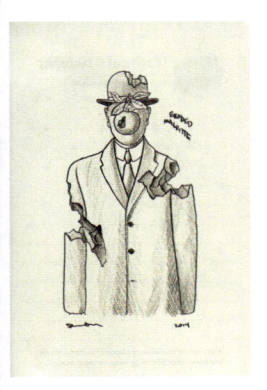

Page 125

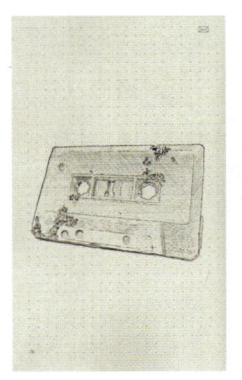

Page 126

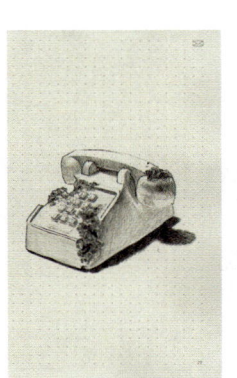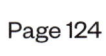

Page 126

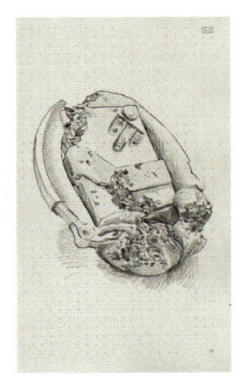

Page 127

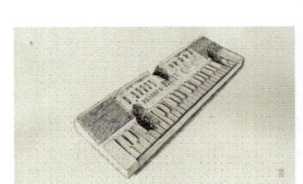

Page 129

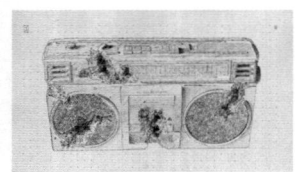

Page 129

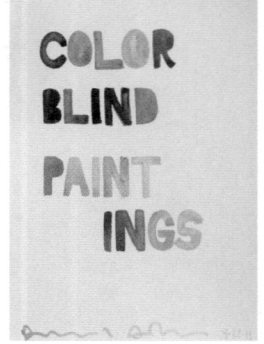

Page 131

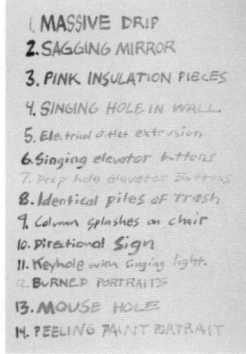

Page 132

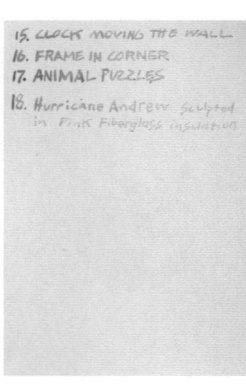

Page 133

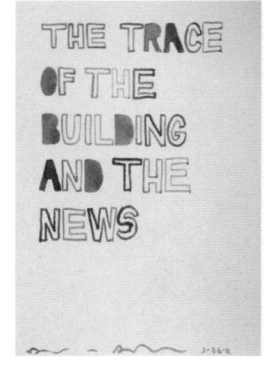

Page 134

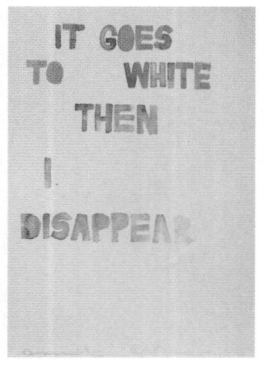

Page 135

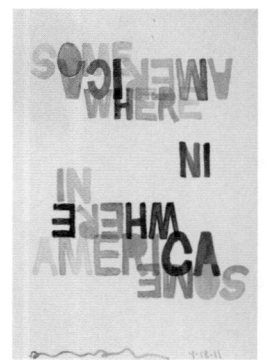

Page 136

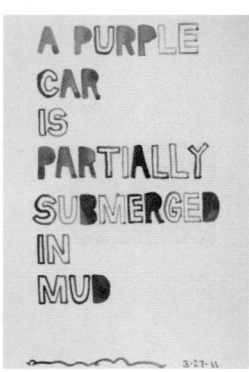

Page 137

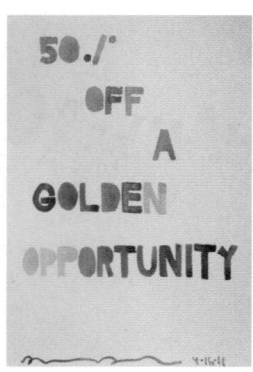

Page 138

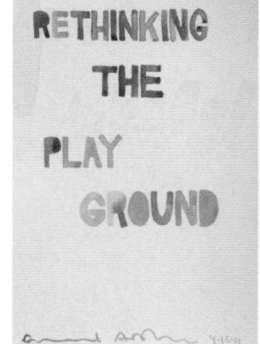

Page 139

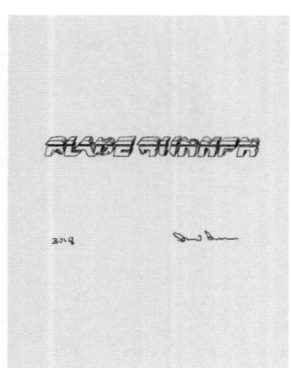

Page 140

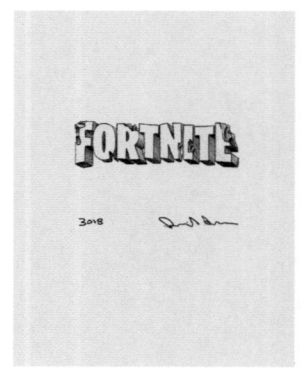

Page 143

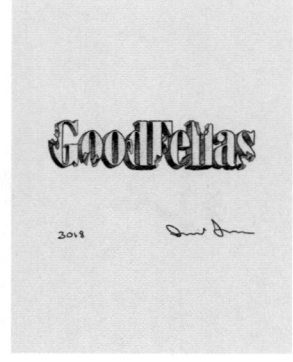

Page 144

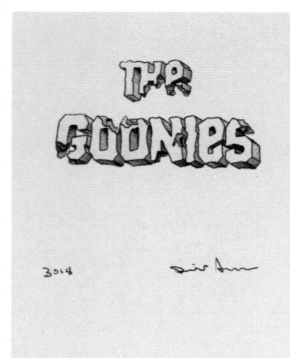

Page 145

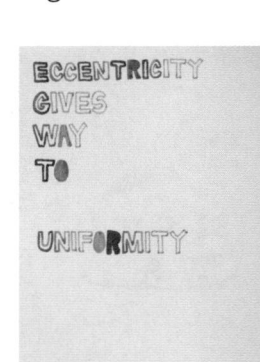

Page 147

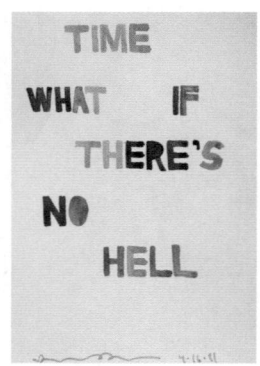

Page 148

Page 150

Page 151

Page 153

Page 154

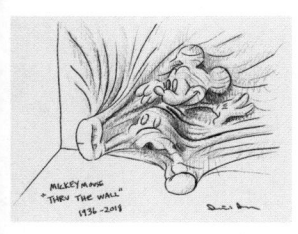

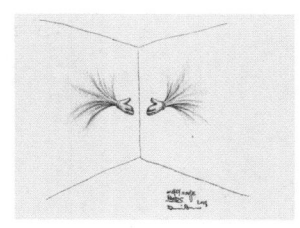

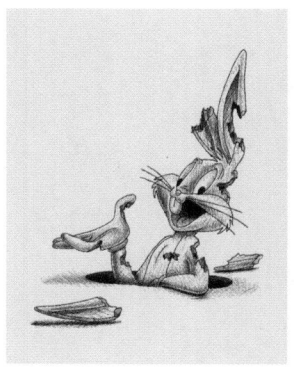

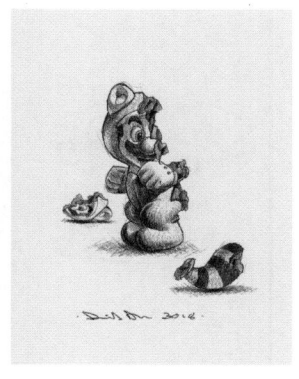

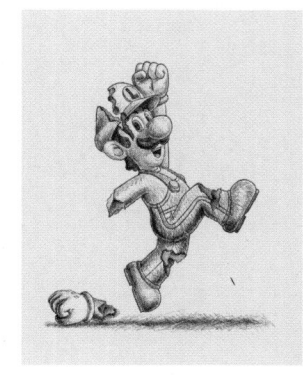

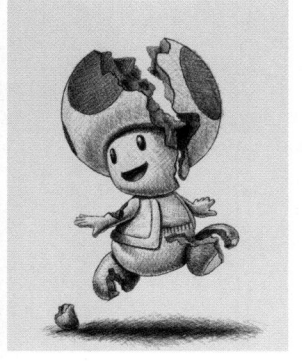

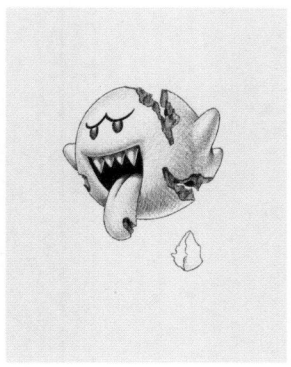

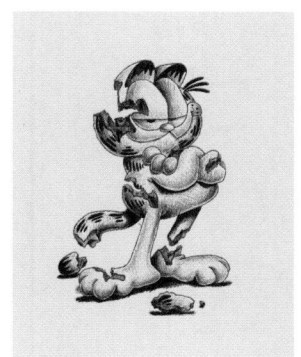

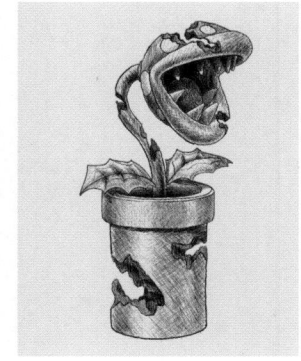

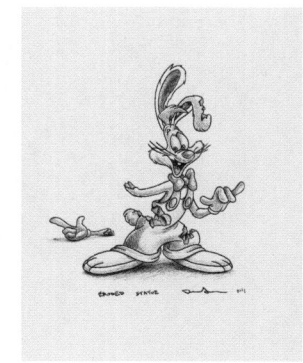

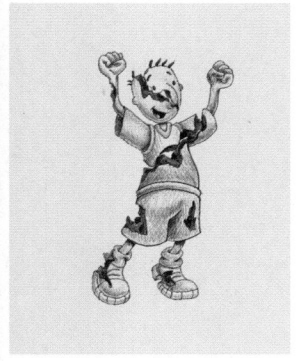

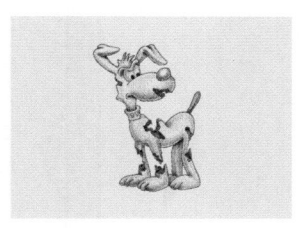

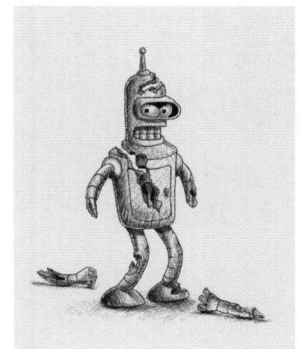

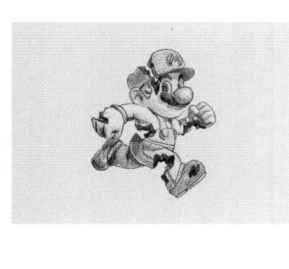

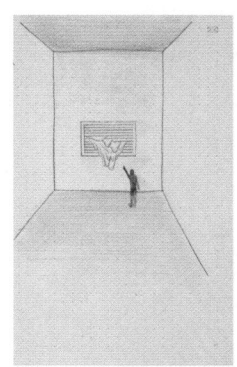

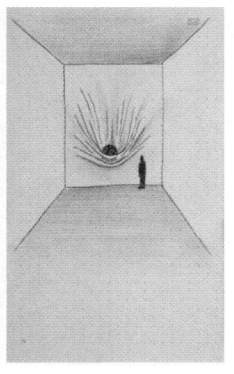

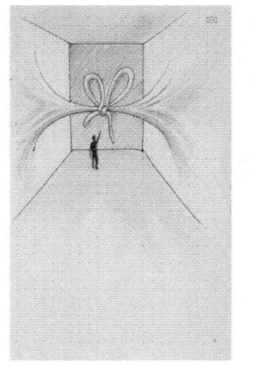

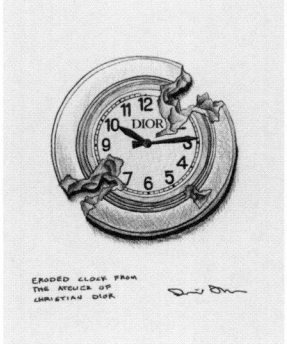

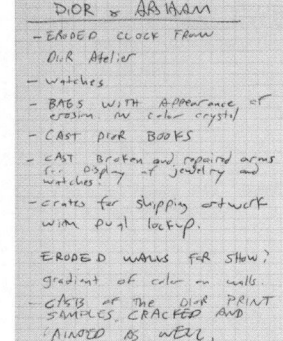

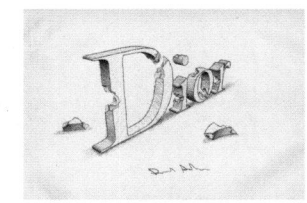

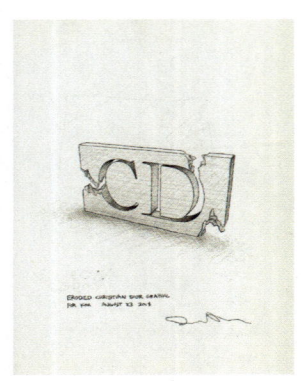

Page 177

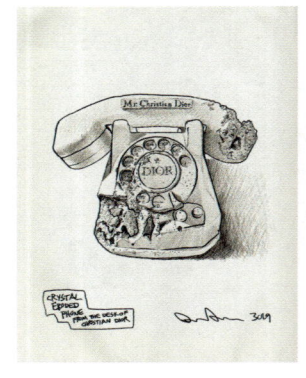

Page 179

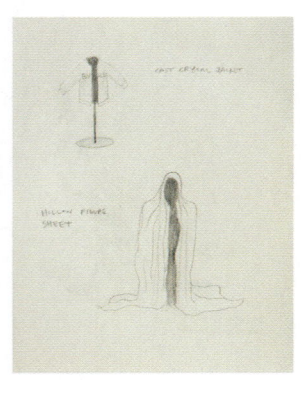

Page 181

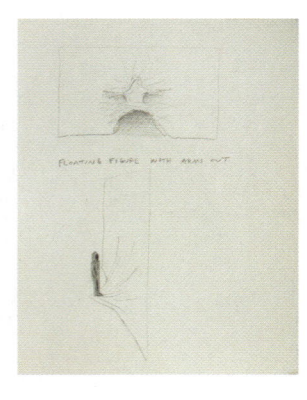

Page 182

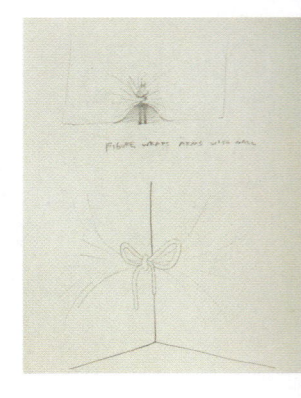

Page 183

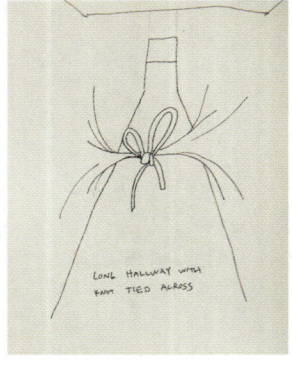

Page 184

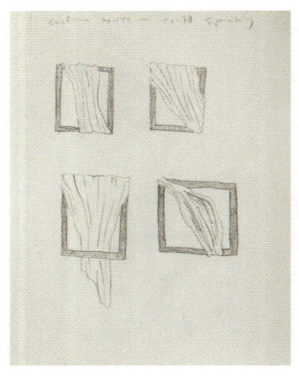

Page 185

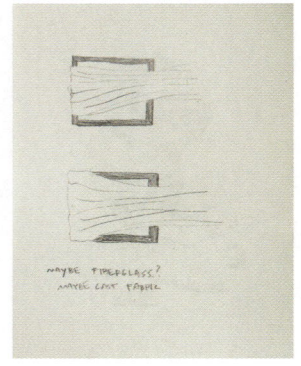

Page 186

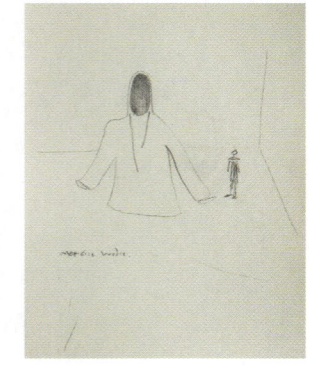

Page 187

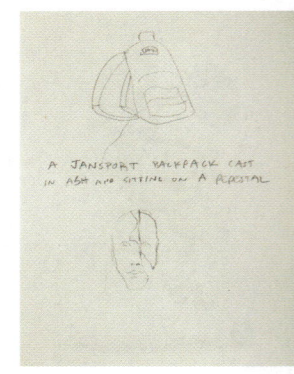

Page 188

Page 189

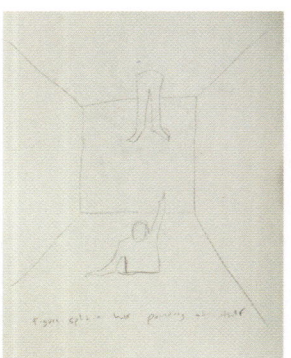

Page 190

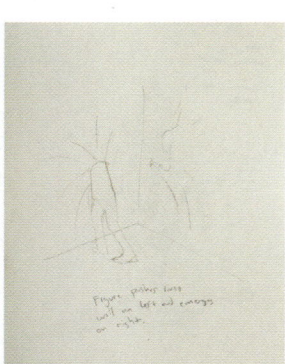

Page 191

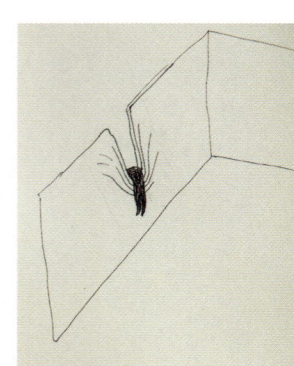

Page 192

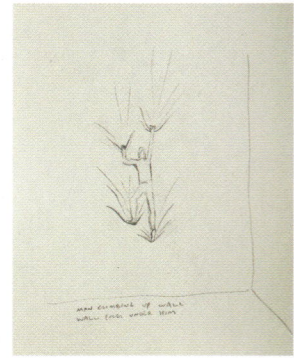

Page 193

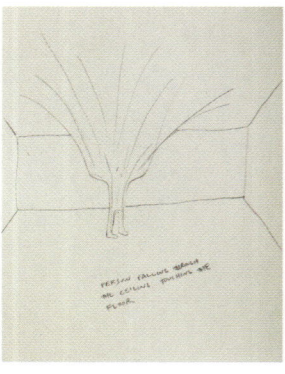

Page 194

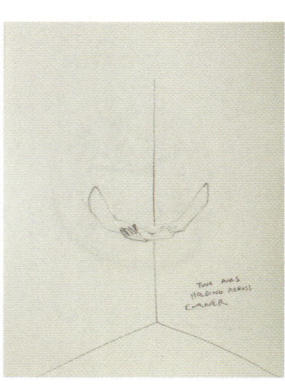

Page 195

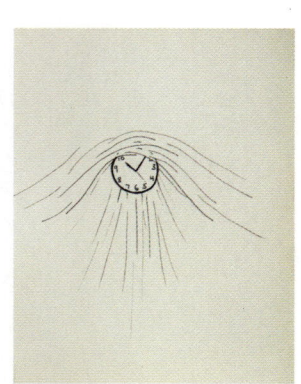

Page 196

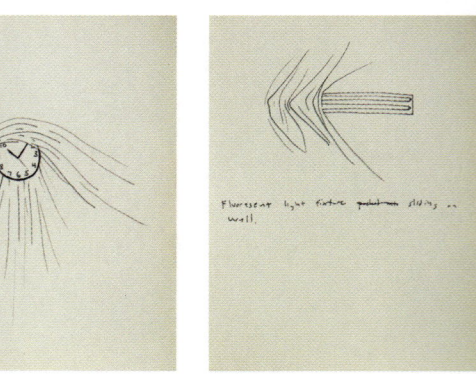

Page 197

Page 198

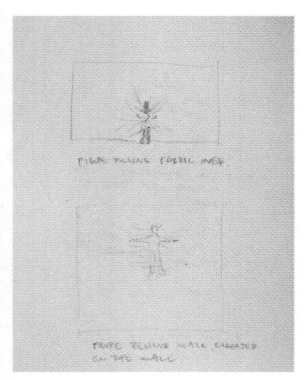

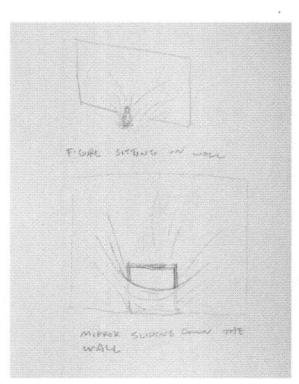

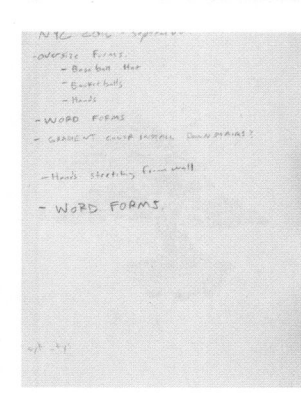

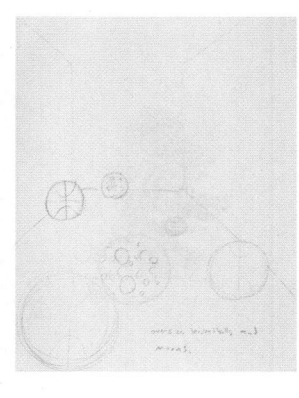

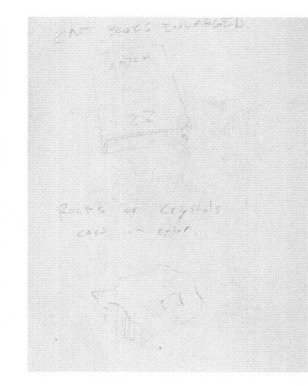

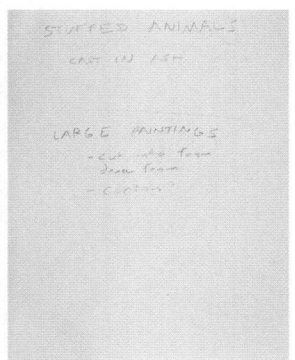

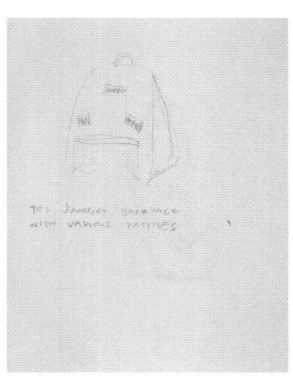

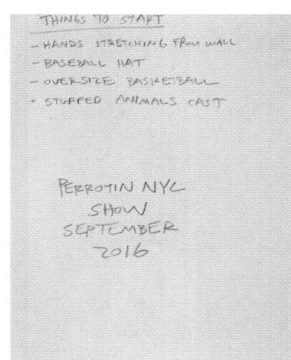

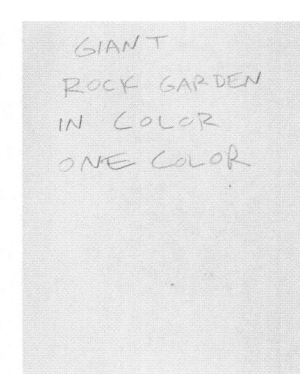

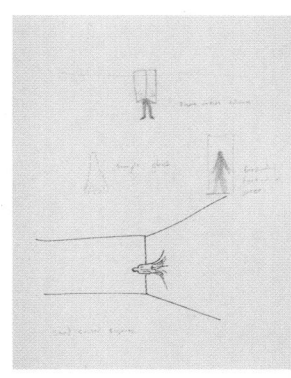

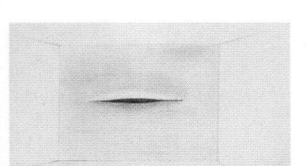

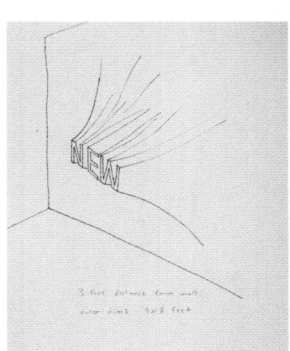

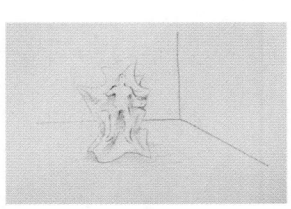

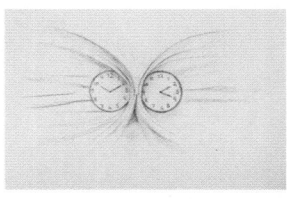

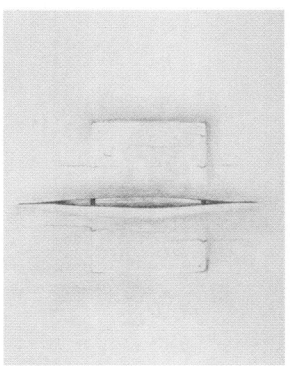

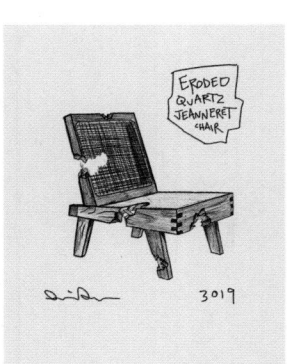

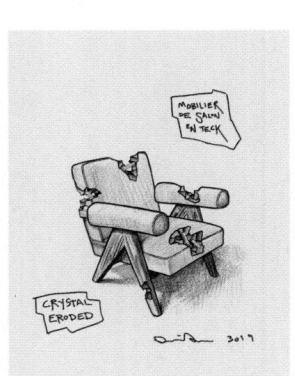

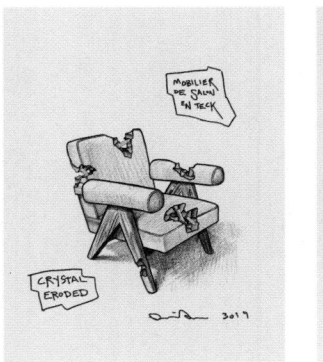

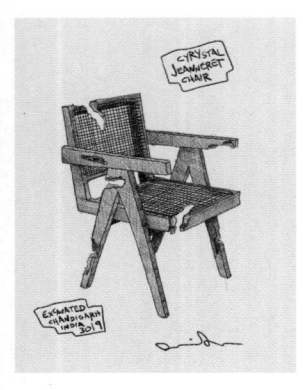

Page 223

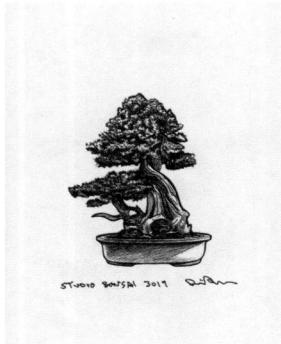

Page 224

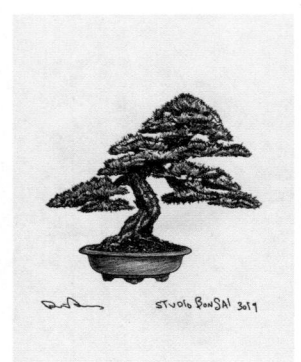

Page 225

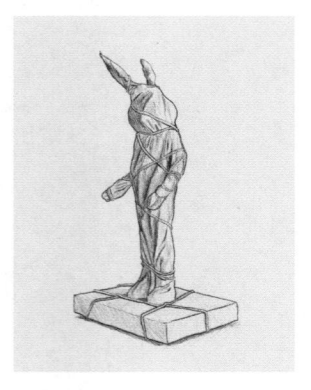

Page 226

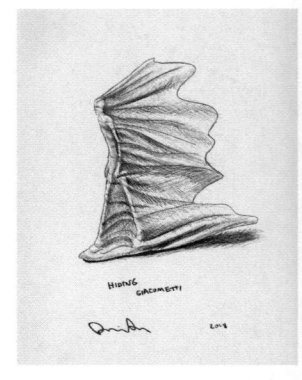

Page 229

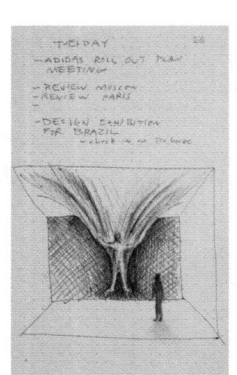

Page 230

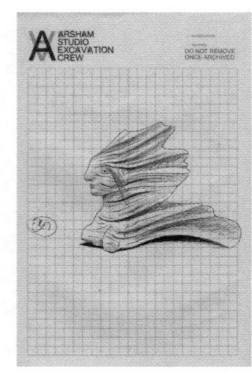

Page 231

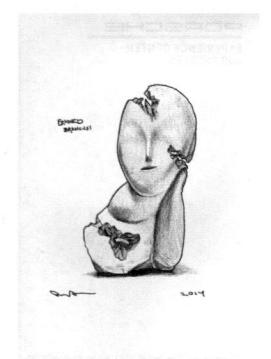

Page 232

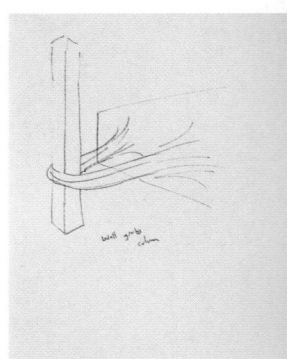

Page 233

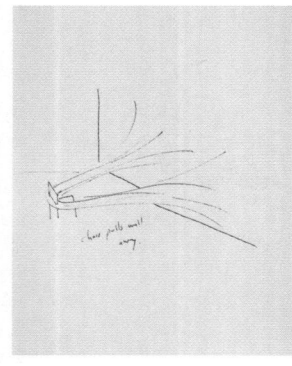

Page 234

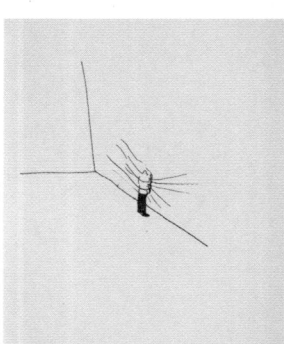

Page 235

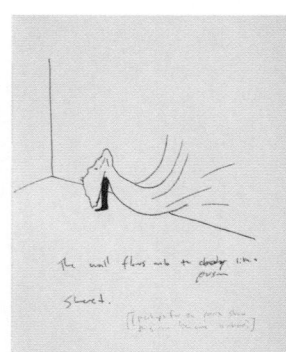

Page 236

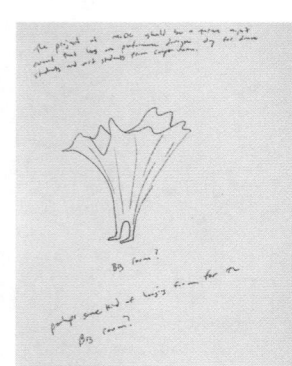

Page 237

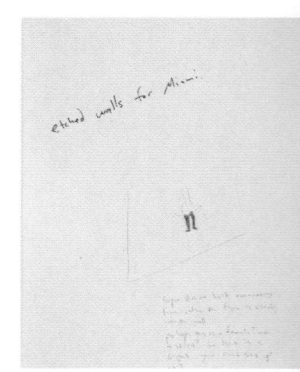

Page 238

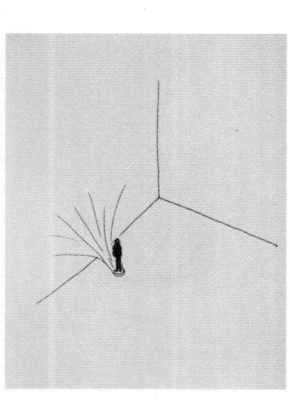

Page 239

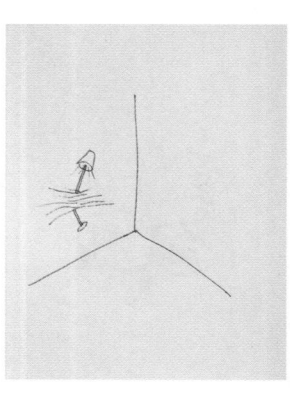

Page 240

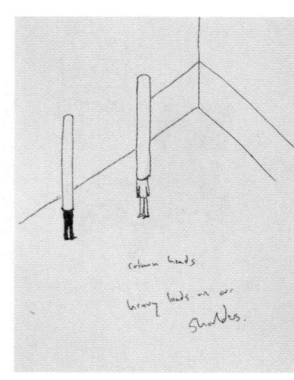

Page 241

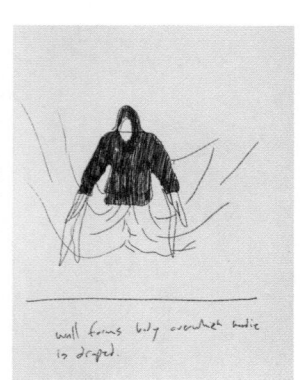

Page 242

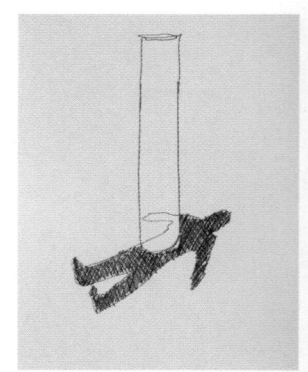

Page 243

Page 244

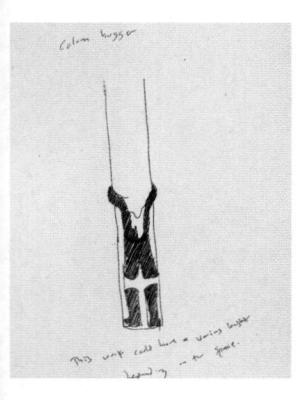

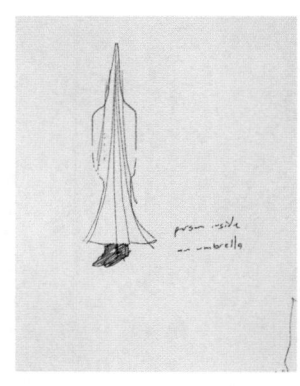

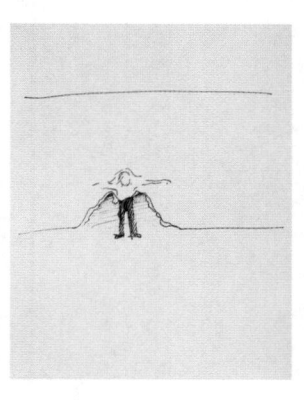

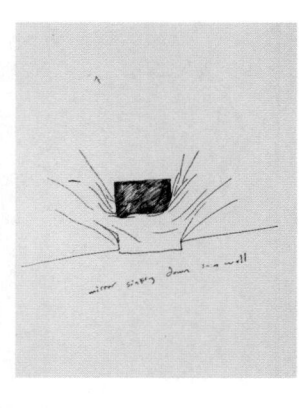

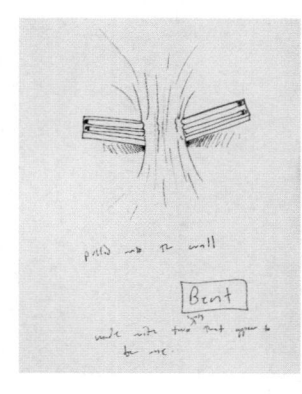

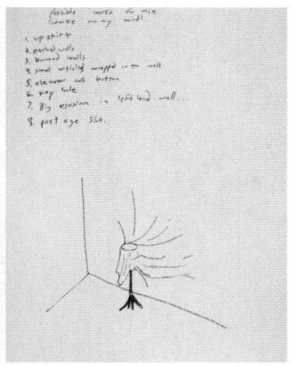

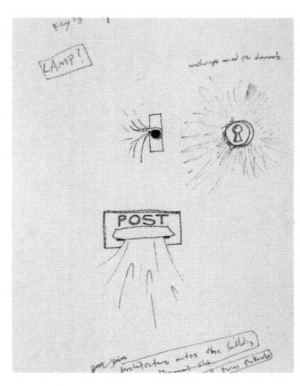

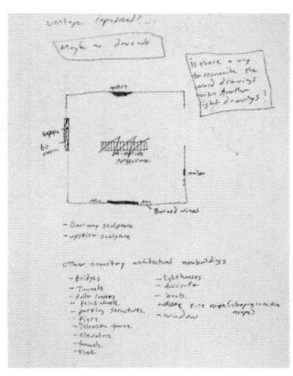

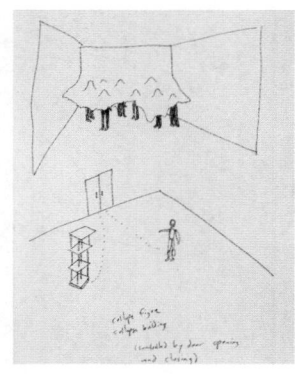

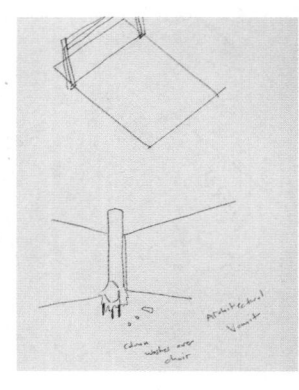

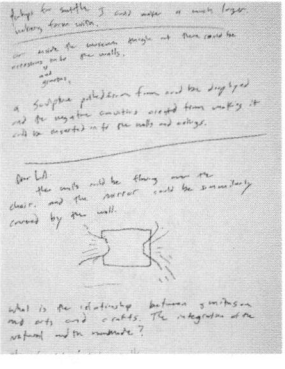

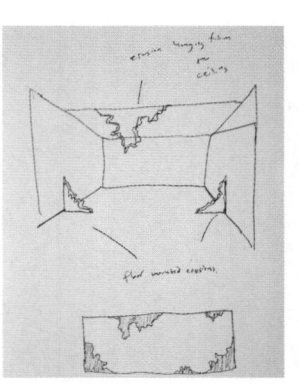

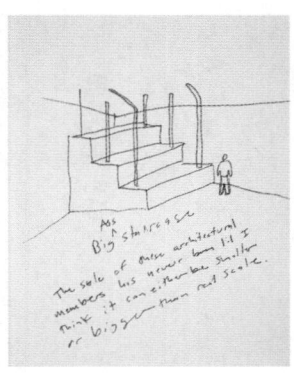

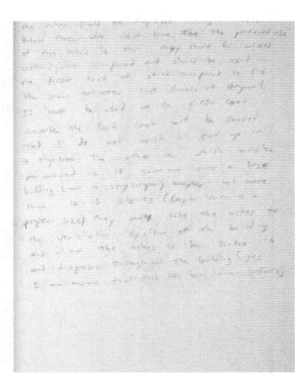

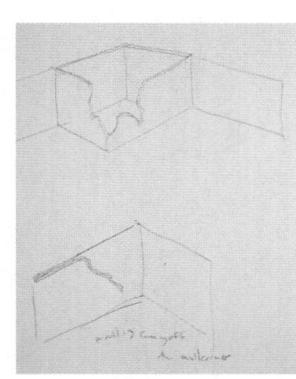

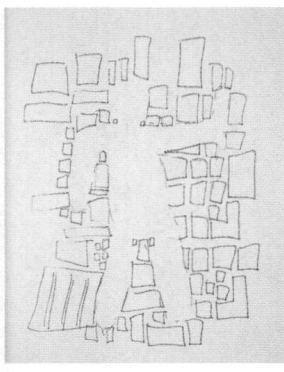

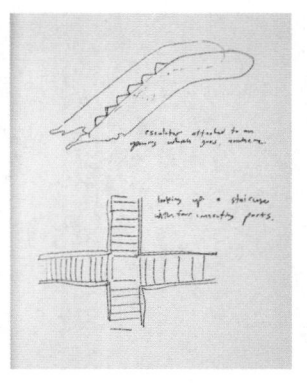

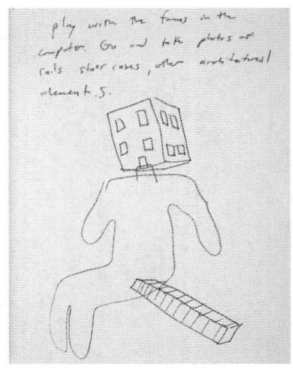

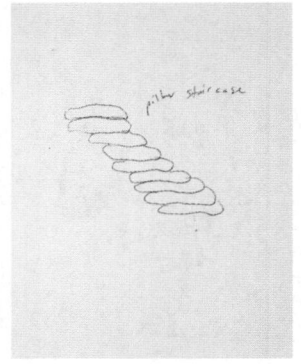

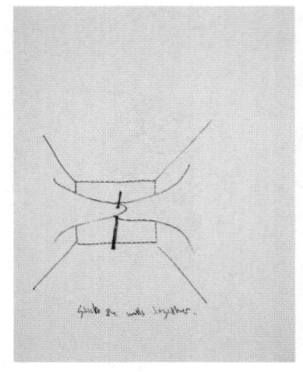

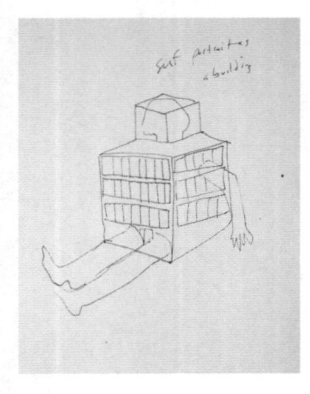

Page 268

Page 269

Page 270

Page 271

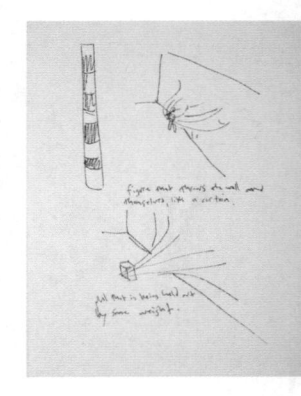

Page 273

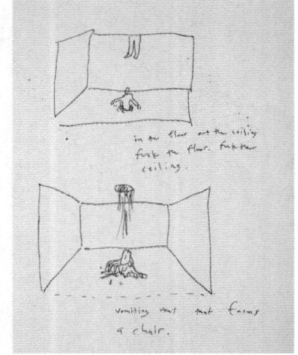

Page 274

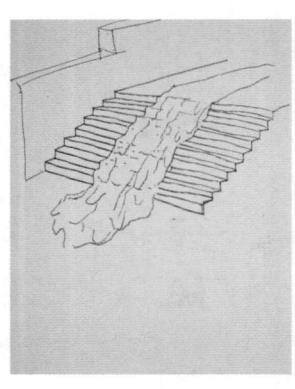

Page 275

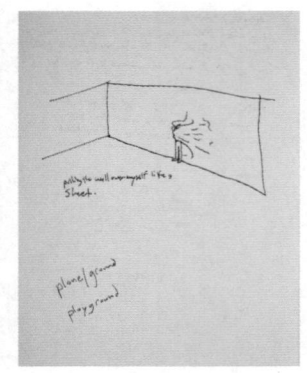

Page 276

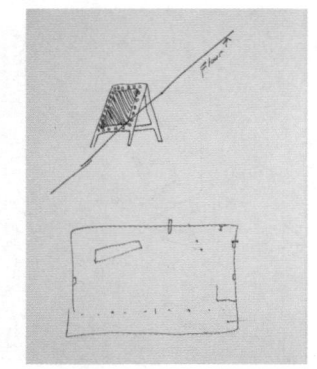

Page 277

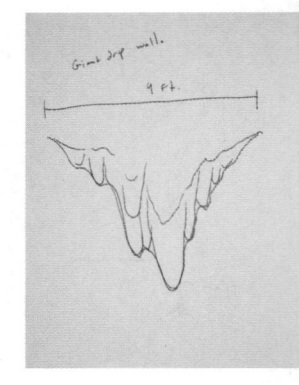

Page 278

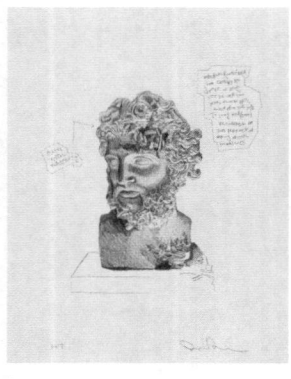

Page 281

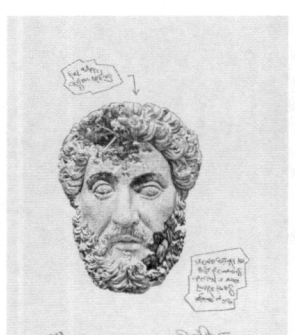

Page 283

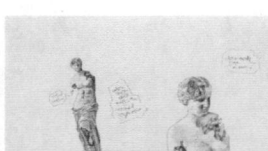

Page 285

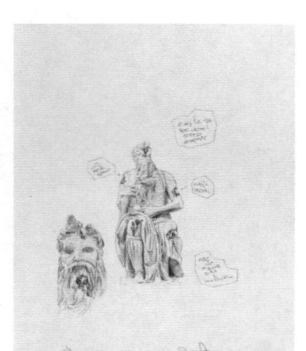

Page 286

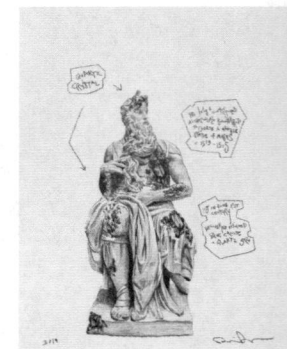

Page 287

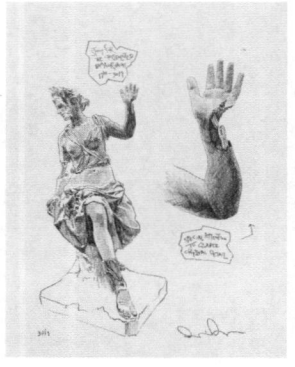

Page 288

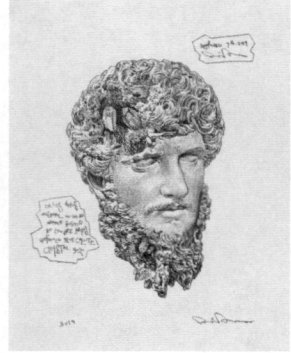

Page 289

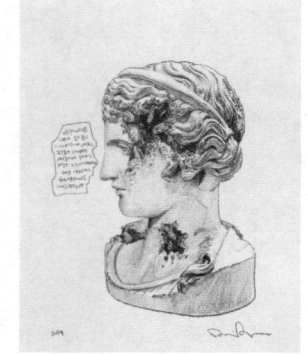

Page 290

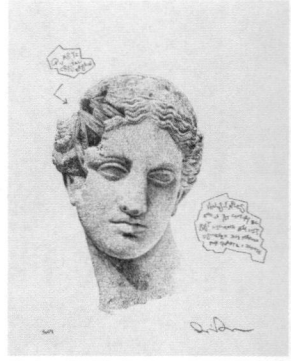

Page 291

Page 293

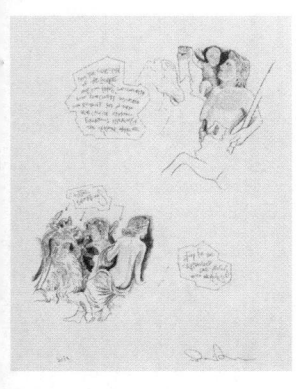

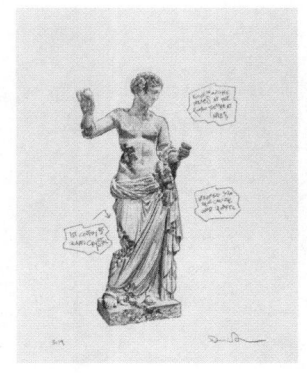

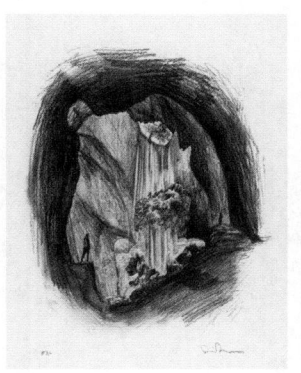

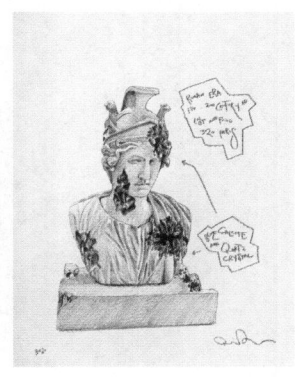

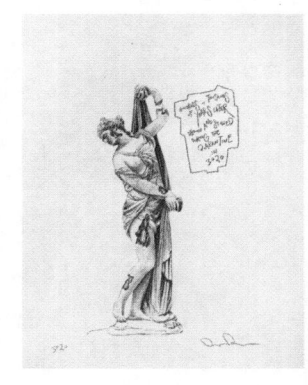

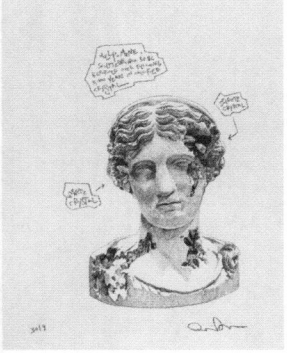

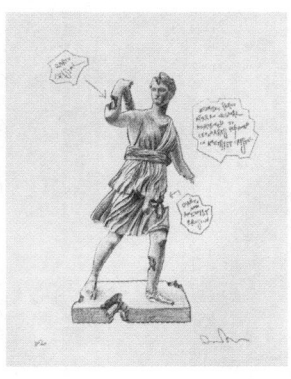

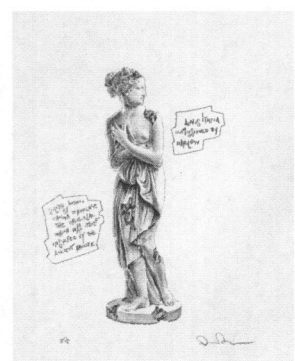

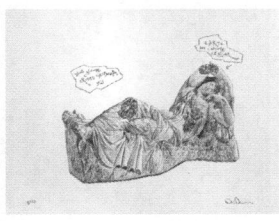

# Acknowledgments

The creation of art relies on many skill sets. All concepts, works and exhibitions utilize the knowledge, ideas, time and effort of many. The people listed here have helped me, or inspired me, to make the things in this book.
— Daniel Arsham

Thank you: Stephanie Jeanroy Arsham; Casper Jeanroy Arsham; Phoenix Jeanroy Arsham; Roger Arsham; Therese Lambert; Katie Arsham; Gerard Jeanroy; Jake Abraham; Natalia Blanco; Cesar Castro; Eunice Chun; Meghan Clohessy; Jude Costello; Karl Cyprien; Matthew Cyprien; Bernie Daroux; Tori Geddes; Hugo Hunt; Sanie Irsay; Thomas Ludacer; Kendell Mahabir; Andrea Martucci; Hayley Martell; Anabella Mazariegos; Ana Menezes; Matthew Mondini; Austin Snyder; Tom Warren; Elise Wunderlich; John Bianchi; Quincy Ellis; Vivek Jayaram; Elsa Arsenault; Louna Bou Ghanem; Alexander Buckeridge; Olivia Colson; Nick Doermann; Clarisse Empaynado; Victor Lee; Marta Llor; Brigitte Lucey; Alex Mustonen; Michie Nimsombun; Greg Pray; Stephanie Tan; Breanna Urquhart; Maria Baro; Marc Benda; Martin Bernard; Anneli Botz; Yuki Itaya; Tat Ito; Johann König; Peggy Leboeuf; Nick Majoor; Ron Mandos; Matthew McCardwell; Shinji Nanzuka; Emmanuel Perrotin; Quentin Schuab; Melissa Timarchi; Michelle Yo; Guillaume Ziccarelli; Matthew Ammirati; Camille Baut; Hayden Cox; Ronnie Fieg; James Law; Sophie Prieto; Chris Stamp.

My thanks to: Daniel Arsham; Hannah Alderfer; Matthew Christensen; Fiona Graham; Meghan Clohessy; Tori Geddes; Sanie Irsay; Austin Snyder; Haley Martell; Eunice Chun; Karl Cyprien; Tom Warren; Haisong Li; Michelle Komie; Christie Henry; Terri O'Prey; Cathy Slovensky; Kenneth Guay; Jodi Price; Kathryn Stevens; Ruthie Rosenstock; Vanessa Lee; Kevin Wong; Keith Estiler; Sarah Sperling; Man Huang; Hassan Ali Khan; Jahan Loh; Mike Dean; Louise Donegan; ASAP Ferg; Carlos "oggizery_los" Desrosiers; Derek Ali; Dan Noble; John Pelosi; John Cahill; Taliesin Thomas; Zara Hoffman; and Steven Rodríguez.

Lastly, my bottomless gratitude to my family: Abbey Warsh; Justin Warsh; Ethan Warsh; Ellie Warsh; Jonah Warsh; and to my mother, Judith.

Larry Warsh
New York City
September 2021

DANIEL ARSHAM is a New York–based artist who explores fine art, architecture, performance, design, and film. Raised in Miami, Arsham attended the Cooper Union in New York City, where he received the Gelman Trust Fellowship Award in 2003. Soon thereafter Arsham toured worldwide with the Merce Cunningham Dance Company as the company's stage designer. Arsham's collaborative practice continues with world-renowned musicians such as Pharrell Williams, Usher, and Nas, alongside fashion brands such as DIOR, Rimowa, and many others.

In 2007 Arsham founded the architecture and design company Snarkitecture with partner Alex Mustonen. The practice has included collaborations with designers Public School and Richard Chai, and created the entrance pavilion for Design Miami, as well as a complete line of functional design objects. Arsham's most recent enterprise in film began in 2014. Productions to date include Arsham's nine-part science fiction film series Future Relic and a short film for Jefferson Hack's MOVEment series.

Arsham's work has been shown at PS1 in New York; the Museum of Contemporary Art in Miami; the Athens Biennale in Athens, Greece; the New Museum in New York; the Contemporary Arts Center in Cincinnati, Ohio; the SCAD Museum of Art in Savannah, Georgia; Carré d'Art de Nîmes, France; and the High Museum of Art, Atlanta, Georgia. Arsham is represented by Galerie Perrotin in Paris, Hong Kong, New York, Seoul, Shanghai, and Tokyo; Baró Galeria in São Paulo; and Ron Mandos in Amsterdam.


LARRY WARSH has been active in the art world for more than thirty years as a publisher and artist-collaborator. An early collector of Keith Haring and Jean-Michel Basquiat, Warsh was a lead organizer for the exhibition Basquiat: The Unknown Notebooks, which debuted at the Brooklyn Museum, New York, in 2015, and later traveled to several American museums. He has served as a curatorial consultant on Keith Haring | Jean-Michel Basquiat: Crossing Lines for the National Gallery of Victoria. The founder of *Museums Magazine*, Warsh has been involved in many publishing projects and is the editor of several other titles published by Princeton University Press, including Weiwei-isms (2012), Basquiatisms (2019), Haring-isms (2020), Futura-isms (2021), Abloh-isms (2021), Arsham-isms (2021), Jean-Michel Basquiat's The Notebooks (2017), and Keith Haring: 31 Subway Drawings, among others. Warsh has served on the board of the Getty Museum Photographs Council, and was a founding member of the Basquiat Authentication Committee until its dissolution in 2012.

NO MORE RULERS (NMR) is a platform representing empowerment, respect, and progression in the art world. NMR partners with leading international institutions, legacy artists, and estates to validate creators through channels of connection, exhibition, and distribution. By connecting audiences with narratives from both top creators and new voices, NMR hopes to empower the creative community and help rethink the status quo.

NO MORE RULERS

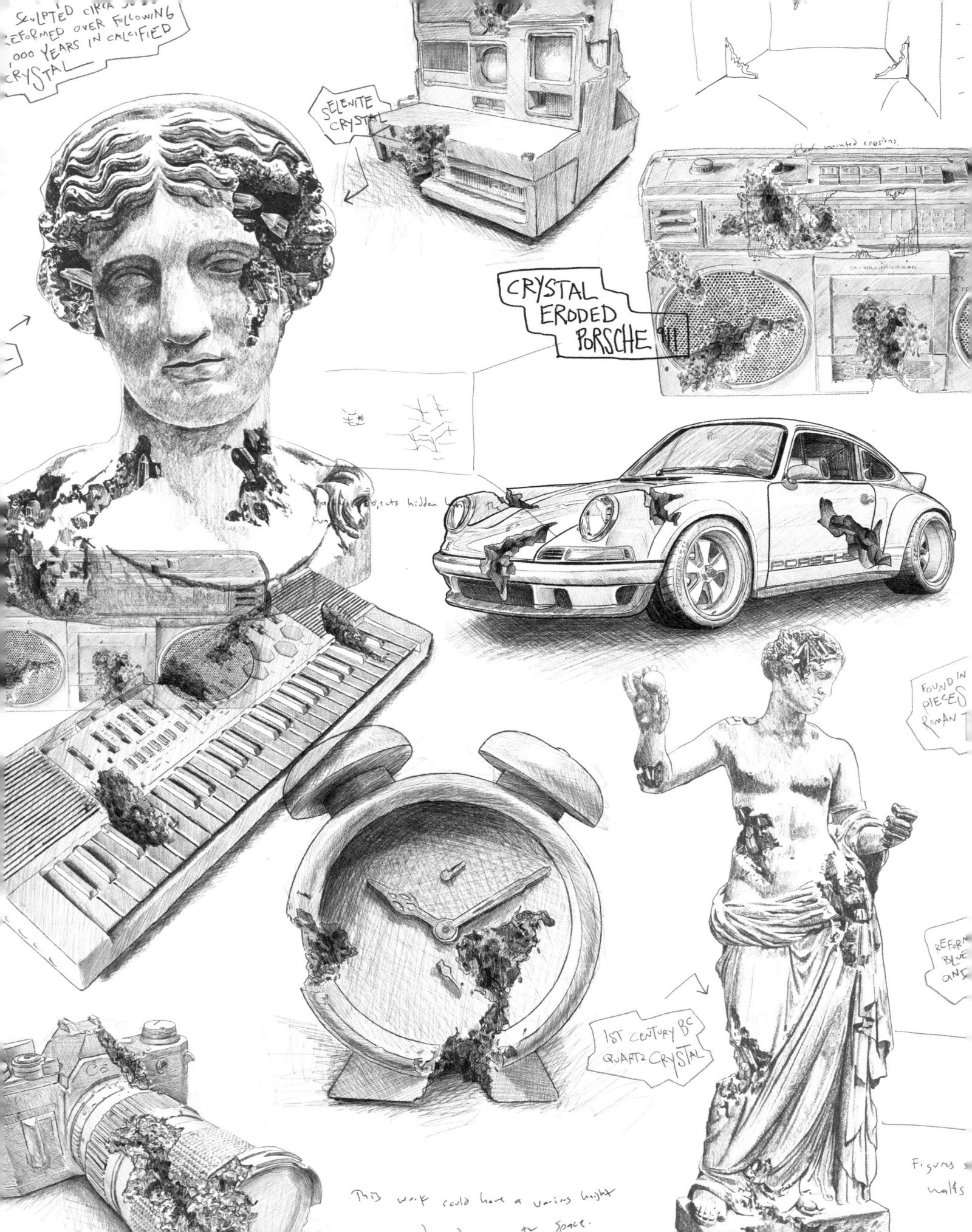

SCULPTED CIRCA [...]
REFORMED OVER FOLLOWING
[...]000 YEARS IN CALCIFIED
CRYSTAL

SELENITE
CRYSTAL

CRYSTAL
ERODED
PORSCHE 911

[...] objects hidden [...]

FOUND IN
PIECES
ROMAN

1ST CENTURY BC
QUARTZ CRYSTAL

REFORM[...]
BLUE
AN[...]

Figure
[...]

This work could have a varing height [...]
[...] to space.